EATCS
Monographs on Theoretical Computer Science
Volume 16

Editors: W. Brauer G. Rozenberg A. Salomaa

Advisory Board: G. Ausiello M. Broy S. Even
J. Hartmanis N. Jones M. Nivat C. Papadimitriou
D. Scott

EATCS Monographs on Theoretical Computer Science

Vol. 1: K. Mehlhorn: Data Structures and Algorithms 1: Sorting and Searching. XIV, 336 pages, 87 figs. 1984.

Vol. 2: K. Mehlhorn: Data Structures and Algorithms 2: Graph Algorithms and NP-Completeness. XII, 260 pages, 54 figs. 1984.

Vol. 3: K. Mehlhorn: Data Structures and Algorithms 3: Multidimensional Searching and Computational Geometry. XII, 284 pages, 134 figs. 1984.

Vol. 4: W. Reisig: Petri Nets. An Introduction. X, 161 pages, 111 figs. 1985.

Vol. 5: W. Kuich, A. Salomaa: Semirings, Automata, Languages. IX, 374 pages, 23 figs. 1986.

Vol. 6: H. Ehrig, B. Mahr: Fundamentals of Algebraic Specification 1. Equations and Initial Semantics. XI, 321 pages. 1985.

Vol. 7: F. Gécseg: Products of Automata. VIII, 107 pages, 18 figs. 1986.

Vol. 8: F. Kröger: Temporal Logic of Programs. VIII, 148 pages. 1987.

Vol. 9: K. Weihrauch: Computability. X, 517 pages. 1987.

Vol. 10: H. Edelsbrunner: Algorithms in Combinatorial Geometry. XV, 423 pages, 93 figs. 1987.

Vol. 11: J. L. Balcázar, J. Díaz, J. Gabarró: Structural Complexity I. IX, 191 pages, 57 figs. 1988.

Vol. 12: J. Berstel, C. Reutenauer: Rational Series and Their Languages. VIII, 151 pages, 1988.

Vol. 13: E. Best, C. Fernández C.: Nonsequential Processes. IX, 112 pages, 44 figs. 1988.

Vol. 14: M. Jantzen: Confluent String Rewriting. Approx. 140 pages, 1988.

Vol. 15: S. Sippu, E. Soisalon-Soininen: Parsing Theory. Volume I: Languages and Parsing. VIII, 228 pages. 1988.

Vol. 16: P. Padawitz: Computing in Horn Clause Theories. XI, 322 pages, 7 figs. 1988.

Peter Padawitz

Computing in Horn Clause Theories

Springer-Verlag
Berlin Heidelberg New York
London Paris Tokyo

Author

Priv.-Doz. Dr. Peter Padawitz
Fakultät für Mathematik und Informatik
Universität Passau, Postfach 2540, D-8390 Passau, FRG

Editors

Prof. Dr. Wilfried Brauer
Institut für Informatik, Technische Universität München
Arcisstraße 21, D-8000 München 2, FRG

Prof. Dr. Grzegorz Rozenberg
Institute of Applied Mathematics and Computer Science
University of Leiden, Niels-Bohr-Weg 1, P.O. Box 9512
NL-2300 RA Leiden, The Netherlands

Prof. Dr. Arto Salomaa
Department of Mathematics, University of Turku
SF-20500 Turku 50, Finland

ISBN-13:978-3-642-73826-5   e-ISBN-13:978-3-642-73824-1
DOI: 10.1007/978-3-642-73824-1

Library of Congress Cataloging-in-Publication Data.
Padawitz, Peter, 1953-. Computing in Horn clause theories / Peter Padawitz. p. cm. -
(EATCS monographs on theoretical computer science ; v. 16)
Bibliography: p. Includes Index.
ISBN-13:978-3-642-73826-5   (U.S.)
1. Logic programming. 2. Horn clauses. I. Title. II. Series.   QA76.6.P327   1988
511.3-dc19   88-20024   CIP

This work is subject to copyright. All rights are reserved, whether the whole or part of the material is concerned, specifically the rights of translation, reprinting, reuse of illustrations, recitation, broadcasting, reproduction on microfilms or in other ways, and storage in data banks. Duplication of this publication or parts thereof is only permitted under the provisions of the German Copyright Law of September 9, 1965, in its version of June 24, 1985, and a copyright fee must always be paid. Violations fall under the prosecution act of the German Copyright Law.

© Springer-Verlag Berlin Heidelberg 1988
Softcover reprint of the hardcover 1st edition 1988

The use of registered names, trademarks, etc. in this publication does not imply, even in the absence of a specific statement, that such names are exempt from the relevant protective laws and regulations and therefore free for general use.

2145/3140-543210   Printed on acid-free paper

Preface

At least four research fields determine the theoretical background of specification and deduction in computer science: recursion theory, automated theorem proving, abstract data types and term rewriting systems. As these areas approach each other more and more, the strong distinctions between functional and relational views, deductive and denotational approaches as well as between specification and programming are relieved in favour of their integration. The book will not expose the lines of this development; conversely, it starts out from the nucleus of Horn clause logic and brings forth both known and unknown results, most of which affect more than one of the fields mentioned above.

Chapter 1 touches on historical issues of specification and prototyping and delimits the topics handled in this book from others which are at the core of related work.

Chapter 2 provides the fundamental notions and notations needed for the presentation and interpretation of *many-sorted Horn clause theories with equality*.

Chapter 3 supplies a number of sample Horn clause specifications ranging from arithmetic through string manipulation to higher data structures and interpreters of programming languages. Some of these examples serve as a reference to illustrate definitions and results, others may throw a light on the strong link between specifications and programs, which are executed by applying deduction rules. Thus we have included examples of how to use *program transformation* methods in specification design.

Chapter 4 is concerned with four denotational views of a Horn clause specification, say SPEC: free semantics, initial semantics, final semantics and the semantics of internalized logic. Each is associated with a certain class of structures that determines the meaning of SPEC. *Free semantics* captures the class of all SPEC-models. It provides the link between model and proof theory in that the *Horn clause calculus* yields the most simple (but least efficient) proof rules for laws obeyed by all SPEC-models. *Initial semantics* adopts the view that each object of discourse is denoted by a (ground) term. *Final semantics* proclaims that two objects are distinguishable only from their visible behaviour. *Internalized logic* embeds (quantifier-free) predicate logic into the functional part of SPEC and thus restricts attention to *consistent* structures that have exactly two truth values. At the end of this chapter, we go into a comparison of Horn clause logic with its natural extension known as *sequent logic*.

Chapter 5 shows the soundness and completeness of *resolution, paramodulation* and *lazy resolution* with respect to deductive goal solutions, i.e. goal solutions that are derivable by the Horn clause calculus. Chapter 4 establishes the link from this calculus to model theory. Hence the soundness and completeness of resolution, etc. is proved with respect to the Horn clause calculus and not - as one usually does - by introducing a particular semantical framework for every new set of inference rules.

Chapter 6 treats the decomposition of a specification SPEC into a base part reserved for (the properties of) *constructors* and a non-base part mainly consisting of (partial) function definitions. This idea is reflected by the proof-theoretical condition that SPEC is a *conservative extension* of the base. Several approaches add the requirement that SPEC be *sufficiently complete,* i.e. all specified functions must be total. However, sufficient completeness is an avoidable assumption, both for the semantics of conservative extensions and for the method of *inductionless induction*.

Chapter 7 generalizes term rewriting to the *goal reduction calculus*. The *Church-Rosser property* of a specification coincides with completeness of this calculus with respect to the Horn clause calculus. We employ several variants of goal reduction because equational rewriting theory has revealed a trade-off with regard to tractable Church-Rosser criteria. The differences mainly concern the places in reduction sequences where base axioms (cf. Chapter 6) may be applied. General criteria for Church-Rosser properties rely on *confluence* conditions. Under certain assumptions, restricted uses of the Goal Reduction Rule, like *strategy-controlled reduction* and *basic reduction*, preserve completeness.

Chapter 8 combines paramodulation and goal reduction to *narrowing*. In contrast to paramodulation, narrowing allows us to substitute into the variables of subgoals, i.e. to compute goal solutions. In contrast to reduction, the completeness of narrowing with respect to goal solutions depends on a Church-Rosser property of the underlying specification. On the other hand, narrowing leads to a considerably smaller search space than paramodulation. This behaviour can be further improved by special uses of the Narrowing Rule such as *strategy-controlled, basic* and *reduced* narrowing. Another way to speed up the derivation process is to alternate narrowing steps with the *optimization* of subgoals. *Lazy narrowing* follows the idea of lazy resolution (cf. Chapter 5) by employing *demand-driven* instead of *data-driven* inference rules.

Chapter 9 goes into the details of Church-Rosser criteria. Based on *critical pair* notions and corresponding *convergence* properties, a number of confluence and compatibility criteria are developed, which come down to three main results, each providing a list of sufficient conditions for a Church-Rosser property. The first requires termination of *congruence class reductions*. The second demands a weaker termination condition, but assumes that all non-base equations are *left-linear*. In the third list, *strong* convergence of critical pairs takes the place of termination. All three criteria are combined to an algorithm for Church-Rosser proofs.

The text is self-contained, although some *tacit knowledge* (see Polanyi) on dealing with syntactical and semantical formalisms is presumed. As proofs often employ inductive arguments, familiarity with such reasoning would be worthwhile. Moreover, the reader who works in one of the traditional fields mentioned above must accept certain changes of notation that were necessary in order to integrate previously separated issues.

We do not only address theoreticians. All results presented center around inference rules and deduction-oriented correctness or completeness conditions that may lead to prototyping tools, being at the heart of programming environments.

The book is an outcome of my ten-years' research and teaching in formal languages, logic, semantics and abstract data types. I am most grateful to all the people who contributed to this monograph with inspiring discussions on its subject and by providing valuable comments on previous versions. They include Peter Bachmann, Manfred Broy, Hartmut Ehrig, Harald Ganzinger, Alfons Geser, Joe Goguen, Rolf Hennicker, Steffen Hölldobler, Dieter Hofbauer, Heinrich Hußmann, Hans-Jörg Kreowski, Ralf Kutsche, Dirk Siefkes, Thomas Streicher and Martin Wirsing. I owe thanks to two anonymous referees, who suggested a number of improvements, and I am particularly indebted to the copy editor of Springer-Verlag, Gillian Hayes, for pointing out numerous typos and incorrect phrases.

Passau, April 1988   Peter Padawitz

Contents

Chapter 1   Introduction 1

Chapter 2   Basic Notions

    2.1   Preliminaries 7
    2.2   The Syntax of Specifications 8
    2.3   Models of a Specification 11

Chapter 3   Sample Specifications

    3.1   Boolean Algebra 16
    3.2   Arithmetic 16
    3.3   Program Transformations 19
    3.4   A Store-based Language Interpreter 22
    3.5   Binary Numbers 25
    3.6   Decoding Binary Numbers 26
    3.7   Sequences 30
    3.8   Palindromes 33
    3.9   Sorting 35
    3.10   Unordered Combinations 38
    3.11   Binary Trees 40
    3.12   Search Trees 41
    3.13   2-3 Trees 44
    3.14   Tree Domains 47
    3.15   A Stream Language Interpreter 50

Chapter 4   Models and Theories

    4.1   Introduction 53
    4.2   The Horn Clause Calculus 55
    4.3   Initial Semantics 61
    4.4   Initial Correctness 68
    4.5   Final Semantics 77
    4.6   Final Correctness 85
    4.7   The Refutation of Inductive Theorems 87

4.8	Internalized Logic	90
4.9	Horn Clause Versus Sequent Logic	104
4.10	Bibliographic Notes	110

Chapter 5   Resolution and Paramodulation

5.1	Introduction	113
5.2	Resolution	114
5.3	Paramodulation	120
5.4	Most General Unification	129
5.5	Lazy Resolution	131
5.6	Bibliographic Notes	136

Chapter 6   The Relevance of Constructors

6.1	Introduction	139
6.2	Partial Semantics	142
6.3	Inductionless Induction	148
6.4	Bibliographic Notes	151

Chapter 7   Reduction

7.1	Introduction	153
7.2	The Classical Approach	155
7.3	The Congruence Class Approach	156
7.4	The Normal Form Approach	159
7.5	The Weak Normal Form Approach	160
7.6	From Equations to Horn Clauses	162
7.7	Term and Goal Reduction	164
7.8	Confluence Properties	173
7.9	Strategy-controlled Reduction	179
7.10	Basic Reduction	181
7.11	Bibliographic Notes	184

Chapter 8   Narrowing

8.1	Introduction	187
8.2	The Narrowing Calculus	188
8.3	Strategy-controlled Narrowing	194

8.4	Narrowing Strategies	198
8.5	Ground Term Generating Term Sets	207
8.6	Basic Narrowing	209
8.7	Reduced Narrowing	214
8.8	Reduced Basic Narrowing	216
8.9	Optimized Narrowing	219
8.10	Optimizing Functions	225
8.11	Lazy Narrowing	231
8.12	Bibliographic Notes	239

Chapter 9   Church-Rosser Criteria

9.1	Introduction	241
9.2	Fully Parallel and Overlapping Reductions	242
9.3	Convergence Properties	247
9.4	Critical Pairs	250
9.5	Confluence of NAX	265
9.6	Strong Confluence of NAX	271
9.7	Confluence of ~NAX	277
9.8	BAX-compatibility of NAX	285
9.9	An Algorithm for Church-Rosser Proofs	292
9.10	Bibliographic Notes	304

References 307

Notation Index 317

Definition Index 319

Chapter 1 Introduction

> *Well*, said Owl, *the customary procedure in such cases is as follows.*
> *What does Crustimoney Proseedcake mean?* said Pooh. *For I am a Bear of Very Little Brain, and long words Bother me.*
> *It means the Thing to Do.*
> *As long as it means that, I don't mind*, said Pooh humbly.
>
> A.A. Milne, Winnie-the-Pooh

Specification is the *process* of translating a problem into a formal description. This should be kept in mind even if we tend to use this term only for the final result of the process. Indeed, it is a characteristic of Western culture that it puts less emphasis on the process than on the form it creates (see Bohm; Whorf). Following Gregory Bateson, development always alternates between process and form. When the process of specification comes up with axioms defining the problem, we start the process of *computation,* for instance, deriving *theorems*. These are expected to improve our understanding of the problem so as to get closer to a solution. But theorems may also reveal flaws in our reasoning, hidden assumptions or undesired effects. In such a case we modify the specification and enter a new cycle of producing forms and initiating processes. Specification and theorem-proving *tools* should support this activity. However, they should not be designed with the intention of relieving us of the whole work. Many decisions are involved for which there is no proper reason to transfer them to a formal system or a machine. We think it necessary to stress this point because computer scientists sometimes ignore the limits of formal methods. Apart from ethical questions, there is no evidence at all that the heart of formal reasoning, namely deduction, plays a significant role in the problem-solving activity of our minds (Dreyfus and Dreyfus; Searle). Formal methods do not stand in their own right. They live with the people who use them (see Naur [1,2]).

The Beginnings

Of course, interest in formal methods does not only result from a philosophical discourse. In the sixties, military projects in the United States made great demands that neither the machines available at that time nor the training of computer scientists could meet. In particular, software products lacked qualities such as modifiability, portability, efficiency and reliability. Enormous financial efforts were undertaken by the U.S. Department of Defense and other institutions to overcome the *software crisis,* giving birth to the discipline of *software engineering* (see Reisin).

Two lines of research were pursued. One line aimed at structuring software systems horizontally and vertically. *Horizontal structuring* divides a problem into subproblems that are interrelated via well-defined interfaces. This *modularization* is carried over to the program that is to solve the problem (see Parnas). *Data types* yield a further concept that complies with horizontal structuring (see Hoare [2]). On the other hand, *vertical structuring* or *stepwise refinement* will close the gap between a specification and a program by going through intermediate descriptions that can be verified against each other (see Dijkstra; Wirth).

We inherited formal methods to describe the *semantics* of programming languages from the other line of research. *Deductive* approaches have been distinguished from *denotational* ones. Probably the first deductive method used in computer science is the *assertion calculus* (see R.W. Floyd; Hoare [1]), associating with a programming language a set of axioms and inference rules for expressions of the form {p}s{q} that are interpreted informally as follows: starting from a *state* that satisfies the assertion p, if the program statement s terminates, then the resulting state satisfies the assertion q.

The informal interpretation is turned into mathematical terms. States are represented by functions from a set X of variables to a set V of values. Program statements denote functions from states to states, and assertions are given by sets of states. The meaning of {p}s{q} is defined as the formula

$$\forall\ f{:}X \longrightarrow V\ (f \in I(p)\ \text{implies}\ I(s)(f) \in I(q))$$

where I is the interpretation function. That I is *second order* is connected with the fact that the assertion calculus actually represents machine behaviour. It meets the demand for a precise and unambiguous semantics. However, problem-oriented abstractness is not one of its characteristics.

The example shows that deductive and denotational methods complement each other. The difference is merely that between proof theory and model theory in mathematical logic. Taking an extreme, but nevertheless remarkable, viewpoint, one may say that every formal method is deductive, since a formalism must have turned into informal knowledge before it can serve to interpret another formalism.

The two lines of research sketched above - structured programming and mathematical semantics - cross in the development of specification languages. These provide facilities for describing problems as well as for implementing solutions. Again, modules, data types and stepwise refinement are the main structuring concepts. Moreover, such languages offer methods for proving the correctness of programs against specifications and supply us with tools for *executing* specifications, *computing* in specifications and *transforming* them into programs.

Computing in specifications is in accordance with the current software engineering paradigm turning away from strict top-down design in favour of a cyclic development, where requirements analysis, prototype construction and target product implementation are undertaken concurrently. The experience clients gain from trying a prototype influences subsequent design decisions. This paradigm complies with what we said above about the process of theory building in general. Besides appropriate tools one needs *on the part of both developers and users a willingness to open themselves to communication and change to a high degree. ... A programming environment suitable for prototyping would support a design methodology that emphasizes creativity, experimentation, learning and evolution* (C. Floyd, pp. 11 and 13).

Various Research Directions

Mathematical research dealing with software concerns has grown out of four fields: recursion theory (REC), automated theorem proving (ATP), abstract data types (ADT) and term rewriting systems (TRS). Each of these areas is associated with its own applications: REC deals with recursive programming and has invented the *fixed point semantics* of programming languages (see Lassez et al.). ATP is used in program verification, database languages and *artificial intelligence* (see Chang and Lee; Boyer and Moore; Nilsson). ADT equips data types and the structured design of specifications with neat syntactical and semantical foundations (see Liskov and Zilles; Guttag; Goguen et al.). TRS is concerned both with decidability problems in algebra (see Huet and Oppen) and with the *operational* semantics of programming languages (see Rosen; Nivat).

Hence REC and ADT adopt the denotational viewpoint, while ATP and TRS ride on the deductive train. REC, ADT and TRS take programming to be the discipline of defining functions, whereas ATP favours relations, certainly influenced by the dominant role of predicates in logic. Consequently, the

REC-language *Lisp* (see Winston and Horn) is purely functional, in contrast to the ATP-language *Prolog* (see Clocksin and Mellish), which propagates relational programming. A further difference between REC, ATP, ADT and TRS concerns the tendency towards specification versus programming: REC is close to programming, and ATP and TRS support the thesis that deduction is programming and programming is deduction. Since deduction is inherent to the activity of specification, ATP and TRS establish a strong link between specification and programming. ADT confirms this link by supplying methods for transforming specifications into programs.

We are now observing the phenomenon that the four research fields are approaching each other more and more. Not only is specification getting closer to programming, but also the exchange between deductive and denotational concepts and between functional and relational views is increasing considerably. However, unifying approaches seem to concentrate more on the development of implementations than on fundamental research. On the other hand, theoretical work is creating a vast number of new results, each of which improves a particular programming environment, but is rarely applicable outside the scope of this one environment.

The objective of this book is to bridge the gap between the general trend towards an integration of methods and the great number of individual achievements, which may lead one to miss the wood for the trees. Starting from the language of *many-sorted Horn logic with equality* we present known methods and results along with new ones. The reasons for adopting this language are as follows.

- It includes the language of (conditional) equations where REC, ADT and TRS are built upon.
- It extends the language of equations up to the point to which the denotational concepts known from ADT can be transferred.
- The language of Horn clauses is easy to use. Where Prolog programs become awkward, i.e. when functions must be translated into relations, we keep to functions and employ *paramodulation, reduction* or *narrowing* instead of *resolution*.
- The theory of a Horn clause specification is completely described by its axioms, congruence axioms for equality symbols and two inference rules: *cut* and *substitution*. This simple calculus serves as a reference for answering questions about the soundness or completeness of more advanced deduction rules.

In summary, Horn logic serves as a nucleus for unfolding a variety of model-theoretic concepts and deduction-oriented methods, which were brought about by the development sketched above. The unified approach should help to locate essential ideas and to categorize related work, even if much of this work cannot be discussed in detail in this book. Its draft version was entitled "Foundations of Specification and Programming with Horn Clauses", but here we have chosen another title in order to stress our focus on deductive methods and to emphasize the viewpoint of *computing* and *deriving* as one and the same activity. The *denotational* background, on the other hand, is only worked out so far as to clarify the differences between several model-theoretic views and their impact on computational procedures.

The presentation of deductive methods comes down from general ones, which permit arbitrary (Horn clause) specifications, to more and more refined ones, which impose more and more restrictions on the underlying specification. Certainly, these restrictions provide a basis for logic and algebraic *programming* techniques. If the one or the other method cannot be used because the given specification/program does not meet the corresponding restrictions, one may either change the specification/program or step backwards and try to apply a more general, but possibly less efficient, method. At best, such attempts will lead to new refinements, which are tailored to specific problem areas.

A short survey of the chapters is given in the preface. Topics not treated in this monograph, but playing a significant role in certain related work are:
- the structuring of specifications by *parameterization* and *abstract implementation* (see Burstall and Goguen; Wand [2]; Ehrig and Mahr),
- *concurrency* in relational and functional programming (see Broy and Bauer; Levi),
- *termination criteria* for rewrite rule systems (see Dershowitz [3]; we take a quick look at *recursive path orderings* in section 9.4),
- *completion procedures* that transform the axioms of an equational specification into a terminating and *confluent* rewrite rule system to decide the theory of the specification (cf. Sections 9.9 and 9.10).

Each of Chapters 4-9 starts with an introduction to the particular issue and ends with bibliographic notes.

Chapter 2 Basic Notions

2.1 Preliminaries

Let A be a set. A binary relation R on A is *irreflexive* if for all $\langle a,b\rangle \in R$, $a \neq b$. R is *Noetherian* if there are no infinite sequences $a_0, a_1, a_2, ...$ of elements of A such that for all $i \in \mathbb{N}$, $\langle a_i, a_{i+1}\rangle \in R$.

Proposition 2.1.1 (Principle of Noetherian Induction; see Cohn, p. 20) Let R be a Noetherian relation on A and $B \subseteq A$ such that the following implication holds true for all $a \in A$:

$$(\forall \langle a,b\rangle \in R : b \in B) \text{ implies } a \in B. \qquad (*)$$

Then $B = A$.

Proof. (see Manna, p. 409) Assume that there is an $a_0 \in A-B$. By (*), there is $\langle a_0, a_1\rangle \in R$ with $a_1 \in A-B$. Again by (*), $\langle a_1, a_2\rangle \in R$ for some $a_2 \in A-B$, and so on. Hence we obtain an infinite sequence $a_0, a_1, a_2,...$ such that for all $i \in \mathbb{N}$, $\langle a_i, a_{i+1}\rangle \in R$, in contradiction to the Noetherian property of R. ∎

Given $n \in \mathbb{N}$, the n-th power of A, A^n, is inductively defined by $A^0 = \{\varepsilon\}$ and $A^{n+1} = A^n \times A$. The elements of A^n are called (finite) *sequences over A* and are written as $\langle a_1,...,a_n\rangle$ where $a_1,...,a_n \in A$. For $a \in A$, the sequence $\langle a\rangle$ is identified with a. a^n denotes the sequence that consists of n occurrences of a. In particular, $a^0 = \varepsilon$. By dropping inner brackets, two sequences v and w are *concatenated* to the sequence vw. Further abbreviations are:

- $A^{<n} = \cup \{A^i \mid i < n\}$,
- $A^{\leq n} = A^{<n} \cup A^n$,
- $A^+ = \cup \{A^n \mid n > 0\}$,
- $A^* = A^+ \cup \{\varepsilon\}$.

Let S be a set whose elements are called *sorts*. An *S-sorted set* is a family $A = \{A_s \mid s \in S\}$ of sets. The elements of A_s, $s \in S$, are said to *have sort s*. Given $w = \langle s_1,...,s_n\rangle \in S^+$, A is extended to an S^+-sorted set by defining

$$A_w = A_{s_1} \times ... \times A_{s_n}$$

For all $s \in S$, let $\sim_s$ be a binary relation on A_s. The family

$$\sim \, = \{\sim_s \mid s \in S\}$$

is called an *S-sorted relation on A*. If all $\sim_s$, $s \in S$, are equivalence relations, then the the *quotient of A by* $\sim$ is given by the family

$$A/\sim \, = \{A_s/\sim_s \mid s \in S\}$$

of corresponding quotient sets.

Given S-sorted sets A and B, a set of functions $f_s : A_s \to B_s$, $s \in S$, is an *S-sorted function,* denoted by $f : A \to B$. Given $w = \langle s_1,...,s_n \rangle \in S^+$ and $\langle a_1,...,a_n \rangle \in A_w$, f is extended to an S^+-sorted function by defining

$$f_w(\langle a_1,...,a_n \rangle) = \langle f_{s_1}(a_1),...,f_{s_n}(a_n) \rangle.$$

id^A denotes the identity function on A. Given an (S-sorted) equivalence relation $\sim$ on A, *nat* stands for the natural mapping from A to $A/\sim$ that assigns to $a \in A$ the set of all $a' \in A$ with $a' \sim a$. • denotes the operator for the sequential composition of functions (from right to left) and relations (from left to right). Function application brackets, the composition operator and sort indices are omitted when they are clear from the context.

2.2 The Syntax of Specifications

Definition A *signature* SIG = $\langle S, OP, PR \rangle$ consists of a set S of sorts and two S^+-sorted sets OP and PR whose elements are called *operation* (or *function*) *symbols* and *predicate symbols,* respectively. S-sorted operation symbols are called *constants.* For $w \in S^+$, $s \in S$ and $\sigma \in OP_{ws}$, w is the *arity* and s the *coarity* of σ. ∎

In definitions and proofs, we use small Greek letters σ, τ, etc. for operation symbols and capital Roman letters P, Q, etc. for predicate symbols. In examples, arbitrary *mixfix* strings are used to denote function and predicate symbols (cf. Chapter 3).

General Assumption We suppose that a signature SIG = $\langle S, OP, PR \rangle$ is given. For all $s \in S$, PR_{ss} implicitly contains a predicate symbol $\equiv_s$ called the *equality predicate for s.* Moreover, we fix an S-sorted set X of *variables* such that for all $s \in S$, X_s is countably infinite. ∎

Composed operations are represented by terms over the signature:

Definition The S-sorted set *T(SIG)* of *terms over SIG* is inductively defined as follows:

- For all $s \in S$, $OP_s \cup X_s \subseteq T(SIG)_s$, i.e. constants and variables are terms,
- for all $w \in S^+$, $s \in S$, $\sigma \in OP_{ws}$ and $t \in T(SIG)_w$, $\sigma t \in T(SIG)_s$.

Given a term t, *root(t)* denotes the leftmost symbol of t. By the definition of S-sorted sets, the sort of t agrees with the coarity of root(t). *size(t)* is the number of operation symbol and variable occurrences in t. *var(t)* denotes the sets of variables occurring in t. *single(t)* consists of all $x \in var(t)$ occurring exactly once in t. t is *linear* if var(t) = single(t), i.e. each variable occurs at most once in t. t is *ground* if var(t) is empty. The set of ground terms over SIG is denoted by *GT(SIG)*. ∎

Typical variables or sequences of variables are x, y and z. Typical terms or sequences of terms are t, u and v.

Definition Let A be an S-sorted set. The set of S-sorted functions from X to A is denoted by A^X. $f \in T(SIG)^X$ is called a *substitution over SIG*. f is *ground* if the range of f consists of ground terms.

The *domain of f*, *dom(f)*, is the set of all variables x such that $f(x) \neq x$. A substitution f is often written as the set of all expressions t/x such that $x \in dom(f)$ and fx = t. (t/x is read as *t for x*.) Accordingly, if $t = \langle t_1,...,t_n \rangle \in T(SIG)^*$ and $x = \langle x_1,...,x_n \rangle \in X^*$, then t/x stands for the set $\{t_1/x_1,...,t_n/x_n\}$. Given a subset V of X, $f \upharpoonright V \in T(SIG)^X$ denotes the restriction of f to V, i.e. $(f \upharpoonright V)(x) = fx$ if $x \in V$, and $(f \upharpoonright V)(x) = x$ otherwise.

Given a term (or sequence of terms) t and a substitution f, the *instance t[f] of t by f* is the term obtained from t by simultaneously replacing all variables occurring in t by their respective values under f, i.e. using the inductive definition of terms given above,

- for all $s \in S$ and $\sigma \in OP_s$, $\sigma[f] = \sigma$,
- for all $s \in S$ and $x \in X_s$, $x[f] = f(x)$,
- for all $w \in S^+$, $s \in S$, $\sigma \in OP_{ws}$ and $t \in T(SIG)_w$, $(\sigma t)[f] = \sigma(t[f])$.

Vice versa, we say that *t is a prefix of t[f]* or that *t subsumes t[f]*. Let $x \in var(t)$ such that $f(x) \in dom(f)$. Then each instance of the term f(x) is said to *overlap t[f]*. Given a further term t', *f unifies t and t'* or *f is a unifier of t and t'* if t[f] = t'[f].

Given a further substitution g, the *sequential composition* of f and g, denoted by f[g], is the substitution defined by

$$(f[g])(x) = (fx)[g]$$

for all x ∈ X. Generalizing the instance notion from terms to substitutions we also call f[g] the *instance of f by g* and *f a prefix of f[g]*.

A unifier f of terms t and t' is *most general* if f is a prefix of every unifier of t and t'.

The *parallel composition* of f and g, denoted by f+g, is the substitution defined by

$$(f+g)(x) = \begin{cases} f(x) & \text{for all } x \in \text{dom}(f)-\text{dom}(g) \\ g(x) & \text{for all } x \in \text{dom}(g)-\text{dom}(f) \\ x & \text{otherwise.} \end{cases}$$

In general, f+g is used only if f and g have distinct domains. ∎

Typical substitutions are f, g and h. The *identity substitution* f with fx = x for all x ∈ X is denoted by *id*.

Some remarks are necessary to justify this notation. On a first reading, f, g, etc. may be confused with function symbols. The reason for our choice of notation is that substitutions are *functions*, while function symbols are *symbols*. Hence we adopt the traditional notation for functions in mathematics and keep Greek letters for syntactical objects such as operation symbols and – see below – goals.

Our notation complies with the algebraic definition of *term instance* and *composed substitution*: each $f \in T(SIG)^X$ induces an S-sorted function f^* on T(SIG): For all $t \in T(SIG)$, $f^*(t)$ is defined as the instance t[f] of t by f (see above). Accordingly, if $f,g \in T(SIG)^X$, then the functional composition $g^* \circ f$ coincides with f[g].

Definition Given $w \in S^+$, $P \in PR_w$ and $u \in T(SIG)_w$, Pu is called an *atom over SIG*. If P is an equality predicate and thus u = ⟨t,t'⟩ for some t,t', then Pu is an *equation*, written t≡t'. For term sequences t and t' with the same sort, t≡t' stands for the set of equations between the respective components of t and t'. For substitutions f and g, f≡g is an abbreviation of the set of equations f(x)≡g(x) where x ∈ X.

Finite sets of atoms over SIG are called *goals over SIG*.

The above definitions of *ground, var, single, linear, instance* and *unifier* are extended to atoms and goals as expected.

The sets of atoms, ground atoms, equations and goals over SIG are denoted by *At(SIG), GAt(SIG), Eq(SIG)* and *Goal(SIG)*, respectively. ∎

Typical atoms are p and q. Typical goals are γ, δ, φ, ψ, ϑ, λ.

Note the difference between the formula t≡t' and the structural identity of two terms t,t' denoted by *t = t'*. The corresponding notational difference, ≡ versus =, is justified for the same reason as reserving Greek letters for function symbols and denoting substitutions by Roman letters were justified (see above). ≡ is a symbol, while = actually *means* equality. As an example of structural identity between formulas, we have

$$(t \equiv t') = (x \equiv t')[t/x] = (t \equiv y)[t'/y]$$

provided that $x \notin var(t')$ and $y \notin var(t)$. The equation $t \equiv t'$ is *equal to* $(x \equiv t')[t/x]$. However, $(x \equiv t')[t/x]$ is *different from* the goal $\{x \equiv t', t \equiv x\}$.

Definition A (definite or positive Horn) *clause over SIG* consists of an atom p and a goal $\gamma = \{p_1,...,p_n\}$ over SIG, written

$$p \Leftarrow \gamma \quad \text{or} \quad p \Leftarrow p_1,...,p_n$$

and read as

$$p \text{ if } \gamma \quad \text{and} \quad p \text{ if } (p_1 \text{ and } ... \text{ and } p_n),$$

respectively. p is the *conclusion*, γ the *premise* of $p \Leftarrow \gamma$. γ may be empty. In that case the implication symbol $\Leftarrow$ is omitted and p is sometimes called a *fact*. $p \Leftarrow \gamma$ is *ground* if p and γ are ground. If p is an equation, then $p \Leftarrow \gamma$ is a called a *conditional equation*.

Let AX be a set of clauses over SIG. The pair <SIG,AX> is called a *specification*. A specification <SIG',AX'> is a *subspecification* of <SIG,AX> if the sorts, function symbols and predicate symbols of SIG' are in SIG and if AX' is a subset of AX. ∎

2.3 Models of a Specification

This section provides general denotations to formalize the semantics of a specification. The notions are in accordance with those used in many-sorted first-order logic.

Definition A *SIG-structure* A consists of
- an S-sorted set called the *carrier* of A,
- an element $\sigma^A \in A_s$ for each constant $\sigma \in OP_s$,
- a function $\sigma^A : A_w \rightarrow A_s$ for each $w \in S^+$, $s \in S$ and $\sigma \in OP_{w,s}$,
- a relation $P^A \subseteq A_w$ for each $w \in S^+$ and $P \in PR_w$.

If equality predicates are the only predicate symbols of SIG, A is also called a *SIG-algebra*.

If, for all $s \in S$, $\equiv_s^A$ is the identity relation on A_s, i.e. $\equiv_s^A = \{<a,a> \mid a \in A\}$, then A is a *SIG-structure with identity*. ∎

Structures with carriers consisting of terms establish the link between the syntax and the semantics of a specification. They arise from Herbrand interpretations (cf. Bundy, Section 16.2):

Definition Let C be an S-sorted subset of T(SIG). C is *closed* if for all $w \in S^*$, $s \in S$ and $\sigma \in OP_{ws}$, $t \in C_w$ implies $\sigma t \in C_s$.

Let C be closed. Then $HU(C) = \{Pt \in At(SIG) \mid t \in C^*\}$ is called the *Herbrand universe* w.r.t. C. Subsets of HU(C) are called *Herbrand interpretations* w.r.t. C.

Given a Herbrand interpretation HI w.r.t. C, the *Herbrand structure HS(C,HI)* is defined as follows. Let A = HS(C,HI).
- for all $s \in S$, $A_s = C_s$,
- for all $w \in S^*$, $s \in S$, $\sigma \in OP_{ws}$ and $t \in C_w$, $\sigma^A(t) = \sigma t$,
- for all $w \in S^+$ and $P \in P_w$, $P^A = \{t \in C_w \mid Pt \in HI\}$. ∎

Chapter 4 deals with several Herbrand structures where the carrier set is either T(SIG) or GT(SIG) and the Herbrand interpretation is a *theory* of <SIG,AX> that determines a class of *models* of AX (see below).

Definition Let A be a SIG-structure. Each $b \in A^X$ is extended to an S-sorted function $b^* : T(SIG) \to A$ in accordance with the inductive definition of terms:
- For all $s \in S$ and $x \in X_s$, $b^*(x) = b(x)$,
- for all $s \in S$ and $\sigma \in OP_s$, $b^*(\sigma) = \sigma^A$,
- for all $w \in S^+$, $s \in S$, $\sigma \in OP_{ws}$ and $t \in T(SIG)_w$, $b^*(\sigma t) = \sigma^A \circ b^*(t)$. ∎

Given $b \in A^X$, b^* *evaluates* a term t by first assigning values to the variables of t according to b, secondly turning the function symbols of t into functions and, thirdly, applying these functions in a stepwise fashion to compute the value of t w.r.t. b.

The instance of t by a substitution f, t[f], can be evaluated in two equivalent ways:
- substitute the terms f(x) with $x \in var(t)$ into t, which gives t[f], and evaluate t w.r.t. b,
- evaluate (w.r.t. b) the terms f(x) with $x \in var(t)$, substitute these values into t, and evaluate the resulting term.

The equivalence is expressed by

Proposition 2.3.1 Let A be a SIG-structure, $b \in A^X$, $t \in T(SIG)$ and $f \in T(SIG)^X$. Then $b^*(t[f]) = (b^* \circ f)^*(t)$.

Proof by induction on size(t).
Case 1. t is a variable, say x. Then $b^*(t[f]) = b^*(x[f]) = b^*(fx) = (b^* \circ f)(x) = (b^* \circ f)^*(x) = (b^* \circ f)^*(t)$.
Case 2. t is a constant, say σ. Then $b^*(t[f]) = b^*(\sigma[f]) = b^*(\sigma) = \sigma^A = (b^* \circ f)^*(\sigma) = (b^* \circ f)^*(t)$.

Case 3. $t = \sigma u$ for some σ and u. By the induction hypothesis, $(\sigma^A \circ b^*)(u[f])$
$= (\sigma^A \circ (b^* \circ f)^*)(u)$. Hence $b^*(t[f]) = b^*(\sigma u[f]) = (\sigma^A \circ b^*)(u[f]) = (\sigma^A \circ (b^* \circ f)^*)(u)$
$= (b^* \circ f)^*(\sigma u) = (b^* \circ f)^*(t)$. ∎

If t is ground, b^*t always returns the same value, regardless of the definition of b. Hence the restriction of b^* to GT(SIG) is denoted by $eval^A$ and called the *evaluation mapping of A*. A is called *term-generated* if each $a \in A$ is the interpretation of a ground term, i.e. if $eval^A$ is surjective.

Definition Let A be a SIG-structure and R be an S-sorted binary relation on A (cf. Section 2.1).
R is *OP-compatible* if for all $w \in S^+$, $s \in S$ and $\sigma \in OP_{ws}$, $\langle a,b \rangle \in R_w$ implies $\langle \sigma^A(a), \sigma^A(b) \rangle \in R$.
R is *PR-compatible* if for all $w \in S^+$, $s \in S$, $P \in PR_w$ and $a \in P^A$, $\langle a,b \rangle \in R_w$ implies $b \in P^A$.
R is a *SIG-congruence relation* if R is an OP- and PR-compatible S-sorted equivalence relation. In that case the quotient $B = A/\sim$ becomes a SIG-structure by defining

$$\sigma^B \circ nat = nat \circ \sigma^A \quad \text{and} \quad P^B = \{nat(a) \mid a \in P^A\}$$

where nat is the natural mapping from A to $A/\sim$. ∎

Note that, if A is a Herbrand structure with carrier set GT(SIG), then the evaluation mapping of $A/\sim$ coincides with the natural mapping from A to $A/\sim$.

Definition Let A be a SIG-structure, $b \in A^X$ and $Pt \in At(SIG)$.
b solves Pt or *is a solution of Pt in A* if $b^*t \in P^A$. *b solves a goal* γ *in A* if b solves all $p \in \gamma$ in A.
An atom *p is valid in A* or *A satisfies p*, written $A \models p$, if all $b \in A^X$ solve p in A. A clause $p \Leftarrow \gamma$ is *valid in A* or *A satisfies* $p \Leftarrow \gamma$, written $A \models p \Leftarrow \gamma$, if all solutions of γ in A solve p in A.
Given a set AX of clauses, a SIG-structure A with identity is a *SIG-model of AX* if A satisfies all $p \Leftarrow \gamma \in AX$. *Mod(SIG,AX)* denotes the class of all SIG-models of AX. ∎

Chapter 3 Sample Specifications

The following Horn clause specifications are designed to illustrate the range of applications expressible within this framework. Some of them are referred to in subsequent chapters. The others should serve as material for the reader's own investigation and assessment of Horn clause specification, programming and deduction using the concepts and calculi developed in this book. It is not the purpose of the present chapter to anticipate all problems and solutions handled in this monograph. (By the way, most of the problems first become obvious in the process of formalization.) The informal explanations given here follow a somewhat loose mode of discourse jumping between several levels which the formal exposition provided later will separate from one another. Moreover, some examples hint at questions and problem areas (e.g. issues of program transformation) which are not treated in the formal exposition. However, we think it necessary to include them here as well, at least to initiate more profound research. All this requires a little effort in the reading of this chapter, which pays off as a deeper insight into both the power and the limits of Horn clause reasoning.

The components of a Horn clause specification, sorts, operation symbols, predicate symbols and axioms, follow the keywords *sorts*, *opns*, *preds* and *axms*, respectively. The keyword *vars* precedes a list of all variables which occur in axioms. Names of previously defined subspecifications follow the keyword *base*. Adding operations or axioms to a specification SPEC sometimes suggests a sort s be renamed as a new sort s'. The modified specification where all occurrences of s have been renamed s' is denoted by SPEC(s **becomes** s').

Mixfix notation is used for operation and predicate symbols, e.g. a binary operation symbol written as _[_] places its first argument before the opening bracket and its second argument between the brackets. To avoid syntactical ambiguities terms may contain additional round brackets. Sort membership is declared as follows. Let $w \in S^+$ and $s \in S$. Then

$\sigma : s$	denotes a constant $\sigma \in OP_s$,
$\sigma : w \rightarrow s$	denotes an operation symbol $\sigma \in OP_{w,s}$,
$P : w$	denotes a predicate symbol $P \in PR_w$,
$x : s$	denotes a variable $x \in X_s$.

3.1 Boolean Algebra

A specification of Boolean algebras is

    BOOL
        sorts :   bool
        opns :   **true** : bool
                      false : bool
                      ¬ _ : bool→bool
                      _ ∧ _ : bool,bool→bool
                      _ ∨ _ : bool,bool→bool
                      _ **impl** _ : bool,bool→bool
                      _ **eq** _ : bool,bool→bool
                      if _ **then** _ **else** _ : bool,bool,bool→bool
        vars :   x,y,z : bool
        axms :   x ∧ y ≡ y ∧ x
                      x ∨ y ≡ y ∨ x
                      x ∧ (y ∧ z) ≡ (x ∧ y) ∧ z
                      x ∨ (y ∨ z) ≡ (x ∨ y) ∨ z
                      x ∧ (y ∨ z) ≡ (x ∧ y) ∨ (x ∧ z)
                      x ∨ (y ∧ z) ≡ (x ∨ y) ∧ (x ∨ z)
                      x ∧ (x ∨ y) ≡ x
                      x ∨ (x ∧ y) ≡ x
                      x ∧ ¬x ≡ **false**
                      x ∨ ¬x ≡ **true**
                      x ∧ **true** ≡ x
                      x ∨ **false** ≡ x
                      x **impl** y ≡ ¬x ∨ y
                      x **eq** y ≡ (x **impl** y) ∧ (y **impl** x)
                      if x **then** y **else** z ≡ (x **impl** y) ∧ (¬x **impl** z)

3.2 Arithmetic

BOOL is completely equational. Our second example, a specification of natural number arithmetic, also includes predicates. The boldface vertical line **|** denotes the successor function, is used as a postfix operator and has the highest priority over all function symbols.

    NAT
        sorts :   nat
        opns :   0 : nat
                      _**|** : nat→nat

preds :   _<_ : nat,nat
          _≤_ : nat,nat
          _≢_ : nat,nat
          _ is even : nat
          _ is odd : nat
vars :   m,n : nat
axms :   0 < n|
          m| < n| ⇐ m < n
          m ≤ n ⇐ m < n
          m ≤ n ⇐ m ≡ n
          m ≢ n ⇐ m < n
          m ≢ n ⇐ n < m
          0 is even
          n| is even ⇐ n is odd
          n| is odd ⇐ n is even

More operations are provided by an extension of NAT:

NAT-ARITHMETIC
  base :   NAT
  opns: 1 : nat
           2 : nat
           3 : nat
           ...
           _ + _ : nat,nat→nat
           _ - _ : nat,nat→nat
           _ * _ : nat,nat→nat
           _ ** _ : nat,nat→nat
  vars :   m,n : nat
  axms :   1 ≡ 0|
           2 ≡ 0||
           3 ≡ 0|||
           ...
           m + 0 ≡ m
           m + n| ≡ (m + n)|
           n - 0 ≡ n
           0 - n ≡ 0
           m| - n| ≡ m - n
           m * 0 ≡ 0
           m * n| ≡ (m * n) + m
           m ** 0 ≡ 1
           m ** n| ≡ (m ** n) * m

Remember our general assumption that equality predicates are implicitly included in each signature (cf. Section 2.2). On the other hand, inequality predicates must be specified explicitly. Note that +, -, * and ** are specified inductively on the structure of their second (or first) argument: each ground term over the *constructors* 0 and _| is an instance of 0 and n|, respectively. *is even* and *is odd* are specified in a mutually recursive manner.

The minimum and maximum of two natural numbers may be specified as projections of a single operation *minmax* that refers to the *pairing* function:

```
NAT-PAIRS
    base :    NAT-ARITHMETIC
    sorts :   nat2
    opns :    <_,_> : nat,nat→nat2
              minmax : nat,nat→nat2
              min : nat→nat
              max : nat→nat
    vars :    m,n,m',n' : nat
    axms :    minmax m n ≡ <m,n>   ⇐   m ≤ n
              minmax m n ≡ <n,m>   ⇐   n < m
              min m n ≡ m'   ⇐   minmax m n ≡ <m',n'>
              max m n ≡ n'   ⇐   minmax m n ≡ <m',n'>
```

Another example for the use of the pairing function is the division of natural numbers as a function that returns both the quotient and the remainder of two natural numbers.

```
NAT-DIV
    base :    NAT-PAIRS
    opns :    _/_ : nat,nat→nat2
    preds :   _ divides _ : nat,nat
              _ does not divide _ : nat,nat
    vars :    m,n,q,r : nat
    axms :    m/n ≡ <0,m>   ⇐   m < n
              m/n ≡ <q|,r>   ⇐   n ≤ m, (m-n)/n ≡ <q,r>
              n divides m   ⇐   m/n ≡ <q,0>
              n does not divide m   ⇐   m/n ≡ <q,r|>
```

We close the section with two alternative specifications of integer numbers.

```
INT 1
    sorts :   int
    opns :    0 : int
              _| : int→int
```

```
        pred _ : int→int
vars :  x : int
axms :  pred x| ≡ x
        (pred x)| ≡ x
```

```
INT2
    sorts :  int
    opns :   0 : int
             _| : int→int
             -_ : int→int
    vars :   x : int
    axms :   -0 ≡ 0
             --x ≡ x
             (-x|)| ≡ -x
```

INT1 and INT2 provide different *constructors*. While INT1 adds the predecessor function to the constructors of NAT, INT2 is based on the inverting operator. Accordingly, we provide two sets of axioms for integer addition.

```
INT1-ADD
    base :   INT1
    opns :   _ + _ : int,int→int
    vars :   x,y : int
    axms :   x + 0 ≡ x
             x + y| ≡ (x + y)|
             x + (pred y) ≡ pred (x + y)
```

```
INT2-ADD
    base :   INT2
    opns :   _ + _ : int,int→int
    vars :   x,y : int
    axms :   x + 0 ≡ x
             x + y| ≡ (x + y)|
             x + (-y) ≡ -(-x + y)
```

3.3 Program Transformations

Let us extend NAT-ARITHMETIC.

```
FIBONACCI
    base :   NAT-ARITHMETIC
```

```
opns :    fib _ : nat⟶nat
vars :    n : nat
axms :    fib 0 ≡ 1
          fib 1 ≡ 1
          fib n|| ≡ (fib n|) + (fib n)
```

Given a ground term of the form *fib t* with t representing the number b, we may regard the previous three axioms as a recursive program, apply it to *fib t* and obtain the result after $2^{b/2}$ recursive calls. Burstall and Darlington transformed the above definition into a linear one using the transformation rules *tupling, fold, unfold, split* and *project*. We reformulate the transformation (cf. Burstall and Darlington, p. 49) using Horn clause syntax and deduction.

```
fib2 n ≡ <fib n|, fib n>                              (tupling)
fib2 0 ≡ <fib 1, fib 0>                               (substitute 0 for n)
       ≡ <1,1>                                        (unfold)
fib2 n| ≡ <fib n||, fib n|>                           (substitute n| for n)
        ≡ <fib n| + fib n, fib n|>                    (unfold)
        ≡ <m+m', m>   ⇐  <m,m'> ≡ <fib n|, fib n>     (split)
        ≡ <m+m', m>   ⇐  <m,m'> ≡ fib2 n              (fold)
fib n ≡ m'   ⇐   fib2 n ≡ <m,m'>                      (project)
```

The corresponding modification of FIBONACCI is based on NAT-PAIRS (cf. Section 3.2):

```
FIBONACCI2
    base :    NAT-PAIRS
    opns :    fib _ : nat⟶nat
              fib2 _ : nat⟶nat2
    vars :    n,m,m' : nat
    axms :    fib n ≡ m'   ⇐   fib2 n ≡ <m,m'>
              fib2 0 ≡ <1,1>
              fib2 n| ≡ <m+m', m>   ⇐   fib2 n ≡ <m,m'>
```

This example shows that the usual program transformations are nothing else but particular *Horn clause* derivations.

Another extension of NAT-ARITHMETIC is given by the well-known recursive program for computing factorials:

```
FACTORIAL
    base :    NAT-ARITHMETIC
    opns :    fact _ : nat⟶nat
```

vars :   n : nat
axms :   fact 0 ≡ 1
         fact n| ≡ (fact n) * n|

Generalize, fold, unfold and *specialize* allow us to turn this program into iterative form (cf. Burstall and Darlington, p. 53 f.):

fact2 n a ≡ (fact n) * a	(generalize)
fact2 0 a ≡ (fact 0) * a	(substitute 0 for n)
≡ 1 * a ≡ a	(unfold)
fact2 n| a ≡ (fact n|) * a	(substitute n| for n)
≡ (((fact n) * n|) * a ≡ (fact n) * (n| * a)	(unfold)
≡ fact2 n (n| * a)	(fold)
fact n ≡ fact2 n 1	(specialize)

The parameter a is called an *accumulator* because it mirrors the intermediate result variable in a corresponding while-program for fact (cf. Sterling and Shapiro, p.126). The transformation leads to

FACTORIAL2
  base :   NAT-ARITHMETIC
  opns :   fact _ : nat→nat
            fact2 _ _ : nat,nat→nat
  vars :   n : nat
  axms :   fact n ≡ fact2 n 1
            fact2 0 a ≡ a
            fact2 n| a ≡ fact2 n (a * n|)

The same transformation schema brings the binary functions of NAT-ARITHMETIC, e.g. multiplication, into iterative form:

mult2 m n a ≡ (m * n) + a	(generalize)
mult2 m 0 a ≡ (m * 0) + a	(substitute 0 for n)
≡ 0 + a ≡ a	(unfold)
mult2 m n| a ≡ (m * n|) + a	(substitute n| for n)
≡ ((m * n) + m) + a ≡ (m * n) + (m + a)	(unfold)
≡ mult2 m n (m + a)	(fold)
m * n ≡ mult2 m n 0	(specialize)

Note that the transformation of FACTORIAL makes use of the multiplicative-monoid property of $\mathbb{N}$. Analogously, the transformation of m*0≡0 and m*n|≡(m*n)+m rests on the fact that $\mathbb{N}$ is an additive monoid.

3.4 A Store-based Language Interpreter

Our goal is to specify an unbounded store with natural number entries. Initially, identifiers are provided by

```
IDENT
    sorts:   ident
    opns:    x0 : ident
             _| : ident→ident
    preds:   _≠_ : ident,ident
    vars:    x,y : ident
    axms:    x0 ≠ x|
             x| ≠ x0
             x| ≠ y| ⇐ x ≠ y
```

A (state of a) store is a partial function from a finite domain of identifiers to a range of values, say natural numbers.

```
STORE
    base:    IDENT, NAT-ARITHMETIC
    sorts:   store
    opns:    ω : store
             _[_←_] : store,ident,nat→store
    vars:    s : store
             x,y : ident
             m,n : nat
    axms:    s[x←m][x←n] ≡ s[x←n]                    (A1)
             s[x←m][y←n] ≡ s[y←n][x←m]  ⇐  x ≠ y    (A2)
```

ω denotes the empty store. (A1) says that an assignment of m to x followed by an assignment of n to x results in the state obtained by only assigning n to x. Two assignments can be exchanged by (A2), provided that the two identifiers to be modified are different.

Horn clause syntax allows us to specify the access to a store in at least two different ways. A *functional* version reads as follows.

```
ACCESS-FUN
    base:    STORE
    opns:    _[_] : store,ident→nat
    vars:    s : store
             x,y : ident
             n : nat
```

axms :   s[x←n][x] ≡ n   (A3)
s[x←n][y] ≡ s[y] ⇐ x ≠ y   (A4)

The empty store ω cannot be accessed. A ground term of the form ω[v] denotes an *undefined* object of sort *nat* because it cannot be identified with a term built up out of the nat-constructors 0 and _| (cf. Section 3.2). On the other hand, a ground term of the form t[u←v] represents a nonempty store obtained from (the store denoted by) t by changing the value of u into v. By (A3), v is the result of accessing u, while (A4) implies that the value of an identifier different from u can only be found in t.

A *relational* version is

ACCESS-REL
  base :   STORE
  preds :   _[_] is _ : store,ident,nat
  vars :   s : store
            x,y : ident
            m,n : nat
  axms :   s[x←n] is n
            s[x←m][y] is n ⇐ s[y] is n, x ≠ y

An ACCESS-REL-atom of the form *t[u] is v* corresponds to the ACCESS-FUN-equation *t[u] ≡ v*.

ACCESS-FUN may be used to specify the meaning of arithmetic expressions.

EXPRESSION
  base :   ACCESS-FUN
  sorts :   exp
  opns :   id _ : ident→exp
            val _ : nat→exp
            _ plus _ : exp,exp→exp
            _ times _ : exp,exp→exp
            evalExp : store,exp→nat
  vars :   s : store
            x : ident
            n : nat
            e,e' : exp
  axms :   evalExp s (id x) ≡ s[x]
            evalExp s (val n) ≡ n
            evalExp s (e plus e') ≡ (evalExp s e) + (evalExp s e')
            evalExp s (e times e') ≡ (evalExp s e) * (evalExp s e')

For instance, given the store $\omega[x0\leftarrow 3]$, evaluating the expression

$$(\text{val } 4) \text{ plus } (\text{id } x0)$$

means carrying out a sequence of unfoldings:

$$\text{evalExp } \omega[x0\leftarrow 3] \, ((\text{val } 4) \text{ plus } (\text{id } x0))$$
$$\equiv (\text{evalExp } \omega[x0\leftarrow 3] \, (\text{val } 4)) + (\text{evalExp } s \, (\text{id } x0))$$
$$\equiv 4 + \omega[x0\leftarrow 3][x0] \equiv 4 + 3 \equiv 0|||| + 0||| \equiv ... \equiv 0||||||| \equiv 7.$$

Optimized expressions are obtained by evaluation steps that do not refer to the *store* argument of evalExp, e.g. the sequence

$$\text{evalExp } s \, (e \text{ plus } (\text{val } 0))$$
$$\equiv (\text{evalExp } s \, e) + (\text{evalExp } s \, (\text{val } 0))$$
$$\equiv (\text{evalExp } s \, e) + 0$$
$$\equiv \text{evalExp } s \, e$$

optimizes (e plus (val 0)) into e.

EXPRESSION is extended to an interpreter of imperative programs.

```
COMMAND
    base :      EXPRESSION
    opns :      _ := _ : ident,exp→com
                _;_ : com,com→com
                if _ is zero then _ else _ : exp,com,com→com
                evalCom : store,com→store
    vars :      s : store
                x : ident
                e : exp
                c,c' : com
    axms :      evalCom s (x := e) ≡ s[x←(evalExp s e)]
                evalCom s (c; c') ≡ evalCom (evalCom s c) c'
                evalCom s (if e is zero then c else c')) ≡ evalCom s c
                    ⇐ evalExp s e ≡ 0
                evalCom s (if e is zero then c else c') ≡ evalCom s c'
                    ⇐ evalExp s e ≢ 0
```

The entire specification of a language with abstraction and communication features is presented along these lines in Padawitz [5].

3.5 Binary Numbers

Starting with natural numbers again, we now specify their binary representation.

```
BINARY
    sorts :    bin
    opns :     0 : bin
               1 : bin
               _0 : bin→bin
               _1 : bin→bin
    preds :    _ < _ : bin,bin
               _ is even : bin
               _ is odd : bin
    vars :     a,b : bin
    axms :     00 ≡ 0                          (E1)
               01 ≡ 1                          (E2)
               0 < 1
               a0 < b0  ⇐  a < b
               a0 < b1  ⇐  a < b
               a0 < b1  ⇐  a ≡ b
               a1 < b0  ⇐  a < b
               a1 < b1  ⇐  a < b
               a0 is even
               a1 is odd
```

Note the difference between the constants 0 and 1 on one hand and the unary (postfix) operators _0 and _1 on the other hand. These symbols are suggested by the usual notation of binary numbers. Using equations (E1) and (E2), ground terms over {0, 1, _0, _1} that represent binary numbers with leading zeros can be reduced to equivalent terms without leading zeros.

We add axioms that define binary addition and multiplication:

```
BINARY-ADD-MULT
    base :     BINARY
    opns :     _ + _ : bin,bin→bin
               _ * _ : bin,bin→bin
    vars :     a,b : bin
    axms :     a + 0 ≡ a
               0 + a ≡ a
               1 + 1 ≡ 10
               a0 + b0 ≡ (a + b)0
               a1 + b0 ≡ (a + b)1
```

$$a0 + b1 \equiv (a + b)1$$
$$a1 + b1 \equiv ((a + b) + 1)0$$
$$a * 0 \equiv 0$$
$$a * 1 \equiv a$$
$$a * b0 \equiv (a * b)0$$
$$a * b1 \equiv (a * b)0 + a$$

The axioms for binary addition can be used to evaluate arithmetic expressions of the form t+t' where t and t' are ground terms over {0, 1, _0, _1} and have the same size. If t and t' have different sizes, the *base* axioms (E1) and (E2) serve to fill up t or t' with zeros such that both terms attain the same size. If function evaluation is not to depend on base axioms, the following axioms must be added to BINARY-ADD-MULT:

$$a0 + 1 \equiv a1$$
$$a1 + 1 \equiv (a + 1)0$$
$$1 + a1 \equiv (a + 1)0$$
$$1 + a0 \equiv a1.$$

3.6 Decoding Binary Numbers

Let us translate binary representations of natural numbers to unary ones.

```
BINARY-TO-NAT
    base :    BINARY, NAT-ARITHMETIC
    opns :    trans _ : bin→nat
    vars :    b : bin
    axms :    trans 0 ≡ 0
              trans 1 ≡ 1
              trans b0 ≡ 2 * (trans b)
              trans b1 ≡ (2 * (trans b))|
```

Following the transformation of FACTORIAL (cf. Section 3.3) we derive an iterative version of BINARY-TO-NAT:

trans2 b n a ≡ ((trans b) * n) + a	(generalize)
trans2 0 n a ≡ ((trans 0) * n) + a	(substitute 0 for b)
≡ (0 * n) + a ≡ a	(unfold)
trans2 1 n a ≡ ((trans 1) * n) + a	(substitute 1 for b)
≡ (1 * n) + a ≡ n + a	(unfold)
trans2 b0 n a ≡ ((trans b0) * n) + a	(substitute b0 for b)
≡ ((2 * (trans b)) * n) + a	(unfold)

$$\equiv ((\text{trans b}) * (2 * n)) + a$$
$$\equiv \text{trans2 b } (2 * n) \text{ a} \qquad \text{(fold)}$$
$$\text{trans2 b1 n a} \equiv ((\text{trans b1}) * n) + a \qquad \text{(substitute b1 for b)}$$
$$\equiv ((2 * (\text{trans b})) * n) + a \qquad \text{(unfold)}$$
$$\equiv (((\text{trans b}) * (2 * n)) + n) + a$$
$$\equiv ((\text{trans b}) * (2 * n)) + (n + a)$$
$$\equiv \text{trans2 b } (2 * n) (n + a) \qquad \text{(fold)}$$
$$\text{trans b} \equiv \text{trans2 b 1 0} \qquad \text{(specialize)}$$

The transformed specification is

```
BINARY-TO-NAT-2
    base :    BINARY, NAT-ARITHMETIC
    opns :    trans _ : bin→nat
              trans2 _ _ _ : bin,nat,nat→nat
    vars :    b : bin
              n,a : nat
    axms :    trans b ≡ trans2 b 1 0
              trans2 0 n a ≡ a
              trans2 1 n a ≡ n + a
              trans2 b0 n a ≡ trans2 b (2 * n) a
              trans2 b1 n a ≡ trans2 b (2 * n) (n + a)
```

In his foundational paper on attributed grammars, Knuth gives a similar example where not only integer, but also non-periodic rational binary numbers are decoded. We present a corresponding extension of BINARY-TO-NAT. Non-negative non-periodic rational binary numbers are provided by

```
BINRAT
    base :    BINARY
    sorts :   binrat
    opns :    _. : bin→binrat
              _0 : binrat→binrat
              _1 : binrat→binrat
```

Non-negative rational unary numbers are represented as pairs of natural numbers:

```
RAT
    base :    NAT-ARITHMETIC
    sorts :   rat, rat2
    opns :    _ : nat→rat
              _/_ : nat,nat→rat
```

```
            _+_ : rat,rat→rat
            _*_ : rat,rat→rat
            <_,_> : rat,rat→rat2
  vars :    m,c,n,d : nat
  axms :    m ≡ m/1
            m/c ≡ n/d  ⇐  m*d ≡ c*n, c ≠ 0, d ≠ 0
            (m/c) + (n/d) ≡ ((m*d) + (c*n)) / (c*d)
            (m/c) * (n/d) ≡ (m*n) / (c*d)
```

Note that RAT admits *undefined* numbers denoted by ground terms of the form t/0.

Now we are ready to extend BINARY-TO-NAT to rational numbers. We write s/2 as shorthand for s*(1/2).

```
BINRAT-TO-RAT
  base :    BINARY-TO-NAT, BINRAT, RAT
  opns :    transrat _ : binrat→rat2
  vars :    b : bin
            c : binrat
            r,s : rat
  axms :    transrat b. ≡ <trans b, 1>
            transrat c0 ≡ <r, s/2>      ⇐  transrat c ≡ <r,s>
            transrat c1 ≡ <r+(s/2), s/2> ⇐  transrat c ≡ <r,s>
```

Given a binary number c, transrat returns two rational numbers. The first, say r, is the translation of c. The second, say s, amounts to 2^{-d} where d is the number of digits following . in c.

Note that NAT-ARITHMETIC is a subspecification of both BINARY-TO-NAT and RAT, while BINARY is a subspecification of both BINARY-TO-NAT and BINRAT. Instead of employing a special concept for *amalgamating* two specifications (cf. Ehrig and Mahr, p. 215 ff.) we establish that sub-specifications with the same name are identified. Hence BINRAT-TO-RAT does not contain two copies of NAT-ARITHMETIC or BINARY.

The iterative version of BINRAT-TO-RAT is accomplished by the following Horn clause derivation (cf. Section 4.2).

```
    transrat2 c x a ≡ <r+(s*a), s*x>              (generalize)    (A)
       ⇐  transrat c ≡ <r,s>
    <r+(s*a), s*x> ≡ transrat2 c x a              (symmetry)      (B)
       ⇐  transrat c ≡ <r,s>
```

```
    transrat2 b. x a ≡ <(trans b)+(1*a), 1*x>     (substitute into A)
       ⇐  transrat .b ≡ <trans b, 1>
```

transrat b. ≡ ⟨trans b, 1⟩	(axiom)
transrat2 .b x a ≡ ⟨(trans b)+(1∗a), 1∗x⟩	(cut)
⟨(trans b)+(1∗a), 1∗x⟩ ≡ ⟨(trans b)+a, x⟩	(RAT-axioms)
transrat2 b. x a ≡ ⟨(trans b)+a, x⟩	(transitivity)

transrat2 c0 x a ≡ ⟨r+((s/2)∗a), (s/2)∗x⟩ ⇐ transrat c0 ≡ ⟨r, s/2⟩	(substitute into A)
transrat c0 ≡ ⟨r, s/2⟩ ⇐ transrat c ≡ ⟨r,s⟩	(axiom)
transrat2 c0 x a ≡ ⟨r+((s/2)∗a), (s/2)∗x⟩ ⇐ transrat c ≡ ⟨r,s⟩	(cut)
⟨r+((s/2)∗a), (s/2)∗x⟩ ≡ ⟨r+(s∗(a/2)), s∗(x/2)⟩	(RAT-axioms)
transrat2 c0 x a ≡ ⟨r+(s∗(a/2)), s∗(x/2)⟩ ⇐ transrat c ≡ ⟨r,s⟩	(transitivity)
⟨r+(s∗(a/2)), s∗(x/2)⟩ ≡ transrat2 c (x/2) (a/2) ⇐ transrat c ≡ ⟨r,s⟩	(substitute into B)
transrat2 c0 x a ≡ transrat2 c (x/2) (a/2) ⇐ transrat c ≡ ⟨r,s⟩	(transitivity)
transrat c ≡ ⟨r,s⟩	(∗)
transrat2 c0 x a ≡ transrat2 c (x/2) (a/2)	(cut)

transrat2 c1 x a ≡ ⟨(r+(s/2))+((s/2)∗a), (s/2)∗x⟩ ⇐ transrat c1 ≡ ⟨r+(s/2), s/2⟩	(substitute into A)
transrat c1 ≡ ⟨r+(s/2), s/2⟩ ⇐ transrat c ≡ ⟨r,s⟩	(axiom)
transrat2 c1 x a ≡ ⟨(r+(s/2))+((s/2)∗a), (s/2)∗x⟩ ⇐ transrat c ≡ ⟨r,s⟩	(cut)
⟨r+(s/2))+((s/2)∗a), (s/2)∗x⟩ ≡ ⟨r+(s∗((a+1)/2)), s∗(x/2)⟩	(RAT-axioms)
transrat2 c1 x a ≡ ⟨r+(s∗((a+1)/2)), s∗(x/2)⟩ ⇐ transrat c ≡ ⟨r,s⟩	(transitivity)
⟨r+(s∗((a+1)/2)), s∗(x/2)⟩ ≡ transrat2 c (x/2) ((a+1)/2) ⇐ transrat c ≡ ⟨r,s⟩	(substitute into B)
transrat2 c1 x a ≡ transrat2 c (x/2) ((a+1)/2) ⇐ transrat c ≡ ⟨r,s⟩	(transitivity)
transrat c ≡ ⟨r,s⟩	(∗)
transrat2 c1 x a ≡ transrat2 c (x/2) ((a+1)/2)	(cut)

transrat c ≡ transrat2 c 1 0	(specialize)

Equation (∗) is valid in the sense that for all ground terms t there are ground terms u,v such that the equation *(transrat t) ≡ ⟨u,v⟩* is derivable from the axioms of BINRAT-TO-RAT.

The transformation results in

BINRAT-TO-RAT-2
    base :   BINARY-TO-NAT, BINRAT, RAT
    opns :   transrat _ : binrat→rat2
               transrat2 _ _ _ : binrat,rat,rat→rat2
    vars :   c : binrat
               b : bin
               x,a : rat
    axms :   transrat c ≡ transrat2 c 1 0
               transrat2 b$_\bullet$ x a ≡ <(trans b)+a, x>
               transrat2 c0 x a ≡ transrat2 c (x/2) (a/2)
               transrat2 c1 x a ≡ transrat2 c (x/2) ((a+1)/2)

3.7 Sequences

The usual functions on finite sequences are provided by

SEQ-OF-NAT
    base :   NAT
    sorts :   seq
    opns :   ε : seq
               _&_ : nat,seq→seq
               head _ : seq→nat
               tail _ : seq→seq
               app _ _ : seq,nat→seq
               conc _ _ : seq,seq→seq
               length _ : seq→nat
               max _ : seq→nat
    vars :   s,s' : seq
               n : nat
    axms :   head n&s ≡ n
               tail n&s ≡ s
               app ε n ≡ n&ε
               app m&s n ≡ m&(app s n)
               conc ε s ≡ s
               conc n&s s' ≡ n&(conc s s')
               length ε ≡ 0
               length n&s ≡ (length s)|
               max n&ε ≡ n
               max m&(n&s) ≡ max n&s   ⇐   m ≤ n
               max m&(n&s) ≡ max m&s   ⇐   n < m

The constructor _&_ adds a natural number to the left of a sequence, while *app* appends elements to the right. _&_ has the highest priority after the successor function _| (cf. Section 3.2). *conc* denotes the concatenation operator.

Based on SEQ-OF-NAT, sequence reversal is specified by

```
REVERSE
    base :   SEQ-OF-NAT
    opns :   rev _ : seq→seq
    vars :   n : nat
             s : seq
    axms :   rev ε ≡ ε
             rev n&s ≡ app (rev s) n
```

Following Section 3.3 we transform REVERSE into an iterative version:

rev2 s s' ≡ conc (rev s) s'	(generalize)
rev2 ε s' ≡ conc (rev ε) s' ≡ conc ε s' ≡ s'	(unfold)
rev2 n&s s' ≡ conc (rev n&s) s'	(unfold)
≡ conc (app (rev s) n) s' ≡ conc (conc (rev s) n&ε) s'	(unfold)
≡ conc (rev s) (conc n&ε s') ≡ conc (rev s) n&(conc ε s')	(unfold)
≡ conc (rev s) n&s' ≡ rev2 s n&s'	(fold)
rev s ≡ rev2 s ε	(specialize)

Hence we obtain

```
REVERSE2
    base :   SEQ-OF-NAT
    opns :   rev _ : seq→seq
             rev2 _ _ : seq,seq→seq
    vars :   n : nat
             s,s' : seq
    axms :   rev s ≡ rev2 s ε
             rev2 ε s' ≡ s'                        (*)
             rev2 n&s s' ≡ rev2 s n&s'
```

As in the case of fact2 (cf. Section 3.3) the second argument of rev2 serves as an accumulator for the result. The final value is returned by (*) when the first argument of rev2 has turned into ε.

The *subsequence* property can be specified by two predicate symbols:

```
SUBSEQ
    base :   SEQ-OF-NAT
```

```
preds :     _ is subseq of _ : seq,seq
            _ begins with _ : seq,seq
vars :      n : nat
            s,s' : seq
axms :      s is subseq of n&s'  ⇐  s is subseq of s'
            s is subseq of n&s'  ⇐  n&s' begins with s
            s begins with ε
            n&s begins with n&s'  ⇐  s begins with s'
```

Factorial sequences ranging from some natural number down to 0 are built up out of

```
FACT-SEQ
    base :   FACTORIAL, SEQ-OF-NAT
    opns :   factseq _ : nat→seq
    vars :   n : nat
    axms :   factseq 0 ≡ 1&ε
             factseq n| ≡ (fact n|)&(factseq n)
```

Burstall and Darlington, p. 50, propose the following optimization of FACT-SEQ where *fact 0, fact 1, fact 2,...* are not computed independently of each other. Instead, the first element of the sequence (denoted by the ground term) *factseq t*, i.e. *fact t*, is used to compute *fact t|* and thus *factseq t|*. The transformation is

```
factseq2 n ≡ <fact n, factseq n>                        (tupling)
factseq2 0 ≡ <fact 0, factseq 0>                        (substitute 0 for n)
          ≡ <1, 1&ε>                                    (unfold)
factseq2 n| ≡ <fact n|, factseq n|>                     (substitute n| for n)
          ≡ <(fact n)*n|, (fact n|)&(factseq n)>        (unfold)
          ≡ <(fact n)*n|, ((fact n)*n|)&(factseq n)>    (unfold)
          ≡ <m*n|, (m*n|)&s>
            ⇐  <m,s> ≡ <fact n, factseq n>              (split)
            ⇐  <m,s> ≡ factseq2 n                       (fold)
factseq n ≡ s  ⇐  factseq2 n ≡ <m,s>.                   (project)
```

It yields

```
FACT-SEQ-2
    base :   FACTORIAL, SEQ-OF-NAT
    sorts :  nat×seq
    opns :   factseq _ : nat→seq
             factseq2 _ : nat→nat×seq
```

vars :   m,n : nat
axms :   factseq n ≡ s ⇐ factseq2 n ≡ <m,s>
         factseq2 0 ≡ <1, 1&ε>
         factseq2 n| ≡ <m∗n|, (m∗n|)&s> ⇐ factseq2 n ≡ <m,s>

<_,_> : nat,seq→nat×seq

3.8 Palindromes

The check whether a sequence s is a palindrome proceeds in two phases. First s is reversed, then the result is tested for equality to s.

    PALINDROME
        base :   REVERSE
        preds : _ is pal : seq
        vars :   s : seq
        axms :   s is pal ⇐ rev s ≡ s

One may ask whether both tasks can be performed concurrently. Following Bird, p. 244 ff., we introduce a function *eqrev* that takes two sequences s and s' and returns the reverse of s if s agrees with s', i.e. eqrev satisfies the equation

$$\text{eqrev s s} \equiv \text{rev s.}$$

Based on eqrev the palindrome predicate is specified by

$$\text{s is pal} \Leftarrow \text{eqrev s s'} \equiv \text{s'}.$$

When calling this clause we initiate the search for a solution of *eqrev s s' ≡ s'*. The axioms for eqrev must ensure that a solution exists if and only if s is a palindrome, i.e. if and only if both s is equal to s' and s' is the reverse of s. We use an auxiliary function *eqrev2* to accumulate the result of eqrev. The axioms for eqrev2 follow those of rev2 (cf. Section 3.7):

    PALINDROME2
        base :   SEQ-OF-NAT
        opns :   eqrev : seq,seq→seq
                 eqrev2 : seq,seq,seq→seq
        preds : _ is pal : seq
        vars :   r,s,s' : seq
        axms :   s is pal ⇐ eqrev s s' ≡ s'
                 eqrev s s' ≡ eqrev2 s s' ε
                 eqrev2 ε ε r ≡ r
                 eqrev2 n&s n&s' r ≡ eqrev2 s s' n&r

For instance, the inverse of the following transformation is a derivation of
2&1&2&ε is pal:

    2&1&2&ε is pal
    eqrev 2&1&2&ε s' ≡ s'   (unfold)
    eqrev2 2&1&2&ε s' ε ≡ s'   (unfold)
    eqrev2 2&1&2&ε 2&r ε ≡ 2&r   (substitute 2&r for s')
    eqrev2 1&2&ε r 2&ε ≡ 2&r   (unfold)
    eqrev2 1&2&ε 1&r' 2&ε ≡ 2&1&r'   (substitute 1&r' for r)
    eqrev2 2&ε r' 1&2&ε ≡ 2&1&r'   (unfold)
    eqrev2 2&ε 2&r" 1&2&ε ≡ 2&1&2&r"   (substitute 2&r" for r')
    eqrev2 ε r" 2&1&2&ε ≡ 2&1&2&r"   (unfold)
    eqrev2 ε ε 2&1&2&ε ≡ 2&1&2&ε   (substitute ε for r")

Since the last equation is an instance of an axiom, namely of *eqrev2 ε ε r ≡ r*, we conclude that *2&1&2&ε is pal* is derivable from PALINDROME2. Many substitutions had to be guessed at in order to achieve the desired result.

Let us now translate Bird's second version of the palindrome test into Horn clauses and compare a corresponding derivation of *2&1&2&ε is pal* with the one given above.

    PALINDROME3
        base :   SEQ-OF-NAT
        opns :   eqrev : seq,seq→seq
                       eqrev2 : seq,seq,seq→seq
        preds :   _ is pal : seq
        vars :   r,r',s,s' : seq
        axms :   s is pal ⇐ eqrev s s' ≡ s'
                       eqrev s s' ≡ eqrev2 s s' ε
                       eqrev2 ε s' r ≡ r ⇐ s' ≡ ε
                       eqrev2 n&s s' r ≡ eqrev2 s (tail s') n&r ⇐ head s' ≡ n

Again, we give a transformation of *2&1&2&ε is pal* the inverse of which is a derivation of this formula. (As in the premise of a Horn clause, the comma denotes a conjunction of atoms.)

    2&1&2&ε is pal
    eqrev 2&1&2&ε s' ≡ s'   (unfold)
    eqrev2 2&1&2&ε s' ε ≡ s'   (unfold)
    eqrev2 1&2&ε (tail s') 2&ε ≡ s',   (unfold)
        head s' ≡ 2

```
    eqrev2 2&ε (tail (tail s')) 1&2&ε ≡ s',           (unfold)
        head (tail s') ≡ 1,
        head s' ≡ 2
    eqrev2 ε (tail (tail (tail s'))) 2&1&2&ε ≡ s',    (unfold)
        head (tail (tail s')) ≡ 2,
        head (tail s') ≡ 1,
        head s' ≡ 2
    2&1&2&ε ≡ s',                                      (unfold)
        tail (tail (tail s')) ≡ ε,
        head (tail (tail s')) ≡ 2,
        head (tail s') ≡ 1,
        head s' ≡ 2
    2&1&2&ε ≡ 2&1&2&ε,                                 (substitute)
        tail (tail (tail 2&1&2&ε)) ≡ ε,
        head (tail (tail 2&1&2&ε)) ≡ 2,
        head (tail 2&1&2&ε) ≡ 1,
        head 2&1&2&ε ≡ 2
```

Since the four equations of the last conjunctive formula follow from axioms of SEQ-OF-NAT, we conclude that *2&1&2&ε is pal* is derivable from PALINDROME3. In contrast to the previous derivation there is only one substitution step and this need not be guessed at because the goal for solving 2&1&2&ε ≡ s' determines the instantiation of s' by 2&1&2&ε. This behaviour results from the fact that the left-hand sides of PALINDROME3-equations have free variables in *both* output parameters (i.e. the second and third arguments) of eqrev2, while PALINDROME2 enforces suitable instantiations of the second argument in order to match the first, the input parameter.

3.9 Sorting

We proceed with some sorting algorithms. First, we look at *sort by insertion*:

```
INSERTION-SORT
    base :   SEQ-OF-NAT
    opns :   sort _ : seq → seq
             insert _ _ : nat,seq → seq
    vars :   s : seq
             m,n : nat
    axms :   sort ε ≡ ε
             sort n&s ≡ insert n (sort s)
             insert m ε ≡ m&ε
```

insert m n&s ≡ m&(n&s) ⇐ m ≤ n
insert m n&s ≡ n&(insert m s) ⇐ n < m

Secondly, *mergesort* may be specified as follows.

```
MERGESORT
    base :   SEQ-OF-NAT
    opns :   sort _ : seq→seq
             merge _ _ : seq,seq→seq
    vars :   s,s' : seq
             m,n : nat
    axms :   sort ε ≡ ε                                                    (1)
             sort (conc s s') ≡ merge (sort s) (sort s')
                ⇐ length s ≤ length s', length s' ≤ (length s)|           (2)
             merge ε s ≡ s
             merge s ε ≡ s
             merge m&s n&s' ≡ m&(merge s n&s')  ⇐  m ≤ n
             merge m&s n&s' ≡ n&(merge m&s s')  ⇐  n < m
```

By (2), sorting a sequence begins with dividing it in half and ends with merging the sorted halves. The dividing in half may be carried out by the functions

    split _ _ _ : seq,seq,seq→seq2
    ⟨_,_⟩ : seq,seq→seq2

with axioms

    split m&n&s s' s" ≡ split s m&s' n&s"
    split m&ε s' s" ≡ ⟨m&s',s"⟩
    split ε s' s" ≡ ⟨s',s"⟩.

Accordingly, axioms (1) and (2) are replaced by the clause

    sort s ≡ merge (sort s') (sort s") ⇐ split s ε ε ≡ ⟨s',s"⟩.

Thirdly, we have *quicksort*:

```
QUICKSORT
    base :   SEQ-OF-NAT
    sorts :  seq2
    opns :   sort _ : seq→seq
             partition _ _ : seq,nat→seq2
             ⟨_,_⟩ : seq,seq→seq2
    vars :   s,s',l,g : seq
             n : nat
```

axms: sort ε ≡ ε
       sort (conc s n&s') ≡ conc (sort l) n&(sort g)   (∗)
              ⇐ partition (conc s s') n ≡ ⟨l,g⟩
       partition ε n ≡ ⟨ε,ε⟩
       partition m&s n ≡ ⟨m&l, g⟩
              ⇐ m ≤ n, partition s n ≡ ⟨l,g⟩
       partition m&s n ≡ ⟨l, m&g⟩
              ⇐ n < m, partition s n ≡ ⟨l,g⟩

The result of *partition s n* is a pair ⟨l,g⟩ of sequences such that l consists of all elements of s less than or equal to n, while g consists of all elements of s greater than n. The right-hand side of (∗) includes an application of *conc* that can be avoided by providing an auxiliary function

$$\text{sort2}\ \_\_\ :\ \text{seq seq} \rightarrow \text{seq}$$

with a second argument serving as an accumulator for the result of *sort s*. The first two axioms of QUICKSORT are replaced by

       sort ε ≡ sort2 s ε
       sort2 ε s ≡ s
       sort2 (conc s n&s') s" ≡ sort2 l n&(sort2 g s")
              ⇐ partition (conc s s') n ≡ ⟨l,g⟩

A Prolog version of this quicksort program can be found in Kluzniak and Szpakowicz, p. 138.

It is a simple task to specify sortedness:

    SORTED
       base: SEQ-OF-NAT
       preds: _ is sorted : seq
       vars: s : seq
                m,n : nat
       axms: ε is sorted   (3)
                n&ε is sorted   (4)
                m&(n&s) is sorted ⇐ m ≤ n, n&s is sorted   (5)

Consequently, a sorting algorithm is correct if for all t ∈ GT(SIG)$_{seq}$ (cf. Section 2.2) the formula *(sort t) is sorted* can be derived from (3)-(5) and the axioms for *sort*, which represent the sorting algorithm.

3.10 Unordered Combinations

We begin with multisets (also called bags) of, say, natural numbers. In contrast to sequence elements the order of multiset elements is irrelevant, but in contrast to sets multiple occurrences of the same elements do count.

```
FINBAG
    base :    NAT
    sorts :   bag
    opns :    ∅ : bag
              insert _ _ : nat,bag→bag
    vars :    m,n : nat
              b : bag
    axms :    insert m (insert n b) ≡ insert n (insert m b)           (A1)
```

(A1) defines *insert* as a commutative operation reflecting the property of a bag to represent unordered combinations. FINBAG can be combined with SEQ-OF-NAT to specify the permutation property of sequences:

```
PERMUTATION
    base :    SEQ-OF-NAT, FINBAG
    opns :    makeBag _ : seq→set
    preds :   _ is perm of _ : seq,seq
    vars :    n : nat
              s,s' : seq
    axms :    makeBag ε ≡ ∅
              makeBag n&s ≡ insert n (makeBag s)
              s is perm of s'  ⇐  makeBag s ≡ makeBag s'
```

Consequently, the equivalence relation induced by (A1) agrees with *is perm of*.

FINBAG is extended by an operation that counts the number of occurrences of a given element in a bag. It reflects the characterization of bags as functions from ℕ to ℕ.

```
FINBAG-COUNT
    base :    FINBAG
    opns :    _[_] : bag,nat→nat
    vars :    m,n : nat
              b : bag
    axms :    ∅[m] ≡ 0
              (insert m b)[m] ≡ b[m]|
              (insert m b)[n] ≡ b[n]  ⇐  m ≠ n
```

To remove occurrences of a given element from a bag we provide

    FINBAG-REMOVE
        base :   FINBAG
        opns :   remove _ _ : nat,bag→bag
        vars :   m,n : nat
                   b : bag
        axms :   remove m $\emptyset \equiv \emptyset$
                  remove m (insert m b) $\equiv$ b   (*)
                  remove m (insert n b) $\equiv$ insert n (remove m b) ⇐ m $\neq$ n

To proceed from bags to sets *insert* must be made idempotent and the counting operation replaced by the membership predicate:

    FINSET
        base :   FINBAG(bag becomes set)
        preds :   _ is in _ : nat,set
        vars :   m,n : nat
                   s : set
        axms :   insert m (insert m s) $\equiv$ insert m s   (A2)
                  m is in (insert m s)
                  m is in (insert n s) ⇐ m is in s

To remove an element from a set means to delete *all* its occurrences. Hence (*) is replaced by (A3):

    FINSET-REMOVE
        base :   FINSET
        opns :   remove _ _ : nat,set→set
        vars :   m,n : nat
                 s : set
        axms :   remove m $\emptyset \equiv \emptyset$
                  remove m (insert m s) $\equiv$ remove m s   (A3)
                  remove m (insert n s) $\equiv$ insert n (remove m s) ⇐ m $\neq$ n
                                                                     (A4)

Adding the constant **all** to denote a universe of elements allows us to represent not only finite sets (by terms over $\emptyset$ and *insert*) but also sets with finite complement (by terms over **all** and *remove*). Consequently, *remove* becomes a constructor like *insert*.

    COFINSET
        base :   FINSET-REMOVE

opns :   all : set
vars :   m,n : nat
axms :   insert m all ≡ all
          insert m (remove m s) ≡ insert m s
          remove m (remove m s) ≡ remove m s
          remove m (remove n s) ≡ remove n (remove m s)
          m is in all
          m is in (remove n s) ⇐ m is in s, m ≠ n

COFINSET is extended by the complementing operator.

COFINSET-COMPL
    base :   COFINSET
    opns :   compl _ : set → set
    vars :   m,n : nat
              s : set
    axms :   compl ∅ ≡ all
              compl all ≡ ∅
              compl (insert m s) ≡ remove m (compl s)
              compl (remove m s) ≡ insert m (compl s) ⇐ m is in s
              compl (remove m s) ≡ compl s ⇐ m is in (compl s)

3.11 Binary Trees

Two constructors build up binary trees with natural number entries at the leaves: ⟦x⟧⟦y⟧ denotes a tree with left subtree x and right subtree y. ⟦n⟧ stands for a leaf with entry $n \in \mathbb{N}$.

BINTREE
    base :   NAT-PAIRS
    sorts :   tree
    opns :   ⟦_⟧ : nat → tree
              ⟦_⟧⟦_⟧ : tree,tree → tree

Bird, p. 241, presents a function *transform* that takes a tree and replaces all its entries by the minimal one:

TREE-TRANSFORM
    base :   BINTREE
    opns :   transform _ : tree → tree
              replace _ _ : tree,nat → tree
              minEntry _ : tree → nat

vars :   x,y : tree
         m,n : nat
axms :   transform x ≡ replace x (minEntry x)
         replace ⟦m⟧ n ≡ ⟦n⟧
         replace ⟦x⟧⟦y⟧ n ≡ ⟦replace x n⟧⟦replace y n⟧
         minEntry ⟦m⟧ ≡ m
         minEntry ⟦x⟧⟦y⟧ ≡ min (minEntry x) (minEntry y)

As was necessary in PALINDROME (cf. Section 3.8) the data structure must be traversed twice before the result of a single operation is obtained. Bird solves the problem by providing a function *repmin* that performs two tasks concurrently, i.e. *repmin* satisfies the equation

(∗)   repmin x m ≡ ⟨replace x m, minEntry x⟩.

Based on *repmin* the tree transformation is specified by

                transform x ≡ y   ⇐   repmin x m ≡ ⟨y,m⟩.

Hence the goal is to solve the premise equation *repmin x m ≡ ⟨y,m⟩*. If ⟨y,m⟩ is a solution, we conclude from (∗) that y is the tree obtained from x by replacing all entries with m and additionally that m is the minimal entry of x. It remains to specify *repmin* such that (∗) holds true.

TREE-TRANSFORM-2
    base :   BINTREE
    sorts : tree×nat
    opns :   transform _ : tree→tree
             repmin _ _ : tree,nat→tree×nat
             ⟨_,_⟩ : tree,nat→tree×nat
    vars :   x,y,x',y' : tree
             m,n,mx,my : nat
    axms :   transform x ≡ y   ⇐   repmin x m ≡ ⟨y,m⟩
             repmin ⟦n⟧ m ≡ ⟨⟦m⟧,n⟩
             repmin ⟦x⟧⟦y⟧ m ≡ ⟨⟦x'⟧⟦y'⟧, min mx my⟩
                 ⇐ repmin x m ≡ ⟨x',mx⟩, repmin y m ≡ ⟨y',my⟩

3.12 Search Trees

A binary tree with entries in *all* nodes is a search tree if the element stored at the left successor of any node N is less than the element stored at N and the element stored at the right successor of N is greater than the element stored at N. The insertion of elements maintains this property.

SEARCHTREE
   base :   NAT-PAIRS
   sorts :   tree
   opns :   ω : tree
               ⟦_⟧_⟦_⟧ : tree,nat,tree→tree
               insert _ _ : nat,tree→tree
   preds :   _ is in _ : nat,tree
   vars :   i,n : nat
               x,y : tree
   axms :   insert i ω ≡ ⟦ω⟧i⟦ω⟧
               insert i ⟦x⟧i⟦y⟧ ≡ ⟦x⟧i⟦y⟧
               insert i ⟦x⟧n⟦y⟧ ≡ ⟦insert i x⟧n⟦y⟧ ⇐ i < n
               insert i ⟦x⟧n⟦y⟧ ≡ ⟦x⟧n⟦insert i y⟧ ⇐ n < i
               i is in ⟦x⟧i⟦y⟧
               i is in ⟦x⟧n⟦y⟧ ⇐ i < n, i is in x
               i is in ⟦x⟧n⟦y⟧ ⇐ n < i, i is in y

A search tree is balanced if all paths from the root to a leaf, or, equivalently, the longest and the shortest paths, have the same length.

BALANCED
   base :   SEARCHTREE
   opns :   minmax _ : tree→nat2
   preds :   _ is balanced : tree
               _ is not balanced : tree
   vars :   m,n,mx,nx,my,ny : nat
               x,y : tree
   axms :   x is balanced ⇐ minmax x ≡ ⟨m,m⟩
               x is not balanced ⇐ minmax x ≡ ⟨m,n⟩, m ≠ n
               minmax ω ≡ ⟨0,0⟩
               minmax ⟦x⟧n⟦y⟧ ≡ ⟨(min mx my)|, (max nx ny)|⟩
                  ⇐ minmax x ≡ ⟨mx,nx⟩, minmax y ≡ ⟨my,ny⟩

For instance, a sequence of unfoldings and two substitutions yields a proof of the balancedness of the tree ⟦⟦ω⟧1⟦ω⟧⟧3⟦⟦ω⟧4⟦ω⟧⟧:

   ⟦⟦ω⟧1⟦ω⟧⟧3⟦⟦ω⟧4⟦ω⟧⟧ is balanced
   minmax ⟦⟦ω⟧1⟦ω⟧⟧3⟦⟦ω⟧4⟦ω⟧⟧ ≡ ⟨m,m⟩   (unfold)
   ⟨(min mx my)|, (max nx ny)|⟩ ≡ ⟨m,m⟩,   (unfold)
      minmax ⟦ω⟧1⟦ω⟧ ≡ ⟨mx,nx⟩,
      minmax ⟦ω⟧4⟦ω⟧ ≡ ⟨my,ny⟩

⟨(min mx my)|, (max nx ny)|⟩ ≡ ⟨m,m⟩,
    ⟨(min mx' my')|, (max nx' ny')|⟩ ≡ ⟨mx,nx⟩,   (unfold)
    minmax ω ≡ ⟨mx',nx'⟩, minmax ω ≡ ⟨my',ny'⟩,
    ⟨(min mx" my")|, (max nx" ny")|⟩ ≡ ⟨my,ny⟩,   (unfold)
    minmax ω ≡ ⟨mx",nx"⟩, minmax ω ≡ ⟨my",ny"⟩
⟨(min mx my)|, (max nx ny)|⟩ ≡ ⟨m,m⟩,
    ⟨(min mx' my')|, (max nx' ny')|⟩ ≡ ⟨mx,nx⟩,
    ⟨0,0⟩ ≡ ⟨mx',nx'⟩, ⟨0,0⟩ ≡ ⟨my',ny'⟩,   (unfold)
    ⟨(min mx" my")|, (max nx" ny")|⟩ ≡ ⟨my,ny⟩,
    ⟨0,0⟩ ≡ ⟨mx",nx"⟩, ⟨0,0⟩ ≡ ⟨my",ny"⟩   (unfold)
⟨(min mx my)|, (max nx ny)|⟩ ≡ ⟨m,m⟩,
    ⟨(min 0 0)|, (max 0 0)|⟩ ≡ ⟨mx,nx⟩,   (substitute 0)
    ⟨(min 0 0)|, (max 0 0)|⟩ ≡ ⟨my,ny⟩   (substitute 0)
⟨(min mx my)|, (max nx ny)|⟩ ≡ ⟨m,m⟩,
    ⟨1,1⟩ ≡ ⟨mx,nx⟩,   (unfold)
    ⟨1,1⟩ ≡ ⟨my,ny⟩   (unfold)
⟨(min 1 1)|, (max 1 1)|⟩ ≡ ⟨m,m⟩   (substitute 1)
⟨2,2⟩ ≡ ⟨m,m⟩   (unfold)

The last equation is solved by substituting 2 for m.

An alternative specification of *balanced* does not refer to *min* and *max* and is completely relational. The atom *height t is n* is solvable only if all paths of the tree represented by t have length n:

BALANCED2
    base :   SEARCHTREE
    preds :   _ is balanced : tree
              _ is not balanced : tree
              height _ is _ : tree,nat
    vars :   m,n,n' : nat
              x,y : tree
    axms :   x is balanced ⇐ height x is n
              height ω is 0
              height ⟦x⟧m⟦y⟧ is n| ⇐ height x is n, height y is n
              ⟦x⟧m⟦y⟧ is not balanced
                                ⇐ height x is n, height y is n', n ≠ n'
              ⟦x⟧m⟦y⟧ is not balanced ⇐ x is not balanced
              ⟦x⟧m⟦y⟧ is not balanced ⇐ y is not balanced

The balancedness of ⟦⟦ω⟧1⟦ω⟧⟧3⟦⟦ω⟧4⟦ω⟧⟧ is now derived as follows:

    ⟦⟦ω⟧1⟦ω⟧⟧3⟦⟦ω⟧4⟦ω⟧⟧ is balanced
    height ⟦⟦ω⟧1⟦ω⟧⟧3⟦⟦ω⟧4⟦ω⟧⟧ is n   (unfold)

height ⟦⟦ω⟧1⟦ω⟧⟧3⟦⟦ω⟧4⟦ω⟧⟧ is m| (substitute m| for n)
height ⟦ω⟧1⟦ω⟧ is m, height ⟦ω⟧4⟦ω⟧ is m   (unfold)
height ⟦ω⟧1⟦ω⟧ is k|, height ⟦ω⟧4⟦ω⟧ is k| (substitute k| for m)
height ω is k   (unfold)

We conclude ⟦⟦ω⟧1⟦ω⟧⟧3⟦⟦ω⟧4⟦ω⟧⟧ is balanced from the axiom height ω is 0.

3.13 2-3 Trees

There are binary trees which cannot be balanced. However, if three successors of a node are allowed as well, every insertion of an element can be followed by rebalancing the whole tree. A corresponding equational program has been given by Hoffman and O'Donnell (Example 3.1; see also O'Donnell [2], Section 16.3), which, however, does not satisfy the Definition Principle (cf. Section 7.8) demanding that *non-base* equations start with *non-base* functions. The version developed below fulfils the Definition Principle.

Search trees with either two or three successors of any node are called 2-3 trees.

```
TWO-THREE-TREE
   base :    NAT-ARITHMETIC
   sorts :   tree
   opns :    ω : tree
             ⟦_⟧_⟦_⟧ : tree,nat,tree → tree
             ⟦_⟧_⟦_⟧_⟦_⟧ : tree,nat,tree,nat,tree → tree
```

We leave it to the reader to specify a predicate *is in* analogously to our specification of the one for SEARCHTREE, presuming that in the case of a node N with two entries m and n and three successors the element stored at the left successor of N is less than m, the element stored at the middle successor of N is greater than m and less than n and the element stored at the right successor of N is greater than n.

The *balanced* predicate of BALANCED2 can be adapted immediately to 2-3-trees:

```
BALANCED3
   base :    TWO-THREE-TREE
   preds :   _ is balanced : tree
             height _ is _ : tree,nat
   vars :    m,n,k : nat
```

```
            x,y,z : tree
axms :      x is balanced  ⇐ height x is n
            height ω is 0
            height 〖x〗m〖y〗 is k|  ⇐ height x is k, height y is k
            height 〖x〗m〖y〗n〖z〗 is k|
                    ⇐ height x is k, height y is k, height z is k
```

When specifying the insertion operator with subsequent rebalancing we have to take into account that rebalancing must be finished *before* further insertions are started. This suggests the introduction of the sort *frozenTree*, which stands for trees whose rebalancing has not been finished. The operation *insert* takes a tree, inserts a number and returns a frozen tree, while *insertAndBalance* subsequently rebalances the frozen tree and *thaws* it by changing its sort from *frozenTree* to *tree*. Let us first specify *insert*:

```
INSERT
    base :   BALANCED3
    sorts :  frozenTree
    opns :   insert _ _ : nat,tree→frozenTree
             freeze1 _ : tree→frozenTree
             freeze2 _ _ _ : tree,nat,tree→frozenTree
             〖_〗_〖_〗 : frozenTree,nat,tree→frozenTree
             〖_〗_〖_〗 : tree,nat,frozenTree→frozenTree
             〖_〗_〖_〗_〖_〗 : frozenTree,nat,tree,nat,tree→frozenTree
             〖_〗_〖_〗_〖_〗 : tree,nat,frozenTree,nat,tree→frozenTree
             〖_〗_〖_〗_〖_〗 : tree,nat,tree,nat,frozenTree→frozenTree
    vars :   x,y,z : tree
             i,m,n : nat
    axms :   insert i 〖x〗i〖y〗 ≡ freeze1 〖x〗i〖y〗
             insert i 〖x〗i〖y〗m〖z〗 ≡ freeze1 〖x〗i〖y〗m〖z〗
             insert i 〖x〗m〖y〗i〖z〗 ≡ freeze1 〖x〗m〖y〗i〖z〗
             insert i ω ≡ freeze2 ω i ω
             insert i 〖x〗m〖y〗 ≡ 〖insert i x〗m〖y〗  ⇐ i < m
             insert i 〖x〗m〖y〗 ≡ 〖x〗m〖insert i y〗  ⇐ m < i
             insert i 〖x〗m〖y〗n〖z〗 ≡ 〖insert i x〗m〖y〗n〖z〗  ⇐ i < m
             insert i 〖x〗m〖y〗n〖z〗 ≡ 〖x〗m〖insert i y〗n〖z〗  ⇐ m < i, i < n
             insert i 〖x〗m〖y〗n〖z〗 ≡ 〖x〗m〖y〗n〖insert i z〗  ⇐ n < i
```

The subtrees enclosed in boldface brackets 〖 and 〗 yield the path from the root of the tree down to the node where i either occurs or must be inserted. In the first case a frozen subtree of the form *freeze1 x* is generated. In the second case a new leaf *freeze2 ω i ω* is appended.

Rebalancing is performed along the path given by the boldface bracketed subtrees. freeze1 indicates that no element has been inserted and thus the tree structure has not changed. Hence the frozen tree is thawed just by shifting freeze1 up to the root:

REBALANCE1
    base :   INSERT
    vars :   x,y,z : tree
              m,n : tree
    axms :   [freeze1 x]m[y] ≡ freeze1 [x]m[y]
               [x]m[freeze1 y] ≡ freeze1 [x]m[y]
               [freeze1 x]m[y]n[z] ≡ freeze1 [x]m[y]n[z]
               [x]m[freeze1 y]n[z] ≡ freeze1 [x]m[y]n[z]
               [x]m[y]n[freeze1 z] ≡ freeze1 [x]m[y]n[z]

Actual rebalancing takes place only if a new leaf, i.e. a subtree of the form *freeze2 x i y* has been generated. Then it depends on the parent node of *freeze2 x i y* within the tree to be rebalanced how to proceed.

If the parent node, say N, has three successors, then N bears two new children N1 and N2, each with two successors, and i becomes the entry of N1 or N2. For instance, the following transformation takes place if *freeze2 x i y* is the left subtree of N:

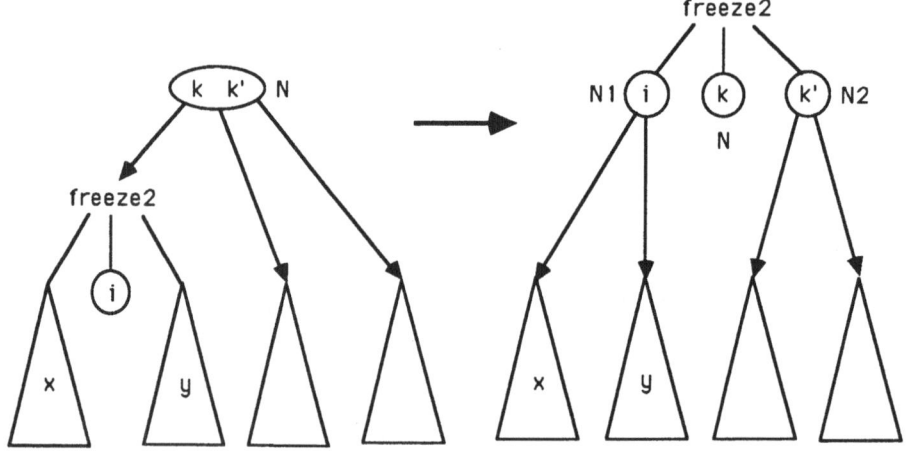

Provided that the whole tree was balanced before insertion this step rebalances the subtree with root N. Moreover, freeze2 is shifted from a child of N up to N.

If the parent node of *freeze2 x i y* has only two successors, then N gets a third one where i is inserted, and freeze1 signals the end of rebalancing:

REBALANCE2
- base : REBALANCE1
- vars : x,y,z,z' : tree
  - i,m,n : tree
- axms : 〚freeze2 x i y〛m〚z〛n〚z'〛 ≡ freeze2 (〚x〛i〚y〛) m (〚z〛n〚z'〛)
  - 〚x〛i〚freeze2 y m z〛n〚z'〛 ≡ freeze2 (〚x〛i〚y〛) m (〚z〛n〚z'〛)
  - 〚x〛i〚y〛m〚freeze2 z n z'〛 ≡ freeze2 (〚x〛i〚y〛) m (〚z〛n〚z'〛)
  - 〚freeze2 x i y〛m〚z〛 ≡ freeze1 〚x〛i〚y〛m〚z〛
  - 〚x〛i〚freeze2 y m z〛 ≡ freeze1 〚x〛i〚y〛m〚z〛

Hence either freeze1 or freeze2 eventually reaches the root whereupon *thaw* removes freeze1 or freeze2 and changes the frozen tree into a tree such that further elements can be inserted.

INSERT-AND-BALANCE
- base : REBALANCE2
- opns : insertAndBalance _ _ : nat,tree→tree
  - thaw _ : frozenTree→tree
- vars : x,y : tree
  - i,n : tree
- axms : insertAndBalance i x ≡ thaw (insert i x)
  - thaw (freeze1 x) ≡ x
  - thaw (freeze2 x i y) ≡ 〚x〛i〚y〛

In Example 4.3.4, we show the correctness of insertAndBalance by presenting a proof of the clause

$$(\text{insertAndBalance } u\ t) \text{ is balanced} \Leftarrow t \text{ is balanced}$$

with arbitrary ground terms u and t.

3.14 Tree Domains

A tree domain is the domain of a partial function from $\mathbb{N}^*$ to a set of entries, say natural numbers, which represents a tree with finite node degree. For instance, if

$$\text{dom}(f) = \{\varepsilon, 0, 1, 2, 10, 11\},$$
$$f(\varepsilon) = 0,\ f(0) = 1,\ f(1) = 2,\ f(2) = 5,\ f(10) = 3 \text{ and } f(11) = 4,$$

then f stands for the tree

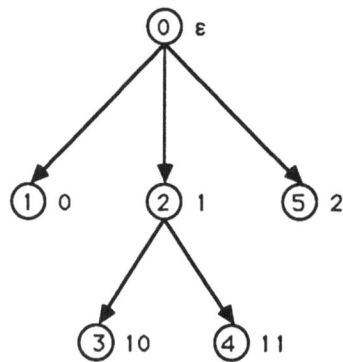

In general, the empty sequence ε denotes the root, while a sequence of the form wn with w ∈ ℕ* and n ∈ ℕ represents the (n+1)th successor of the node given by w. This interpretation leads to the following axioms that characterize a set D ⊆ ℕ* as a tree domain:

- w0 ∈ D implies w ∈ D,
- w(n+1) ∈ D implies wn ∈ D.

A first approach to a corresponding Horn clause specification follows the lines of STORE (cf. Section 3.4).

    TREE
        base :   SEQ-OF-NAT(seq **becomes** dom)
        sorts :   tree
        opns :   ω : tree
                    _[_←_] : tree,dom,nat→tree
        preds :   ≠ : dom,dom
        vars :   x : tree
                    d,d' : dom
                    m,n,i,k : nat
        axms :   x[d←m][d←n] ≡ x[d←n]
                    x[d←m][d'←n] ≡ x[d'←n][d←m] ⇐ d ≠ d'
                    ε ≠ i&d
                    i&d ≠ ε
                    i&d ≠ k&d' ⇐ i ≠ k
                    i&d ≠ k&d' ⇐ d ≠ d'

The problem with this solution is that it does not reflect the tree domain axioms given above: there are terms representing trees with "holes". For instance, a term of the form t[(app d 0)←m] such that there is no valid equation t ≡ t'[d←n] represents a tree with non-root node app d 0, but without a defined parent node of app d 0. We suggest two possibilities to overcome this problem. One is to adopt a "behavioural" viewpoint (cf. Section 4.5), i.e. to specify the context in which trees occur - here, the access operator - only for trees without holes.

TREE-ACCESS
    base :   TREE
    opns :   _[_] : tree,dom→nat
    preds :   _ is defined at _ : tree,dom
    vars :   x : tree
              d,d' : dom
              i,n : nat
    axms :   x[d←n][d] ≡ n ⇐ x is defined at d
              x[ε←n] is defined at ε
              x[(app d 0)←n] is defined at (app d 0) ⇐ x is defined at d
              x[(app d i|)←n] is defined at (app d i|)
                  ⇐ x is defined at (app d i)
              x[d←n][d'] ≡ x[d'] ⇐ d ≢ d'

A more rigorous solution starts out from tree constructors which do not allow trees with holes at all.

TREE2
    base :   NAT
    sorts :   tree, treeSeq
    opns :   ε : treeSeq
              _&_ : tree,treeSeq→treeSeq
              _⟦_⟧ : nat,treeSeq→tree

Here a tree is either ε or of the form n⟦s⟧ where n is the entry of its root and s is the sequence of its maximal proper subtrees. For instance, the tree given above is represented by the term

$$0⟦1⟦ε⟧ \& 2⟦3⟦ε⟧ \& 4⟦ε⟧ \& ε⟧ \& 5⟦ε⟧ \& ε⟧.$$

The access operators for trees and tree sequences - both denoted by _[_] - are specified by mutual recursion:

TREE2-ACCESS
    base :   TREE2, SEQ-OF-NAT(seq becomes dom)
    opns :   _[_] : tree,dom→nat
              _[_] : treeSeq,dom→nat
    vars :   n,i : nat
              s : treeSeq

```
                    d : dom
    axms :   n⟦s⟧[ε] ≡ n
             n⟦s⟧[i&d] ≡ s[i&d]
             (x&s)[0&d] ≡ x[d]
             (x&s)[i|&d] ≡ s[i&d]
```

3.15 A Stream Language Interpreter

The programs constructable from the interpreter specification COMMAND (cf. Section 3.4) refer to a store of numbers. In the sequel we are concerned with a language that processes number sequences directly. It is based upon the *deterministic stream processing language* DSPL introduced by Broy et al., Section 6. Expressions are formed as in Section 3.4. However, the rôle of commands is taken over by *agents*:

```
AGENT
    base :   EXPRESSION
    sorts :  agent
    opns :   _ := _; _ : ident,exp,agent → agent
             read _; _ : ident,agent → agent
             write _; _ : exp,agent → agent
             _; _ : agent → agent
             if _ is zero then _ else _ : exp,agent,agent → agent
             stop : agent
```

Assignments are not evaluated by modifying a store of values, but by directly substituting values for variables (identifiers). Hence we need two operators, denoted by _[_←_], for substituting numbers into expressions and agents, respectively.

```
SUBSTITUTE
    base :   SEQ-OF-NAT
    opns :   _[_←_] : exp,ident,nat → exp
             _[_←_] : agent,ident,nat → agent
    vars :   x,y : ident
             m,n : nat
             e,e' : exp
             a,a' : agent
    axms :   (id x)[x←n] ≡ val n
             (id x)[y←n] ≡ id x   ⇐   x ≠ y
             (val m)[y←n] ≡ val m
             (e plus e')[y←n] ≡ e[y←n] plus e'[y←n]
```

$(e \text{ times } e')[y \leftarrow n] \equiv e[y \leftarrow n] \text{ times } e'[y \leftarrow n]$
$(x := e; a)[x \leftarrow n] \equiv x := e[x \leftarrow n]; a$
$(x := e; a)[y \leftarrow n] \equiv x := e[y \leftarrow n]; a[y \leftarrow n] \Leftarrow x \not\equiv y$
$(\text{read } x; a)[x \leftarrow n] \equiv \text{read } x; a$
$(\text{read } x; a)[y \leftarrow n] \equiv \text{read } x; a[y \leftarrow n] \Leftarrow x \not\equiv y$
$(\text{write } e; a)[y \leftarrow n] \equiv \text{write } e[y \leftarrow n]; a[y \leftarrow n]$
$(a; a')[y \leftarrow n] \equiv a[y \leftarrow n]; a'[y \leftarrow n]$
$(\text{if } e \text{ is zero then } a \text{ else } a')[y \leftarrow n]$
$\qquad \equiv \text{if } e[y \leftarrow n] \text{ is zero then } a[y \leftarrow n] \text{ else } a'[y \leftarrow n]$
$\text{stop}[y \leftarrow n] \equiv \text{stop}$

Given a number sequence s, an agent is evaluated sequentially. If a read command is encountered, say *read x; a*, then the first element is taken from the number sequence s and assigned to x. Vice versa, the evaluation of *write (val n)* results in appending n to the left of s. The whole interpreter of (non-recursive) agents reads as follows.

```
EVAL-AGENT
    base :  SUBSTITUTE
    opns :  evalAgent _ _ : seq,agent→seq
    vars :  s : seq
            x : ident
            n : nat
            a,a' : agent
    axms :  evalAgent s (x := (val n); a) ≡ evalAgent s a[x←n]
            evalAgent n&s (read x; a) ≡ evalAgent s a[x←n]
            evalAgent s (write (val n); a) ≡ n&(evalAgent s a)
            evalAgent s (a; a') ≡ evalAgent (evalAgent s a) a'
            evalAgent s (if (val 0) is zero then a else a') ≡ evalAgent s a
            evalAgent s (if (val n) is zero then a else a') ≡ evalAgent s a'
                ⇐ n ≠ 0
            evalAgent s stop ≡ ε
```

To evaluate recursive agent declarations one needs a substitution operator for agent identifiers obeying the *fixpoint* equation

$$\text{let } x \text{ be } a \equiv a[x \leftarrow (\text{let } x \text{ be } a)].$$

A corresponding specification is

```
REC-AGENT
    base :  EVAL-AGENT
    opns :  let _ be _ : ident,agent→agent
```

	call _ : ident⟶agent
	_[_←_] : agent,ident,agent⟶agent
vars :	x,y : ident
	a,a',a" : agent
	e : exp
	n : nat
axms :	let x be a ≡ a[x←(let x be a)]
	(call x)[x←a] ≡ a
	(call x)[y←a] ≡ call x ⇐ x ≢ y
	(call x)[y←n] ≡ call x
	(x := e; a)[y←a'] ≡ x := e; a[y←a']
	(read x; a)[y←a'] ≡ read x; a[y←a']
	(write e; a)[y←a'] ≡ write e; a[y←a']
	(a; a")[y←a'] ≡ a[y←a']; a"[y←a']
	(if e is zero then a else a")[y←a']
	≡ if e[y←n] is zero then a[y←a'] else a"[y←a']
	stop[y←a] ≡ stop

Chapter 4 Models and Theories

4.1 Introduction

This chapter deals with several theories derived from a Horn clause specification. Each theory is *complete* with respect to a subclass of Mod(SIG,AX) (cf. Section 2.3). Different theories represent different concepts of semantical abstraction. Some of them correspond to the theory of a single SIG-structure, say B. Vice versa, if we start out from a SIG-structure A as the formalization of a data type, an axiom set AX is called *correct w.r.t. A* if A coincides with B.

It is not only the sort of axioms that determines on which semantical concept should be adopted. Different kinds of questions also suggest different theories. For instance, if we expect a positive answer, *free or initial semantics* is mostly the right choice, while *final semantics* is more suitable for finding a refutation.

We begin with the *Horn clause calculus* consisting of the *Substitution Rule* and the *Cut Rule*. The latter agrees with Gentzen's cut rule when restricted to Horn clauses. Gentzen works with *sequents* $\delta \Leftarrow \gamma$ where - in contrast to Horn clauses - the conclusion δ need not be a single atom, but a set of atoms representing the *disjunction* of its elements. Accordingly, $\emptyset \Leftarrow \gamma$ denotes the negation of γ. Therefore sequents allow inconsistencies to be expressed, which Horn clauses do not. Indeed, sequents provide the full expressive power of quantifier-free first-order logic (see Kowalski, Chapter 10, for the conversion of first-order formulas into sequents). More details about the gap between Horn clauses and sequents are given in Section 4.9.

Strong reasons for keeping to Horn clauses were listed in Chapter 1. For further motivation we cite Kowalski: *The majority of formalisms for computer programming bear greater resemblance to Horn clauses than they do to 'non-Horn' clauses. In addition, most of the models for problem-solving which have been developed in artificial intelligence can be regarded as models for problems expressed by means of Horn clauses* (Kowalski, p. 17).

On the other hand, a syntax of specifications that only admits unconditional equations as axioms has turned out to be too restrictive. For example, axioms for *is even* (cf. Section 3.2) such as

$$0 \text{ is even}$$
$$n\| \text{ is even} \Leftarrow n \text{ is even}$$

that do not use other functions like *is odd* cannot be transformed into a purely equational specification (cf. Thatcher et al., Theorem 5). The reason is that the above axioms lead to a semi-decision procedure for even numbers, whereas *is even* must be turned into a total function

$$\text{even}\_ : \text{nat} \to \text{bool}$$

(cf. Section 3.1) so that it can be specified by equational axioms. Therefore we need an additional function telling us when a number is *not* even. The negation operator, for example, would do:

$$\text{even } 0 \equiv \text{true}$$
$$\text{even } 1 \equiv \text{false}$$
$$\text{even } n|| \equiv \neg(\text{even } n|).$$

Given a specification <SIG,AX>, the set of atoms derivable from AX and *equality axioms* by the Horn clause calculus is called the *deductive theory* of <SIG,AX> (cf. Section 4.2). Together with Mod(SIG,AX) on the denotational side the deductive theory represents the *free* (or *loose*) *semantics* of <SIG,AX>. The other concepts restrict the class of models and thus extend the deductive theory.

Initial semantics means to confine the models to be taken into account to term-generated ones (cf. Section 2.3). The corresponding theory is called the *inductive theory* because induction on the structure of ground terms plays the dominant rôle in proofs of theorems that are valid in all term-generated SIG-models of AX (cf. Section 4.3). The inductive theory of <SIG,AX> is captured by the *initial structure,* and AX is called *initially correct* w.r.t. a SIG-structure A if A is isomorphic to the initial structure (cf. Section 4.4).

Final semantics results from a black-box view of specifications. *Objects of interest* (see Guttag) are distinguished by observing their input-output behaviour, i.e. their effect on *visible* objects. In particular, programming languages give rise to final semantics because programs are considered to be equivalent if they implement the same input-output relation. Final semantics starts out from *contexts* given by formulas with a "hole", that is a distinguished free variable x_o with non-visible sort. The *inductive contextual theory* identifies all non-visible terms t,t' such that for all contexts c, $c[t/x_o]$ is derivable iff $c[t'/x]$ is derivable (cf. Section 4.5). The inductive contextual theory is complete with respect to each model that is *visibly initial,* i.e. agrees with the initial <SIG,AX>-structure only on visible objects. The least visibly initial model is called the *final structure* Z(SIG,AX). Analogously to initial correctness (cf. Section 4.4) AX is *finally correct* w.r.t. a SIG-structure A if A is isomorphic to the final structure (cf. Section 4.6). Final semantics is especially useful for disproving inductive theorems (cf. Section 4.7).

Internalized logic is the way of equipping a Horn clause specification with quantifier-free logic by including a specification of Boolean algebra (cf. Section 3.1). If predicates are translated into Boolean-valued functions, the laws of Boolean algebra allow us to derive all quantifier-free first-order theorems. However, this logic resides on the level of terms, and thus we are no longer interested in all models of AX, but only in *consistent* ones where the Boolean carrier consists of two elements. Deduction-oriented conditions allow us to transform non-consistent models into consistent ones such that the deductive (respectively, inductive) theory is complete w.r.t. the class of consistent (term-generated) models (cf. Section 4.8).

General Assumption (continued; cf. Section 2.2) We suppose that a set AX of Horn clauses and thus a specification <SIG,AX> are given. Moreover, SIG is assumed to be *inhabited,* i.e. for all $s \in S$, the set of ground terms with sort s is nonempty. ∎

Definition (cf. Section 2.3) Let A be a SIG-structure with identity. A is a *SIG-model of AX* if A satisfies all clauses of AX. *Mod(SIG,AX)* denotes the class of all SIG-models of AX. ∎

Since SIG is inhabited, each carrier set of a SIG-structure A is nonempty. Without this assumption A^X could be empty and we would be faced with the crude consequence that all atoms are valid in A. The discussion on empty carrier sets is summarized by Goguen and Meseguer [2]. Permitting empty carrier sets is useful if one is dealing with specifications including a formal parameter part. Here we do not employ such specifications and dispense with empty carrier sets.

Definition Let A be a SIG-structure and let SAT(A) denote the set of atoms satisfied by A. A goal γ is *sound w.r.t. A* if $\gamma \subseteq SAT(A)$. γ is *complete w.r.t. A* if $SAT(A) \subseteq \gamma$. γ is sound w.r.t. a class A of SIG-structures if γ is sound w.r.t. all $A \in \mathbf{A}$. γ is complete w.r.t. **A** if γ is complete w.r.t. all $A \in \mathbf{A}$. ∎

4.2 The Horn Clause Calculus

Let F be a set of formulas, e.g. all clauses over SIG, and let R be a set of *inference rules*. Given $C \subseteq F$ and $c \in F$, a *derivation of c from C via R* is a sequence $\langle c_1,...,c_n \rangle \in F^*$ such that $c_n = c$ and for all $1 \leq i \leq n$ either $c_i \in C$ or R contains a rule of the form

(∗) $$\frac{c_{i_1},...,c_{i_k}}{c_i}$$

where $i_j < i$ for all $1 \le j \le k$. R induces an *inference relation* denoted by $\vdash$ and defined as follows: given $C \subseteq F$ and $c \in F$,

$$C \vdash c \quad \text{iff} \quad \text{there is a derivation of } c \text{ from } C \text{ via } R.$$

If C is a singleton, say $\{c_0\}$, we simply write $c_0 \vdash c$.

To be more precise, we should call (*) a rule *instance* rather than a rule. An inference rule only bears the *schema* of formulas before and after a transformation step.

Definition The *Horn clause calculus* consists of the following two inference rules:

Substitution Rule Let $p \Leftarrow \gamma$ be a clause and f be a substitution. Then

$$\frac{p \Leftarrow \gamma}{p[f] \Leftarrow \gamma[f]}.$$

Cut Rule Let p,q be atoms and γ, δ be goals. Then

$$\frac{p \Leftarrow \gamma \cup \{q\},\ q \Leftarrow \delta}{p \Leftarrow \gamma \cup \delta}.$$

The corresponding inference relation is denoted by $\vdash$.

The set *EAX* of *equality axioms* consists of all clauses of the form

$$x \equiv x$$
$$y \equiv x \Leftarrow x \equiv y$$
$$x \equiv z \Leftarrow x \equiv y,\ y \equiv z$$
$$\sigma\langle x_1,\dots,x_n\rangle \equiv \sigma\langle y_1,\dots,y_n\rangle \Leftarrow x_1 \equiv y_1,\ \dots,\ x_n \equiv y_n$$
$$P\langle y_1,\dots,y_n\rangle \Leftarrow P\langle x_1,\dots,x_n\rangle,\ x_1 \equiv y_1,\ \dots,\ x_n \equiv y_n$$

where $x,y,z,x_1,\dots,x_n,y_1,\dots,y_n \in X$, $\sigma \in OP$ and $P \in PR$.

The *(deductive) theory* of $\langle SIG, AX \rangle$, *DTh(SIG,AX)*, consists of all atoms p such that $AX \cup EAX \vdash p$. Elements and subsets of DTh(SIG,AX) are called *(deductive) $\langle SIG,AX \rangle$-theorems*. ∎

The restriction to atoms (instead of all clauses) is needed to ensure the completeness of DTh(SIG,AX) w.r.t. Mod(SIG,AX) (cf. Theorem 4.2.2).

Example 4.2.1 Let <SIG,AX> = BINARY (cf. Section 3.5). A derivation of the atom *11<100* from AX∪EAX via the Horn clause calculus reads as follows:

a1 < b0 ⇐ a < b	∈ AX
01 < 10 ⇐ 0 < 1	(substitution)
0 < 1	∈ AX
01 < 10	(cut)
01≡1	∈ AX
x≡x	∈ EAX
10≡10	(substitution)
$y_1 < y_2$ ⇐ $x_1 < x_2$, $x_1 \equiv y_1$, $x_2 \equiv y_2$	∈ EAX
1 < 10 ⇐ 01 < 10, 01≡1, 10≡10	(substitution)
1 < 10 ⇐ 01≡1, 10≡10	(cut)
1 < 10	(cut, cut)
a1 < b0 ⇐ a < b	∈ AX
11 < 100 ⇐ 1 < 10	(substitution)
11 < 100	(cut).

Hence *11<100* is a BINARY-theorem. ∎

Definition The equality axioms EAX ensure that the binary relation ~ on T(SIG) defined by

$$t \sim t' \quad \text{iff} \quad t \equiv t' \in DTh(SIG,AX)$$

is a SIG-congruence relation on the Herbrand structure

$$DH = HS(T(SIG), DTh(SIG,AX))$$

(cf. Section 2.3). The quotient of DH by ~ is called the *free <SIG,AX>-structure, F(SIG,AX)*, i.e. F(SIG,AX) = DH/~. ∎

Theorem 4.2.2 *Soundness and completeness of the deductive theory w.r.t. the class of all models*
DTh(SIG,AX) is sound and complete w.r.t. Mod(SIG,AX) and w.r.t. F(SIG,AX).

Proof. Mod(SIG,AX) satisfies the deductive theory of <SIG,AX> because EAX is valid in all A ∈ Mod(SIG,AX) and the Horn clause calculus preserves validity in A. The latter is shown by consulting the Substitution Rule and the Cut Rule separately. One has to check that
(1) for all clauses c and substitutions f, if A satisfies c, then A satisfies c[f],
(2) for all atoms p,q and goals γ,δ, if A satisfies p⇐γ∪{q} and q⇐δ, then A satisfies p⇐γ∪δ.

(2) is verified immediately. For (1), we apply Proposition 2.3.1: let $c = (Pt \Leftarrow P_1 t_1,...,P_n t_n)$ be valid in A and $b \in A^X$ such that for all $1 \le i \le n$, $b^*(t_i[f]) \in P_i^A$. Then by Proposition 2.3.1, $(b^* \circ f)^* t_i \in P_i^A$. Since A satisfies c, $(b^* \circ f)^* t \in P^A$ as well. Again by Proposition 2.3.1, $b^*(t[f]) \in P^A$. Thus $c[f]$ is valid in A, and we conclude (1) holds.

Conversely, let $A = DH$, $B = F(SIG,AX)$, nat : $A \rightarrow B$ be the corresponding natural mapping and Pt be an atom satisfied by all SIG-models of AX.

Suppose that B is a SIG-model of AX. Then Pt is valid in B., i.e. for all $b \in B^X$, $b^* t \in P^B$. In particular, $(nat \circ id^X)^* t \in P^B$. Hence $nat(t) \in P^B$ and thus $t \in P^A$. By definition of A, we conclude that Pt is a $\langle SIG,AX \rangle$-theorem. It remains for us to show that B is a SIG-model of AX.

B is a SIG-structure *with identity* because for all $s \in S$, the relation $\equiv_s^B$ on B is given by all pairs $\langle nat(t), nat(t') \rangle$ such that $t \equiv_s t'$ is a $\langle SIG,AX \rangle$-theorem.

Moreover, B satisfies AX: let $Pt \Leftarrow P_1 t_1,...,P_n t_n$ be in AX and $b \in B^X$ such that for all $1 \le i \le n$, $b^* t_i \in P_i^B$. Since $nat \circ f = b$ for some substitution f, we have $t_i[f] \in P_i^A$, i.e. $P_i t_i[f]$ is a $\langle SIG,AX \rangle$-theorem for all $1 \le i \le n$. By the Substitution and the Cut Rule, $Pt[f]$ is a $\langle SIG,AX \rangle$-theorem, too, and thus $t[f] \in P^A$. Hence $b^* t \in P^B$. ∎

Note that the step from validity of Pt in B to derivability of Pt does not hold if Pt is replaced by a non-atomic clause. For instance, all SIG-models of AX satisfy $p \Leftarrow \{p\}$, although there is no derivation of $p \Leftarrow \{p\}$ via the Horn clause calculus. Corollary 4.2.4 below provides a way to derive clauses with non-empty premises as well. First we show how solutions in structures (cf. Section 2.3) are related to *deductive* solutions.

Definition A substitution f is called a *deductive $\langle SIG,AX \rangle$-solution* of a goal γ if $\gamma[f]$ is a $\langle SIG,AX \rangle$-theorem. ∎

Corollary 4.2.3 *Solvability in structures is equivalent to solvability in the deductive theory*

A goal γ has a deductive $\langle SIG,AX \rangle$-solution iff for all SIG-models A of AX, some $b \in A^X$ solves γ.

Proof. Let $\gamma[f] \subseteq DTh(SIG,AX)$. By Theorem 4.2.2, $\gamma[f]$ is valid in Mod(SIG,AX), i.e. for all SIG-models A of AX, $b \in A^X$ and $Pt \in \gamma$, $b^*(t[f]) \in P^A$. Hence by Proposition 2.3.1, $(b^* f)^* t \in P^A$, i.e. $b^* f$ is a solution of γ in A.

Conversely, if for all $A \in Mod(SIG,AX)$ some b solves γ in A, then in particular, some $b = nat \circ f$ solves γ in the free $\langle SIG,AX \rangle$-structure. Therefore $\gamma[f]$ is a $\langle SIG,AX \rangle$-theorem. ∎

Corollary 4.2.4 *The derivation of non-atomic theorems*

Let $c = (p \Leftarrow \gamma)$ be a clause and $x_1,...,x_n$ be the variables of γ. Fix new constants $k_1,...,k_n$ with $sort(k_i) = sort(x_i)$. Let

$$SIG' = \langle S, OP \cup \{k_1,...,k_n\}, PR \rangle,$$

$$p' = p[k_1/x_1,...,k_n/x_n] \text{ and } \gamma' = \gamma[k_1/x_1,...,k_n/x_n].$$

Then $Mod(SIG,AX)$ satisfies c iff p' is a $\langle SIG', AX \cup \gamma' \rangle$-theorem.

Proof. By Theorem 4.2.2, it is sufficient to show that $Mod(SIG,AX)$ satisfies c iff $Mod(SIG',AX\cup\gamma')$ satisfies p'.

Suppose that $Mod(SIG,AX)$ satisfies c and let A be a SIG'-model of $AX\cup\gamma'$. Clearly, A is also a SIG-model of AX. Thus by assumption, A satisfies c. So let $b \in A^X$ such that $bx_i = k_i^A$ for all $1 \le i \le n$. Since γ' is valid in A, b is a solution of γ in A. Hence b solves p in A because A satisfies c. Therefore A satisfies p'.

Conversely, suppose that $Mod(SIG',AX\cup\gamma')$ satisfies p' and let A be a SIG-model of AX. Furthermore, let b be a solution of γ in A. A is extended to a SIG'-structure by defining $k_i^A = bx_i$ for all $1 \le i \le n$. Since b solves γ in A, A satisfies γ'. Hence A is a SIG'-model of $AX \cup \gamma'$ and thus by assumption, p' is valid in A. Therefore b is a solution of p in A, and we conclude that A satisfies c. ∎

The addition of constants - usually called *skolemization* - prevents the variables of $p \Leftarrow \gamma$ from being instantiated during the derivation process. Having turned $x_1,...,x_n$ into constants $k_1,...,k_n$ we are actually inferring the formula $\forall x_1... \forall x_n (p \Leftarrow \gamma)$, while in case when instantiations of $x_1,...,x_n$ are allowed we might come up with a proof of the weaker statement $(\forall x_1... \forall x_n p) \Leftarrow (\forall x_1... \forall x_n \gamma)$ which does not comply with our interpretation of $p \Leftarrow \gamma$ (cf. Section 2.3). A complete calculus for deriving conditional equations without skolemization is given by Selman, Section 5.

Example 4.2.5 Let $\langle SIG,AX \rangle$ = BINARY-ADD-MULT (cf. Section 3.5) and let c be the clause

$$a + b \equiv a \Leftarrow b \equiv 0.$$

We show that $Mod(SIG,AX)$ satisfies c. Referring to additional constants k and k' we conclude from Corollary 4.2.4 that it is sufficient to derive the equation $(k+k') \equiv k$ from $AX \cup EAX \cup \{k' \equiv 0\}$. A suitable derivation reads as follows.

k'≡0	
$x_1+x_2 \equiv y_1+y_2 \Leftarrow x_1 \equiv y_1, x_2 \equiv y_2$	∈ EAX
k+k' ≡ k+0 ⇐ k≡k, k'≡0	(substitution)
k+k' ≡ k+0 ⇐ k≡k	(cut)
x≡x	∈ EAX

$$
\begin{array}{ll}
k \equiv k & \text{(substitution)} \\
k+k' \equiv k+0 & \text{(cut)} \\
a+0 \equiv a & \in AX \\
k+0 \equiv k & \text{(substitution)} \\
x \equiv z \Leftarrow x \equiv y,\ y \equiv z & \in EAX \\
k+k' \equiv k \Leftarrow k+k' \equiv k+0,\ k+0 \equiv k & \text{(substitution)} \\
k+k' \equiv k \Leftarrow k+k' \equiv k+0 & \text{(cut)} \\
k+k' \equiv k & \text{(cut).}
\end{array}
$$

Using quantifiers,

$$\text{Mod}(SIG, AX) \models (a + b \equiv a \Leftarrow b \equiv 0)$$

means that the formula

$$\forall a\ \forall b\ (a + b \equiv a \Leftarrow b \equiv 0).$$

is valid in Mod(SIG,AX). On the other hand, there are SIG-models of AX that do not satisfy the formula

$$\forall a\ \forall b\ (a + b \equiv 0 \Leftarrow b \equiv 0).$$

However, if the variables a and b are *not* turned into constants, we obtain a derivation of (a+b)≡0 from AX∪EAX∪{b≡0}:

$$
\begin{array}{lll}
(*) & b \equiv 0 & \\
& a \equiv 0 & \text{(substitution)} \\
& x_1+x_2 \equiv y_1+y_2 \Leftarrow x_1 \equiv y_1,\ x_2 \equiv y_2 & \in EAX \\
& a+b \equiv 0+0 \Leftarrow a \equiv 0,\ b \equiv 0 & \text{(substitution)} \\
& a+b \equiv 0+0 \Leftarrow a \equiv 0 & \text{(cut)} \\
& a+b \equiv 0+0 & \text{(cut)} \\
& a+0 \equiv a & \in EAX \\
& 0+0 \equiv 0 & \text{(substitution)} \\
& x \equiv z \Leftarrow x \equiv y,\ y \equiv z & \in EAX \\
& a+b \equiv 0 \Leftarrow a+b \equiv 0+0,\ 0+0 \equiv 0 & \text{(substitution)} \\
& a+b \equiv 0 \Leftarrow a+b \equiv 0+0 & \text{(cut)} \\
& a+b \equiv 0 & \text{(cut).}
\end{array}
$$

This example shows that skolemization is necessary: The instantiation at (∗) would have been prevented if the variable b had been replaced by a constant. ∎

Another way to deal with non-atomic clauses is to incorporate Boolean algebra into the Horn clause calculus and to confine oneself to consistent models (cf. Section 4.8).

4.3 Initial Semantics

The following two sections deal with term-generated models and, in particular, with the initial <SIG,AX>-structure, I(SIG,AX), which is the *greatest* term-generated model of AX: each term-generated model is a quotient of I(SIG,AX). Initial semantics identifies data types with initial structures and presumes that equality relations have been specified explicitly, i.e. things are equal only if they are provably equal.

Viewed from the subset ordering on the power set of ground atoms, I(SIG,AX) is the *least* model of AX: ground atoms are valid only if they are provably valid. (For the corresponding fixpoint characterization of I(SIG,AX), see Lloyd, Theorem 6.5.) It is easy to see that a specification including non-Horn clauses may lack a least model. *Disjunctive* axioms such as Pt∨Qu give rise to several minimal models, and *negated* atoms, which lead to contradictions such as Pt∧¬Pt, rule out any model.

A model-theoretic correctness notion and a proof-theoretic correctness criterion will explicate the nature of initial semantics (cf. Section 4.4). First we establish the completeness result corresponding to Theorem 4.2.2.

Definition *Gen(SIG,AX)* denotes the class of term-generated SIG-models of AX. The *inductive theory of <SIG,AX>*, *ITh(SIG,AX)*, consists of all atoms all ground instances of which are derivable from AX∪EAX. Elements and subsets of ITh(SIG,AX) are called *inductive <SIG,AX>-theorems*. ∎

Of course, the restriction of ITh(SIG,AX) to ground atoms coincides with the deductive theory of <SIG,AX> (cf. Section 4.2).

Example 4.3.1 Let <SIG,AX> = NAT-ARITHMETIC (cf. Section 3.2). An inductive - but non-deductive - NAT-ARITHMETIC-theorem is the commutativity law

$$m+n \equiv n+m.$$

A straightforward induction shows that for all ground terms t over NAT-ARITHMETIC there is a ground term u over NAT such that t≡u is a <SIG,AX>-theorem. Hence (m+n)≡(n+m) is an inductive theorem iff for all ground terms t,t' over NAT,

(1)   (t+t')≡(t'+t) is a deductive theorem.

The specification of +, namely the axioms

$$m+0 \equiv m$$
$$m+(n|) \equiv (m+n)|$$

(cf. Section 3.2), suggests we consider the following two cases:
(i) $t' = 0$,
(ii) $t' = u|$ for some ground term u over NAT.
By induction on size(t'), we obtain (1). Note that the proof needs the inductive theorems
$$0+m \equiv m$$
$$m|+n \equiv (m+n)|$$
as lemmata. ∎

Definition Let *GDTh(SIG,AX)* be the restriction of DTh(SIG,AX) to ground atoms. The equality axioms EAX ensure that the binary relation ~ on GT(SIG) defined by

$$t \sim t' \quad \text{iff} \quad t \equiv t' \in GDTh(SIG,AX)$$

is a SIG-congruence relation on the Herbrand structure

$$IH = HS(GT(SIG), GDTh(SIG,AX))$$

(cf. Section 2.3). The quotient of IH by ~ is called the *initial <SIG,AX>-structure, I(SIG,AX),* i.e. I(SIG,AX) = IH/~. ∎

Theorem 4.3.2 *Soundness and completeness of the inductive theory w.r.t. the class of term-generated models*
ITh(SIG,AX) is sound and complete w.r.t. Gen(SIG,AX) and w.r.t. I(SIG,AX).

Proof. Let Pt ∈ ITh(SIG,AX) and A ∈ Gen(SIG,AX). Since EAX is valid in A and since the Horn clause calculus preserves validity in A (cf. the proof of Theorem 4.2.2), A is a model of all ground instances of Pt. Moreover, A satisfies Pt.

Let b ∈ A^X. Since A is term-generated, there is a ground substitution f with $eval^A \circ f = b$. Since Pt[f] is valid in A, we obtain $b^*t \in P^A$. Hence A satisfies Pt.

Let A = IH, B = I(SIG,AX) and nat : A⟶B be the corresponding natural mapping. The validity of AX in B as well as the fact that B is a SIG-structure with identity can be shown analogously to the proof of Theorem 4.2.2.

Therefore B ∈ Mod(SIG,AX). Of course, B is term-generated. It remains for us to show that all atoms Pt that are valid in B are inductive <SIG,AX>-theorems.

So let f be a ground substitution and for all b in B^X, $b^*t \in P^B$. In particular,

$(nat \circ f)^* t \in P^B$. Hence by Proposition 2.3.1, $nat(t[f]) \in P^B$ and thus $t[f] \in P^A$. Since $A = IH$, we conclude that $Pt[f]$ is a $\langle SIG, AX \rangle$-theorem. Therefore Pt is an inductive $\langle SIG, AX \rangle$-theorem. ∎

As far as non-atomic clauses $p \Leftarrow \gamma$ are concerned we have to distinguish between two kinds of inductive theorems. In contrast to atoms, validity in Gen(SIG,AX) does not coincide with validity in I(SIG,AX). The first is equivalent to the derivability of all ground instances of p from AX, EAX and corresponding instances of γ. This is captured by the following corollary, which resembles the Deduction Theorem of first-order logic (cf. Barnes and Mack, Chapter IV) as well as Corollary 4.2.4.

Corollary 4.3.3 *The derivation of non-atomic inductive theorems*
Given a clause $c = (p \Leftarrow \gamma)$, Gen(SIG,AX) satisfies c iff, for all ground substitutions f,

(1) $\qquad AX \cup EAX \cup \gamma[f] \vdash p[f]$.

Proof. Since $p[f]$ is ground, $p[f]$ is derivable from $AX \, EAX \cup \gamma[f]$ iff $p[f]$ is an inductive $\langle SIG, AX \cup \gamma[f] \rangle$-theorem. Hence by Theorem 4.3.2, it is sufficient to show that Gen(SIG,AX) satisfies c iff for all ground substitutions f, Gen(SIG,AX$\cup\gamma$[f]) satisfies p[f].

Suppose that Gen(SIG,AX) satisfies c. Let f be a ground substitution and A be a term-generated SIG-model of $AX \cup \gamma[f]$. By assumption, A satisfies c. So let $b \in A^X$ such that for all $x \in var(\gamma)$, $bx = eval^A(fx)$. Since $\gamma[f]$ is valid in A, b is a solution of γ in A. Hence b solves p in A because A satisfies c. Therefore A satisfies p[f].

Conversely, suppose that for all ground substitutions f and all term-generated SIG-models B of $AX \cup \gamma[f]$, B satisfies p[f]. Let A be a term-generated SIG-model of AX. Furthermore, let b be a solution of γ in A. Since A is term-generated, there is a ground substitution f with $eval^A \circ f = b$. Since b solves γ in A, A satisfies $\gamma[f]$. Hence A is a SIG-model of $AX \cup \gamma[f]$ and by assumption, A satisfies p[f]. Therefore b is a solution of p in A, and we conclude that A satisfies c. ∎

Alternatively, the inductive theory (for arbitrary clauses) may be defined as the set of all $p \Leftarrow \gamma$ such that, for all ground substitutions f,

(2) $\qquad (AX \cup EAX \vdash \gamma[f])$ implies $(AX \cup EAX \vdash p[f])$.

However, as one may verify immediately, (2) means that $p \Leftarrow \gamma$ is valid in the initial $\langle SIG, AX \rangle$-structure. The following example outlines a sample proof of (2) and shows that, indeed, (1) is stronger than (2).

Example 4.3.4 Let ⟨SIG,AX⟩ = INSERT-AND-BALANCE (cf. Section 3.13) and p⇐γ be given by the clause

(insertAndBalance i x) is balanced ⇐ x is balanced.

A straightforward induction shows that for all ground terms t over INSERT-AND-BALANCE there is a ground term t' over TWO-THREE-TREE such that t≡t' is a ⟨SIG,AX⟩-theorem. Hence (2) is equivalent to the following condition: for all ground terms t,u over TWO-THREE-TREE with sort *tree* (or *nat*),

(3)   (AX ∪ EAX ⊢ t is balanced)
       implies   (AX ∪ EAX ⊢ (insertAndBalance u t) is balanced).

By AX, (3) is equivalent to

(4)   (AX ∪ EAX ⊢ t is balanced)
       implies   (AX ∪ EAX ⊢ (thaw (insert u t)) is balanced.

Of course, we want to show (4) by induction on size(t). As is often the case with inductive proofs, there is some point where the conjecture turns out to be too weak to be used as an induction hypothesis. Then it must be *generalized*. (For notes on generalization techniques, cf. Bundy, Section 11.4.) If the conjecture has the form of an implication

(∗)   (AX ∪ EAX ⊢ γ) implies (AX ∪ EAX ⊢ δ)

such as (4), antecedents of γ (δ) w.r.t. proofs of γ (δ) might lead to a tractable generalization of (∗). For instance, if every derivation of γ includes some γ', and if δ can be derived from δ' as well as from δ", then (∗) follows from

(∗∗)   AX ∪ EAX ⊢ γ' implies AX ∪ EAX ⊢ δ' or AX ∪ EAX ⊢ δ".

This kind of generalization is applied to (4) and - consulting our knowledge about INSERT-AND-BALANCE (cf. Section 3.13) - we claim that

(5)   AX ∪ EAX ⊢ height t is v
       implies   AX ∪ EAX ⊢ (insert u t ≡ freeze1 t_o,
                              height t_o is v) for some t_o
       or   AX ∪ EAX ⊢ (insert u t ≡ freeze2 t_o u_o t_1,
                        height t_o is v,
                        height t_1 is v) for some t_o, u_o, t_1.

Before showing (5) we infer (4) from (5). Let *t is balanced* be derivable from AX∪EAX. Then for some v, *height t is v* is derivable as well. Hence by (5), we have two cases:

Case 1.
$$\text{AX} \cup \text{EAX} \quad \vdash \quad \{\text{insert } u \ t \equiv \text{freeze1 } t_o, \text{height } t_o \text{ is } v\}.$$

Then
$$\text{AX} \cup \text{EAX} \quad \vdash \quad \{\text{thaw (insert } u \ t) \equiv \text{thaw (freeze1 } t_o),$$
$$\text{height } t_o \text{ is } v\}$$
$$\vdash \quad \{\text{thaw (insert } u \ t) \equiv t_o, t_o \text{ is balanced}\}$$
$$\vdash \quad (\text{thaw (insert } u \ t)) \text{ is balanced}.$$

Case 2.
$$\text{AX} \cup \text{EAX} \quad \vdash \quad \{\text{insert } u \ t \equiv \text{freeze2 } t_o \ u_o \ t_1,$$
$$\text{height } t_o \text{ is } v, \text{height } t_1 \text{ is } v\}.$$

Then
$$\text{AX} \cup \text{EAX} \quad \vdash \quad \{\text{thaw (insert } u \ t) \equiv \text{thaw (freeze2 } t_o \ u_o \ t_1),$$
$$\text{height } t_o \text{ is } v, \text{height } t_1 \text{ is } v\}$$
$$\vdash \quad \{\text{thaw (insert } u \ t) \equiv [\![t_o]\!]u_o[\![t_1]\!],$$
$$\text{height } [\![t_o]\!]u_o[\![t_1]\!] \text{ is v}|\}$$
$$\vdash \quad \{\text{thaw (insert } u \ t) \equiv [\![t_o]\!]u_o[\![t_1]\!],$$
$$[\![t_o]\!]u_o[\![t_1]\!] \text{ is balanced}\}$$
$$\vdash \quad (\text{thaw (insert } u \ t)) \text{ is balanced}.$$

Now we turn to the proof of (5), employing induction on size(t). So let

(6) $\quad$ AX ∪ EAX $\quad \vdash \quad$ height t is v.

Case 1. $t = \omega$. Then $v = 0$ and
$$\text{AX} \cup \text{EAX} \quad \vdash \quad \text{insert } u \ t \equiv \text{freeze2 } \omega \ u \ \omega.$$

With $t_o = t_1 = \omega$ and $u_o = u$ we conclude
$$\text{AX} \cup \text{EAX} \quad \vdash \quad \{\text{insert } u \ t \equiv \text{freeze2 } t_o \ u_o \ t_o,$$
$$\text{height } t_o \text{ is } v, \text{height } t_1 \text{ is } v\}.$$

Case 2. $t = [\![t']\!]u'[\![t'']\!]$ for some t', u', t''. By (6), there is v' such that $v'| = v$ and
$$\text{AX} \cup \text{EAX} \quad \vdash \quad \{\text{height } t' \text{ is } v', \text{height } t'' \text{ is } v'\}.$$

Case 2.1. AX ∪ EAX $\vdash u \equiv u'$. Then
$$\text{AX} \cup \text{EAX} \quad \vdash \quad \text{insert } u \ t \equiv \text{freeze1 } t.$$

With $t_o = t$ we conclude
$$\text{AX} \cup \text{EAX} \quad \vdash \quad \{\text{insert } u \ t \equiv \text{freeze1 } t_o, \text{height } t_o \text{ is } v\}.$$

Case 2.2. AX ∪ EAX ⊢ u < u'. Then

AX ∪ EAX   ⊢   insert u t ≡ ⟦insert u t'⟧u'⟦t"⟧.

By the induction hypothesis, we have two subcases:

Case 2.2.1.

AX ∪ EAX   ⊢   {insert u t' ≡ freeze1 t_o', height t_o' is v'}.

Then

AX ∪ EAX   ⊢   {insert u t ≡ ⟦freeze1 t_o'⟧u'⟦t"⟧,
                 height t_o' is v', height t" is v'}
            ⊢   {insert u t ≡ freeze1 ⟦t_o'⟧u'⟦t"⟧,
                 height ⟦t_o'⟧u'⟦t"⟧ is v}.

With t_o = ⟦t_o'⟧u'⟦t"⟧ we conclude

AX ∪ EAX   ⊢   {insert u t ≡ freeze1 t_o, height t_o is v}.

Case 2.2.2.

AX ∪ EAX   ⊢   {insert u t' ≡ freeze2 t_o' u_o' t_1',
                 height t_o' is v', height t_1' is v'}.

Then

AX ∪ EAX   ⊢   {insert u t ≡ ⟦freeze2 t_o' u_o' t_1'⟧u'⟦t"⟧,
                 height t_o' is v', height t_1' is v', height t" is v'}
            ⊢   {insert u t ≡ freeze1 ⟦t_o'⟧u_o'⟦t_1'⟧u'⟦t"⟧,
                 height ⟦t_o'⟧u_o'⟦t_1'⟧u'⟦t"⟧ is v}.

With t_o = ⟦t_o'⟧u_o'⟦t_1'⟧u'⟦t"⟧ we conclude

AX ∪ EAX   ⊢   {insert u t ≡ freeze1 t_o, height t_o is v}.

Case 2.3. AX ∪ EAX ⊢ u' < u, analogously to Case 2.2.

Case 3. t = ⟦t'⟧u'⟦t"⟧u"⟦t_2⟧ for some t',u',t",u",t_2. By (6), there is v' such that v'| = v and

AX ∪ EAX   ⊢   {height t' is v', height t" is v', height t_2 is v'}.

Case 3.1. AX ∪ EAX ⊢ u≡u', analogously to Case 2.1.

Case 3.2. AX ∪ EAX ⊢ u < u'. Then

AX ∪ EAX   ⊢   insert u t ≡ ⟦insert u t'⟧u'⟦t"⟧u"⟦t_2⟧.

By the induction hypothesis, we have two subcases:

Case 3.2.1.

AX ∪ EAX   ⊢   {insert u t' ≡ freeze1 t_o', height t_o' is v'}.

Then
$$AX \cup EAX \quad \vdash \quad \{insert\ u\ t \equiv [freeze1\ t_o']u'[t'']u''[t_2],$$
$$height\ t_o'\ is\ v',\ height\ t''\ is\ v',\ height\ t_2\ is\ v'\}$$
$$\vdash \quad \{insert\ u\ t \equiv freeze1\ [t_o']u'[t'']u''[t_2],$$
$$height\ [t_o']u'[t'']u''[t_2]\ is\ v\}.$$

With $t_o = [t_o']u'[t'']u''[t_2]$ we conclude
$$AX \cup EAX \quad \vdash \quad \{insert\ u\ t \equiv freeze1\ t_o,\ height\ t_o\ is\ v\}.$$

Case 3.2.2.
$$AX \cup EAX \quad \vdash \quad \{insert\ u\ t' \equiv freeze2\ t_o'\ u_o'\ t_1',$$
$$height\ t_o'\ is\ v',\ height\ t_1'\ is\ v'\}.$$
Then
$$AX \cup EAX \quad \vdash \quad \{insert\ u\ t \equiv [freeze2\ t_o'\ u_o'\ t_1']u'[t'']u''[t_2],$$
$$height\ t_o'\ is\ v',\ height\ t_1'\ is\ v',\ height\ t''\ is\ v',$$
$$height\ t_2\ is\ v'\}$$
$$\vdash \quad \{insert\ u\ t \equiv freeze2\ ([t_o']u_o'[t_1'])\ u'\ ([t'']u''[t_2]),$$
$$height\ [t_o']u_o'[t_1']\ is\ v,\ height\ [t'']u''[t_2]\}.$$

With $t_o = [t_o']u_o'[t_1']$, $u_o = u'$ and $t_1 = [t'']u''[t_2]$ we conclude
$$AX \cup EAX \quad \vdash \quad \{insert\ u\ t \equiv freeze2\ t_o\ u_o\ t_1,$$
$$height\ t_o\ is\ v,\ height\ t_o\ is\ v\}.$$

Case 3.3. $AX \cup EAX \vdash \{u' < u,\ u < u''\}$, analogously to Case 3.2.

Case 3.4. $AX \cup EAX \vdash u \equiv u''$, analogously to Case 2.1.

Case 3.5. $AX \cup EAX \vdash u'' < u$, analogously to Case 3.2.

This concludes the proof of (5) from which we have already inferred (3).

Let us now use Corollary 4.3.3 to show that the corresponding instance of (1), i.e.

(7) $AX \cup EAX \cup \{t\ is\ balanced\} \vdash (insertAndBalance\ u\ t)\ is\ balanced$

does not hold. By Corollary 4.3.3, it is sufficient to construct a term-generated SIG-model B of AX that does not satisfy $p \Leftarrow \gamma$.

Let A be the Herbrand structure $HS(GT(SIG), \delta)$ where

$$\delta = GDTh(SIG, AX) \cup \{t_o\ is\ balanced\}$$

and

$$t_o = [\omega]0[[\omega]1[\omega]].$$

A is defined in the same manner as IH, the Herbrand structure underlying I(SIG,AX), except that the atom t_o *is balanced* has been added to the Herbrand interpretation that determines IH (cf. Section 2.3). Let ~ be the binary relation on T(SIG) defined by

$$t \sim t' \quad \text{iff} \quad t \equiv t' \in \text{GDTh}(\text{SIG},\text{AX})$$

and $B = A/\sim$. B satisfies AX. Let $Pt \Leftarrow P_1 t_1,...,P_n t_n$ be in AX and $b \in B^X$ such that for all $1 \leq i \leq n$, $b*t_i \in P_i^B$. Since $nat \cdot f = b$ for some substitution f, we have $t_i[f] \in P_i^A$, i.e. $P_i t_i[f] \in \delta$ for all $1 \leq i \leq n$. Since the predicate symbol *is balanced* does not occur in axiom premises, $P_i t_i[f]$ must be a <SIG,AX>-theorem. By the Substitution and the Cut Rule, $Pt[f]$ is a <SIG,AX>-theorem as well. Therefore $t[f] \in P^A$, i.e. $b*t \in P^B$.

Hence B is a term-generated SIG-model of AX.

It remains for us to show that B does not satisfy $p \Leftarrow \gamma$.

Let $b \in A^X$ such that $b(x) = t_o$ and $b(i) = 2$ where x and i are the two variables of $p \Leftarrow \gamma$. Since

$$b(x) = t_o \in \{t \in GT(SIG) \mid (t \text{ is balanced}) \in \delta\} = (\_ \text{ is balanced})^A,$$

b solves γ in A and thus $nat \cdot b$ solves γ in B where nat is the natural mapping from A to B.

On the other hand, assume that $nat \cdot b$ solves p in B. Then b is a solution of p in A, i.e.

$$((\text{insertAndBalance } 2\ t_o) \text{ is balanced}) \in \delta.$$

Since

$$\text{AX} \cup \text{EAX} \vdash \text{insertAndBalance } 2\ t_o \equiv t_1$$

where $t_1 = [\omega]0[[\omega]1[\omega]2[\omega]]]$, we conclude

$$(t_1 \text{ is balanced}) \in \delta.$$

But this is a contradiction because $t_1 \neq t_o$ and t_1 *is balanced* is not derivable from AX∪EAX. Hence $nat \cdot b$ does not solve p in B. ∎

4.4 Initial Correctness

Starting out from a SIG-structure A as the formal description of a data type, the question arises as to what is meant by a set AX of clauses being a correct axiomatization of A. The answer given by initial semantics is that A must be isomorphic to the initial <SIG,AX>-structure. Then AX is called *initially correct w.r.t. A*. Initial correctness can be characterized by a *universal* property that does not refer to I(SIG,AX): AX is initially correct w.r.t. A if and only if for each SIG-model B of AX there is a unique *homomorphism* from A to B.

Definition Let A and B be two SIG-structures. An S-sorted function h : A⟶B is *(SIG-)homomorphic* or a *(SIG-)homomorphism* if for all $\sigma \in$ OP and P $\in$ PR,
$$h \bullet \sigma^A = \sigma^B \bullet h \quad \text{and} \quad h(P^A) \subseteq P^B.$$

If, in addition, $P^B \subseteq h(P^A)$ and
- h is bijective or, equivalently,
- some function g : B⟶A satisfies g•h = id^A and h•g = id^B,

then h is a *(SIG)-isomorphism,* and A and B are called *(SIG)-isomorphic*.

Given a SIG-model A of AX, AX is *initially correct w.r.t. A* if for all SIG-models B of AX there is a unique homomorphism from A to B called ini^B. ∎

Lemma 4.4.1 AX is initially correct w.r.t. I(SIG,AX).

Proof. Let A = I(SIG,AX), B $\in$ Mod(SIG,AX) and nat be the natural mapping from GT(SIG) to A. ini^B : A⟶B is well-defined by $ini^B \bullet$ nat = $eval^B$. ini^B is homomorphic: for all ground terms σt,

$$ini^B \bullet \sigma^A \bullet nat(t) = ini^B \bullet nat(\sigma t) = eval^B(\sigma t) = \sigma^B \bullet eval^B(t) = \sigma^B \bullet ini^B \bullet nat(t).$$

For all ground atoms Pt, nat(t) $\in P^A$ implies AX ⊢ Pt. Hence B satisfies Pt, and thus
$$ini^B \bullet nat(t) = eval^B(t) \in P^B.$$

Conversely, let h : A⟶B be homomorphic. h = ini^B follows by induction on the size of ground terms. Let σ be a constant. Then

$$h \bullet nat(\sigma) = h(\sigma^A) = \sigma^B = eval^B(\sigma) = ini^B \bullet nat(\sigma).$$

Let $\sigma t \in$ GT(SIG). By the induction hypothesis, $h \bullet \sigma^A \bullet nat(t) = \sigma^B \bullet h \bullet nat(t)$. Hence

$$h \bullet nat(\sigma t) = h \bullet \sigma^A \bullet nat(t) = \sigma^B \bullet h \bullet nat(t) = \sigma^B \bullet eval^B(t) = eval^B(\sigma t)$$
$$= ini^B \bullet nat(\sigma t). \; \blacksquare$$

The definition of initial correctness yields

Proposition 4.4.2 Let AX be initially correct w.r.t. a SIG-structure A. AX is initially correct w.r.t. a SIG-structure B iff A and B are isomorphic. ∎

Therefore Lemma 4.4.1 amounts to

Theorem 4.4.3 Let A be a SIG-structure. A and I(SIG,AX) are isomorphic iff AX is initially correct w.r.t. A. ∎

Theorem 4.4.3 gives rise to a proof method for initial correctness. Define a unique homomorphism from A to an arbitrary model of AX. Since the concrete representation of A plays an important rôle in such a definition, purely deductive criteria to guide correctness proofs are not available. However, Goguen et al.; Bergstra and Tucker; Klären; Nourani; and Beierle and Voß have investigated term structures (called *canonical term structures* or *traversals*) that are isomorphic to I(SIG,AX). Not only do these structures have a term carrier; the terms are canonical in the sense that they *uniquely* represent the elements of the given model A. Canonical term structures can either be defined directly or derived as the image of a *representation function* rep^A from the given model A to the set of ground terms.

Definition Let A be a SIG-structure and nat be the natural mapping from GT(SIG) to I(SIG,AX). An S-sorted mapping $rep^A : A \rightarrow GT(SIG)$ is called an *initial representation function for A* if

- rep^A is a *coretraction* w.r.t. $eval^A$, i.e. $eval^A \cdot rep^A = id^A$,
- rep^A satisfies the *representation condition*, i.e. $nat \cdot rep^A$ is homomorphic or, equivalently, for all $w \in S^*$, $s \in S$, $\sigma \in OP_{ws}$ and $a \in A_w$,

$$AX \cup EAX \vdash \sigma rep^A(a) \equiv rep^A \cdot \sigma^A(a)$$

and for all $P \in PR$ and $a \in P^A$,

$$AX \cup EAX \vdash Prep^A(a). \blacksquare$$

Theorem 4.4.4 *Proof-theoretical criterion for initial correctness*

AX is initially correct w.r.t. a SIG-structure A iff A satisfies AX and has an initial representation function rep^A.

Proof. Let AX be initially correct relative to A. Then AX is valid in A and there is a unique homomorphism ini^B from A to B = I(SIG,AX) which can be decomposed into a function $rep^A : A \rightarrow GT(SIG)$ and the natural mapping nat from GT(SIG) to B. Moreover, id^A is the unique homomorphism from A to A. By Lemma 4.4.1, AX is initially correct w.r.t. B. Hence the unique homomorphism ini^A from B to A is defined by $ini^A \cdot nat = eval^A$. Therefore

$$eval^A \bullet rep^A = ini^A \bullet nat \bullet rep^A = ini^A \bullet ini^B = id^A$$

and thus rep^A is an initial representation function for A.

Conversely, suppose that A satisfies AX and has an initial representation function rep^A. It is sufficient to show that the unique homomorphism ini^A from B = I(SIG,AX) to A is an isomorphism.

$nat \bullet rep^A$ and thus $nat \bullet rep^A \bullet ini^A$ are homomorphic. Hence

$$nat \bullet rep^A \bullet ini^A = id^B$$

because id^B is the unique homomorphism from B to B. Furthermore,

$$ini^A \bullet nat \bullet rep^A = eval^A \bullet rep^A = id^A.$$

Thus ini^A is an isomorphism. ■

Corollary 4.4.5 Let AX be initially correct w.r.t. a SIG-structure A with initial representation function rep^A.
(1) For all ground terms t, AX∪EAX ⊢ $rep^A(eval^A(t)) \equiv t$.
(2) For all ground atoms Pt, A ⊨ Pt implies AX∪EAX ⊢ Pt.

Proof. (1) Let B = I(SIG,AX) and ini^A be the unique homomorphism from B to A. Since $eval^A$ and id^B are unique homomorphisms from GT(SIG) to A (from B to B), we obtain

$$nat \bullet rep^A \bullet eval^A = nat \bullet rep^A \bullet ini^A \bullet nat = id^B \bullet nat = nat.$$

Hence AX∪EAX ⊢ $rep^A(eval^A(t)) \equiv t$.

(2) Let A satisfy the ground atom Pt, i.e. $eval^A(t) \in P^A$. By the representation condition, AX∪EAX ⊢ $Prep^A(eval^A(t))$. Therefore (1) implies AX∪EAX ⊢ Pt. ■

Each SIG-structure A with respect to which AX is initially correct induces a term structure that is isomorphic to A.

Proposition 4.4.6 Let AX be initially correct w.r.t. a SIG-structure A. Then there is a SIG-structure B such that AX is initially correct w.r.t. B and
(1) for all $s \in S$, $B_s \subseteq GT(SIG)_s$,
(2) for all $w \in S^*$, $s \in S$, $\sigma \in OP_{ws}$ and $t \in GT(SIG)_w$,
 $\sigma t \in B_s$ implies AX∪EAX ⊢ $t \equiv t'$ and $\sigma^B(t') = \sigma t$ for some $t' \in B_w$.

Proof. By Theorem 4.4.4, A satisfies AX and has an initial representation function rep^A. Define B as follows:

- For all $s \in S$, $B_s = rep^A(A_s)$.
- For all $w \in S^*$, $s \in S$, $\sigma \in OP_{ws}$ and $a \in A_w$, $\sigma^B(rep^A(a)) = rep^A(\sigma^A(a))$.
- For all $P \in PR$, $P^B = rep^A(P^A)$.

Of course, (1) holds true. Since $eval^A \cdot rep^A = id^A$, σ^B is well-defined. Let $\sigma \in OP_{ws}$, $t \in GT(SIG)_w$ and $\sigma t \in B_s$. By Corollary 4.4.5 (1),

$$AX \cup EAX \vdash t \equiv rep^A(eval^A(t)).$$

Moreover, $\sigma t \in B_s$ implies $\sigma t = rep^A(a)$ for some $a \in A_s$. Thus

$$\sigma^B(rep^A(eval^A(t))) = rep^A(\sigma^A(eval^A(t))) = rep^A(eval^A(\sigma t)) = rep^A(a) = \sigma t.$$

Therefore (2) is valid. By definition of B, the image restriction of rep^A is a surjective homomorphism from A to B. Since $eval^A \cdot rep^A = id^A$, rep^A is injective. Since $P^B = rep^A(P^A)$, we conclude that A and B are isomorphic. Hence by Proposition 4.4.2, AX is initially correct w.r.t. B. ∎

Proposition 4.4.6 suggests we confine ourselves to the following class of term structures when designing the model of a data type.

Definition A SIG-structure A is called a *canonical term structure* if
(1)   for all $s \in S$, $A_s \subseteq GT(SIG)_s$,
(2)   for all $w \in S^*$, $s \in S$, $\sigma \in OP_{ws}$ and $t \in GT(SIG)_w$,
      $\sigma t \in A_s$ implies $t \in A_w$ and $\sigma^A(t) = \sigma t$. ∎

Note that this notion is more general than the notion of a Herbrand structure (cf. Section 2.2): while these structures have a fixed interpretation of function symbols, namely $\sigma^A(t) = \sigma t$ for all $t \in A_w$, canonical term structures demand that definition only if $\sigma t \in A$.

In fact, it is easier to characterize initial correctness w.r.t. a canonical term structure than w.r.t. an arbitrary SIG-structure.

Corollary 4.4.7 Let A be a canonical term structure. AX is initially correct w.r.t. A iff A satisfies AX and the following conditions:
(1)   for all $w \in S^*$, $s \in S$, $\sigma \in OP_{ws}$ and $t \in A_w$, $AX \cup EAX \vdash \sigma t \equiv \sigma^A(t)$,
(2)   for all $P \in PR$ and $t \in P^A$, $AX \cup EAX \vdash Pt$.

Proof. Since A is canonical, we have $eval^A(t) = t$ for all $t \in A$. This follows by induction on size(t): if t is a constant, then $eval^A(t) = t^A = t$. If $t = \sigma u$ for some σ and u, then by the induction hypothesis,

$$eval^A(t) = \sigma^A(eval^A(u)) = \sigma^A(u) = \sigma u = t.$$

Suppose that A satisfies AX as well as (1) and (2). Let rep^A be the inclusion mapping from A to GT(SIG). Since $\text{eval}^A(t) = t$ for all $t \in A$, rep^A is a coretraction w.r.t. eval^A. Hence by assumption and Theorem 4.4.4, AX is initially correct w.r.t. A.

Conversely, suppose that AX is initially correct w.r.t. A. Then AX is valid in A and there is a unique homomorphism ini^B from A to B = I(SIG,AX) which can be decomposed into the inclusion mapping rep^A from A to GT(SIG) and the natural mapping nat from GT(SIG) to B. Hence for all $w \in S^*$, $s \in S$, $\sigma \in OP_{ws}$ and $t \in A_w$,

$$\text{nat}(\sigma t) = \sigma^B \bullet \text{nat}(t) = \sigma^B \bullet \text{nat} \bullet \text{rep}^A(t) = \sigma^B \bullet \text{ini}^B(t) = \text{ini}^B \bullet \sigma^A(t)$$
$$= \text{nat} \bullet \text{rep}^A \bullet \sigma^A(t) = \text{nat} \bullet \sigma^A(t)$$

and thus AX∪EAX ⊢ $\sigma t \equiv \sigma^A(t)$. Moreover, for all $P \in PR$ and $t \in P^A$,

$$\text{nat}(t) = \text{nat} \bullet \text{rep}^A(t) = \text{ini}^B(t) \in P^B$$

and thus AX∪EAX ⊢ Pt. ∎

Example 4.4.8 Let <SIG,AX> = INT1 (cf. Section 3.2) and let A be the canonical term structure with carrier set

$$A_{int} = \{0|^n \mid n \in \mathbb{N}\} \cup \{(\text{pred}^n\ 0) \mid n \in \mathbb{N}\}.$$

The function and predicate symbols of SIG are interpreted as follows:

- $0^A = 0$, $\text{pred}^A(0) = (\text{pred}\ 0)$,
- for all $n \in \mathbb{N}$, $|^A(0|^n) = 0|^{n+1}$,
- for all $n \geq 1$, $|^A(\text{pred}^n\ 0) = (\text{pred}^{n-1}\ 0)$, $\text{pred}^A(0|^n) = 0|^{n-1}$ and $\text{pred}^A(\text{pred}^n\ 0) = (\text{pred}^{n+1}\ 0)$,
- $\equiv^A = \{<t,t> \mid t \in A_{int}\}$.

Let us verify conditions (1) and (2) of Corollary 4.4.7. For the constant 0 we have $0 = 0^A$. For the unary operations _| and pred, let $t \in A_{int}$.

Case 1. $t = 0$. Then $t| = 0| = |^A(0)$ and $(\text{pred}\ t) = (\text{pred}\ 0) = \text{pred}^A(0)$.
Case 2. $t = 0|^n$ for some $n \geq 1$. Then $t| = 0|^{n+1} = |^A(0|^n) = |^A(t)$ and

$$(\text{pred}\ t) = (\text{pred}\ 0|^n) = 0|^{n-1} = \text{pred}^A(0|^n) = |^A(t).$$

Case 3. $t = (\text{pred}^n\ 0)$ for some $n \geq 1$. Then

$$\text{AX} \ \vdash\ t| = (\text{pred}^n\ 0)| \equiv (\text{pred}^{n-1}\ 0) = |^A(\text{pred}^n\ 0) = |^A(t)$$

and

$$AX \vdash (\text{pred } t) = (\text{pred } 0|^n) \equiv 0|^{n-1} = \text{pred}^A(\text{pred}^n \; 0) = \text{pred}^A(t).$$

Let $\langle t,t' \rangle \in \equiv^A$. Then $t = t'$ and thus $EAX \vdash t \equiv t'$.

Therefore (1) and (2) are valid, and we conclude from Corollary 4.4.7 that the axiom set of INT1 is initially correct w.r.t. A. ∎

Example 4.4.9 Let $\langle SIG, AX \rangle =$ INT2 (cf. Section 3.2) and A be the canonical term structure with carrier set

$$A_{int} = \{0|^n \mid n \in \mathbb{N}\} \cup \{-0|^n \mid n \geq 1\}.$$

The function and predicate symbols of SIG are interpreted as follows:

- $0^A = 0$, $-^A(0) = 0$,
- for all $n \in \mathbb{N}$, $|^A(0|^n) = 0|^{n+1}$,
- for all $n \geq 1$, $|^A(-0|^n) = 0|^{n-1}$, $-^A(0|^n) = -0|^n$ and $-^A(-0|^n) = 0|^n$.
- $\equiv^A = \{\langle t,t \rangle \mid t \in A_{int}\}$.

Let us verify conditions (1) and (2) of Corollary 4.4.7. For the constant 0 we have $0 = 0^A$. For the unary operations $\_|$ and pred, let $t \in A_{int}$.

Case 1. $t = 0$. Then $t| = 0| = |^A(0)$ and

$$AX \vdash -t = -0 \equiv 0 = -^A(0).$$

Case 2. $t = 0|^n$ for some $n \geq 1$. Then $t| = 0|^{n+1} = |^A(0|^n) = |^A(t)$ and $-t = -0|^n = -^A(0|^n) = -^A(t)$.

Case 3. $t = -0|^n$ for some $n \geq 1$. Then

$$AX \vdash t| = (-0|^n)| \equiv -0|^{n-1} = |^A(-0|^n) = |^A(t)$$

and

$$AX \vdash -t = --0|^n \equiv 0|^n = -^A(-0|^n) = -^A(t).$$

Let $\langle t,t' \rangle \in \equiv^A$. Then $t = t'$ and thus $EAX \vdash t \equiv t'$.

Therefore (1) and (2) are valid, and we conclude from Corollary 4.4.7 that the axiom set of INT2 is initially correct w.r.t. A. ∎

Example 4.4.10 Let $\langle SIG, AX \rangle =$ BINARY (cf. Section 3.5) and let A be the canonical term structure with carrier set

$$A_{bin} = \{0\} \cup \{1w \mid w \in \{0,1\}^*\}.$$

The function and predicate symbols of SIG are interpreted as follows: $0^A = 0$, $1^A = 1$ (*constants* 0 *and* 1 !),

$0^A(0) = 0$, $1^A(0) = 1$, for all $w \in \{0,1\}^*$, $0^A(1w) = 1w0$ and $1^A(1w) = 1w1$,

$\equiv^A = \{\langle t,t\rangle \mid t \in A_{bin}\}$,

$<^A$ is inductively defined by:
- $\{\langle 0,1w\rangle \mid w \in \{0,1\}^*\} \subseteq <^A$,
- $\{\langle 1,1w\rangle \mid w \in \{0,1\}^+\} \subseteq <^A$,
- $\{\langle 1w0,1w1\rangle \mid w \in \{0,1\}^*\} \subseteq <^A$,
- for all $x,y \in \{0,1\}$, $\langle u,u'\rangle \in <^A$ implies $\langle ux,u'y\rangle \in <^A$.

(is even)^A = $\{0\} \cup \{1w0 \mid w \in \{0,1\}^*\}$,

(is odd)^A = $\{1\} \cup \{1w1 \mid w \in \{0,1\}^*\}$.

Let us verify conditions (1) and (2) of Corollary 4.4.7. For the constants 0 and 1 we have $0 = 0^A$ and $1 = 1^A$. For the unary operations $\_0$ and $\_1$, let $t \in A_{bin}$.

Case 1. $t = 0$. Then
$$AX \vdash t0 = 00 \equiv 0 = 0^A(0) = 0^A(t)$$
and
$$AX \vdash t1 = 01 \equiv 1 = 1^A(0) = 1^A(t).$$

Case 2. $t = 1w$ for some $w \in \{0,1\}^*$. Then
$$t0 = 1w0 = 0^A(1w) = 0^A(t) \text{ and } t1 = 1w1 = 1^A(1w) = 1^A(t).$$

Let $\langle t,t'\rangle \in \equiv^A$. Then $t = t'$ and thus $EAX \vdash t \equiv t'$.

Let $\langle t,t'\rangle \in <^A$.
Case 1. $t = 0$ and $t' = 1w$ for some $w \in \{0,1\}^n$ and $n \in \mathbb{N}$. Then
$$AX \cup EAX \vdash \{0 \equiv 00^n, 00^n < 1w\} \vdash t < t'.$$

Case 2. $t = 1$ and $t' = 1w$ for some $w \in \{0,1\}^n$ and $n \geq 1$. Then
$$AX \cup EAX \vdash \{1 \equiv 00^{n-1}1, 00^{n-1}1 < 1w\} \vdash t < t'.$$

Case 3. $t = 1w0$ and $t' = 1w1$ for some $w \in \{0,1\}^*$. Then
$$AX \cup EAX \vdash \{1w \equiv 1w\} \vdash t < t'.$$

Case 4. $t = ux$ and $t' = u'y$ for some $\langle u,u'\rangle \in <^A$ and $x,y \in \{0,1\}$. By the induction hypothesis,

$$AX \cup EAX \vdash u < u' \vdash t < t'.$$

Let $t \in (\text{is even})^A$.
  Case 1. $t = 0$. Then
  $$AX \cup EAX \vdash \{0 \equiv 00, 00 \text{ is even}\} \vdash \{t \text{ is even}\}.$$

  Case 2. $t = 1w0$ for some $w \in \{0,1\}^+$. Then $AX \vdash \{t \text{ is even}\}$.

Let $t \in (\text{is odd})^A$.
  Case 1. $t = 1$. Then
  $$AX \cup EAX \vdash \{1 \equiv 01, 01 \text{ is odd}\} \vdash \{t \text{ is odd}\}.$$

  Case 2. $t = 1w1$ for some $w \in \{0,1\}^+$. Then $AX \vdash \{t \text{ is odd}\}$.

Therefore (1) and (2) are valid, and we conclude from Corollary 4.4.7 that the axiom set of BINARY is initially correct w.r.t. A. ∎

Correctness proofs help to find axioms for a data type. One proceeds up to the verification of conditions (1) and (2) of Corollary 4.4.7 where the needed axioms become apparent (cf. Examples 4.4.8,9,10).

Chapter 6 introduces the decomposition of <SIG,AX> into a base part and an extension part. Provided that <SIG,AX> is a *conservative extension* of the base (cf. Section 6.1), it is sufficient to show that the base axioms are correct w.r.t. the base part, say B, of the given SIG-structure A because this implies the correctness of AX w.r.t. the *initial SIG-extension* of B (cf. Corollary 6.2.5).

A goal is an inductive <SIG,AX>-theorem if *all* its ground instances are <SIG,AX>-theorems. An initial representation function rep^A allows us to consider only those ground substitutions that assign terms in the range of rep^A.

Theorem 4.4.11 *Inductive theory criterion based on a representation function*
  Let A be a SIG-model of AX with initial representation function rep^A.
(1) An atom p is an inductive <SIG,AX>-theorem iff for all $f \in rep^A(A)^X$, p[f] is derivable from $AX \cup EAX$.
(2) Given a clause $p \Leftarrow \gamma$, Gen(SIG,AX) satisfies $p \Leftarrow \gamma$ iff for all $f \in rep^A(A)^X$, p[f] is derivable from $AX \cup EAX \cup \gamma[f]$.

Proof. (1) Let p be an inductive <SIG,AX>-theorem and g be a ground substitution. By assumption,

$$AX \cup EAX \vdash p[rep^A \circ eval^A \circ g]$$

and thus by Corollary 4.4.5 (2), AX∪EAX ⊢ p[g]. Hence p is an inductive
<SIG,AX>-theorem.

The converse is trivial.

(2) Suppose that Gen(SIG,AX) satisfies p⇐γ. Let f ∈ rep^A(A)^X. Then f is a
ground substitution and we conclude from Corollary 4.3.3 that p[f] is
derivable from AX∪γ[f].

Conversely, suppose that for all f ∈ rep^A(A)^X, p[f] is derivable from
AX∪EAX∪γ[f]. Then by Theorem 4.2.2,

(3) $$\text{Mod}(SIG, AX \cup \gamma[f]) \models p[f].$$

Suppose that B is a term-generated SIG-model of AX. We show that B
satisfies p⇐γ.

Let b be a solution of γ in B. Since B is term-generated, there is a ground
substitution g with eval^B∘g = b. By Corollary 4.4.5 (1),

(4) $$AX \cup EAX \vdash \text{rep}^A \circ \text{eval}^A \circ g \equiv g.$$

Let f = rep^A∘eval^A∘g. Since B satisfies AX, (4) implies eval^B∘f = eval^B∘g.
Therefore eval^B∘f = b. Since b solves γ in B, γ[f] is valid in B. Hence B is a
SIG-model of AX∪γ[f] and thus by (3), B satisfies p[f]. Therefore b solves p
in B, and we conclude that B satisfies p⇐γ. ∎

4.5 Final Semantics

This approach is complementary to initial semantics. Distinguishing a set
VS of *visible* sorts, we restrict our attention to *visibly initial* models that
differ from the initial structure by their freedom concerning the *behavioural
equivalence,* that is the interpretation of equality predicates for non-visible
sorts. The final <SIG,AX>-structure, Z(SIG,AX), is the *smallest* visibly initial
model of AX: Z(SIG,AX) is a quotient of every visibly initial model. Final
semantics identifies data types with final structures and propagates *full
abstractness*: Things are different only if they are provably different.

The visibility concept stems from automata theory, which deals with
methods of obtaining *observable realizations* of input-output functions. The
behavioural equivalence *of structures* has played a more major rôle along
these lines than have deductive aspects of final semantics (cf. Goguen and
Meseguer [5], Section 7.1).

As in the case of initial semantics, we present a model-theoretic
correctness notion and a proof-theoretic correctness criterion (cf. Section
4.6). The refutation of inductive theorems is often facilitated by employing
final semantics (cf. Section 4.7).

For the following three Sections, 4.5, 4.6 and 4.7, which are devoted to final semantics, we assume that a subset VS of *visible sorts* has been distinguished from the set S of all sorts.

Definition An atom Pt is *visible* if the predicate symbol P is an equality predicate *only if* P is an equality predicate for a visible sort. A goal is visible if all its atoms are visible. ∎

In the framework of equational specifications, *contexts* for a non-visible sort s are given by all terms with visible sort and a distinguished variable x_o with sort s. Consequently, the behavioural equivalence consists of all term pairs $\langle t,t'\rangle$ such that for all contexts c of t,

$$AX \cup EAX \vdash c[t/x_o] \equiv c[t'/x_o]. \qquad (1)$$

In the sequel, this approach is generalized in accordance with Sannella and Tarlecki's *abstractor* specifications where contexts occur as additional formulas and are part of the specification. Horn clause logic allows arbitrary visible atoms to serve as contexts. The context that is given by the *term* c corresponds to the visible atom $c \equiv x$, and (1) is turned into the following equivalence: for all ground terms u,

$$AX \cup EAX \vdash c[t/x_o] \equiv u \quad iff \quad AX \cup EAX \vdash c[t'/x_o] \equiv u. \qquad (2)$$

Hence the generalization of behavioural equivalence to contexts represented as a set C of visible atoms reads as follows. For all $p \in C$ and ground substitutions f,

$$AX \cup EAX \vdash p[t/x_o][f] \quad iff \quad AX \cup EAX \vdash p[t'/x_o][f]. \qquad (3)$$

To obtain a well-defined final semantics, C must be chosen in such a way that the interpretation of each equality predicate becomes a SIG-congruence relation (cf. Section 2.3).

Definition Let s be a non-visible sort. An *s-context* is a visible atom with a unique occurrence of the fixed variable $x_o \in X_s$. ∎

In general, the fixed variable x_o is not the only variable occurring in a context. There are other variables as well that serve as *input parameters* (cf. Examples 4.5.1-4.5.4).

Definition For each $s \in S-VS$ let C_s be a set of s-contexts. The *contextual theory of* $\langle SIG,AX \rangle$, $CTh(SIG,AX)$, consists of

- all visible ⟨SIG,AX⟩-theorems and
- all equations $t \equiv_s t'$ with non-visible sort s such that, for all s-contexts p and ground substitutions f, (3) holds true.

$$AX \cup EAX \vdash p[t/x_0][f] \quad \text{iff} \quad AX \cup EAX \vdash p[t'/x_0][f].$$

Elements and subsets of CTh(SIG,AX) are called *contextual ⟨SIG,AX⟩-theorems*.

The *inductive contextual theory of ⟨SIG,AX⟩*, *ICTh(SIG,AX)*, consists of all atoms all ground instances of which are contextual ⟨SIG,AX⟩-theorems. Elements and subsets of ICTh(SIG,AX) are called *inductive contextual ⟨SIG,AX⟩-theorems*.

Let *GCTh(SIG,AX)* be the restriction of CTh(SIG,AX) to ground atoms. The binary relation $\approx$ on GT(SIG) defined by

$$t \approx t' \quad \text{iff} \quad t \equiv t' \in GCTh(SIG,AX)$$

is called the *behavioural ⟨SIG,AX⟩-equivalence*. ∎

Of course, $\approx$ is an S-sorted equivalence relation. But in order to proceed to the definition of a final structure we need the additional assumption that $\approx$ is OP- and PR-compatible (cf. Section 2.3). To see what this means let t,t' be two ground terms with the same non-visible sort, say s, such that t and t' are not behaviourally equivalent. Then there are an s-context p and a ground substitution f such that either $p[t/x_0][f]$ or $p[t'/x_0][f]$ is derivable from AX∪EAX. For this reason contexts are also called *discriminators* (see Burstall) or *distinguishing formulas* (see Kamin).

Definition Suppose that the behavioural ⟨SIG,AX⟩-equivalence is OP- and PR-compatible. Then the quotient of the Herbrand structure

$$CH = HS(GT(SIG), GCTh(SIG,AX))$$

by $\approx$ is called the *final ⟨SIG,AX⟩-structure, Z(SIG,AX)*, i.e. $Z(SIG,AX) = CH/\approx$. ∎

Hence Z(SIG,AX) does not only depend on ⟨SIG,AX⟩. It also depends on the choice of contexts for non-visible sorts and the assumption that the induced behavioural equivalence is OP- and PR-compatible. Let us give examples of specifications that are equipped with contexts. Their signatures include a list of contexts preceded by the keyword *conts*. The non-visible sort a context belongs to is determined by the sort of the distinguished variable x_0, which occurs in the list of variables.

Example 4.5.1 Let ⟨SIG,AX⟩ = STORE-FINAL where

STORE-FINAL
   base : IDENT
   sorts : store
   opns : ω : store
           _[_←_] : store,ident,nat→store
           _[_] : store,ident→nat
   vars : s, x_o : store
          x,y : ident
          m,n : nat
   axms : s[x←n][x] ≡ n
           s[x←n][y] ≡ s[y] ⇐ x ≠ y
   conts : x_o[x] ≡ n

STORE-FINAL coincides with ACCESS-FUN (cf. Section 3.4) except that the *base* axioms (A1) and (A2) of ACCESS-FUN were omitted. OP-compatibility of the behavioural STORE-FINAL-equivalence amounts to the following condition:

- Let t,t' ∈ GT(SIG)$_{store}$ such that for all ground terms u,v,
    AX ∪ EAX ⊢ t[u]≡v   implies   AX ∪ EAX ⊢ t'[u]≡v.   (∗)
Then for all ground terms u,u',v,v',
    AX ∪ EAX ⊢ t[u←v][u']≡v'   implies   AX ∪ EAX ⊢ t'[u←v][u']≡v'.

So let (∗) hold true and t[u←v][u']≡v' be derivable from AX∪EAX. Then either u≡u' and v≡v' or t[u']≡v' is derivable from AX∪EAX. In the second case, (∗) implies that t'[u']≡v' is derivable from AX∪EAX. Therefore AX∪EAX ⊢ t'[u←v][u']≡v'. ∎

Example 4.5.2 Let ⟨SIG,AX⟩ = FINBAG-FINAL where

FINBAG-FINAL
   base : NAT
   sorts : bag
   opns : $\emptyset$: bag
           insert _ _ : nat,bag→bag
           _[_] : bag,nat→nat
   vars : m,n : nat
          b, x_o : bag
   axms : $\emptyset$[m] ≡ 0
           (insert m b)[m] ≡ b[m]|
           (insert m b)[n] ≡ b[n] ⇐ m ≠ n
   conts : x_o[m] ≡ n

FINBAG-FINAL agrees with FINBAG-COUNT (cf. Section 3.10) except that we omitted the *base* axiom (A1) of FINBAG-COUNT. OP-compatibility of the behavioural FINBAG-FINAL-equivalence amounts to the following condition:

* Let t,t' ∈ GT(SIG)$_{bag}$ such that for all ground terms u,v,
    AX ∪ EAX ⊢ t[u]≡v   implies   AX ∪ EAX ⊢ t'[u]≡v.   (∗)
  Then for all ground terms u,u',v,
    AX ∪ EAX ⊢ (insert u' t)[u]≡v
           implies   AX ∪ EAX ⊢ (insert u' t')[u]≡v.

So let (∗) hold true and (insert u' t)[u]≡v be derivable from AX∪EAX. Then either u≡u' and t[u]|≡v or t[u]≡v is derivable from AX∪EAX. Hence by (∗), either u≡u' and t'[u]|≡v or t'[u]≡v is derivable from AX∪EAX. Therefore AX∪EAX ⊢ (insert u' t')[u]≡v. ∎

Example 4.5.3 Let <SIG,AX> = FINSET-FINAL where

FINSET-FINAL
  base : NAT
  sorts : set
  opns : ∅ : set
          insert _ _ : nat,set→set
  preds : _ is in _ : nat,set
  vars : m,n : nat
          s,x$_o$: set
  axms : m is in (insert m s)
          m is in (insert n s) ⇐ m is in s
  conts : m is in x$_o$

FINSET-FINAL agrees with FINSET (cf. Section 3.10) except that the *base* axioms (A1) and (A2) of FINSET were omitted. The behavioural FINSET-FINAL-equivalence is PR-compatible if the following condition holds true:

* Let t,t' ∈ GT(SIG)$_{set}$ such that for all ground terms u,
    AX ∪ EAX ⊢ u is in t   implies   AX ∪ EAX ⊢ u is in t'.   (∗)
  Then for all ground terms u,u',
    AX ∪ EAX ⊢ u is in (insert u' t)
           implies   AX ∪ EAX ⊢ u is in (insert u' t').

So let (∗) hold true and (u is in (insert u' t)) be derivable from AX∪EAX. Then either u≡u' or (u is in t) is derivable from AX∪EAX. In the second case (∗)

implies that (u is in t') is derivable from AX∪EAX. Therefore

$$AX \cup EAX \vdash u \text{ is in (insert } u' \text{ } t'\text{)}. \blacksquare$$

Example 4.5.4 Let <SIG,AX> = SEQ-FINAL where

SEQ-FINAL
    base : NAT
    sorts : seq
    opns : ε : seq
           _&_ : nat,seq→seq
           head _ : seq→nat
           tail _ : seq→seq
    vars : s, s', x_0 : seq
           n : nat
    axms : head n&s ≡ n
           tail n&s ≡ s
    conts : head ($tail^k$ x_0) ≡ n   for all k ∈ $\mathbb{N}$

The behavioural SEQ-FINAL-equivalence is OP-compatible if the following condition holds true:

- Let t,t' ∈ GT(SIG)$_{seq}$ such that for all ground terms u and k ∈ $\mathbb{N}$,
$$AX \cup EAX \vdash head (tail^k t) \equiv u$$
implies $AX \cup EAX \vdash head (tail^k t') \equiv u.$ (*)
Then for all ground terms u,u' and k ∈ $\mathbb{N}$,
$$AX \cup EAX \vdash head (tail^k u\&t) \equiv u'$$
implies $AX \cup EAX \vdash head (tail^k u\&t') \equiv u'$
and
$$AX \cup EAX \vdash head (tail^k (tail\ t)) \equiv u'$$
implies $AX \cup EAX \vdash head (tail^k (tail\ t')) \equiv u'.$

So let (*) hold true and (head ($tail^k$ u&t) ≡ u') be derivable from AX∪EAX. We show
$$AX \cup EAX \vdash head (tail^k u\&t') \equiv u' \qquad (1)$$

by induction on k. If k = 0, then AX∪EAX ⊢ u≡u', and the proof is complete. Otherwise (head ($tail^{k-1}$ t) ≡ u') is derivable from AX∪EAX. Hence by (*),

$$AX \cup EAX \vdash head (tail^{k-1} t') \equiv u'.$$

Therefore (1) holds true.

Secondly, let (head (tail^k (tail t)) $\equiv$ u') be derivable from AX$\cup$EAX. Then by (∗),

$$AX \cup EAX \vdash head (tail^k (tail\ t')) \equiv u'. \blacksquare$$

The structures we are concerned with in final semantics are term-generated. Moreover, all visible atoms they satisfy are inductive theorems:

Definition A term-generated SIG-structure A is *visibly initial w.r.t. AX* if for all visible atoms p

$$A \vDash p \quad \text{implies} \quad p \in ITh(SIG,AX).$$

The class of visibly initial SIG-models of AX is denoted by *VI(SIG,AX)*. ∎

Hence by Theorem 4.3.2, for all visibly initial models A and all visible atoms p, A satisfies p *if and only if* p is an inductive theorem.

Theorem 4.5.5 Suppose that for all $q\Leftarrow\vartheta \in AX$, ϑ is visible. Then Z(SIG,AX) is a visibly initial SIG-model of AX.

Proof. Let B = Z(SIG,AX). We show that B satisfies AX. Let $Pt\Leftarrow P_1t_1,...,P_nt_n$ be in AX and $b \in B^X$ such that for all $1 \le i \le n$, $b*t_i \in P_i^B$. Then $b = nat \cdot f$ for some ground substitution f and the natural mapping nat from GT(SIG) to B. Hence for all $1 \le i \le n$, $nat(t_i[f]) \in P_i^B$, and thus $P_it_i[f]$ is a contextual <SIG,AX>-theorem. By assumption, $P_it_i[f]$ is visible. Hence by definition of contextual theorems, $P_it_i[f]$ and thus Pt[f] are <SIG,AX>-theorems. Therefore Pt[f] is a contextual <SIG,AX>-theorem, i.e. $b*t = nat(t[f]) \in P^B$. We conclude that B satisfies $Pt\Leftarrow P_1t_1,...,P_nt_n$.

B is a SIG-structure with identity because for all $s \in S$, the relation $\equiv_s^B$ on B is given by all pairs <nat(t),nat(t')> with $t \approx t'$.

B is visibly initial. Let Pt be a visible atom satisfied by B. Then nat(t) $\in$ P^B. Hence Pt is a contextual and thus a deductive <SIG,AX>-theorem. ∎

Corollary 4.5.6 Suppose that for all $q\Leftarrow\vartheta \in AX$, ϑ is visible. Then ICTh(SIG,AX) is sound w.r.t. Z(SIG,AX).

Proof. Let B = Z(SIG,AX) and Pt $\in$ ICTh(SIG,AX). Then for all ground substitutions f, Pt[f] is either a visible deductive <SIG,AX>-theorem or an equation, say $u\equiv_s u'$, with non-visible sort s. Let $b \in B^X$. Since B is term-generated, there is a ground substitution f with $nat\cdot f = eval^B\cdot f = b$.

By Theorem 4.5.5, B is a SIG-model of AX. Since B satisfies EAX and the Horn clause calculus preserves validity in B (cf. the proof of Theorem 4.2.2), B satisfies all deductive <SIG,AX>-theorems. Thus if Pt[f] $\in$ DTh(SIG,AX), Pt[f] is valid in B, i.e. $b*t \in P^B$, and we conclude that B satisfies Pt.

If Pt is an equation, say $u \equiv u'$, then $u[f] \equiv u'[f]$ is a contextual theorem, i.e. $u[f] \approx u'[f]$. Hence $nat(u[f]) = nat(u'[f])$ where nat is the natural mapping from CH to B. Therefore $b^*u = b^*u'$, i.e. B satisfies Pt. ∎

Whereas the inductive theory is sound w.r.t. the class of *all* term-generated models, there is no corresponding result in final semantics stating that *all* visibly initial models satisfy the inductive contextual theory. This is not surprising because, given a model A of AX, the property of visible initiality does not entail that all behaviourally equivalent terms be identified by A. It is only the final <SIG,AX>-structure that does not distinguish between behaviourally equivalent terms. On the other hand, we have

Theorem 4.5.7 ICTh(SIG,AX) is complete w.r.t. *each* visibly initial SIG-model of AX.

Proof. Let A be a visibly initial SIG-model of AX, let Pt be an atom satified by A and let f be a ground substitution. We have to show that Pt[f] is a contextual <SIG,AX>-theorem. There are two cases:

Case 1. $Pt[f] = (u \equiv_s u')$ for some non-visible sort s. Let $Qv \in C_s$ and g be a ground substitution. Suppose that $q = Qv[u/x_o][g]$ is a <SIG,AX>-theorem. Then A satisfies q and thus $q' = Qv[u'/x_o][g]$ because $u \equiv_s u'$ is valid in A. Since Q is not an equality predicate for a non-visible sort, we conclude from visible initiality of A that q' is a <SIG,AX>-theorem. Analogously, if q' is a <SIG,AX>-theorem, then q is a <SIG,AX>-theorem as well. Therefore Pt[f] is a contextual <SIG,AX>-theorem.

Case 2. Pt[f] is visible. Since A is visibly initial, Pt[f] is a deductive and thus a contextual <SIG,AX>-theorem. ∎

The following characterization of visibly initial models suggests calling Z(SIG,AX) the *final* <SIG.AX>-structure. It also shows that final semantics is complementary to initial semantics.

Corollary 4.5.8 *Characterization of visibly initial models*
A term-generated SIG-model A of AX is visibly initial iff there is a homomorphism $abs^A : A \longrightarrow Z(SIG,AX)$ called an *abstraction homomorphism*.

Proof. Let A be a visibly initial SIG-model of AX, B = Z(SIG,AX) and nat be the natural mapping from GT(SIG) to B.

Suppose that A is visibly initial. By Theorem 4.5.7, for all ground equations $t \equiv t'$,

(1) $\qquad A \models t \equiv t' \quad \text{implies} \quad t \equiv t' \in CTh(SIG,AX)$.

Hence abs^A is well-defined by $abs^A \bullet eval^A = nat$. Moreover, abs^A is homomorphic. Let $w \in S^*$, $s \in S$, $\sigma \in OP_{ws}$ and $a \in A_w$. Then there is a ground term t such that $eval^A(t) = a$, and one obtains

$$abs^A \bullet \sigma^A(a) = abs^A \bullet \sigma^A \bullet eval^A(t) = abs^A \bullet eval^A(\sigma t) = nat(\sigma t) = \sigma^B \bullet nat(t)$$
$$= \sigma^B \bullet abs^A \bullet eval^A(t) = \sigma^B \bullet abs^A(a).$$

Let $P \in PR$ and $a \in P^A$. Again, $eval^A(t) = a$ for some ground term t. Hence A satisfies Pt, and we conclude from Theorem 4.5.7 that Pt is a contextual $<SIG,AX>$-theorem. Therefore

$$abs^A(a) = abs^A \bullet eval^A(t) = nat(t) \in P^B.$$

Conversely, let $abs^A : A \to B$ be a homomorphism. By uniqueness of the homomorphism from $GT(SIG)$ to B, $abs^A \bullet eval^A$ coincides with the natural homomorphism nat from $GT(SIG)$ to B. Let Pt be a visible atom satisfied by A. Then $eval^A(t) \in P^A$. Hence

$$nat(t) = abs^A \bullet eval^A(t) \in P^B$$

and thus $Pt \in CTh(SIG,AX)$. Therefore Pt is a $<SIG,AX>$-theorem, and we conclude that A is visibly initial. ∎

4.6 Final Correctness

It is a small step from Corollary 4.5.8 to the following correctness notion that inverts the notion of initial correctness (cf. Section 4.4).

Definition Given a SIG-structure B that is visibly initial w.r.t. AX, AX is *finally correct* w.r.t. B if for all $A \in VI(SIG,AX)$ there is a unique SIG-homomorphism from A to B, called fin^A. ∎

Lemma 4.6.1 Suppose that for all $q \Leftarrow \vartheta \in AX$, ϑ is visible. Then AX is finally correct w.r.t. $Z(SIG,AX)$.

Proof. By Theorem 4.5.5, $Z(SIG,AX) \in VI(SIG,AX)$. For all visibly initial SIG-models A of AX, Corollary 4.5.8 establishes a homomorphism abs^A from A to $Z(SIG,AX)$ such that $abs^A \bullet eval^A = nat$. Since *every* homomorphism h from A to $Z(SIG,AX)$ fulfils the equation $h \bullet eval^A = nat$, abs^A is the only one, and we define $fin^A = abs^A$. ∎

The definition of final correctness yields

Proposition 4.6.2 Let AX be finally correct w.r.t. a SIG-structure A. ⟨SIG,AX⟩ is finally correct w.r.t. a SIG-structure B iff A and B are isomorphic. ∎

Therefore Lemma 4.6.1 amounts to

Theorem 4.6.3 Suppose that for all $q \Leftarrow \delta \in AX$, δ is visible. Let A be a SIG-structure. A and Z(SIG,AX) are isomorphic iff AX is finally correct w.r.t. A. ∎

As in the case of initial correctness we provide a method for carrying out proofs of final correctness that uses representations functions:

Definition Let A be a SIG-structure and nat be the natural mapping from GT(SIG) to Z(SIG,AX). An S-sorted mapping $rep^A : A \rightarrow GT(SIG)$ is called a *final representation function* if
- rep^A is a coretraction of $eval^A$, i.e. $eval^A \cdot rep^A = id^A$,
- $nat \cdot rep^A$ is injective, i.e. for all $a,a' \in A$, $rep^A(a) \equiv rep^A(a') \in CTh(SIG,AX)$ implies $a = a'$. ∎

Theorem 4.6.4 *Proof-theoretical criterion for final correctness*

Suppose that for all $q \Leftarrow \delta \in AX$, δ is visible. AX is finally correct w.r.t. a SIG-structure A iff A is visibly initial and satisfies AX and there is a final representation function rep^A.

Proof. Let AX be finally correct w.r.t. A. By Theorem 4.5.5, Z(SIG,AX) is a visibly initial SIG-model of AX. Since by Theorem 4.6.3, A and Z(SIG,AX) are isomorphic, A is a visibly initial SIG-model of AX as well. In particular, A is term-generated, implying $eval^A \cdot rep^A = id^A$ for some $rep^A : A \rightarrow GT(SIG)$. Let $a,a' \in A$ such that $rep^A(a) \equiv rep^A(a')$ is a contextual ⟨SIG,AX⟩-theorem. Then Z(SIG,AX) satisfies $rep^A(a) \equiv rep^A(a')$, and thus

$$eval^A \cdot rep^A(a) = eval^A \cdot rep^A(a')$$

because A and Z(SIG,AX) are isomorphic. Since rep^A is a coretraction of $eval^A$, we obtain $a = a'$.

Therefore $nat \cdot rep^A$ is injective.

Conversely, suppose that $A \in VI(SIG,AX)$ admits a final representation function rep^A. We prove that A and Z(SIG,AX) are isomorphic. By Corollary 4.5.8, there is a homomorphism abs^A from A to Z(SIG,AX) with $abs^A \cdot eval^A = nat$. Hence abs^A is surjective. It remains for us to check that abs^A is injective.

So let $abs^A(a) = abs^A(a')$. Since rep^A is a coretraction of $eval^A$,

$$abs^A = abs^A \bullet eval^A \bullet rep^A = nat \bullet rep^A.$$

Hence $nat \bullet rep^A(a) = nat \bullet rep^A(a')$, and we conclude $a = a'$ from injectivity of $nat \bullet rep^A$. ∎

4.7 The Refutation of Inductive Theorems

Comparing the specifications ACCESS-FUN (cf. Section 3.4), FINBAG-COUNT and FINSET (cf. Section 3.10) with their *final counterparts* given by Examples 4.5.1-4.5.3 one observes that the latter were obtained from the former (subsequently called *initial* specifications) by dropping those equational axioms which only involve *constructor* functions. Each *final* specification was equipped with contexts in such a way that all equivalences induced by the additional axioms of the initial specification return as behavioural equivalences of the final one.

It is the abstraction homomorphism that maps the inductive theorems of an initial specification to inductive contextual theorems of its final counterpart. But the existence of an abstraction homomorphism depends on the visible initiality of its domain structure (cf. Corollary 4.5.8). So we have to ensure that the initial structure of an initial specification is visibly initial with respect to the axioms of its final counterpart. Remember that, by definition of visible initiality, I(SIG,AX) is visible initial w.r.t. AX.

Proposition 4.7.1 *From inductive to inductive contextual theorems*
Let AX' be a set of clauses including AX. I(SIG,AX') is visibly initial w.r.t. AX iff every inductive ⟨SIG,AX'⟩-theorem is an inductive contextual ⟨SIG,AX⟩-theorem.

Proof. Let $A = I(SIG,AX')$ be visibly initial w.r.t. AX and $B = Z(SIG,AX)$. By Corollary 4.5.8, there is a homomorphism $abs^A : A \rightarrow B$. Moreover, $abs^A \bullet eval^A$ = nat where nat is the natural mapping from GT(SIG) to B.

Let $Pt \in ITh(SIG,AX')$ and let f be a ground substitution. Then A satisfies $Pt[f]$, i.e. $eval^A(t[f]) \in P^A$. Hence

$$nat(t[f]) = abs^A \bullet eval^A(t[f]) \in P^B$$

and thus $Pt[f] \in CTh(SIG,AX)$. Therefore $Pt \in ICTh(SIG,AX)$.

Conversely, suppose that every inductive ⟨SIG,AX'⟩-theorem is an inductive contextual ⟨SIG,AX⟩-theorem. Then in particular, for all ground terms t and t', $t \equiv t' \in GTh(SIG,AX')$ implies $t \equiv t' \in GCTh(SIG,AX)$, i.e. $eval^A(t) =$

$eval^A(t')$ implies $t \approx t'$. Hence $h : A \rightarrow B$ with $h \circ eval^A$ = nat is a well-defined homomorphism. By Corollary 4.5.8, B is visibly initial w.r.t. AX. ∎

Sometimes the initial and the final versions of a specification coincide. For instance, SEQ-FINAL (cf. Example 4.5.4) is such a case where AX' is AX and thus, by Proposition 4.7.1, the set of inductive <SIG,AX>-theorems agrees with the set of inductive contextual <SIG,AX>-theorems. In other words, the initial SEQ-FINAL-structure and the final SEQ-FINAL-structure are the same. However, if AX is a *proper* subset of AX', we need a tractable criterion to show that I(SIG,AX') is visibly initial in order to make use of Proposition 4.7.1. Such a criterion is given by the following condition, applied to the clauses of AX'-AX.

Definition A set C of clauses *follows contextually from AX* if
- for all $u \equiv u' \Leftarrow \vartheta \in C$, visible atoms p, $x \in var(p)$ and ground substitutions f,

  AX ∪ EAX ⊢ $(\{p[u/x]\} \cup \vartheta)[f]$ iff   AX ∪ EAX ⊢ $(\{p[u'/x]\} \cup \vartheta)[f]$,
- for all $q \Leftarrow \vartheta \in C$ and ground substitutions f such that q is visible, but not an equation,

  AX ∪ EAX ⊢ $\vartheta[f]$ implies   AX ∪ EAX ⊢ $q[f]$. ∎

We claim that, if AX'-AX follows contextually from AX, then each inductive contextual <SIG,AX'>-theorem is already an inductive contextual <SIG,AX>-theorem, and thus, in particular, every inductive <SIG,AX'>-theorem is an inductive contextual <SIG,AX>-theorem, or, in terms of Proposition 4.7.1, I(SIG,AX') is visibly initial w.r.t. AX. Before stating the precise result we illustrate the criterion at some examples.

Example 4.7.2 Let <SIG,AX> = STORE-FINAL (cf. Example 4.5.1). Adding the axioms

(A1) $s[x \leftarrow m][x \leftarrow n] \equiv s[x \leftarrow n]$
(A2) $s[x \leftarrow m][y \leftarrow n] \equiv s[y \leftarrow n][x \leftarrow m] \Leftarrow x \neq y$

to <SIG,AX> we obtain ACCESS-FUN (cf. Section 3.4).

The only visible atoms that can be instantiated by the left-hand or right-hand side of (A1) or (A2) are instances of the *store*-context $x_o[x] \equiv n$. Hence (A1) and (A2) follow contextually from AX if the following implications hold true for all ground terms t,u,u',u",v,v',v":

$$\text{AX} \cup \text{EAX} \vdash t[u \leftarrow v][u \leftarrow v'][u"] \equiv v"$$
iff $$\text{AX} \cup \text{EAX} \vdash t[u \leftarrow v'][u"] \equiv v",$$

$$\text{AX} \cup \text{EAX} \vdash \{t[u \leftarrow v][u' \leftarrow v'][u"] \equiv v", u \neq u'\}$$

iff   AX ∪ EAX ⊢ {t[u'←v][u←v'][u"]≡v", u≠u'}.

The proof using induction on size(t) is straightforward. ∎

Example 4.7.3 Let <SIG,AX> = FINBAG-FINAL (cf. Example 4.5.2). Adding the axiom

(A1)   insert m (insert n s) ≡ insert n (insert m s)

to <SIG,AX> we obtain FINBAG-COUNT (cf. 3.10).

The only visible atoms that can be instantiated by the left-hand or right-hand side of (A1) are instances of the *bag*-context $x_o[m] \equiv n$. Hence (A1) follows contextually from AX if the following implication holds true for all ground terms t,u,u',v,v':

AX ∪ EAX ⊢ (insert u (insert u' t))[v]≡v'
iff   AX ∪ EAX ⊢ (insert u' (insert u t))[v]≡v'.

The proof using induction on size(t) is straightforward. ∎

Example 4.7.4 Let <SIG,AX> = FINSET-FINAL (cf. Example 4.5.3). Adding the axioms

(A1)   insert m (insert m s) ≡ insert m s
(A2)   insert m (insert n s) ≡ insert n (insert m s)

to <SIG,AX> we obtain FINSET (cf. 3.10).

The only visible atoms that can be instantiated by the left-hand or right-hand side of (A1) or (A2) are instances of the *set*-context m is in x_o. Hence (A1) and (A2) follow contextually from AX if the following implications hold true for all ground terms t,u,u',v:

AX ∪ EAX ⊢ v is in (insert u (insert u t))
iff   AX ∪ EAX ⊢ v is in (insert u t),

AX ∪ EAX ⊢ v is in (insert u (insert u' t))
iff   AX ∪ EAX ⊢ v is in (insert u' (insert u t)).

The proof using induction on size(t) is straightforward. ∎

Theorem 4.7.5 *Criterion for visible initiality of initial structures*
Let AX' be a set of clauses such that AX ⊆ AX' and for all q⇐ϑ ∈ AX', ϑ is visible. If AX'−AX follows contextually from AX, then I(SIG,AX') is visibly initial w.r.t. AX.

Proof The proof uses the fact that <SIG,AX'>-theorems can be proved by paramodulation. Hence we postpone it to the end of Section 5.3. ∎

Example 4.7.6 Let us combine the previous theorem with Proposition 4.7.1 in order to show that the equation s≡ω (where s is a variable) is *not* an inductive ACCESS-FUN-theorem (cf. Section 3.4).

By Example 4.7.2, the two axioms (A1) and (A2) distinguishing ACCESS-FUN from STORE-FINAL follow contextually from the axioms of STORE-FINAL. Hence by Theorem 4.7.5, the initial ACCESS-FUN-structure is visibly initial w.r.t. the axioms of STORE-FINAL. Thus by Proposition 4.7.1, s≡ω is not an inductive ACCESS-FUN-theorem if s≡ω is not an inductive *contextual* STORE-FINAL-theorem.

To show the latter we need a ground term t such that t≡ω is not a contextual STORE-FINAL-theorem. Since $x_o[x]\equiv n$ is the only *store*-context, we need ground terms t,u,v such that either t[u]≡v or ω[u]≡v is derivable from the axioms of STORE-FINAL, say AX, and EAX. Take t = ω[x0←0], u = x0 and v = 0. Then AX∪EAX ⊢ t[u]≡v, but ω[u]≡v is not derivable from AX∪EAX. (The latter is an immediate consequence of the Church-Rosser property of STORE-FINAL; see chapters 6 and 9.)

One may object that there is no great difference between the tasks of refuting a visible atom like ω[u]≡v on one hand and disproving the original goal (here s≡ω) on the other hand. However, in the latter case we must take into account all axioms of the initial specification (here ACCESS-FUN), while it is often easier to see that there is no derivation of a visible atom from the (smaller set of) axioms of the final specification. ∎

4.8 Internalized Logic

Horn clause specifications are always consistent because they have free and initial models. This follows from the syntax of Horn clauses that forbids negative statements. We have also mentioned the fact that the initial structure is the only model with a minimal number of valid ground atoms because Horn clause logic does not allow disjunctive formulas (cf. Section 4.3). Two suggestions for overcoming these restrictions while keeping to Horn clause syntax are common. The first is to specify new predicates that stand for the negation or the disjunction of predicates already present. However, this relationship cannot be proved within Horn clause logic: *Q is ¬P* only means that for all (ground) terms t, *either* Pt *or* Qt is derivable from the axioms. A similar suggestion is to employ Negation as Failure, which takes ¬Pt as being proved if Pt has no deductive solution (cf. Section 4.2). The soundness of Negation as Failure will be treated at the end of Section 5.2.

In the present section, we introduce a third way to simulate quantifier-free first-order logic within Horn clause logic. We assume that BOOL (cf. Section 3.1) is a subspecification of <SIG,AX> and extend <SIG,AX> by characteristic functions of predicates of SIG.

Then we are faced with two levels of logical reasoning: the clause level and the term level. On both levels, deduction is guided by the Horn clause calculus, but, since the laws of Boolean algebra are part of <SIG,AX>, we can simulate the inference rules of quantifier-free first-order logic on the term level. However, to work on both levels simultaneously is reasonable only if we restrict ourselves to *consistent* structures.

Definition A SIG-structure A is *consistent* if A_{bool} has exactly two elements, which are the interpretations of the constants **true** and **false** (cf. Section 3.1). The class of consistent (consistent and term-generated) SIG-models of AX is denoted by *CMod(SIG,AX)* (*CGen(SIG,AX)*, respectively). ∎

Of course, consistent SIG-models of AX do not exist if <SIG,AX> is contradictory in the sense that the equation **true≡false** is derivable from AX∪EAX. The converse holds true as well if <SIG,AX> is BOOL-complete.

Definition <SIG,AX> is *BOOL-complete* if for all ground terms t with sort bool, t≡**true** or t≡**false** is a <SIG,AX>-theorem. ∎

Example 4.8.1 A purely equational specification of natural numbers reads as follows (cf. Section 3.2).

```
NAT-EQ
   base :  BOOL
   sorts : nat
   opns :  0 : nat
           _| : nat→nat
           _ eq _ : nat,nat→bool
           _ less _ : nat,nat→bool
           _ less or eq _ : nat,nat→bool
           _ neq _ : nat,nat→bool
           even _ : nat→bool
           odd _ : nat→bool
   vars :  m,n : nat
   axms :  (0 eq 0) ≡ true                    (A1)
           (0 eq n|) ≡ false                  (A2)
           (n| eq 0) ≡ false                  (A3)
           (m| eq n|) ≡ (m eq n)              (A4)
           (0 less n|) ≡ true                 (A5)
           (n less 0) ≡ false                 (A6)
```

$(m|\text{ less }n|) \equiv (m \text{ less } n)$ (A7)
$(m \text{ less or eq } n) \equiv ((m \text{ less } n) \lor (m \text{ eq } n))$
$(m \text{ neq } n) \equiv \neg(m \text{ eq } n)$
$(\text{even } 0) \equiv \text{true}$
$(\text{even } n|) \equiv \neg(\text{even } n)$
$(\text{odd } n) \equiv \neg(\text{even } n)$

NAT-EQ is BOOL-complete. For instance, all ground terms of the form t *less* t' can be reduced to **true** or **false**. Employ induction on size(t)+size(t'):

Case 1. $t = 0$ and $t' = u|$ for some u. Then

$(0 \text{ less } n|) \equiv \text{true}$ (A5)
$\vdash (t \text{ less } t') \equiv \text{true}$ (substitution).

Case 2. $t' = 0$. Then

$(n \text{ less } 0) \equiv \text{false}$ (A6)
$\vdash (t \text{ less } t') \equiv \text{false}$ (substitution).

Case 3. $t = u|$ and $t' = v|$ for some u,v. Then

$\phantom{\text{AX}\cup\text{EAX}}\ \ (m|\text{ less }n|) \equiv (m \text{ less } n)$ (A7)
$\phantom{\text{AX}\cup\text{EAX}}\ \vdash (t \text{ less } t') \equiv (u \text{ less } v)$ (substitution)
$\text{AX}\cup\text{EAX} \vdash (u \text{ less } v) \equiv b \in \{\text{true},\text{false}\}$ (by induction hypothesis)
$\phantom{\text{AX}\cup\text{EAX}}\ \ x \equiv z \Leftarrow x \equiv y, y \equiv z$ (equality axiom)
$\phantom{\text{AX}\cup\text{EAX}}\ \vdash (t \text{ less } t') \equiv b$ (substitution)
$\phantom{\text{AX}\cup\text{EAX}}\ \ \ \Leftarrow (t \text{ less } t') \equiv (u \text{ less } v), (u \text{ less } v) \equiv b$
$\phantom{\text{AX}\cup\text{EAX}}\ \vdash (t \text{ less } t') \equiv b$ (cut). ∎

Lemma 4.8.2 Let ⟨SIG,AX⟩ be BOOL-complete. There are no consistent (term-generated) SIG-models of AX iff **true≡false** is a ⟨SIG,AX⟩-theorem.

Proof. Let **true≡false** be derivable from AX∪EAX. Since DTh(SIG,AX) is sound w.r.t. Mod(SIG,AX) (cf. Theorem 4.2.2), we have $\text{true}^A = \text{false}^A$ for all SIG-models A of AX. Hence CMod(SIG,AX) and thus CGen(SIG,AX) are empty.

Conversely, suppose that **true≡false** is not derivable from AX∪EAX. Then by completeness of ITh(SIG,AX) w.r.t. Gen(SIG,AX) (cf. Theorem 4.3.2), $\text{true}^A \neq \text{false}^A$ for some term-generated SIG-model A of AX. Hence for all $a \in A_{\text{bool}}$ there is a ground term t with $\text{eval}^A(t) = a$. Since ⟨SIG,AX⟩ is BOOL-complete, $\text{eval}^A(t) \in \{\text{true}^A, \text{false}^A\}$. Therefore A is consistent, i.e. CGen(SIG,AX) and thus CMod(SIG,AX) are nonempty. ∎

Definition Let $w \in S^+$ and $P \in PR_w$. The operation symbol $\sigma_P \in OP_{w,bool}$ is called the *characteristic function of P*. Characteristic functions of equality predicates are denoted by eq. The characteristic function of $\equiv_{bool}$ agrees with Boolean equivalence (cf. Section 3.1).

A SIG-model A of AX is *conversion-complete w.r.t.* $P \in PR$ if the following conditions hold true:

- SIG contains the characteristic function σ_P of P.
- A satisfies the clause

$$Px \Leftarrow \sigma_P x \equiv true$$

called the *conversion axiom for P*.

- If P is the equality predicate for $s \in S$, then, for some $x \in X_s$, A satisfies the equation

$$(x \text{ eq } x) \equiv true$$

called the *functional reflexivity axiom for s*. ∎

Proposition 4.8.3 All SIG-models of AX are conversion-complete w.r.t. the equality predicate for bool.

Proof. Since the characteristic function of $\equiv_{bool}$ is the Boolean equivalence whose specification is part of <SIG,AX>, we can derive the functional reflexivity axiom for bool from AX∪EAX. Moreover, the conversion axiom for $\equiv_{bool}$ is given by

(CA) $\qquad\qquad x \equiv_{bool} y \Leftarrow (x \text{ eq } y) \equiv true$.

By Corollary 4.2.4, Mod(SIG,AX) satisfies (CA) if for additional constants k,k',

$$AX \cup EAX \cup \{(k \text{ eq } k') \equiv true\} \vdash k \equiv k'.$$

A suitable derivation is

k eq k' ≡ true	(assumption)
k ∧ true ≡ k	(axiom instance)
k ∧ (k eq k') ≡ k	
k ∧ (¬k ∨ k') ∧ (¬k' ∨ k) ≡ k	
k ∧ (¬k ∨ k') ≡ k	
false ∨ (k ∧ k') ≡ k	
k ∧ k' ≡ k.	

Analogously, one derives

$$k' \wedge k \equiv k.$$

Hence AXuEAX ⊢ k≡k'. ∎

Example 4.8.4 Let ⟨SIG,AX⟩ = NAT-EQ (cf. Example 4.8.1). By Proposition 4.8.3, the initial ⟨SIG,AX⟩-structure is conversion-complete w.r.t. $\equiv_{bool}$. We show that I(NAT-EQ) is conversion-complete w.r.t. $\equiv_{nat}$ as well.

Of course, the functional reflexivity axiom for nat is an inductive NAT-EQ-theorem. Hence by Theorem 4.3.2, I(NAT-EQ) satisfies this axiom. The conversion axiom for $\equiv_{nat}$ is valid in I(NAT-EQ) if for all ground terms t,t' of sort nat,

$$(AX \cup EAX \vdash (t\ eq\ t') \equiv true) \quad \text{implies} \quad (AX \cup EAX \vdash t \equiv t').$$

Given a derivation of (t eq t')≡true from AXuEAX we employ induction on size(t)+size(t') to conclude that t≡t' is derivable as well:

Case 1. t = 0. Then t' = 0. Hence t = t'.

Case 2. t = u| for some u. Then AXuEAX ⊢ (u eq v)≡true for some v with v| = t'. By the induction hypothesis, AXuEAX ⊢ u≡v. Hence AXuEAX ⊢ t≡t'.

The reader might prove in addition that F(SIG,AX) is *not* conversion-complete w.r.t. $\equiv_{nat}$. ∎

BOOL- and conversion-completeness allow us to characterize the existence of consistent models as follows.

Theorem 4.8.5 Let ⟨SIG,AX⟩ be BOOL-complete and F(SIG,AX) (or I(SIG,AX)) be conversion-complete w.r.t. all predicate symbols. Then Mod(SIG,AX) (Gen(SIG,AX), respectively) includes consistent structures iff not all atoms are deductive (inductive, respectively) ⟨SIG,AX⟩-theorems.

Proof. Let CMod(SIG,AX) (or CGen(SIG,AX)) be empty and Pt ∈ At(SIG). By Lemma 4.8.2, true≡false is a ⟨SIG,AX⟩-theorem. Thus we obtain the following derivation of $\sigma_P t \equiv true$:

$\sigma_P t \wedge true \equiv \sigma_P t$	(axiom instance)
$true \equiv false$	(assumption)
$\sigma_P t \wedge false \equiv \sigma_P t$	
$\sigma_P t \vee false \equiv \sigma_P t$	(axiom instance)
$(\sigma_P t \wedge false) \vee false \equiv \sigma_P t$	
$false \vee (false \wedge \sigma_P t) \equiv false$	(axiom instance)
$\sigma_P t \equiv false$	
$true \equiv false$	(assumption)
$\sigma_P t \equiv true.$	

Hence Mod(SIG,AX) satisfies $\sigma_P t \equiv true$. Since the conversion axiom for P is valid in F(SIG,AX) (or I(SIG,AX)), we conclude that Pt is a deductive (inductive, respectively) <SIG,AX>-theorem.

Conversely, if all atoms are deductive (inductive) <SIG,AX>-theorems, then in particular, $true \equiv false$ is a <SIG,AX>-theorem, and we conclude from Lemma 4.8.2 that CMod(SIG,AX) and CGen(SIG,AX) are empty. ∎

The question arises whether the assumptions of Theorem 4.8.5 can be weakened. We do not see how to get rid of conversion-completeness. However, BOOL-completeness is a much stronger requirement which actually demands the negation of each predicate be specified. Indeed, we can dispense with BOOL-completeness if each axiom has an *equational counterpart* such that all proofs can be simulated on the level of equational deduction.

Definition Let $s \in S$. The function symbol

$$\text{if } \_ \text{ then } \_ \text{ else } \_ : bool, s, s \to s$$

is called the *conditional function for s*. The conditional function for *bool* agrees with the Boolean if-then-else function (cf. Section 3.1).

Given a conditional equation $c = (t \equiv_s t' \Leftarrow P_1 t_1, \ldots, P_n t_n)$ with $n \geq 1$, let eq(c) be the equation

$$t \equiv (\text{if } \sigma_{P_1} t_1 \wedge \ldots \wedge \sigma_{P_n} t_n \text{ then } t' \text{ else } t).$$

Given an atom Pt such that P is not an equality predicate, let eq(Pt) be the equation

$$\sigma_P t \equiv true.$$

Given $c = (Pt \Leftarrow P_1 t_1, \ldots, P_n t_n)$ with $n \geq 1$ such that P is not an equality predicate, let eq(c) be the equation

$$(\sigma_{P_1} t_1 \wedge \ldots \wedge \sigma_{P_n} t_n \text{ impl } \sigma_P t) \equiv true.$$

For each clause c, eq(c) is called the *equational counterpart of c*.

A SIG-model A of AX is *equationally complete* if A satisfies
- the equational counterpart of each $c \in AX$,
- the equation
  $$\text{if true then } x \text{ else } y \equiv x$$
  for each conditional function in OP,
- the equation
  $$\sigma \langle x_1, \ldots, x_i, (\text{if } x \text{ then } y \text{ else } z), z_1, \ldots, z_n \rangle$$
  $$\equiv \text{if } x \text{ then } \sigma \langle x_1, \ldots, x_i, y, z_1, \ldots, z_n \rangle \text{ else } \sigma \langle x_1, \ldots, x_i, z, z_1, \ldots, z_n \rangle$$

for each conditional function in OP and each $\sigma \in$ OP without Boolean arguments. ∎

Equational completeness allows us to simulate applications of the Cut Rule (cf. Section 4.2) by term replacement steps using conditional functions and Boolean implication. Furthermore, we must ensure that our simulation maintains the separation of *logical* from *non-logical* operations.

Definition SIG *respects logical syntax* if, for all $\sigma \in$ OP with at least one Boolean argument,
(1) coarity(σ) = bool implies $\sigma \in$ BOOL,
(2) coarity(σ) ≠ bool implies that σ is a conditional function. ∎

(1) guarantees that SIG takes all logical functions from BOOL. (2) says that the only functions that map Booleans to non-Booleans are conditional functions.

Example 4.8.6 A purely equational version of FINSET-REMOVE (cf. Section 3.10) using conditional functions is

```
FINSET-EQ
    base : BOOL
    sorts : set,nat
    opns :  ∅ : set
            insert __ __ : nat,set→set
            remove __ __ : nat,set→set
            0 : nat
            _| : nat→nat
            _ eq _ : set,set→bool
            _ eq _ : nat,nat→bool
            if _ then _ else _ : bool,set,set→set
    vars :  s,s',s" : set
            m,n : nat
            b : bool
    axms :  insert m (insert m s) ≡ insert m s
            insert m (insert n s) ≡ insert n (insert m s)
            remove m ∅ ≡ ∅
            remove m (insert n s)
                ≡ if (m eq n) then (remove m s)
                              else (insert n (remove m s))
            s eq s ≡ true                                    (A1)
            if true then s else s' ≡ s                       (A2)
            if (s eq s') then s else s' ≡ s'                 (A3)
```

$$\text{insert m (if b then s else s')}$$
$$\equiv \text{if b then (insert m s) else (insert m s')} \quad (A4)$$
$$\text{remove m (if b then s else s')}$$
$$\equiv \text{if b then (remove m s) else (remove m s')} \quad (A5)$$
$$\text{(if b then s else s') eq s''}$$
$$\equiv \text{if b then (s eq s'') else (s' eq s'')} \quad (A6)$$
$$\text{s'' eq (if b then s else s')}$$
$$\equiv \text{if b then (s'' eq s) else (s'' eq s')} \quad (A7)$$
$$\text{n eq n} \equiv \text{true}$$
$$\text{if true then m else n} \equiv \text{m}$$
$$\text{if (m eq n) then m else n} \equiv \text{n}$$

Of course, FINSET-EQ is not BOOL-complete, but it respects logical syntax. Let A be the initial FINSET-EQ-structure. By Proposition 4.8.3, A is conversion-complete w.r.t. $\equiv_{bool}$. For conversion-completeness w.r.t. $\equiv_{set}$ (and, analogously, w.r.t. $\equiv_{nat}$), the clause

$$s \equiv s' \Leftarrow (s \text{ eq } s') \equiv \text{true}$$

must be valid in A. This follows from (A2) and (A3).

Hence A is conversion-complete w.r.t. all predicates of FINSET-EQ. Moreover, A is equationally complete because
- all axioms are already unconditional equations,
- the equations to be valid in A and involving conditional functions are axioms. ∎

Compare FINSET-EQ with a BOOL-complete specification like NAT-EQ (cf. Example 4.8.1): if FINSET-EQ were BOOL-complete, equations (A2) and

$$\text{if false then s else s'} \equiv \text{s'}$$

would suffice to derive (A3)-(A7) as inductive theorems. In general, we have

Proposition 4.8.7 Let <SIG,AX> be BOOL-complete. A ∈ Gen(SIG,AX) is equationally complete if A is conversion-complete w.r.t. all predicate symbols and satisfies the equations

$$\text{if true then x else y} \equiv \text{x} \quad (B1)$$
$$\text{if false then x else y} \equiv \text{y} \quad (B2)$$
$$\sigma_P x \equiv \text{true} \Leftarrow Px \quad (B3)$$

for all conditional functions and all non-equality predicates P.

Proof. Let $c = (t \equiv_s t' \Leftarrow P_1 t_1,...,P_n t_n) \in AX$ with $n \geq 1$, and $b \in A^X$. By BOOL-completeness of $\langle SIG, AX \rangle$ we have two cases:

Case 1. $b^*(\sigma_{P_1} t_1 \wedge ... \wedge \sigma_{P_n} t_n) = true^A$. Since A satisfies the conversion axioms for PR, we conclude $b^*(t_i) \in P_i^A$ for all $1 \leq i \leq n$. Since A satisfies c and (B1),

$$b^*(t) = b^*(t') = b^*(\text{if true then } t' \text{ else } t)$$
$$= b^*(\text{if } \sigma_{P_1} t_1 \wedge ... \wedge \sigma_{P_n} t_n \text{ then } t' \text{ else } t).$$

Case 2. $b^*(\sigma_{P_1} t_1 \wedge ... \wedge \sigma_{P_n} t_n) = false^A$. Since A satisfies (B2),

$$b^*(t) = b^*(\text{if false then } t' \text{ else } t)$$
$$= b^*(\text{if } \sigma_{P_1} t_1 \wedge ... \wedge \sigma_{P_n} t_n \text{ then } t' \text{ else } t).$$

Thus, in both cases, the equational counterpart of c is valid in A.

Let $c = (Pt \Leftarrow P_1 t_1,...,P_n t_n) \in AX$ such that P is not an equality predicate. Again we have two cases:

Case 1. $b^*(\sigma_{P_1} t_1 \wedge ... \wedge \sigma_{P_n} t_n) = true^A$. Since A satisfies the conversion axioms for PR, we conclude $b^*(t_i) \in P_i^A$ for all $1 \leq i \leq n$. Since A satisfies c, $b^*(t) \in P^A$. Since A satisfies BOOL-axioms and (B3),

$$b^*(\sigma_{P_1} t_1 \wedge ... \wedge \sigma_{P_n} t_n \text{ impl } \sigma_P t) = b^*(\text{true impl } \sigma_P t) = b^*(\sigma_P t) = b^*(\text{true}).$$

Case 2. $b^*(\sigma_{P_1} t_1 \wedge ... \wedge \sigma_{P_n} t_n) = false^A$. Since A satisfies BOOL-axioms,

$$b^*(\sigma_{P_1} t_1 \wedge ... \wedge \sigma_{P_n} t_n \text{ impl } \sigma_P t) = b^*(\text{false impl } \sigma_P t) = b^*(\text{true}).$$

Thus, in both cases, the equational counterpart of c is valid in A.

Since A satisfies (B1) and (B2), the equations to be valid in A and involving conditional functions can be deduced immediately. ∎

The previous proposition implies that equational completeness of term-generated models is not stronger than BOOL-completeness of $\langle SIG, AX \rangle$. Let us now present the crucial lemma that will be referred to in the completeness theorem for consistent models (Theorem 4.8.9). It employs the *Prime Ideal Theorem* (or its dual version called *Ultrafilter Theorem*), which plays an important rôle in completeness proofs of first-order logic (cf. Bell and Slomson, Theorem 3.4; Rasiowa/Sikorski, Sections I.8 and II.5; or Richter, Lemma 1.5.11).

Lemma 4.8.8 *Transformation of models into consistent ones such that a given unsolvable atom remains unsolvable*

Suppose that <SIG,AX> respects logical syntax. Let A be a SIG-model of AX that is equationally complete and conversion-complete w.r.t. all predicate symbols. Let p be an atom and $f \in A^X$ such that *f does not solve p in A*.

Then there is an OP-compatible equivalence relation $\sim$ on A such that $A/\sim$ is a consistent SIG-model of AX and *nat•f does not solve p in $A/\sim$* (where nat is the OP-compatible natural mapping from A to $A/\sim$).

Proof. Let p = Pt. f does not solve p in A, i.e. $f^*t \notin P^A$. By the Boolean Assumption, A satisfies the clause $Px \Leftarrow \sigma_P x \equiv true$. Hence $f^*(\sigma_P t) \neq true^A$. Since A_{bool} is a Boolean algebra, there is a *prime ideal* PI of A_{bool}, i.e. a maximal proper subset of A_{bool} including $f^*(\sigma_P t)$ and satisfying the equivalence

$$a,b \in PI \quad iff \quad a \vee b \in PI.$$

An S-sorted equivalence relation $\sim$ on A is inductively defined as follows:

(1) $\sim_{bool} = \{<a,b> \in A_{bool} \mid a,b \in PI \text{ or } a,b \notin PI\}$,

(2)   for all $s \in S-\{bool\}$ and $a \in A_s$, $a \sim_s a$,

(3)   for all conditional functions and suitable a,b,c,a',b',c',
$a \sim a'$, $b \sim b'$ and $c \sim c'$
imply $(if^A \text{ a then b else c}) \sim (if^A \text{ a' then b' else c'})$.

OP-compatibilty of $\sim$ is checked by induction on the definition of $\sim$:
Let $s_1,...,s_n, s \in S$, $\sigma \in OP_{s_1,...,s_n,s}$ and for all $1 \le i \le n$, $a_i, b_i \in A_{s_i}$ such that $a_i \sim b_i$. We have to show

(4) $\sigma^A(a_1,...,a_n) \sim \sigma^A(b_1,...,b_n).$

Case 1. σ is a conditional function. Then (4) follows from (3).

Case 2. s = bool and s_i = bool for some $1 \le i \le n$. Since <SIG,AX> respects logical syntax, σ is already in BOOL. Hence (4) follows from the fact that $\sim_{bool}$ is compatible with all Boolean algebra operators.

Case 3. $s_i \neq$ bool for all $1 \le i \le n$.

Case 3.1. $a_i = b_i$ for all $1 \le i \le n$. Then (4) follows immediately.

Case 3.2. There are $1 \le j \le n$ and c,d,c',d',c",d" $\in$ A such that

$a_j = (if^A \text{ c then c' else c"}), \quad b_j = (if^A \text{ d then d' else d"}),$

$c \sim d$, $c' \sim d'$ and $c'' \sim d''$. By the induction hypothesis,

$$\sigma^A(a_1,...,a_{i-1}, c', a_{i+1},...,a_n) \sim \sigma^A(b_1,...,b_{i-1}, d', b_{i+1},...,b_n)$$

and

$$\sigma^A(a_1,...,a_{i-1}, c'', a_{i+1},...,a_n) \sim \sigma^A(b_1,...,b_{i-1}, d'', b_{i+1},...,b_n).$$

By (3),

$(if^A \ c \ then \ \sigma^A(a_1,...,a_{i-1}, c', a_{i+1},...,a_n) \ else \ \sigma^A(a_1,...,a_{i-1}, c'', a_{i+1},...,a_n))$
$\sim (if^A \ d \ then \ \sigma^A(a_1,...,a_{i-1}, d', a_{i+1},...,a_n) \ else \ \sigma^A(a_1,...,a_{i-1}, d'', a_{i+1},...,a_n)).$

Since A is equationally complete, A satisfies the equation

$\sigma\langle x_1,...,x_{i-1},$ (if x then y else z), $x_{i+1},...,x_n\rangle$
$\equiv$ if x then $\sigma\langle x_1,...,x_{i-1}, y, x_{i+1},...,x_n\rangle$ else $\sigma\langle x_1,...,x_{i-1}, z, x_{i+1},...,x_n\rangle.$

Thus we conclude (4).

Let $B = A/\sim$. From (1) we conclude that B_{bool} consists of two distinct elements $true^B$ and $false^B$, i.e. B is consistent. B becomes a SIG-structure with identity by defining

$$\equiv_s^B = \{\langle b,b\rangle \mid b \in B_s\}$$

for all $s \in S$ and

$$Q^B = \{b \in B_w \mid \sigma_Q^B(b) = true^B\}$$

for all non-equality predicates $Q \in PR_w$.

Next we show that B satsifies AX. Let $c = (Qu \Leftarrow Q_1u_1,...,Q_nu_n) \in AX$ and $h \in B^X$ such that for all $1 \le i \le n$, $h^*u_i \in Q_i^B$. Of course, there is $g \in A^X$ with $nat \cdot g = h$.

Case 1. c has no premises and Qu is an equation, say $v \equiv v'$. Then $g^*v = g^*v'$ because A satisfies Qu. Hence $h^*v = nat(g^*v) = nat(g^*v') = h^*v'$, i.e. $h^*u \in Q^B$.

Case 2. c has no premises and Qu is not an equation. Since A is equationally complete, A satisfies the equation $\sigma_Q u \equiv true$. Hence $g^*(\sigma_Q u) = true^A$ and thus

$$h^*(\sigma_Q u) = nat \cdot g^*(\sigma_Q u) = nat(true^A) = true^B,$$

i.e. $h^*u \in Q^B$.

Case 3. c has premises. W.l.o.g. assume that there is $1 \le k \le n$ such that for all $0 \le i \le k$, $Q_i u_i$ is an equation, say $v_i \equiv v_i'$, and for all $k < i \le n$, $Q_i u_i$ is not an equation. Hence for all $0 \le i \le k$, $h^*v_i = h^*v_i'$, i.e. $g^*v_i \sim g^*v_i'$ and thus

$$g^*(\sigma_{Q_i}u_i) = (g^*v_i \text{ eq}^A g^*v_i') \sim (g^*v_i \text{ eq}^A g^*v_i) = \text{true}^A$$

because $\sim$ is compatible with eq^A and A satisfies the equation $(x \text{ eq } x) \equiv \text{true}$, while for all $k \leq i \leq n$, $h^*u_i \in Q_i^B$, i.e. $g^*(\sigma_{Q_i}u_i) \sim \text{true}^A$.

Hence for all $1 \leq i \leq n$

(5) $\qquad\qquad\qquad g^*(\sigma_{Q_i}u_i) \sim \text{true}^A.$

Case 3.1. Qu is an equation, say $v \equiv v'$. Since A is equationally complete, A satisfies the equation
$$v \equiv (\text{if } \sigma_{Q_1}u_1 \wedge ... \wedge \sigma_{Q_n}u_n \text{ then } v' \text{ else } v).$$
Hence
$$\begin{aligned}g^*v &= (\text{if}^A \ g^*(\sigma_{Q_1}u_1) \wedge^A ... \wedge^A g^*(\sigma_{Q_n}u_n) \text{ then } g^*v' \text{ else } g^*v) \\ &\sim (\text{if}^A \text{ true}^A \text{ then } g^*v' \text{ else } g^*v) = g^*v'.\end{aligned}$$

Thus $h^*v = h^*v'$, i.e. $h^*u \in Q^B$.

Case 3.2. Qu is not an equation. Since A is equationally complete, A satisfies the equation
$$(\sigma_{Q_1}u_1 \wedge ... \wedge \sigma_{Q_n}u_n \text{ impl } \sigma_Q u) \equiv \text{true}.$$
Hence
$$\begin{aligned}g^*(\sigma_Q u) &= (\text{true}^A \text{ impl}^A g^*(\sigma_Q u)) \\ &\sim (g^*(\sigma_{Q_1}u_1) \wedge^A ... \wedge^A g^*(\sigma_{Q_n}u_n) \text{ impl}^A \sigma_Q^A(g^*u)) = \text{true}^A.\end{aligned}$$

Thus $h^*(\sigma_Q u) = \text{true}^B$, i.e. $h^*u \in Q^B$.

It remains for us to show that nat$\bullet$f does not solve Pt in A. First, $f^*(\sigma_P t) \in PI$ implies $f^*(\sigma_P t) \not\sim \text{true}^A$. Hence, if Pt is an equation, say $v \equiv v'$, then

(6) $\qquad\qquad\qquad (f^*v \text{ eq}^A f^*v') \not\sim \text{true}^A.$

Assume that $f^*v \sim f^*v'$. Since $\sim$ is compatible with eq^A and A satisfies the equation $(x \text{ eq } x) \equiv \text{true}$, we would obtain

$$(f^*v \text{ eq}^A f^*v') \sim (f^*v \text{ eq}^A f^*v) = \text{true}^A,$$

in contradiction to (6). Therefore $f^*v \not\sim f^*v'$, i.e. $(\text{nat}\bullet f)^*v \neq (\text{nat}\bullet f)^*v'$ and thus $(\text{nat}\bullet f)^*t \notin P^B$. If Pt is not an equation, then by definition of P^B, $(\text{nat}\bullet f)^*t \notin P^B$. ∎

Theorem 4.8.9 *Soundness and completeness of the deductive theory w.r.t. the class of consistent models*

Suppose that $\langle SIG,AX \rangle$ respects logical syntax and F(SIG,AX) (I(SIG,AX)) is equationally complete and conversion-complete w.r.t. all predicate symbols.

The deductive (inductive) theory of <SIG,AX> is sound and complete w.r.t. CMod(SIG,AX) (CGen(SIG,AX), respectively).

Proof Soundness follows from Theorem 4.2.2 (4.3.2) because CMod(SIG,AX) (CGen(SIG,AX)) is a subclass of Mod(SIG,AX) (Gen(SIG,AX)).

Conversely, suppose that some atom Pt is not a deductive (inductive) <SIG,AX>-theorem. By Theorem 4.2.2 (4.3.2), Pt is not valid in A = F(SIG,AX) (A = I(SIG,AX)). Hence there is f ∈ A^X such that f does not solve Pt in A. By Lemma 4.8.8, there is a consistent quotient B of A that satisfies AX, but does not satisfy Pt. Hence Pt is not valid in CMod(SIG,AX) (CGen(SIG,AX)). ∎

Example 4.8.10 In Example 4.8.6, we have shown that <SIG,AX> = FINSET-EQ satisfies all assumptions of Theorem 4.8.9 for I(SIG,AX). Thus we conclude that the inductive theory of FINSET-EQ agrees with the theory of CGen(FINSET-EQ). For instance, it is obvious that the equation

$$\text{remove } m \text{ (remove } n \text{ } s) \equiv \text{remove } n \text{ (remove } m \text{ } s) \quad (1)$$

is valid in all consistent and term-generated SIG-models of AX. Since remove was specified *completely*, (1) is an inductive <SIG,AX>-theorem if

$$\text{remove } m \text{ (remove } n \text{ } t) \equiv \text{remove } n \text{ (remove } m \text{ } t) \quad (2)$$

is a deductive one for each term t over {∅,insert,if-then-else}∪X_{nat}. Let us prove this.

Case 1. t = ∅. Then
    AX ∪ EAX ⊢ remove m (remove n t)) ≡ remove m ∅
                  ⊢ remove m (remove n t)) ≡ ∅
                  ⊢ remove m (remove n t)) ≡ remove n ∅
                  ⊢ remove m (remove n t)) ≡ remove n (remove m t)).

Case 2. t = (insert x u) for some x,u. Then
    AX ∪ EAX ⊢ remove m (remove n t))
              ≡ remove m (if (n eq x) then (remove n u)
                               else (insert x (remove n u)))
          ⊢ remove m (remove n t))
            ≡ if (n eq x) then remove m (remove n u)
                     else remove m (insert x (remove n u)))
          ⊢ remove m (remove n t))
            ≡ if (n eq x) then remove m (remove n u)
                     else if (m eq x)

$$\text{then (remove m (remove n u))}$$
$$\text{else (insert x (remove m (remove n u)))}$$
$\vdash$ remove m (remove n t))
$$\equiv \text{if (n eq x) then remove n (remove m u)}$$
$$\text{else if (m eq x)}$$
$$\text{then (remove n (remove m u))}$$
$$\text{else (insert x (remove n (remove m u)))}$$

(by the induction hypothesis).
Using abbreviations we have shown:

$$\text{AX} \cup \text{EAX} \vdash \text{remove m (remove n t))} \equiv u(n,m) \qquad (3)$$

where $u(n,m) = $ if (n eq x) then t_o else (if (m eq x) then t_o else t_1),
$t_o = $ (remove n (remove m u)) and $t_1 = $ (insert x t_o).
Symmetrically, one achieves

$$\text{AX} \cup \text{EAX} \vdash \text{remove n (remove m t))} \equiv u(m,n) \qquad (4)$$

(without employing the induction hypothesis). Proceeding with (A6) and (A7) (cf. Example 4.8.6) we obtain

AX ∪ EAX $\vdash$ u(n,m) eq u(m,n)
$$\equiv \text{if (n eq x) then } (t_o \text{ eq } u(m,n))$$
$$\text{else if (m eq x)}$$
$$\text{then } (t_o \text{ eq } u(m,n))$$
$$\text{else } (t_1 \text{ eq } u(m,n))$$
$\vdash$ u(n,m) eq u(m,n)
$$\equiv \text{if (n eq x) then if (m eq x)}$$
$$\text{then } (t_o \text{ eq } t_o)$$
$$\text{else if (n eq x) then } (t_o \text{ eq } t_o)$$
$$\text{else } (t_o \text{ eq } t_1)$$
$$\text{else if (m eq x)}$$
$$\text{then if (m eq x)}$$
$$\text{then } (t_o \text{ eq } t_o)$$
$$\text{else if (n eq x) then } (t_o \text{ eq } t_o)$$
$$\text{else } (t_o \text{ eq } t_1)$$
$$\text{else if (m eq x)}$$
$$\text{then } (t_1 \text{ eq } t_o)$$
$$\text{else if (n eq x) then } (t_1 \text{ eq } t_o)$$
$$\text{else } (t_1 \text{ eq } t_1).$$

Let v denote this conditional term. Then BOOL-axioms (cf. Section 3.1) lead to

$$\text{AX} \cup \text{EAX} \vdash v \equiv \text{true}.$$

Hence

$$\text{AX} \cup \text{EAX} \vdash u(n,m) \text{ eq } u(m,n) \equiv \text{true}. \qquad (5)$$

By (A2) and (A3) (cf. Example 4.8.6),

$$AX \cup EAX \vdash u(n,m) \equiv u(m,n).$$
By (3) and (4), we have derived (2).

Case 3. $t = $ (**if** z **then** u **else** u') for some z,u,u'. A derivation of (2) is obtained immediately by applying (A5) (cf. Example 4.8.6) and the induction hypothesis (to u and u'). ∎

We are now in a position to present a generalized version of Theorem 4.8.5 that does not presume BOOL-completeness. From Proposition 4.8.7 we know that the substitutes for BOOL-completeness are not stronger. On the contrary, Example 4.8.6 suggests that the new conditions are much weaker than BOOL-completeness: if we are dealing with a purely equational specification, then conversion-completeness and equational completeness of any model is captured by axioms like (A1)-(A7) (cf. Example 4.8.6).

Corollary 4.8.11 Suppose that <SIG,AX> respects logical syntax and that F(SIG,AX) (I(SIG,AX)) is equationally complete and conversion-complete w.r.t. all predicate symbols. Then the following conditions are equivalent:
(1) CMod(SIG,AX) (CGen(SIG,AX)) is empty.
(2) All atoms are deductive (inductive) <SIG,AX>-theorems.
(3) **true≡false** is a <SIG,AX>-theorem.

Proof. (1) implies (2): Let CMod(SIG,AX) (resp. CGen(SIG,AX)) be empty. Then, trivially, this class satisfies all atoms. Hence by Theorem 4.8.9, all atoms are deductive (resp. inductive) <SIG,AX>-theorems.
(2)=>(3) and (3)=>(1) follow immediately. ∎

4.9 Horn Clause Versus Sequent Logic

In the previous section, we explored the consequences of logical reasoning on the term level. The purpose was to make available first-order quantifier-free logic *within* Horn clause logic. We think the end of this chapter on models and theories to be a good place for having a closer look at sequent logic (cf. Section 4.1). Sequent logic extends Horn clause logic by permitting implications of the form $\delta \Leftarrow \gamma$ where γ and δ are goals, but δ is regarded as the *disjunction* of its atoms. These formulas also cover full quantifier-free logic.

We generalize the Horn clause calculus of Section 4.2 to a calculus for sequents and present a completeness proof to reveal the gap between Horn clause logic and its extensions. The gain in expressiveness is paid for by losing the guarantee that every set of axioms is *consistent,* i.e., that it has models. This (usual) notion of consistency is strongly related to consistent

models in the sense of Section 4.8: we have shown that under the assumptions of Lemma 4.8.2 or Theorem 4.8.9
- a set AX of Horn clauses has no consistent models iff the equation true≡false is derivable from AX∪EAX.

On the other hand,
- a set AX of sequents has no models iff the *empty sequent* $\emptyset \Leftarrow \emptyset$ can be derived from AX∪EAX.

Definition A *sequent* (over SIG) consists of two goals $\delta = \{p_1,...,p_m\}$ and $\gamma = \{q_1,...,q_n\}$, written

$$\delta \Leftarrow \gamma \quad \text{or} \quad p_1,...,p_m \Leftarrow q_1,...,q_n$$

and read as

$$\delta \text{ if } \gamma \quad \text{or} \quad (p_1 \text{ or ... or } p_m) \text{ if } (q_1 \text{ and ... and } q_n).$$

δ or γ may be empty. If γ is empty and δ is a singleton, say $\delta = \{p\}$, the sequent $\delta \Leftarrow \gamma$ is identified with the atom p. Conversely, if δ is empty and γ is a singleton, say $\gamma = \{p\}$, the sequent $\delta \Leftarrow \gamma$ is identified with the *negated* atom ¬p. p and ¬p are called *literals*. ∎

Definition Let A be a SIG-structure and let $\delta \Leftarrow \gamma$ be a sequent. $\delta \Leftarrow \gamma$ is *valid in A* or *A satisfies* $\delta \Leftarrow \gamma$ if γ or δ is nonempty and either δ is nonempty and all solutions of γ in A solves *some* p ∈ δ in A or δ is empty and γ is not solvable in A.

Given a set AX of sequents, a SIG-structure A *with identity* is a *SIG-model of AX* if A satisfies all $\delta \Leftarrow \gamma$ ∈ AX. *Mod(SIG,AX)* denotes the class of all SIG-models of AX. ∎

Since the empty goal is solvable in every SIG-structure, there is no SIG-structure that satisfies the *empty sequent* $\emptyset \Leftarrow \emptyset$. Indeed, it represents contradiction.

Definition The *sequent calculus* consists of the following two inference rules:

Substitution Rule Let $\delta \Leftarrow \gamma$ be a sequent and f be a substitution. Then

$$\frac{\delta \Leftarrow \gamma}{\delta[f] \Leftarrow \gamma[f]}.$$

Cut Rule Let p be an atom and $\delta, \gamma, \varphi, \psi$ be goals. Then

$$\delta \Leftarrow \gamma u(p), \{p\}u\varphi \Leftarrow \psi$$
$$\overline{\delta u \varphi \Leftarrow \gamma u \psi.}$$

The corresponding inference relation is denoted by $\vdash$, while $\vdash_{cut}$ stands for restriction to applications of the Cut Rule. A derivation of the empty sequent from a sequent set S is called a *refutation of S*. S is *consistent* if there is no refutation of S. S is *cut-consistent* if there is no refutation of S via the Cut Rule, i.e. $S \vdash_{cut} \emptyset \Leftarrow \emptyset$ does not hold true. ∎

Proposition 4.9.1 Let S be a set of sequents and

$$\text{sub}(S) = \{\delta[f] \Leftarrow \gamma[f] \mid \delta \Leftarrow \gamma \in S, f \in T(SIG)^X\}.$$

(1) If $\text{sub}(S) \vdash_{cut} \delta \Leftarrow \gamma$, then $S \vdash \delta \Leftarrow \gamma$.
(2) If $S \vdash \delta \Leftarrow \gamma$, then for all substitutions f, $\text{sub}(S) \vdash_{cut} \delta[f] \Leftarrow \gamma[f]$.

Proof. (1) follows immediately. For (2), let $\langle d_1,...,d_n \rangle$ be a shortest derivation of $\delta \Leftarrow \gamma$ from S. The statement is shown by induction n. If $\delta \Leftarrow \gamma \in \text{sub}(S)$, the proof is complete. Otherwise there are i,j < n, goals $\varphi, \psi, \lambda, \vartheta$, atoms p,p' and substitutions g,h such that

$$d_i = (\varphi \Leftarrow \lambda u\{p\}), \quad d_j = (\{p'\}u\psi \Leftarrow \vartheta),$$

$\varphi[g]u\psi[h] = \delta$, $p[g] = p'[h]$ and $\lambda[g]u\vartheta[h] = \gamma$. By the induction hypothesis, for all substitutions h',

(1) $\quad\quad\quad \text{sub}(S) \vdash_{cut} d_i[h']$ and $\text{sub}(S) \vdash_{cut} d_j[h']$.

Let f be a substitution. In particular, (1) implies

(2) $\quad\quad\quad \text{sub}(S) \vdash_{cut} d_i[g][f]$ and $\text{sub}(S) \vdash_{cut} d_j[h][f]$.

Since $p[g][f] = p'[h][f]$, we can apply the Cut Rule:

(3) $\{d_i[g][f], d_j[h][f]\}$
$\quad\quad \vdash_{cut} (\varphi[g][f]u\psi[h][f] \Leftarrow \lambda[g][f]u\vartheta[h][f]) = (\delta[f] \Leftarrow \gamma[f])$.

(2) and (3) yield $\text{sub}(S) \vdash_{cut} \delta[f] \Leftarrow \gamma[f]$. ∎

Refutations of a literal c via the Cut Rule can be transformed into derivations of the negation of c:

Lemma 4.9.2 *From cut-refutations to cut-derivations*
Let S be a cut-consistent set of sequents. Then for all atoms p,

(1) $\qquad$ $S \cup \{p\} \vdash_{cut} \emptyset \Leftarrow \emptyset$ implies $S \vdash_{cut} \neg p$,

(2) $\qquad$ $S \cup \{\neg p\} \vdash_{cut} \emptyset \Leftarrow \emptyset$ implies $S \vdash_{cut} p$.

Proof Let $\langle d_1,\ldots,d_n \rangle$ be a shortest refutation of $S \cup \{p\}$ ($S \cup \{\neg p\}$, respectively). We show (1) ((2)) by induction on the number m of indices $1 \le i \le n$ with $d_i = p$ ($\neg p$). Since S is cut-consistent, $\langle d_1,\ldots,d_n \rangle$ involves an application of the Cut Rule to p ($\neg p$). Hence there are $1 \le i, j < k \le n$ and goals δ, γ such that $d_i = \delta \Leftarrow \gamma \cup \{p\}$ ($\{p\} \cup \delta \Leftarrow \gamma$), $d_j = p$ (resp. $\neg p$), $d_k = \delta \Leftarrow \gamma$ and $\langle d_1,\ldots,d_i \rangle$ is a derivation of d_i from S.

Case 1. $S \cup \{d_k\}$ is not cut-consistent. Then there is a refutation $\langle \delta_1 \Leftarrow \gamma_1,\ldots,\delta_s \Leftarrow \gamma_s \rangle$ of $S \cup \{d_k\}$. It can be transformed into a derivation $\langle e_1,\ldots,e_s \rangle$ from $S \cup \{d_i\}$ such that for all $1 \le j \le s$, $e_j = \delta_j \Leftarrow \gamma_j$ or $e_j = \delta_j \Leftarrow \gamma_j \cup \{p\}$ ($\{\delta_j \cup \{p\} \Leftarrow \gamma_j\}$), In particular, $e_s = \emptyset \Leftarrow \emptyset$ or $e_s = \neg p$ ($e_s = p$).

Hence $\langle d_1,\ldots,d_i,e_1,\ldots,e_s \rangle$ is a derivation of $\emptyset \Leftarrow \emptyset$ or $\neg p$ (p) from S. The empty sequent cannot be derived because S is cut-consistent. Therefore $S \vdash_{cut} \neg p$ (S $\vdash_{cut} p$).

Case 2. $S \cup \{d_k\}$ is cut-consistent. Since $d_j = p$ (resp. $\neg p$), $\langle d_1,\ldots,d_{j-1}, d_{j+1},\ldots,d_n \rangle$ is a derivation of $\emptyset \Leftarrow \emptyset$ from $S \cup \{d_k\}$ whose number of indices i with $d_i = p$ ($\neg p$) is less than m. Hence by the induction hypothesis,

$$S \cup \{d_k\} \vdash_{cut} \neg p \ (S \cup \{d_k\} \vdash_{cut} p).$$

Let $\langle \delta_1 \Leftarrow \gamma_1,\ldots,\delta_s \Leftarrow \gamma_s \rangle$ be a derivation of $\neg p$ (p) from $S \cup \{d_k\}$. It can be transformed into a derivation $\langle e_1,\ldots,e_s \rangle$ from $S \cup \{d_i\}$ such that for all $1 \le j \le s$, $e_j = \delta_j \Leftarrow \gamma_j$ or $e_j = \delta_j \Leftarrow \gamma_j \cup \{p\}$ ($\{\delta_j \cup \{p\} \Leftarrow \gamma_j\}$), In particular, $e_s = \neg p$ (p). Hence $\langle d_1,\ldots,d_i,e_1,\ldots,e_s \rangle$ is a derivation of $\neg p$ (p) from S. Therefore $S \vdash_{cut} \neg p$ (S $\vdash_{cut} p$). ∎

Definition Let AX be a set of sequents. The *(deductive) theory of* $\langle SIG,AX \rangle$, *DTh(SIG,AX)*, consists of all literals c such that $AX \cup EAX \vdash c$. Elements and subsets of DTh(SIG,AX) are called *(deductive)* $\langle SIG,AX \rangle$-*theorems*. ∎

Theorem 4.9.3 *Sequent version of Theorem 4.2.2*
Let $AX \cup EAX$ be a consistent set of sequents. Then DTh(SIG,AX) is sound and complete w.r.t. Mod(SIG,AX).

Proof Mod(SIG,AX) satisfies the deductive theory of $\langle SIG,AX \rangle$ because EAX is valid in all $A \in Mod(SIG,AX)$ and the sequent calculus preserves validity in A. (cf. the proof of Theorem 4.2.2.)

The completeness proof of Theorem 4.2.2 cannot be transferred to sequents. Although one might define a free structure F(SIG,AX) as in the case of Horn clauses, there is no guarantee that F(SIG,AX) satisfies AX. Instead, we proceed indirectly. Let c be a literal that is not derivable from AX∪EAX. W.l.o.g. suppose that c is an atom. Let S = sub(AX∪EAX) (cf. Proposition 4.9.1). We claim that Su{¬c} is cut-consistent. Otherwise, by Lemma 4.9.2, S ⊢$_{cut}$ c, which contradicts our assumption that c is not derivable from AX∪EAX. Therefore Su{¬c} is cut-consistent.

Let f : $\mathbb{N}$ → At(SIG) be an enumeration of all atoms. We add f(0), f(1), etc., to Su{¬c} up to the first i ∈ $\mathbb{N}$ such that Su{¬c,f(0),f(1),...,f(i)} is no longer cut-consistent. Such an i exists because Su{¬c,c} is not cut-consistent. So let

$$M_0 = \emptyset, \quad M_{i+1} = \begin{cases} M_i \cup \{f(i)\} & \text{if } M_i \cup Su\{¬c,f(i)\} \text{ is cut-consistent} \\ M_i & \text{otherwise} \end{cases}$$

and M = ∪{M_i | i ∈ $\mathbb{N}$}. Of course, M = M_k = M_{k+n} for some k ∈ $\mathbb{N}$ and all n ∈ $\mathbb{N}$. Hence

(1)   M∪Su{¬c} is cut-consistent.

Furthermore, let p ∈ At(SIG)−M. Of course, p = f(i) for some i ∈ $\mathbb{N}$. Since p ∉ M and M_{i+1} ⊆ M, we conclude p ∉ M_{i+1}. Hence by definition of M_{i+1}, M_i∪Su{¬c,p} and thus M∪Su{¬c,p} are not cut-consistent. Therefore M is maximal w.r.t. (1), i.e.

(2)   for all p ∈ At(SIG)−M, M∪Su{¬c,p} is not cut-consistent.

The equality axioms EAX ensure that the binary relation ~ on T(SIG) defined by

t ~ t'   iff   t≡t' ∈ DTh(SIG,AX)

is a SIG-congruence relation on the Herbrand structure

DH(c) = HS(T(SIG),M)

(cf. Section 2.3). Thus, compared with Horn clause logic (cf. Section 4.2), the free <SIG,AX>-structure is replaced by the quotient DH(c)/~. In fact, DH(c)/~ satisfies AX, which is shown below. However, note the difference between the Herbrand interpretations underlying F(SIG,AX) on one hand and DH(c)/~ on the other hand. In the first case it is just the set of all atoms derivable from AX∪EAX, while in the second case it is a maximal set M of atoms such that M∪sub(AX∪EAX)∪{¬c} is cut-consistent. Hence DH(c)/~ depends on c, and this dependence is crucial because DH(c)/~ will serve as a model of AX that *does not satisfy c*.

So let $A = DH(c)$, $B = DH(c)/\sim$, nat be the natural mapping from A to B and s = $(P_1t_1,...,P_mt_m \Leftarrow Q_1u_1,...,Q_nu_n) \in AX$.

Case 1. $m > 0$. Let $b \in B^X$ such that for all $1 \le i \le n$, $b^*u_i \in Q_i^B$. Then $b = nat \cdot f$ for some substitution f. Hence for all $1 \le i \le n$, $u_i[f] \in Q_i^A$, i.e. $Q_iu_i[f] \in M$. Assume that for all $1 \le i \le m$, $P_it_i[f] \notin M$. Then by (2), for all $1 \le i \le m$,

$$M \cup S \cup \{\neg c, P_it_i[f]\} \vdash_{cut} \emptyset \Leftarrow \emptyset$$

and thus by Lemma 4.9.2,

$$M \cup S \cup \{\neg c\} \vdash_{cut} \neg P_it_i[f].$$

Since $s[f] \in S$, m applications of the Cut Rule result in

$$M \cup S \cup \{\neg c\} \vdash_{cut} \emptyset \Leftarrow Q_1u_1[f],...,Q_nu_n[f],$$

and, since $\{Q_1u_1[f],...,Q_nu_n[f]\} \subseteq M$, further n applications of the Cut Rule yield

(3) $$M \cup S \cup \{\neg c\} \vdash_{cut} \emptyset \Leftarrow \emptyset,$$

in contradiction to (1). Therefore $P_it_i[f] \in M$ for some $1 \le i \le m$. Hence $t_i[f] \in P_i^A$ and thus $b^*t_i \in P_i^B$.

Case 2. $m = 0$. We must show that $\{Q_1u_1,...,Q_nu_n\}$ is not solvable in B. Assume that there is $b \in B^X$ such that $b^*u_i \in Q_i^B$ for all $1 \le i \le n$. Then $b = nat \cdot f$ for some substitution f. Hence for all $1 \le i \le n$, $u_i[f] \in Q_i^A$, i.e. $Q_iu_i[f] \in M$. Since $s[f] \in S$, n applications of the Cut Rule lead to (3), in contradiction to (1). Therefore $\{Q_1u_1,...,Q_nu_n\}$ is not solvable in B.

Thus, in both cases, B satisfies s. Finally, assume that B satisfies c. Let c = Pt. Then for all $b \in B^X$, $b^*t \in P^B$. In particular, $nat(t) = (nat \cdot id^X)^*t \in P^B$ and thus $t \in P^A$, i.e. $Pt \in M$. A single application of the Cut Rule yields (3), in contradiction to (1). Hence c is not valid in B.

In summary, B is a SIG-model of AX that does not satisfy the non-derivable literal c. So we conclude that all literals satisfied by Mod(SIG,AX) are derivable from AX∪EAX. ∎

Let us recall the main idea of the preceding completeness proof. Given a consistent axiom set AX and a non-derivable literal c, we first stated that, roughly speaking, AX∪{¬c} is consistent as well. Secondly, we built up a maximal goal M such that M∪AX∪{¬c} is consistent. Thirdly, M served as a Herbrand interpretation and led to a model of AX that does not satisfy c. (By the way, c and M correspond to the value $f^*(\sigma_P t)$ and the prime ideal PI, respectively, employed in the proof of Lemma 4.8.8.) This model takes over the rôle of the free structure induced by a Horn clause specification. The Herbrand interpretation that underlies the free structure consists of all atoms *derivable from AX*, while the construction of M follows an arbitrary enumeration of At(SIG) as long as *consistency with AX∪{¬c}* is guaranteed.

We hope to have thrown some light on the borderline between Horn clause logic and sequent logic by bringing them together as close as possible. What remains to be done is to explore sequent logic with regard to its use for specification and programming. First of all, the sequent calculus must be further developed, preferably along the lines of refinements of the Horn clause calculus such as resolution, paramodulation, reduction and narrowing (cf. Chapters 5, 7 and 8). TABLOG seems to pursue such a goal (see Malachi et al.).

4.10 Bibliographic Notes

Kowalski has drawn our attention to the expressiveness of Horn clauses. Goguen and Meseguer [3] combined Horn clause logic with equational logic and the theory of abstract data types, which was built upon algebraic concepts. When restricted to equations, the Horn clause calculus coincides with Birkhoff's *equational calculus* that led to the notion of the "term congruence generated by AX" (cf. Ehrig and Mahr, p. 119). Kaplan [1] generalized it to conditional equations. Goguen and Meseguer [1] discovered that the equational calculus is incorrect if the underlying signature is not inhabited (cf. Section 4.1). They propose a modified calculus where each equation is equipped with variable declarations to be taken into account by corresponding inference rules (see also Ehrig and Mahr, Sections 5.5 and 5.6).

The research on algebraic specifications was started in the mid-seventies by Liskov and Zilles, Guttag, and Goguen et al. Guttag was guided by the idea of final semantics, while Goguen et al. propagated initial semantics. The latter three authors, as well as Bergstra and Tucker, Klaeren, Nourani, and Beierle and Voß emphasized the proof-theoretical significance of representation functions. The state of the art of initial semantics can be found in Ehrig and Mahr. In contrast to Ehrig and Mahr, we have reserved the notion *initial structure* for the canonical construction as a quotient of a Herbrand structure (cf. Section 4.3). The reason for this is that the deduction-oriented results refer to this construction more frequently than to the *universal* property that I(SIG,AX) admits a unique homomorphism into every model of AX.

Final semantics was elaborated by Giarratana et al., Guttag and Horning, Kamin, Sannella and Tarlecki, Wand [1], and Wirsing et al.

Proposals to extend the equational syntax of specifications range from conditional equations (see Thatcher et al.; Kaplan [1]) through partial functions (see Broy and Wirsing; Reichel) up to higher-order logic (see

Poigné). The impact of such broader settings on the existence of initial or final structures was investigated by Broy et al. and by Mahr and Makowsky. Other extensions aim at operators to build up new specifications out of given ones. Here *parameterized specifications* play the most important rôle and provide further reasons for breaking the bonds of pure equational logic (see Thatcher et al.; Burstall and Goguen; Ehrich; Ehrig and Mahr; Navarro and Orejas; Padawitz [1,2,3]; Wirsing). Computability issues were treated by Bergstra and Tucker and by Meseguer and Goguen. Recent approaches use a partial order on the sort set and promise to cover *sort inheritance* as well as partiality and overloading of function definitions (see Goguen and Meseguer [4]).

Chapter 5   Resolution and Paramodulation

5.1   Introduction

The previous chapter was devoted to theories of a Horn clause specification <SIG,AX> and their connection to classes of SIG-models of AX. All this was based upon the Horn clause calculus with its two simple inference rules: the Substitution and the Cut Rule (cf. Section 4.2). Derivations via the Horn clause calculus proceed *bottom-up* from the axioms to the goal to be proved. From an operational point of view, this might lead to a completely untractable *search space*. Cut and substitution capture the consequences of an axiomatization. To have these rules in mind allows us to check, more or less intuitively, whether AX is already what we want. But the pure Horn clause calculus is not appropriate to executing proofs automatically. For this purpose one should work *top-down* from the goal to be proved (or solved) by applying axioms *backwards* until a *reduced* (e.g. empty) goal has been achieved that indicates the validity (or solvability) of the initial goal. This is what the rules presented in Chapters 5, 7 and 8 do.

Let us begin with resolution and paramodulation. In contrast to classical introductions (see Chang and Lee, or Lloyd) we do not relate these rules to a model-theoretic level, but compare them directly with the Horn clause calculus: the *Resolution Rule* is a special combination of cut and substitution. Actually, we restrict ourselves to *input resolution* where one of the two clauses resolved upon is an axiom. *Paramodulation* simulates resolution with conditional equations by term replacement.

The purpose of resolution and paramodulation is to find one or more deductive solutions of a goal γ (cf. Section 4.2). If the identity on X is one of the computed solutions, we can conclude that γ is a deductive theorem, i.e. that γ could also be derived from AX∪EAX via the Horn clause calculus.

We do not adopt the classical view that regards resolution and paramodulation as *refutation* procedures for inconsistent goals. Instead, we define resolution and paramodulation as rules that transform a pair $<\gamma,f>$ of a goal and a substitution into another pair $<\gamma',f[g]>$ such that, if some h solves γ', then g[h] solves γ. Hence by induction, if a sequence of rule applications transforms $<\gamma,id>$ into $<\emptyset,f>$, then we can conclude that f solves γ. Thus resolution and paramodulation do not only solve a goal, but also compute a solution by extending stepwise the identity substitution until the empty goal has been derived.

We also diverge from the classical presentation in that the restriction of solution components to most general unifiers (cf. Section 2.2) is not part of the original rules, but is treated as a refinement and therefore added later. This allows us to separate soundness or completeness questions from the particular problem of *lifting* arbitrary derivations to most general ones.

Thirdly, our notion of a goal as a *set* of atoms abstracts from the order as well as from multiple occurrences of the same atom in a goal. Hence *factoring* is not an issue we are concerned with.

Finally, our completeness proofs simulate a calculus (resolution or paramodulation) by another one (the Horn clause calculus) and thus avoid model-theoretic constructions like *semantic trees* (see Chang and Lee) or *fixpoints* (see Lloyd). As the link from deductive solutions (based on the Horn clause calculus) to solutions in models was established by Corollary 4.2.3, we do need a particular semantics for resolution or paramodulation.

Section 5.2 deals with resolution, Sections 5.3 and 5.4 handle paramodulation. Section 5.5 tackles the recent approach in which term unification is separated from resolution and simulated by additional rules. The connection between *Negation as Failure* and solvability in free and initial structures is outlined at the end of Section 5.2.

Variable Assumption From now on we fix an infinite set XG of variables that is disjoint from all variables occurring in AXuEAX. The elements of XG are called *goal variables*: given a goal-substitution pair $\langle \gamma, f \rangle$ with $var(\gamma) \subseteq XG$ and a derivation step from $\langle \gamma, f \rangle$ to $\langle \gamma', f' \rangle$, we assume that all $x \in var(\gamma')-XG$ are renamed as variables of XG before $\langle \gamma', f' \rangle$ is subjected to further deduction steps. ∎

5.2 Resolution

The Resolution Rule takes an axiom $q \Leftarrow \vartheta$ and tries to unify q with an atom p of the goal to be solved. If the unification succeeds, there is a substitution g such that $p[g] = q[g]$ and $\vartheta[g]$ *implies* $p[g]$: a solution of $\vartheta[g]$ would be a solution of p as well. Therefore, the Resolution Rule replaces p by $\vartheta[g]$ and thus shifts the solvability question from p to $\vartheta[g]$.

If this step belongs to a *successful* derivation, i.e. if further resolution steps lead to the empty goal, then g is a prefix of a solution, say f, of the goal the derivation started out from. (Of course, to achieve the empty goal we must eventually resolve with *unconditional* axioms.) f is composed of all the unifiers, each of which is generated as part of a derivation step, i.e. an application of the Resolution Rule.

Definition The *resolution calculus* (w.r.t. AXuEAX) consists of the following inference rule:

Resolution Rule Let γ be a goal, p be an atom, $q \Leftarrow \delta \in AX \cup EAX$, f be a substitution and g be a unifier of p and q. Then

$$\frac{\langle \gamma \cup \{p\}, f \rangle}{\langle (\gamma \cup \delta)[g], f[g \upharpoonright XG] \rangle}.$$

$\gamma \cup \{p\}$ and $q \Leftarrow \delta$ are the clauses *resolved upon*. $(\gamma \cup \delta)[f]$ is the *resolvent* of the clauses resolved upon.

Recall the general notions concerning deductive systems given at the beginning of Section 4.2.

Let γ, γ' be goals and f,f' be substitutions. A derivation of $\langle \gamma', f' \rangle$ from $\langle \gamma, f \rangle$ via the resolution calculus is called a *resolving expansion* of $\langle \gamma, f \rangle$ to $\langle \gamma', f' \rangle$ (w.r.t. $AX \cup EAX$). If γ' is empty, the expansion is *successful*. If, in addition, f is the identity substitution *id*, then f' is called an *R-solution* of γ (w.r.t. $AX \cup EAX$). If γ' is nonempty and the Resolution Rule is not applicable to $\langle \gamma', f' \rangle$, then the expansion is *failing*.

The corresponding inference relation is denoted by $\vdash_{AX}^{R}$. ∎

Note that the domains of R-solutions are subsets of XG. First of all, dom(id) is empty and thus is a subset of XG. Moreover, a resolution step $\langle \gamma, f \rangle \vdash_{AX}^{R}$ $\langle \gamma', f[g \upharpoonright XG] \rangle$ with dom(f) ⊆ XG yields

$$\text{dom}(f[g \upharpoonright XG]) \subseteq \text{dom}(f) \cup \text{dom}(g \upharpoonright XG) \subseteq XG.$$

To apply the Resolution Rule effectively one uses an algorithm that checks whether f unifies p and q (cf. Robinson [1], Section 5.8). Actually, Robinson's unification algorithm constructs a *most general* unifier (cf. Section 2.2). It also rests on the Variable Assumption: the variables of p must be disjoint from the variables of q. Even if this is guaranteed, the procedure might reduce the unification problem to another pair of atoms, which *do* share variables. For instance, let p = P⟨x,x⟩ and q = P⟨y,σy⟩. The algorithm substitutes y for x and generates p' = P⟨y,y⟩ and q' = P⟨y,σy⟩. Now y occurs both in p' and in q'. This will not be recognized at once. But when the task is to substitute the term σy for the variable y, the procedure stops because y occurs in the term to be substituted for y. In general, before substituting a term t for a variable x, the algorithm tests whether x occurs in t. It stops if this test – called the *occur check* (cf. Lloyd, p. 22) – succeeds. *Lazy resolution* does not need an occur check because unification is performed by rule applications (cf. Section 5.5).

Example 5.2.1 Let ⟨SIG,AX⟩ = BINARY-ADD-MULT (cf. Section 3.5). A resolving expansion of the equation x+11≡100 w.r.t. AX∪EAX reads as follows.

⟨{x+11≡100}, id⟩
⊢$_{AX}^{R}$ ⟨{x+11≡(1+1)0, (1+1)0≡100}, id⟩ (resolution with a≡c ⇐ a≡b, b≡c)
⊢$_{AX}^{R}$ ⟨{(1+1)0≡100}, {1/x}⟩ (resolution with 1+a1≡(1+a)0)
⊢$_{AX}^{R}$ ⟨{1+1≡10}, {1/x}⟩ (resolution with a0≡b0 ⇐ a≡b)
⊢$_{AX}^{R}$ ⟨∅, {1/x}⟩ (resolution with 1+1≡10).

Hence {1/x} is an R-solution of x+11≡100. ∎

Example 5.2.2 Let ⟨SIG,AX⟩ = BALANCED2 (cf. Section 3.12) and p be the atom

$$\text{height } [\![\omega]\!]0[\![\omega]\!]3[\![\omega]\!]1[\![\omega]\!]2[\![\omega]\!]] \text{ is n.}$$

A resolving expansion of p w.r.t. AX is

⟨{p}, id⟩
⊢$_{AX}^{R}$ ⟨{height $[\![\omega]\!]0[\![\omega]\!]$ is k, height $[\![\omega]\!]1[\![\omega]\!]2[\![\omega]\!]$ is k}, {k|/n}⟩
⊢$_{AX}^{R}$ ⟨{height ω is k'}, {k|/n}[k'|/k]⟩
⊢$_{AX}^{R}$ ⟨∅, {k|/n}[k'|/k][0/k']⟩.

Hence {k|/n}[k'|/k][0/k'] = {0||/n, 0|/k, 0/k'} is an R-solution of p. ∎

Resolution provides the basis for more "effective" goal-solving rules such as paramodulation (cf. Section 5.3), goal reduction (cf. Chapter 7) and narrowing (cf. Chapter 8). We have already established the step from solutions in models of AX to deductive solutions (Corollary 4.2.3). Theorem 5.2.4 given below transforms *bottom-up* derivations via the Horn clause calculus into *top-down* resolving expansions. Later we simulate the derivation of R-solutions by paramodulation (Theorem 5.3.4) and continue the hierarchy of refinements in Chapters 7 and 8 by turning paramodulating expansions into goal reductions (Theorem 7.8.2) and narrowing expansions (Lemma 8.2.4).

For completeness of resolution w.r.t. deductive solutions we need the following lemma, which is the restriction of Proposition 4.9.1 (2) to Horn clauses. Derivations from a clause set C via the Substitution *and* the Cut Rule can be reduced to derivations from instances of C via the Cut Rule:

Lemma 5.2.3 Let ⊢$_{cut}$ stand for the restriction of ⊢ to applications of the Cut Rule, let C be a set of clauses and

$$\text{sub}(C) = \{p[f] \Leftarrow \gamma[f] \mid p \Leftarrow \gamma \in C, f \in T(SIG)^X\}.$$

If C ⊢ q⇐δ, then for all substitutions f, sub(C) ⊢$_{cut}$ q[f]⇐δ[f]. ∎

Theorem 5.2.4 *Soundness and completeness of resolution w.r.t. deductive solutions*

Let γ be a goal and f be a substitution such that $var(\gamma) \cup dom(f) \subseteq XG$. f is a deductive $\langle SIG,AX \rangle$-solution of γ iff f is an R-solution of γ w.r.t. $AX \cup EAX$.

In particular, γ is a $\langle SIG,AX \rangle$-theorem iff the identity substitution id is an R-solution of γ w.r.t. $AX \cup EAX$.

Proof. Let $\langle \gamma, id \rangle \vdash^R_{AX} \langle \emptyset, f \rangle$. Then there are $\gamma_0,\ldots,\gamma_n, f_0,\ldots,f_{n-1}$ such that $\langle \gamma, id \rangle = \langle \gamma_0, f_0 \rangle$, for all $0 \le i < n$, $\langle \gamma_i, f_0[f_1]\ldots[f_{i-1}] \rangle$ expands to $\langle \gamma_{i+1}, f_0[f_1]\ldots[f_i] \rangle$ by applying the Resolution Rule, γ_n is empty and $f_0[f_1]\ldots[f_{n-1}] = f$. We show the following condition:

(1)   For all $0 \le i \le n$ and $p \in \gamma_{n-i}$, $AX \cup EAX \vdash p[f_{n-i}]\ldots[f_{n-1}]$.

(1) is proved by induction on i. If $i = 0$, the proof is complete because γ_n is empty. Let $i > 0$. Then $\langle \gamma_{n-i}, f_0[f_1]\ldots[f_{n-i-1}] \rangle$ expands to $\langle \gamma_{n-i+1}, f_0[f_1]\ldots[f_{n-i}] \rangle$ by applying the Resolution Rule, i.e. there are a goal δ, an atom p and $q \Leftarrow \delta \in AX \cup EAX$ such that $\gamma_{n-i} = \delta \cup \{p\}$, $p[f_{n-i}] = q[f_{n-i}]$ and $(\delta \cup \delta)[f_{n-i}] = \gamma_{n-i+1}$. By the induction hypothesis,

(2)   for all $r \in \gamma_{n-i+1}$, $AX \cup EAX \vdash r[f_{n-i+1}]\ldots[f_{n-1}]$.

Let $p' \in \gamma_{n-i}$. We have to show

(3) $AX \cup EAX \vdash p'[f_{n-i}]\ldots[f_{n-1}]$.

Case 1. $p' = p$. Since $\delta[f_{n-i}] \subseteq \gamma_{n-i+1}$, (2) implies

$$AX \cup EAX \vdash \delta[f_{n-i}][f_{n-i+1}]\ldots[f_{n-1}].$$

Hence by the Cut Rule, (3) holds true.

Case 2. $p' \in \delta$. Since $\delta[f_{n-i}] \subseteq \gamma_{n-i+1}$, (2) implies (3).

This finishes the proof of (1). The case $i=n$ implies that $\gamma[f]$ is a $\langle SIG,AX \rangle$-theorem.

Conversely, suppose that $\gamma[f]$ is $\langle SIG,AX \rangle$-theorem and the following condition holds true: For all clause sets C and clauses $p \Leftarrow \delta$,

(4)   if $C \vdash_{cut} p \Leftarrow \delta$, then id is an R-solution of p w.r.t. $C \cup \delta$.

In particular, for all atoms p,

(5)   if $C \vdash_{cut} p$, then id is an R-solution of p w.r.t. C.

Since $\gamma[f]$ is a $\langle SIG,AX \rangle$-theorem, we conclude from Lemma 5.2.3 that $\gamma[f]$ is derivable from sub(AX∪EAX) by applying only the Cut Rule. Hence by (5), id is an R-solution of $\gamma[f]$ w.r.t. sub(AX∪EAX), i.e. we have a resolving expansion $\langle d_1,...,d_n \rangle$ of $\langle \gamma[f],id \rangle$ and goals $\gamma_1,...,\gamma_n$ such that $\gamma_1 = \gamma[f]$, $\gamma_n = \emptyset$ and for all $1 \leq i \leq n$, $d_i = \langle \gamma_i, id \rangle$.

In particular, there are λ, p, g and $q \Leftarrow \vartheta \in$ AX∪EAX such that $\gamma = \lambda u(p)$, $p[f] = q[g]$ and $\gamma_2 = \lambda[f] \cup \vartheta[g]$. Let $f_1 = f + g\upharpoonright(X-XG)$. W.l.o.g. var($\gamma$) $\subseteq$ XG. Hence $p[f_1]$ = $p[f] = q[g] = q[f_1]$, and we obtain the resolution step

(6) $\langle \gamma, id \rangle = \langle \lambda u(p), id \rangle \vdash^R_{AX} \langle (\lambda u \vartheta)[f_1], f_1 \upharpoonright XG \rangle = \langle \gamma_2, f \rangle$.

Furthermore, for all $1 < i < n$ there is $q_i \Leftarrow \vartheta_i \in$ sub(AX∪EAX) such that resolution of γ_i with $q_i \Leftarrow \vartheta_i$ leads to γ_{i+1}. Hence $q_i \Leftarrow \vartheta_i = p_i[f_i] \Leftarrow \varphi_i[f_i]$ for some $p_i \Leftarrow \varphi_i \in$ AX∪EAX and substitutions f_i with $f_i \upharpoonright XG$ = id. Since we assume that the variables of γ_{i+1} belong to XG, we have

(7) $\langle \gamma_i, f \rangle \vdash^R_{AX} \langle \gamma_{i+1}[f_i], f[f_i \upharpoonright XG] \rangle = \langle \gamma_{i+1}, f \rangle$.

For all $1 < i \leq n$, let $e_i = \langle \gamma_i, f \rangle$. By (6) and (7), $\langle \langle \gamma, id \rangle, e_2,...,e_n \rangle$ is a resolving expansion of $\langle \gamma, id \rangle$. Since $e_n = \langle \gamma_n, f \rangle = \langle \emptyset, f \rangle$, we conclude that f is an R-solution of γ w.r.t. AX∪EAX.

It remains for us to show (4). We proceed by induction on a shortest derivation $\langle d_1,...,d_n \rangle$ of $p \Leftarrow \delta$ from C. If $p \Leftarrow \delta \in C$, the proof is complete because resolving p upon $p \Leftarrow \delta$ yields δ and further resolution steps of atoms of δ with themselves lead to the empty goal. If $p \Leftarrow \delta \notin C$, then $\langle d_1,...,d_n \rangle$ contains a Cut Rule application from some $d_i = (p \Leftarrow \lambda u(q))$ and some $d_j = (q \Leftarrow \varphi)$ to $p \Leftarrow \delta$, i.e. $\delta = \lambda u \varphi$. Since $i, j < n$, the induction hypothesis implies that id is an R-solution of both p w.r.t. C∪$\lambda u(q)$ and q w.r.t. C∪φ. Hence we have resolving expansions $\langle c_1,...,c_k \rangle$ of p w.r.t. C∪$\lambda u(q)$ and $\langle e_1,...,e_m \rangle$ of q w.r.t C∪φ such that $c_k = e_m = \langle \emptyset, id \rangle$.

Of course, $\langle c_1,...,c_k \rangle$ can be transformed into a resolving expansion $\langle c_1, c_2',...,c_s' \rangle$ of p w.r.t. C∪λ where for all $1 < i \leq s$ there is $1 < j \leq k$ such that $c_j = \langle \psi, id \rangle$ implies $c_i' = c_j$ or $c_i' = \langle \psi u(q), id \rangle$. If $c_s' = \langle \emptyset, id \rangle$, then $\langle c_1, c_2',...,c_s' \rangle$ is a resolving expansion of p w.r.t. C∪δ because $\lambda \subseteq \delta$. Otherwise $c_s' = \langle (q), id \rangle$, and thus $\langle c_1, c_2',...,c_s', e_1,...,e_m \rangle$ is a resolving expansion of p w.r.t. C∪δ.

Therefore, id is an R-solution of p w.r.t. C∪δ. ∎

From Corollary 4.2.3 and Theorem 5.2.4 we obtain

Corollary 5.2.5 *Soundness and completeness of resolution w.r.t. solvability in structures*

A goal γ with $\mathrm{var}(\gamma) \subseteq XG$ has an R-solution w.r.t. $AX \cup EAX$ iff for all SIG-models A of AX, some $b \in A^X$ solves γ. ∎

R-solutions are related to solutions in initial structures via representation functions (cf. Section 4.4):

Corollary 5.2.6 *Soundness and completeness of resolution w.r.t. solutions in initial structures*

Let γ be a goal with $\mathrm{var}(\gamma) \subseteq XG$ and let A be a SIG-model of AX with initial representation function rep^A.

$b \in A^X$ solves γ in A iff $(\mathrm{rep}^A \circ b) \upharpoonright XG$ is an R-solution of γ w.r.t. $AX \cup EAX$.

Proof. Let b be a solution of γ in A. Then for all $Pt \in \gamma$, $b^*t \in P^A$ and thus for $B = I(SIG,AX)$,

$$\mathrm{nat}(t[\mathrm{rep}^A \circ b]) = \mathrm{nat} \circ \mathrm{rep}^A(b^*t) \in P^B.$$

Hence for all $Pt \in \gamma$, $Pt[\mathrm{rep}^A \circ b]$ is a $\langle SIG,AX \rangle$-theorem. By Theorem 5.2.4, $(\mathrm{rep}^A \circ b) \upharpoonright XG$ is an R-solution of γ w.r.t. $AX \cup EAX$.

Conversely, if $\langle \gamma, id \rangle \vdash^R_{AX} \langle \emptyset, (\mathrm{rep}^A \circ b) \upharpoonright XG \rangle$, then by Theorem 5.2.4, for all $Pt \in \gamma$, $Pt[\mathrm{rep}^A \circ b]$ is a $\langle SIG,AX \rangle$-theorem. Thus we have

$$b^*t = (\mathrm{eval}^A \circ \mathrm{rep}^A \circ b)^*t = \mathrm{eval}^A(t[\mathrm{rep}^A \circ b]) \in P^A,$$

i.e. b solves γ in A. ∎

Negation as Failure stands for the viewpoint that the negation of a goal γ is valid if all expansions of $\langle \gamma, id \rangle$ are failing ones (see Clark). This holds true under the *closed world assumption* where AX is supposed to include a complete specification of the predicates occurring in γ. In other words, validity is restricted to the initial $\langle SIG,AX \rangle$-structure. Several approaches such as *completed definitions* (see Lloyd, chapter 3) and Prolog's cut operator aim at the control of failing expansions (see Sterling and Shapiro, Chapter 11).

An immediate consequence of Theorems 4.2.2, 4.3.2, 5.2.4 and our assumption that SIG is inhabited (cf. Section 4.1) is

Corollary 5.2.7 Let γ be a goal. The following conditions are equivalent:
- γ has no R-solution w.r.t. $AX \cup EAX$.
- γ has no solution in the free $\langle SIG,AX \rangle$-structure.
- γ has no solution in the initial $\langle SIG,AX \rangle$-structure. ∎

If BOOL is a subspecification of $\langle SIG,AX \rangle$ (cf. Section 3.1), this result can be refined to

Corollary 5.2.8 Suppose that <SIG,AX> is BOOL-complete, I(SIG,AX) is conversion-complete w.r.t. P ∈ PR and there are consistent SIG-models of AX (cf. Section 4.8). Let Pt be an atom and I(SIG,AX) satisfy the inverse conversion axiom $\sigma_{Pt} \equiv true \Leftarrow Pt$. Then Pt has no R-solution w.r.t. AX∪EAX iff $\sigma_{Pt} \equiv false$ is an inductive <SIG,AX>-theorem.

Proof. By Corollary 5.2.7, it is sufficient to show that I(SIG,AX) does not solve Pt iff $\sigma_{Pt} \equiv false \in ITh(SIG,AX)$.

If Pt has no solution in I(SIG,AX), then by conversion-completeness of I(SIG,AX) w.r.t. P, $\sigma_{Pt} \equiv true$ has no solution either. Since <SIG,AX> is BOOL-complete, I(SIG,AX) satisfies $\sigma_{Pt} \equiv false$. Hence by Theorem 4.3.2, $\sigma_{Pt} \equiv false$ is an inductive <SIG,AX>-theorem.

Vice versa, let $\sigma_{Pt} \equiv false \in ITh(SIG,AX)$. Since <SIG,AX> is BOOL-complete and there are consistent models of AX, we conclude from Lemma 4.8.2 that true≡false is not derivable from AX∪EAX. Thus for all ground substitutions f, $\sigma_{Pt}[f] \equiv true$ is not derivable from AX∪EAX either. Since I(SIG,AX) satisfies $\sigma_{Pt} \equiv true \Leftarrow Pt$, we conclude that Pt[f] is not derivable from AX∪EAX. Therefore by Theorem 4.3.2, Pt has no solution in I(SIG,AX). ∎

5.3 Paramodulation

The Paramodulation Rule simulates resolution with conditional equations by term replacement. It takes an axiom u≡u'⇐δ and tries to unify u with a subterm t of the goal γ to be solved, i.e. $\gamma = \delta[t/x]$ for some goal δ and x ∈ var(δ). If the unification succeeds, there is a substitution g such that t[g] = u[g], and ($\delta \cup \delta[u'/x])[g]$ *implies* $\gamma[g]$: a solution of ($\delta \cup \delta[u'/x])[g]$ would be a solution of γ as well. Therefore, the Paramodulation Rule replaces γ by ($\delta \cup \delta[u'/x])[g]$ and thus shifts the solvability question from γ to ($\delta \cup \delta[u'/x])[g]$.

Paramodulation steps are composed in the same way as resolution steps. The Paramodulation Rule alone, however, is not complete for deductive solutions. Certain resolution steps are still necessary, namely resolution with the reflexivity axiom x≡x and with all axioms that are not conditional equations. Moreover, in contrast to the Narrowing Rule discussed in Chapter 8, for each axiom u≡u'⇐δ we must admit paramodulation with the inverse axiom u'≡u⇐δ. Last, but not least, we are sometimes forced to apply a conditional equation to a *proper* subterm of an instance of the goal to be solved. This means that we are actually applying a conditional equation of the form t[u/x]≡t[u'/x]⇐δ instead of the axiom u≡u'⇐δ. We call t[u/x]≡t[u'/x]⇐δ a prefixed axiom:

Definition Let *CE(AX)* denote the set of conditional equations of AX. *Pre(AX)*, the set of *prefixed axioms*, is the smallest superset of CE(AX) which satisfies the following closure property:
- If $u \equiv u' \Leftarrow \vartheta$ is a prefixed axiom, then for all terms t of the form $\tau \langle x_1,...,x_n \rangle$ and all $1 \leq i \leq n$ such that sort(x_i) = sort(u), $t[u/x_i] \equiv t[u'/x_i] \Leftarrow \vartheta$ is a prefixed axiom as well. ∎

In fact, completeness of paramodulation is guaranteed only if we allow a goal to be instantiated before applying an axiom of CE(AX), or conversely, if the axiom is extended by a prefix before one of its sides is substituted into a variable of the goal to be solved. Just these extensions are captured by Pre(AX).

Definition The *paramodulation calculus* (w.r.t. AX) consists of the following three inference rules:

Paramodulation Rule Let δ be a goal, $x \in$ single(δ) (cf. Section 2.2), t be a term, $u \equiv u' \Leftarrow \vartheta$ (or $u' \equiv u \Leftarrow \vartheta$) $\in$ Pre(AX), f be a substitution and g be a unifier of t and u. Then

$$\frac{\langle \delta[t/x], f \rangle}{\langle (\delta[u'/x] \cup \vartheta)[g], f[g \restriction XG] \rangle .}$$

$\delta[t/x]$ and $u \equiv u' \Leftarrow \vartheta$ are the clauses *paramodulated upon*. $(\delta[u'/x] \cup \vartheta)[g]$ is the *paramodulant* of the clauses paramodulated upon.

Restricted Resolution Rule Let γ be a goal, p be an atom, $q \Leftarrow \vartheta \in$ AX-CE(AX), f be a substitution and g be a unifier of p and q. Then

$$\frac{\langle \gamma \cup \{p\}, f \rangle}{\langle (\gamma \cup \vartheta)[g], f[g \restriction XG] \rangle .}$$

Unification Rule Let γ be a goal, $t \equiv t'$ be an equation, f be a substitution and g be a unifier of t and t'. Then

$$\frac{\langle \gamma \cup \{t \equiv t'\}, f \rangle}{\langle \gamma[g], f[g] \rangle .}$$

Let γ, γ' be goals and f,f' be substitutions. A derivation of $\langle \gamma', f' \rangle$ from $\langle \gamma, f \rangle$ via the paramodulation calculus is called a *paramodulating expansion* of $\langle \gamma, f \rangle$ to $\langle \gamma', f' \rangle$ (w.r.t. AX). If γ' is empty, the expansion is *successful*. If, in addition, f = id, then f' is a *P-solution* of γ (w.r.t. AX). If γ' is nonempty and no rule of the paramodulation calculus is applicable to $\langle\gamma',f'\rangle$, then the expansion is *failing*.

The corresponding inference relation is denoted by $\vdash^P_{AX}$. ∎

The Restricted Resolution Rule and the Unification Rule cover the two remaining classes of resolution steps mentioned above: resolution with axioms of AX-CE(AX) and with x≡x. On the other hand, applications of the Resolution Rule to CE(AX) or to other equality axioms than reflexivity are no longer necessary.

Example 5.3.1 Let $\langle SIG,AX\rangle$ = BINARY-ADD-MULT (cf. Section 3.5). A paramodulating expansion of x+10≡11 w.r.t. AX is

$\qquad \langle\{x+10\equiv 11\}, id\rangle$
$\vdash^P_{AX} \langle\{11\equiv 11\}, \{1/x\}\rangle$ (paramodulation with 1+a0 ≡ a1)
$\vdash^P_{AX} \langle\emptyset, \{1/x\}\rangle$ (unification).

A paramodulating expansion of x+11≡100 w.r.t. AX reads as follows (cf. Example 5.2.1).

$\qquad \langle\{x+11\equiv 100\}, id\rangle$
$\vdash^P_{AX} \langle\{(1+1)0\equiv 100\}, \{1/x\}\rangle$ (paramodulation with 1+a1≡(1+a)0)
$\vdash^P_{AX} \langle\{100\equiv 100\}, \{1/x\}\rangle$ (paramodulation with 1+1≡10)
$\vdash^P_{AX} \langle\emptyset, \{1/x\}\rangle$ (unification). ∎

The following lemma allows us to *lift* every expansion of $\langle\gamma[h],f\rangle$ to an expansion of $\langle\gamma,f\rangle$. This result rests on the possibility of paramodulating upon prefixed axioms.

Lemma 5.3.2 *Backward lifting of paramodulating expansions*
Let $\langle\gamma[h],id\rangle \vdash^P_{AX} \langle\varphi,g\rangle$ and $var(\gamma)\cup dom(h) \subseteq XG$. Then $\langle\gamma,id\rangle \vdash^P_{AX} \langle\varphi,h[g]\rangle$.

Proof. By assumption there is a paramodulating expansion $\langle d_1,...,d_n\rangle$ of $\langle\gamma[h],id\rangle$ to $\langle\varphi,g\rangle$. Let $d_2 = \langle\varphi',g'\rangle$ and g'[g"] = g. Then

(1) $\qquad\qquad\qquad \langle\varphi',id\rangle \vdash^P_{AX} \langle\varphi,g"\rangle$.

Of course, (1) implies

(2) $\qquad\qquad\qquad \langle\varphi',h[g']\rangle \vdash^P_{AX} \langle\varphi,h[g]\rangle$.

Suppose that

(3) $\qquad \langle\gamma,\text{id}\rangle \vdash^P_{AX} \langle\varphi',h[g']\rangle.$

Then the proof is complete by composing (3) and (2). To show (3) we have to consider several cases concerning the rule applied to $d_1 = \langle\gamma[h],\text{id}\rangle$ and producing $d_2 = \langle\varphi',g'\rangle$.

Case 1. The Restricted Resolution Rule or the Unification Rule leads from d_1 to d_2. Then (3) follows immediately.

Case 2. The Paramodulation Rule leads from d_1 to d_2, i.e. there are a goal δ, $x \in \text{single}(\delta)$, a term t and $u \equiv u' \Leftarrow \vartheta$ (or $u' \equiv u \Leftarrow \vartheta) \in \text{Pre}(AX)$ such that $\delta[t/x] = \gamma[h]$ and

(4) $\qquad (\delta[u'/x] \cup \vartheta)[g'] = \varphi'.$

W.l.o.g. $\text{hГvar}(u \equiv u' \Leftarrow \vartheta) = \text{id}$. $\delta[t/x] = \gamma[h]$ admits two subcases:

Case 2.1. $\gamma = \delta'[t'/x]$, $\delta = \delta'[\text{hГ}(X-\{x\})]$ and $t = t'[h]$ for some δ',t'. Since $t'[h][g'] = t[g'] = u[g'] = u[h][g']$, $h[g']$ is a unifier of t' and u. Thus by the Paramodulation Rule,

(5) $\qquad \langle\gamma,\text{id}\rangle \vdash^P_{AX} \langle(\delta'[u'/x] \cup \vartheta)[h][g'], h[g']\rangle.$

From (5),

$\delta'[u'/x][h][g'] = \delta'[\text{hГ}(X-\{x\})][u'[h]/x][g'] = \delta[u'[h]/x][g'] = \delta[u'/x][g'],$

$\vartheta[h][g'] = \vartheta[g']$ and (4) one infers (3).

Case 2.2. $\delta = \gamma[h']$ and $h = h'[t/x]$ for some h'. Then there are $z \in \text{single}(\gamma)$, a term v and a substitution h'' such that $x \in \text{var}(v)$, $h' = \{v/z\}[h'']$, $h''x = x$ and $v[u/x] \equiv v[u'/x] \Leftarrow \vartheta$ (or $v[u'/x] \equiv v[u/x] \Leftarrow \vartheta) \in \text{Pre}(AX)$. W.l.o.g. $h''\text{Гvar}(v) = h\text{Гvar}(v)$. Hence

$\qquad z[h][g'] = z[h'][t/x][g']$
$\qquad\qquad = z[h'][u/x][g'] \qquad$ (since g' unifies t and u)
$\qquad\qquad = v[h''][u/x][g'] \qquad$ (since h' = {v/z}[h''])
$\qquad\qquad = v[h''Г(X-\{x\})][u/x][g'] \qquad$ (since h''x = x)
$\qquad\qquad = v[hГ(X-\{x\})][u/x][g'] \qquad$ (since h''Гvar(v) = hГvar(v))
$\qquad\qquad = v[hГ(X-\{x\})][u[h]/x][g'] \qquad$ (since hГvar(u) = id)
$\qquad\qquad = v[u/x][h][g'].$

Therefore $h[g']$ unifies z and $v[u/x]$, and the Paramodulation Rule implies

(6) $\qquad \langle\gamma,\text{id}\rangle \vdash^P_{AX} \langle(\gamma[v[u'/x]/z] \cup \vartheta)[h][g'], h[g']\rangle.$

From $v[h"] = h'z$, $x \in var(v)$ and $h"x = x$ one infers that x occurs in $h'z$. However, $h'z$ is a subterm of $\gamma[h']$ and $x \in single(\delta) = single(\gamma[h'])$. Hence for all $y \in var(\gamma)-\{z\}$, x does not occur in $h'y$, i.e. $x \notin var(\gamma[h'|'(X-\{z\})])$. Thus we have

(7) $\qquad \gamma[h'[t_0/x]]'(X-\{z\})] = \gamma[h'[t_1/x]]'(X-\{z\})]$

for arbitrary terms t_0, t_1. Moreover, we may assume that z occurs neither in $\delta = \gamma[h']$ nor in u'. Hence z does not occur in $\gamma[h'[u'/x]]$ either. Putting all this together we obtain

$\gamma[v[u'/x]/z][h][g']$
$= \gamma[h|'(X-\{z\})][v[u'/x][h]/z][g']$
$= \gamma[h'[t/x]|'(X-\{z\})][v[u'/x][h]/z][g']$
$= \gamma[h'[u'/x]|'(X-\{z\})][v[u'/x][h]/z][g']$ $\qquad$ (by (7))
$= \gamma[h'[u'/x]|'(X-\{z\})][v[h|'(X-\{x\})][u'[h]/x]/z][g']$
$= \gamma[h'[u'/x]|'(X-\{z\})][v[h|'(X-\{x\})][u'/x]/z][g']$ $\qquad$ (since $h|var(u') = id$)
$= \gamma[h'[u'/x]|'(X-\{z\})][v[h"|'(X-\{x\})][u'/x]/z][g']$ $\qquad$ (since $h|var(v) = h'|var(v)$)
$= \gamma[h'[u'/x]|'(X-\{z\})][v[h"][u'/x]/z][g']$ $\qquad$ (since $h"x = x$)
$= \gamma[h'[u'/x]|'(X-\{z\})][h'[u'/x]|'(z)][g']$ $\qquad$ (since $h' = \{v/z\}[h"]$)
$= \gamma[h'[u'/x]][g']$ $\qquad$ (since $z \notin var(\gamma[h'[u'/x]])$)
$= \gamma[h'][u'/x][g']$
$= \delta[u'/x][g']$

and $\delta[h][g'] = \delta[g']$ because $h|var(\delta) = id$. Hence (6) and (4) imply (3). ∎

The following example illustrates the need for prefixed axioms.

Example 5.3.3 (cf. Furbach et al., Section 3.4) Given that $\langle SIG, AX\rangle$ consists of two binary functions f, g and a unary one h, constants a, b and axioms

$\qquad (g\ ha\ hb) \equiv (f\ ha\ hb)$
$\qquad a \equiv b,$

let $\gamma = \{gxx \equiv fxx\}$. Of course, $\gamma[ha/x]$ is a $\langle SIG, AX\rangle$-theorem. For instance, a resolving expansion of $\langle\gamma, id\rangle$ is

$\qquad \langle\gamma, id\rangle$
$\vdash^R_{AX} \langle\{gxx \equiv y, y \equiv fxx\}, id\rangle$ $\qquad$ (resolution with $z \equiv z' \Leftarrow z \equiv y, y \equiv z'$)
$\vdash^R_{AX} \langle\{x \equiv z, x \equiv z', gzz' \equiv fxx\}, \{gzz'/y\}\rangle$
$\qquad\qquad\qquad$ (resolution with $gyy' \equiv gzz' \Leftarrow y \equiv z, y' \equiv z'$)
$\vdash^R_{AX} \langle\{x \equiv z, x \equiv z', gzz' \equiv y, y \equiv fxx\}, \{gzz'/y\}\rangle$
$\qquad\qquad\qquad$ (resolution with $z_0 \equiv z_1 \Leftarrow z_0 \equiv y, y \equiv z_1$)

$\vdash^R_{AX}$ $\langle\{x \equiv ha, x \equiv hb, fhahb \equiv fxx\}, \{gzz'/y\}[fhahb/y]\rangle$
(resolution with ghahb≡fhahb)
$\vdash^R_{AX}$ $\langle\{x \equiv ha, x \equiv hb, ha \equiv x, hb \equiv x\}, \{gzz'/y\}\rangle$
(resolution with fyy'≡fzz' ⇐ y≡z, y'≡z')
$\vdash^R_{AX}$ $\langle\{x \equiv ha, x \equiv hb, hb \equiv x\}, \{gzz'/y\}\rangle$ (resolution with z≡y ⇐ y≡z)
$\vdash^R_{AX}$ $\langle\{x \equiv ha, x \equiv hb\}, \{gzz'/y\}\rangle$ (resolution with z≡y ⇐ y≡z)
$\vdash^R_{AX}$ $\langle\{y \equiv a, hy \equiv hb\}, \{gzz'/y\}[hy/x]\rangle$ (resolution with hy≡hz ⇐ y≡z)
$\vdash^R_{AX}$ $\langle\{y \equiv a, y \equiv b\}, \{gzz'/y\}[hy/x]\rangle$ (resolution with hy≡hz ⇐ y≡z)
$\vdash^R_{AX}$ $\langle\{a \equiv b\}, \{gzz'/y\}[hy/x][a/y]\rangle$ (resolution with z≡z)
$\vdash^R_{AX}$ $\langle \emptyset, \{gzz'/y\}[ha/x] \rangle$ (resolution with a≡b).

A corresponding paramodulating expansion of $\langle\gamma,id\rangle$ reads as follows.

$\quad\langle\gamma, id\rangle$
= $\langle\{(gxy \equiv fxx)[x/y]\}, id\rangle$
$\vdash^P_{AX}$ $\langle\{(gxy \equiv fxx)[hb/y][ha/x]\}, \{ha/x\}\rangle$
= $\langle\{ghahb \equiv fhaha\}, \{ha/x\}\rangle$ (paramodulation with ha≡hb)
$\vdash^P_{AX}$ $\langle\{ghahb \equiv fhahb\}, \{ha/x\}\rangle$ (paramodulation with a≡b)
$\vdash^P_{AX}$ $\langle \emptyset, \{ha/x\} \rangle$ (paramodulation with ghahb≡fhahb).

The reader should convince him- or herself that the prefixed axiom ha≡hb is necessary to obtain {ha/x} as a P-solution. ∎

In general, the completeness proof of paramodulation w.r.t. resolution uses expansion lifting (cf. Lemma 5.3.2) and thus requires prefixed axioms.

Theorem 5.3.4 *Resolution is equivalent to paramodulation*
Let γ, γ' be goals and f be a substitution.
(1) $\quad\langle\gamma,id\rangle \vdash^R_{AX} \langle\emptyset,f\rangle$ implies $\langle\gamma,id\rangle \vdash^P_{AX} \langle\emptyset,f\rangle$.
(2) $\quad\langle\gamma,id\rangle \vdash^P_{AX} \langle\gamma',f\rangle$ implies $\langle\gamma,id\rangle \vdash^R_{AX} \langle\gamma',f\rangle$.

Proof. (1) Let AX' = (CE(AX) ∪ EAX) - {$x \equiv_s x \mid s \in S$}, i.e. AX' consists of all axioms the paramodulation calculus cannot resolve upon. Let f be a substitution and $\langle d_1,...,d_n\rangle$ be a shortest resolving expansion of $\langle\gamma,id\rangle$ to $\langle\emptyset,f\rangle$. We show $\langle\gamma,id\rangle \vdash^P_{AX} \langle\emptyset,f\rangle$ by induction on n. Suppose that all $q \Leftarrow \delta \in$ AX' commute with paramodulation, i.e. for all goals φ and substitutions g,h

(3) $\quad\langle\varphi \cup \delta[g], id\rangle \vdash^P_{AX} \langle\emptyset,h\rangle$ implies $\langle\varphi \cup \{q[g]\}, id\rangle \vdash^P_{AX} \langle\emptyset,h\rangle$.

Case 1. $\langle d_1,...,d_n\rangle$ is already a paramodulating expansion. Then the proof is complete.
Case 2. $\langle d_1,...,d_n\rangle$ is not a paramodulating expansion. Then $\langle d_1,...,d_n\rangle$ can be splitted into a paramodulating expansion $\langle d_1,...,d_i\rangle$ and a resolving expansion

$\langle d_{i+1},...,d_n \rangle$ such that the step from d_i to d_{i+1} is obtained by applying the Resolution Rule to some $q \Leftarrow \vartheta \in AX'$, i.e.

$$d_i = \langle \varphi u(p), h \rangle \quad \text{and} \quad d_{i+1} = \langle (\varphi u \vartheta)[h'], h[h'] \rangle$$

for some φ, p, h, h' with $p[h'] = q[h']$. Moreover, there is h'' such that $f = h[h'][h'']$. By the induction hypothesis,

$$\langle (\varphi u \vartheta)[h'], id \rangle \vdash^P_{AX} \langle \varnothing, h'' \rangle.$$

Since $q \Leftarrow \vartheta \in AX'$, we conclude

$$\langle (\varphi u(q))[h'], id \rangle \vdash^P_{AX} \langle \varnothing, h'' \rangle$$

from (3). $q[h'] = p[h']$ implies

$$\langle (\varphi u(p))[h'], id \rangle \vdash^P_{AX} \langle \varnothing, h'' \rangle.$$

By Lemma 5.3.2,

$$\langle \varphi u(p), id \rangle \vdash^P_{AX} \langle \varnothing, h'[h''] \rangle$$

and thus

$$\langle \varphi u(p), h \rangle \vdash^P_{AX} \langle \varnothing, f \rangle.$$

Combining $\langle d_1,...,d_i \rangle$ with a paramodulating expansion of $\langle \varphi u(p), h \rangle$ to $\langle \varnothing, f \rangle$ we obtain a paramodulating expansion of $\langle \gamma, id \rangle$ to $\langle \varnothing, f \rangle$. It remains for us to show (3). Let

(4) $$\langle \varphi u \vartheta[g], id \rangle \vdash^P_{AX} \langle \varnothing, h \rangle$$

for some $q \Leftarrow \vartheta \in AX'$. We must infer

(5) $$\langle \varphi u(q[g]), id \rangle \vdash^P_{AX} \langle \varnothing, h \rangle.$$

Case 1. $q \Leftarrow \vartheta$ is a symmetry axiom, say $q = (y \equiv x)$ and $\vartheta = \{x \equiv y\}$. By (4), h is a P-solution of $\vartheta[g]$. Hence $\vartheta[g]$ can be eliminated only by the Unification Rule, i.e. $(gx)[h] = (gy)[h]$. Thus again by the Unification Rule,

$$\langle \varphi u(q[g]), id \rangle = \langle \varphi u(gy \equiv gx), id \rangle \vdash^P_{AX} \langle \varnothing, h \rangle.$$

Case 2. $q \Leftarrow \vartheta$ is a transitivity axiom, say $q = (x \equiv z)$ and $\vartheta = \{x \equiv y, y \equiv z\}$. By (4), h is a P-solution of $\vartheta[g]$. Hence $\vartheta[g]$ can be eliminated only by the Unification Rule, i.e. $(gx)[h] = (gy)[h] = (gz)[h]$. Thus by the Unification Rule,

$$\langle \varphi u(q[g]), id \rangle = \langle \varphi u(gx \equiv gz), id \rangle \vdash^P_{AX} \langle \varnothing, h \rangle.$$

Case 3. $q \Leftarrow \vartheta$ is an OP-compatibility axiom, say $q = (\sigma\langle x_1,...,x_n\rangle \equiv \sigma\langle y_1,...,y_n\rangle)$ and $\vartheta = \{x_1 \equiv y_1,...,x_n \equiv y_n\}$. By (4), h is a P-solution of $\vartheta[g]$. Hence $\vartheta[g]$ can be eliminated only by the Unification Rule, i.e. for all $1 \leq i \leq n$, $(gx_i)[h] = (gy_i)[h]$. Thus by the Unification Rule,

$$\langle \varphi \cup \{q[g]\}, id\rangle = \langle \varphi \cup \{\sigma\langle gx_1,...,gx_n\rangle \equiv \sigma\langle gy_1,...,gy_n\rangle\}, id\rangle \vdash^P_{AX} \langle \emptyset, h\rangle.$$

Case 4. $q \Leftarrow \vartheta$ is a PR-compatibility axiom, say $q = P\langle y_1,...,y_n\rangle$ and $\vartheta = \{P\langle x_1,...,x_n\rangle, x_1 \equiv y_1,...,x_n \equiv y_n\}$. By (4), h is a P-solution of $\vartheta[g]$. Hence $\{x_1 \equiv y_1,...,x_n \equiv y_n\}$ can be eliminated only by the Unification Rule, i.e. for all $1 \leq i \leq n$, $(gx_i)[h] = (gy_i)[h]$. Since $P\langle gx_1,...,gx_n\rangle \in \vartheta[g]$, (4) implies

$$\langle \varphi \cup \{P\langle gy_1,...,gy_n\rangle\}, id\rangle = \langle \varphi \cup \{P\langle gx_1,...,gx_n\rangle\}, id\rangle \vdash^P_{AX} \langle \emptyset, h\rangle.$$

Case 5. $q \Leftarrow \vartheta \in CE(AX)$, say $q = (u \equiv u')$. By paramodulating upon $q[g]$ and $q \Leftarrow \vartheta$ we obtain
$$\langle \varphi \cup \{q[g]\}, id\rangle \vdash^P_{AX} \langle \varphi \cup \{u'[g] \equiv u'[g]\} \cup \vartheta[g], id\rangle.$$

The Unification Rule leads to

$$\langle \varphi \cup \{q[g]\}, id\rangle \vdash^P_{AX} \langle \varphi \cup \vartheta[g], id\rangle,$$

and (4) implies (5).

This finishes part (1) of the theorem, and we conclude that paramodulation is complete w.r.t. resolution.

(2) We have seen that the Restricted Resolution Rule and the Unification Rule are special cases of the Resolution Rule. So it remains for us to show that each application of the Paramodulation Rule can be simulated by a sequence of resolution steps.

A paramodulation step has the form

(6) $\qquad \langle \varphi \cup \{p\}, id\rangle \vdash^P_{AX} \langle (\varphi \cup \{p'\} \cup \vartheta)[g], g\rangle$

where
$$p = P\langle t_1,...,t_i[t/x],...,t_n\rangle, \quad p' = P\langle t_1,...,t_i[v[u'/z]/x],...,t_n\rangle,$$

$u \equiv u' \Leftarrow \vartheta \in AX$ and g is a unifier of t and $v[u/z]$, i.e. $v[u/z] \equiv v[u'/z] \Leftarrow \vartheta$ is the applied prefixed axiom. First, p can be resolved with the equality axiom

$$P\langle y_1,...,y_n\rangle \Leftarrow P\langle x_1,...,x_n\rangle, x_1 \equiv y_1, ..., x_n \equiv y_n.$$

We obtain

$\langle\varphi u(p), \text{id}\rangle \vdash^R_{AX} \langle(\varphi u(p', t_1 \equiv t_1, ..., t_i[v[u'/z]/x] \equiv t_i[t/x], ..., t_n \equiv t_n), \text{id}\rangle.$

Secondly, resolution with reflexivity and OP-compatibility axioms yields

$\langle(\varphi u(p', t_1 \equiv t_1, ..., t_i[v[u'/z]/x] \equiv t_i[t/x], ..., t_n \equiv t_n), \text{id}\rangle$
$\vdash^R_{AX} \langle(\varphi u(p', v[u'/z] \equiv t), \text{id}\rangle.$

Since g unifies t and v[u/z], OP-compatibility axioms lead to

$\langle(\varphi u(p', v[u'/z] \equiv t), \text{id}\rangle \vdash^R_{AX} \langle(\varphi u(p, u' \equiv u))[g], g\rangle.$

By the symmetry axiom,

$\langle(\varphi u(p, u' \equiv u))[g], g\rangle \vdash^R_{AX} \langle(\varphi u(p, u \equiv u'))[g], g\rangle.$

Finally, we resolve with $u \equiv u' \Leftarrow \vartheta$ and obtain

$\langle(\varphi u(p, u \equiv u'))[g], g\rangle \vdash^R_{AX} \langle(\varphi u(p) \cup \vartheta)[g], g\rangle.$

Thus (6) has been simulated by a sequence of resolution steps, and we conclude part (2) of the theorem, i.e. paramodulation is sound w.r.t. resolution. ∎

Theorems 5.2.4 and 5.3.4 imply

Theorem 5.3.5 *Soundness and completeness of paramodulation w.r.t. deductive solutions*
Let γ be a goal and f be a substitution with $\text{var}(\gamma) \cup \text{dom}(f) \subseteq XG$. f is a deductive <SIG,AX>-solution of γ iff f is a P-solution of γ w.r.t. AX.
In particular, γ is a <SIG,AX>-theorem iff id is a P-solution of γ w.r.t. AX. ∎

We are now in a position to prove Theorem 4.7.5 which established a criterion for initial structures to be visibly initial w.r.t. a smaller set of axioms.

Proof of Theorem 4.7.5. Let γ be a ground visible goal. We have to show that if γ is a <SIG,AX'>-theorem, then γ is already derivable from AX∪EAX. So let γ be a <SIG,AX'>-theorem. By Theorem 5.3.5, there is a shortest paramodulating expansion $\langle d_1,...,d_n\rangle$ of $\langle\gamma,\text{id}\rangle$ to $\langle\emptyset,\text{id}\rangle$ w.r.t. AX'. The fact that γ is a <SIG,AX>-theorem will be deduced by induction on n.
If n = 1, then γ is empty and the proof is complete. Otherwise one of the following two cases holds true:

Case 1. The Restricted Resolution Rule or the Unification Rule leads from $d_1 = \langle \gamma, id \rangle$ to d_2, i.e. there are $q \Leftarrow \vartheta \in (AX'-CE(AX')) \cup (x \equiv x)$, a ground goal φ and a ground substitution f such that $\gamma = \varphi \cup \{q[f]\}$ and $d_2 = \langle \varphi \cup \vartheta[f], id \rangle$.

By Theorem 5.3.5, $\varphi \cup \vartheta[f]$ is a $\langle SIG, AX' \rangle$-theorem. Since $\varphi \subseteq \gamma$, φ is visible. By assumption, ϑ is visible. Hence by the induction hypothesis, $\varphi \cup \vartheta[f]$ is a $\langle SIG, AX \rangle$-theorem. It remains for us to show that $q[f]$ is a $\langle SIG, AX \rangle$-theorem.

If $q \Leftarrow \vartheta \in AX$, then $\vartheta[f] \subseteq DTh(SIG,AX)$ implies that $q[f]$ is a $\langle SIG,AX \rangle$-theorem as well. If $q \Leftarrow \vartheta \in AX'-AX$, then by assumption, $q \Leftarrow \vartheta$ follows contextually from AX, and we conclude from the visibility of $q[f] \in \gamma$ and from $\vartheta[f] \subseteq DTh(SIG,AX)$ that $q[f]$ is derivable from $AX \cup EAX$.

Case 2. The Paramodulation Rule leads from $d_1 = \langle \gamma, id \rangle$ to d_2, i.e. there are a goal δ, $x \in single(\delta)$, a ground substitution f and $u \equiv u' \Leftarrow \vartheta$ (or $u' \equiv u \Leftarrow \vartheta$) $\in AX'$ such that $\gamma = \delta[u[f]/x]$ and $d_2 = \langle \delta[u'[f]/x] \cup \vartheta[f], id \rangle$.

By Theorem 5.3.5, $\delta[u'[f]/x] \cup \vartheta[f]$ is a $\langle SIG,AX' \rangle$-theorem. By assumption, ϑ is visible. Moreover, the visibility of $\gamma = \delta[u[f]/x]$ implies the visibility of $\delta[u'[f]/x]$. Hence by the induction hypothesis, $\delta[u'[f]/x] \cup \vartheta[f]$ is derivable from $AX \cup EAX$.

If $u \equiv u' \Leftarrow \vartheta \in AX$, then $\delta[u'[f]/x] \cup \vartheta[f] \subseteq DTh(SIG,AX)$ implies that $\gamma = \delta[u[f]/x]$ is also a $\langle SIG,AX \rangle$-theorem. If $q \Leftarrow \vartheta \in AX'-AX$, then by assumption, $u \equiv u' \Leftarrow \vartheta$ follows contextually from AX, and we conclude from the visibility of δ and from $\delta[u'[f]/x] \cup \vartheta[f] \subseteq DTh(SIG,AX)$ that $\gamma = \delta[u[f]/x]$ is derivable from $AX \cup EAX$. ∎

5.4 Most General Unification

As mentioned in Section 5.1 we treat the restrictions of resolution and paramodulation to most general unifiers (cf. Section 2.2) as refinements that are not needed for correctness considerations, but for an effective use of the inference rules.

Definition A resolving (paramodulating) expansion $\langle d_1, \ldots, d_n \rangle$ is *most general* if for all $1 \leq i < n$ the step from d_i to d_{i+1} is performed by a rule of the resolution (paramodulation) calculus where the respective unifier g is most general.

The corresponding inference relation is denoted by $\vdash_{AX}^{GR}$ ($\vdash_{AX}^{GP}$). If $\langle \gamma, id \rangle \vdash_{AX}^{GR} \langle \varnothing, f \rangle$ ($\langle \gamma, id \rangle \vdash_{AX}^{GP} \langle \varnothing, f \rangle$), then f is a *GR- (GP-) solution* of γ (w.r.t. AX). ∎

Lemma 5.4.1 *Forward lifting of paramodulating expansions*
If $\langle \gamma, id \rangle \vdash_{AX}^{P} \langle \varphi, f \rangle$, then there are φ', f', h such that $\langle \gamma, id \rangle \vdash_{AX}^{GP} \langle \varphi', f' \rangle$, $\varphi'[h] = \varphi$ and $f'[h] = f$.

In particular, if f is a P-solution of γ w.r.t. AX, then there is a GP-solution of γ w.r.t. AX, which subsumes f.

Proof. Let $\langle d_1,...,d_n\rangle$ be a shortest paramodulating expansion of $\langle\gamma,id\rangle$ to $\langle\varphi,f\rangle$. We proceed by induction on n. If $n \leq 2$, then the result follows immediately. Otherwise there are $1<i<n$ and δ,g,h such that $d_i = \langle\delta,g\rangle$, $g[h] = f$ and $\langle\varphi,f\rangle$ is obtained from d_i by applying a rule of the paramodulation calculus. By the induction hypothesis, there are δ',g',h' such that

(1) $\qquad \langle\gamma,id\rangle \vdash^{GP}_{AX} \langle\delta',g'\rangle$, $\delta'[h'] = \delta$ and $g'[h'] = g$.

Hence $\langle\delta,g\rangle \vdash^{P}_{AX} \langle\varphi,g[h]\rangle$ implies

$$\langle\delta,id\rangle \vdash^{P}_{AX} \langle\varphi,h\rangle.$$

By Lemma 5.3.2,

$$\langle\delta',id\rangle \vdash^{P}_{AX} \langle\varphi,h'[h]\rangle.$$

Again by the induction hypothesis,

(2) $\qquad \langle\delta',id\rangle \vdash^{GP}_{AX} \langle\varphi',g''\rangle$, $\varphi'[h''] = \varphi$ and $g''[h''] = h'[h]$

for some φ',g'',h''. Hence $\langle\delta',g'\rangle \vdash^{GP}_{AX} \langle\varphi',g'[g'']\rangle$, and (1) yields

$\langle\gamma,id\rangle \vdash^{GP}_{AX} \langle\varphi',g'[g'']\rangle$, $\varphi'[h''] = \varphi$ and $g'[g''][h''] = g'[h'][h] = g[h] = f'$. ∎

Of course, the lifting of paramodulating expansions to expansions with most general unifiers applies to resolving expansions as well. (The analogue of Lemma 5.3.2 for $\vdash^{R}_{AX}$ instead of $\vdash^{P}_{AX}$ is trivial.) In the following chapters, we use paramodulating expansions rather than resolving expansions when reasoning about deductive solutions.

Theorem 5.3.5 and Lemma 5.4.1 amount to

Theorem 5.4.2 *Soundness and completeness of most general paramodulation w.r.t. deductive solutions*

Let γ be a goal and let f be a substitution with $var(\gamma)\cup dom(f) \subseteq XG$. f is a deductive $\langle SIG,AX\rangle$-solution of γ iff $f = g[h]$ for some GP-solution g of γ w.r.t. AX and some substitution h.

In particular, γ is a $\langle SIG,AX\rangle$-theorem iff id is a GP-solution of γ w.r.t. AX. ∎

Finally, Corollary 4.2.3 and Theorem 5.4.2 relate GP-solutions to solutions in structures:

Corollary 5.4.3 *Soundness and completeness of most general paramodu-*

lation w.r.t. solvability in structures

A goal γ has a GP-solution w.r.t. AX iff for all SIG-models A of AX, some b solves γ in A. ∎

Corollary 5.4.4 *Soundness and completeness of most general paramodulation w.r.t. solutions in initial structures*

Let γ be a goal with var(γ) ⊆ XG and let A be a SIG-model of AX with initial representation function rep^A. b ∈ A^X solves γ in A iff $(rep^A \cdot b)\upharpoonright XG = g[h]$ for some GP-solution g of γ w.r.t. AX and some substitution h.

Proof. Corollary 5.2.6, Theorem 5.3.4 and Lemma 5.4.1. ∎

Theorems 4.4.7 (1) and 5.4.2 provide the following inductive theory criterion.

Theorem 5.4.5 *Inductive theory criterion*

Let A be a SIG-model of AX with initial representation function rep^A. A goal γ with var(γ) ⊆ XG is an inductive <SIG,AX>-theorem iff for all f ∈ $rep^A(A)^X$ some GP-solution g of γ w.r.t. AX and some substitution h satisfy $g[h] = f\upharpoonright XG$. ∎

5.5 Lazy Resolution

Let us return to Section 5.2. The crucial condition for applying the Resolution Rule is that the conclusion of an axiom be unifiable with an atom of the goal to be solved. The unification task is transferred to an algorithm that is not part of the calculus. Alternatively, this task may be simulated by (a sequence of) rule applications the first of which takes an axiom Pu⇐ϑ and transforms an atom Pt into the goal {t≡u,Pu}∪ϑ.

Instead of unifying t and u, the equation(s) t≡u are expanded. This procedure is called *demand-driven* or *lazy* resolution because corresponding inference rules demand a solution of t≡u. The Resolution Rule of Section 5.2, on the other hand, is *data-driven* or *eager*, since it can be applied only if the datum given by the unifier of t and u is already present. Jaffar et al. call the expansion of t≡u *generalized unification* because it may involve arbitrary resolution steps, whereas to unify t and u means to resolve t≡u only with the reflexivity axiom x≡x.

Definition The *lazy resolution calculus* (w.r.t. AX∪EAX) consists of the Unification Rule (only for most general unifiers; cf. Section 5.3) and the

Lazy Resolution Rule Let γ be a goal, Pt be an atom, Pu⇐ϑ ∈ AX∪EAX and f be a substitution. Then

$$\frac{\langle \gamma \cup \{Pt\}, f \rangle}{\langle \gamma \cup \{t \equiv u\} \cup \vartheta, f \rangle}.$$

(Remember that $t \equiv u$ stands for the set of all equations between corresponding components of t and u; cf. Section 2.2.)

Let γ, γ' be goals and f, f' be substitutions. A derivation of $\langle \gamma', f' \rangle$ from $\langle \gamma, f \rangle$ via the lazy resolution calculus is called a *lazily resolving expansion* of $\langle \gamma, f \rangle$ to $\langle \gamma', f' \rangle$ (w.r.t. AX∪EAX).

The corresponding inference relation is denoted by $L\vdash_{AX}^{GR}$. If $\langle \gamma, id \rangle \ L\vdash_{AX}^{GR} \ \langle \emptyset, f \rangle$, then f is called an *LGR-solution* of γ (w.r.t. AX∪EAX). ∎

Example 5.5.1 (cf. Example 5.2.1) Let ⟨SIG,AX⟩ = BINARY-ADD-MULT (cf. Section 3.5). A lazily resolving expansion of the equation x+11≡100 w.r.t. AX∪EAX reads as follows.

$\langle \{x+11 \equiv 100\}, id \rangle$
$L\vdash_{AX}^{GR}$ $\langle \{x+11 \equiv z, 100 \equiv z\}, id \rangle$ (lazy resolution with z≡z)
$L\vdash_{AX}^{GR}$ $\langle \{x+11 \equiv 1+a1, y \equiv (1+a)0, 100 \equiv z\}, id \rangle$
                                                (lazy resolution with 1+a1≡(1+a)0)
$L\vdash_{AX}^{GR}$ $\langle \{100 \equiv (1+1)0\}, \{1/x, 1/a, 100/z\} \rangle$
                                                (unification)
$L\vdash_{AX}^{GR}$ $\langle \{100 \equiv z0, (1+1)0 \equiv z'0, z \equiv z'\}, \{1/x, 1/a, 100/z\} \rangle$
                                                (lazy resolution with z0≡z'0 ⇐ z≡z')
$L\vdash_{AX}^{GR}$ $\langle \{10 \equiv 1+1\}, \{1/x, 1/a, 100/z\}[10/z, (1+1)/z'] \rangle$
                                                (unification)
$L\vdash_{AX}^{GR}$ $\langle \{10 \equiv z', 1+1 \equiv z, z \equiv z'\}, \{1/x, 1/a, 100/z\}[(1+1)/z'] \rangle$
                                                (lazy resolution with z'≡z ⇐ z≡z')
$L\vdash_{AX}^{GR}$ $\langle \{1+1 \equiv 10\}, \{1/x, 1/a, 100/z\}[(1+1)/z'][10/z', (1+1)/z] \rangle$
                                                (unification)
$L\vdash_{AX}^{GR}$ $\langle \{1+1 \equiv 1+1, 10 \equiv 10\}, \{1/x, 1/a, 100/z\}[(1+1)/z'] \rangle$
                                                (lazy resolution with 1+1≡10)
$L\vdash_{AX}^{GR}$ $\langle \emptyset, \{1/x, 1/a, 100/z\}[(1+1)/z'] \rangle$ (unification).

Hence $\{1/x, 1/a, 100/z\}[(1+1)/z'] = \{1/x, 1/a, 100/z, (1+1)/z'\}$ is an LGR-solution of x+11≡100. ∎

Lemma 5.5.2 *Soundness of lazy resolution w.r.t. deductive solutions*
Let γ be a goal. Every LR-solution of γ w.r.t. AX∪EAX is a deductive ⟨SIG,AX⟩-solution.

Proof. We proceed along the lines of the proof of Theorem 5.2.4.

Let $\langle \gamma, id \rangle$ $L\vdash^{GR}_{AX}$ $\langle \emptyset, f \rangle$. Then there are $\gamma_0, ..., \gamma_n, f_0, ..., f_{n-1}$ such that $\langle \gamma, id \rangle = \langle \gamma_0, f_0 \rangle$, for all $0 \leq i < n$, $\langle \gamma_i, f_0[f_1]...[f_{i-1}] \rangle$ expands to $\langle \gamma_{i+1}, f_0[f_1]...[f_i] \rangle$ by applying the Lazy Resolution or the Unification Rule, γ_n is empty and $f_0[f_1]...[f_{n-1}] = f$. We show the following condition:

(1)   For all $0 \leq i \leq n$ and $p \in \gamma_{n-i}$, $AX \cup EAX \vdash p[f_{n-i}]...[f_{n-1}]$.

(1) is proved by induction on i. If $i = 0$, the proof is complete because γ_n is empty. Let $i > 0$.

   Case 1. $\langle \gamma_{n-i}, f_0[f_1]...[f_{n-i-1}] \rangle$ expands to $\langle \gamma_{n-i+1}, f_0[f_1]...[f_{n-i}] \rangle$ by applying the Lazy Resolution Rule, i.e. there are a goal δ, an atom Pt and Pu$\Leftarrow\delta$ $\in$ AX$\cup$EAX such that $\gamma_{n-i} = \delta u\{Pt\}$, $\delta u\{t \equiv u\} \cup \delta = \gamma_{n-i+1}$ and $f_{n-i} = id$. By induction hypothesis,

(2)   for all $r \in \gamma_{n-i+1}$, $AX \cup EAX \vdash r[f_{n-i+1}]...[f_{n-1}]$.

Let $p' \in \gamma_{n-i}$. We have to show

(3) $AX \cup EAX \vdash p'[f_{n-i}]...[f_{n-1}]$.

   Case 1.1. $p' = Pt$. Since $\delta \subseteq \gamma_{n-i+1}$ and $f_{n-i} = id$, (2) implies

$$AX \cup EAX \vdash \delta[f_{n-i}][f_{n-i+1}]...[f_{n-1}].$$

Hence by the Cut Rule, (3) holds true.

   Case 1.2. $p' \in \delta$. Since $\delta \subseteq \gamma_{n-i+1}$ and $f_{n-i} = id$, (2) implies (3).

   Case 2. $\langle \gamma_{n-i}, f_0[f_1]...[f_{n-i-1}] \rangle$ expands to $\langle \gamma_{n-i+1}, f_0[f_1]...[f_{n-i}] \rangle$ by applying the Unification Rule, i.e. there are δ, t, u such that $\gamma_{n-i} = \delta u\{t \equiv u\}$, $t[f_{n-i}] = u[f_{n-i}]$ and $\delta[f_{n-i}] = \gamma_{n-i+1}$. By the induction hypothesis, (2) holds true. Let $p' \in \gamma_{n-i}$. We have to show (3).

   Case 2.1. $p' = (t \equiv u)$. Then we conclude (3) from $t[f_{n-i}] = u[f_{n-i}]$.

   Case 2.2. $p' \in \delta$. Since $\delta[f_{n-i}] = \gamma_{n-i+1}$, (2) implies (3).

This finishes the proof of (1). The case $i=n$ implies that $\gamma[f]$ is a $\langle SIG, AX \rangle$-theorem. ∎

Lemma 5.5.3 *Completeness of lazy resolution w.r.t. most general resolution*

   $\langle \gamma, id \rangle \vdash^{GR}_{AX} \langle \delta, f \rangle$ implies $\langle \gamma, id \rangle L\vdash^{GR}_{AX} \langle \delta, f \rangle$.

Proof. Let $\gamma u\{p\}$ be a goal, $q \Leftarrow \delta \in AX \cup EAX$ and g be a most general unifier of p and q. Then there are P, t, u such that $Pt = p$, $Pu = q$ and g unifies u and t. The resolution step from $\langle \gamma u\{p\}, id \rangle$ to $\langle (\gamma u \delta)[g], g \rangle$ can be simulated by an application of the Lazy Resolution Rule, namely

$$\langle \gamma \cup \{p\}, id \rangle \vdash_{AX}^{GR} \langle \gamma \cup \{t \equiv u\} \cup \vartheta, id \rangle,$$

followed by an application of the Unification Rule:

$$\langle \gamma \cup \{t \equiv u\} \cup \vartheta, id \rangle \vdash_{AX}^{GR} \langle (\gamma \cup \vartheta)[g], g \rangle. \blacksquare$$

Let us now decompose applications of the Unification Rule into elementary rule applications, namely resolution steps with OP-compatibility axioms (Splitting Rule), followed by the elimination of equations with an isolated variable on one side:

Splitting Rule Let γ be a goal and $\sigma t \equiv \sigma u$ be an equation. Then

$$\frac{\langle \gamma \cup \{\sigma t \equiv \sigma u\}, f \rangle}{\langle \gamma \cup \{t \equiv u\}, f \rangle}.$$

Absorption Rule Let γ be a goal and $x \in X$. Then

$$\frac{\langle \gamma \cup \{x \equiv x\}, f \rangle}{\langle \gamma, f \rangle}.$$

Expansion Rule Let γ be a goal and $x \equiv t$ be an equation such that $x \in$ X-var(t). Then

$$\frac{\langle \gamma \cup \{x \equiv t\}, f \rangle}{\langle \gamma[t/x], f[t/x] \rangle}$$

and

$$\frac{\langle \gamma \cup \{t \equiv x\}, f \rangle}{\langle \gamma[t/x], f[t/x] \rangle}.$$

Definition With regard to their inventors the above rules are called *Martelli-Montanari rules*. The inference relation induced by these rules and the Lazy Resolution rule is denoted by $LM\vdash_{AX}^{GR}$. If $\langle \gamma, id \rangle \ LM\vdash_{AX}^{GR} \langle \emptyset, f \rangle$, then f is called an *LMGR-solution* of γ (w.r.t. AX∪EAX). ∎

Lemma 5.5.4 *Soundness of LMGR-solutions w.r.t. deductive solutions*
Let γ be a goal. Every LMGR-solution of γ w.r.t. AX∪EAX is a deductive ⟨SIG,AX⟩-solution of γ.

Proof. We adopt the proof of Lemma 5.5.2. Case 2 (application of the Unification Rule) falls into four subcases:

Case 2.1. $\langle \gamma_{n-i}, f_0[f_1]...[f_{n-i-1}] \rangle$ expands to $\langle \gamma_{n-i+1}, f_0[f_1]...[f_{n-i}] \rangle$ by applying the Splitting Rule, i.e. there are a goal δ and an equation $\sigma t \equiv \sigma u$ such that $\gamma_{n-i} = \delta \cup \{\sigma t \equiv \sigma u\}$, $\gamma_{n-i+1} = \delta \cup \{t \equiv u\}$ and $f_{n-i} = id$. By the induction hypothesis,

(2) $\qquad$ for all $r \in \gamma_{n-i+1}$, $AX \cup EAX \vdash r[f_{n-i+1}]...[f_{n-1}]$.

Let $p' \in \gamma_{n-i}$. We have to show

(3) $\qquad\qquad AX \cup EAX \vdash p'[f_{n-i}]...[f_{n-1}]$.

Case 2.1.1. $p' = (\sigma t \equiv \sigma u)$. Since $t \equiv u \in \gamma_{n-i+1}$ and $f_{n-i} = id$, (2) implies (3).
Case 2.1.2. $p' \in \delta$. Since $\delta \subseteq \gamma_{n-i+1}$ and $f_{n-i} = id$, (2) implies (3).
Case 2.2. $\langle \gamma_{n-i}, f_0[f_1]...[f_{n-i-1}] \rangle$ expands to $\langle \gamma_{n-i+1}, f_0[f_1]...[f_{n-i}] \rangle$ by applying the Absorption Rule, i.e. there are a goal δ and an equation $t \equiv x$ such that $\gamma_{n-i} = \delta \cup \{x \equiv x\}$, $\gamma_{n-i+1} = \delta$ and $f_{n-i} = id$. By the induction hypothesis, (2) holds true. Let $p' \in \gamma_{n-i}$. We have to show (3).
Case 2.2.1. $p' = (x \equiv x)$. Then (3) holds true.
Case 2.2.2. $p' \in \delta$. Since $\delta = \gamma_{n-i+1}$ and $f_{n-i} = id$, (2) implies (3).
Case 2.3. $\langle \gamma_{n-i}, f_0[f_1]...[f_{n-i-1}] \rangle$ expands to $\langle \gamma_{n-i+1}, f_0[f_1]...[f_{n-i}] \rangle$ by applying the Expansion Rule, i.e. there are a goal δ and an equation $x \equiv t$ such that $x \notin var(t)$, w.l.o.g. $\gamma_{n-i} = \delta \cup \{x \equiv t\}$, $\gamma_{n-i+1} = \delta[t/x]$ and $f_{n-i} = (t/x)$. By the induction hypothesis, (2) holds true. Let $p' \in \gamma_{n-i}$. We have to show (3).
Case 2.3.1. $p' = (x \equiv t)$. Since $x \notin var(t)$, we have $x[f_{n-i}] = t[f_{n-i}]$. Thus (3) holds true.
Case 2.3.2. $p' \in \delta$. Since $\delta[f_{n-i}] = \gamma_{n-i+1}$, (2) implies (3). ∎

Lemma 5.5.5 *Completeness of LMGR-expansions w.r.t. lazy resolution*
$\langle \gamma, id \rangle \vdash^{GR}_{AX} \langle \delta, f \rangle$ implies $\langle \gamma, id \rangle LM\vdash^{GR}_{AX} \langle \delta, f \rangle$.

Proof. Let $\gamma \cup \{t \equiv u\}$ be a goal and g be a most general unifier of t and u. It is sufficient to show that the unification step from $\langle \gamma \cup \{t \equiv u\}, id \rangle$ to $\langle \gamma[g], g \rangle$ can be simulated by applications of lazy unification rules. We proceed by induction on $size(t) + size(u)$.

Case 1. t is a variable, say $t = x$, such that $x \notin var(u)$. Since g is most general, w.l.o.g. $g = \{u/x\}$. Hence by the Expansion Rule,

$$\langle \gamma \cup \{t \equiv u\}, id \rangle \; LM\vdash^{GR}_{AX} \; \langle \gamma[u/x], \{u/x\} \rangle = \langle \gamma[g], g \rangle.$$

Case 2. Both t and u are the same variable, say x. Since g is most general, w.l.o.g. $g = id$. Hence by the Absorption Rule,

$$\langle \gamma \cup \{t \equiv u\}, \text{id} \rangle \ \text{LM}|_{AX}^{GR} \ \langle \gamma, \text{id} \rangle = \langle \gamma[g], g \rangle.$$

Case 3. t is a variable that occurs in u, but u is not a variable. Then t and u are not unifiable, which contradicts our assumption that g unifies t and u.

Case 4. u is a variable. Then proceed analogously to cases 1 and 3.

Case 5. $t = \sigma t'$ and $u = \sigma u'$ for some σ, t', u'. Then by the Splitting Rule,

$$\langle \gamma \cup \{t \equiv u\}, \text{id} \rangle \ \text{LM}|_{AX}^{GR} \ \langle \gamma \cup \{t' \equiv u'\}, \text{id} \rangle.$$

Since g unifies t' and u', the induction hypothesis implies

$$\langle \gamma \cup \{t' \equiv u'\}, \text{id} \rangle \ \text{LM}|_{AX}^{GR} \ \langle \gamma[g], g \rangle.$$

Case 6. $t = \sigma t'$ and $u = \tau u'$ for some σ, τ, t', u' such that $\sigma \neq \tau$. Then t and u are not unifiable, which contradicts our assumption that g unifies t and u. ∎

The Expansion Rule eliminates an equation $x \equiv t$ only if x does not occur in t. If x occurs in t, then only the Lazy Resolution Rule can expand $x \equiv t$. When this rule is not applicable either, $x \equiv t$ is unsolvable. One may regard $x \equiv t$ as a representation of the infinite term $t^A = t[t[...t/x...]/x]$. From this point of view, an expansion of $\langle \gamma, \text{id} \rangle$ to $\langle \{x \equiv t\}, f \rangle$ indicates that the substitution $f[t^A/x]$ is a solution of γ. Therefore, the Martelli-Montanari rules do not only simulate the Unification Rule. They may also create *infinite* solutions, which the unification algorithm called by the Resolution Rule rejects, since the occur check fails (cf. Section 5.2).

Theorem 5.5.6 *Soundness and completeness of LMGR-solutions w.r.t. deductive solutions*

Let γ be a goal and f be a substitution such that $\text{var}(\gamma) \cup \text{dom}(f) \subseteq XG$. f is a deductive $\langle SIG, AX \rangle$-solution theorem iff $f = g[h]$ for some LMGR-solution g of γ w.r.t. $AX \cup EAX$ and some substitution h.

In particular, γ is a $\langle SIG, AX \rangle$-theorem iff id is an LMGR-solution of γ w.r.t. $AX \cup EAX$.

Proof. Theorem 5.2.4 and Lemmata 5.5.2-5.5.5. ∎

5.6 Bibliographic Notes

Resolution was introduced as a refutation procedure for inconsistent (Horn as well as non-Horn) clause sets (see Robinson [1], and Chang and Lee). The variant we employ here is called *SLD-resolution* (linear resolution with selection function for definite clauses; see Kowalski and Kuehner, and Apt and van Emden), *LUSH-resolution* (linear resolution with unrestricted selection function for Horn clauses; see Hill, and Robinson [2]) or *input resolution* (see Chang and Lee, Section 7.3). Our proof that resolution is sound (cf. Theorem 5.2.4) follows the lines of Apt and van Emden, Theorem 5.1, but avoids the detour via fixpoint semantics. Interpreters of the programming language Prolog use SLD- resolution with control components (see Clocksin and Mellish, and Sterling and Shapiro). Negation as Failure stems from Clark. Goguen [2] mentioned the connection between initial structures and the closed world assumption.

Paramodulation is due to Robinson and Wos whose completeness proof presumes the *functionally reflexive axioms,* that are all equations of the form $\sigma\langle x_1,...,x_n\rangle \equiv \sigma\langle x_1...,x_n\rangle$. Chang and Lee refined paramodulation to *hyperparamodulation,* which no longer applies to negated equations. Even hyperparamodulation demands functionally reflexive axioms to ensure completeness (cf. Chang and Lee, p. 173; see also Furbach et al.). When paramodulating upon a goal and a functionally reflexive axiom, say $\sigma\langle x_1,...,x_n\rangle \equiv \sigma\langle x_1...,x_n\rangle$, the goal either remains unchanged or one of its variables is instantiated by $\sigma\langle x_1,...,x_n\rangle$. We have seen in Section 5.3 (particularly in Example 5.3.3) that such instantiations are sometimes necessary to build up a prefix of the left- or right-hand side of an axiom to be applied subsequently. But instead of presuming functionally reflexive axioms we have generalized the paramodulation rule so as to capture exactly those applications of functionally reflexive axioms that guarantee the completeness of paramodulation. Theorem 5.3.4 disproves the *paramodulation conjecture* (cf. Bundy, p. 64) by showing that certain applications of functionally reflexive axioms cannot be omitted.

Plotkin and Kornfeld were early apologists for combining equational deduction with resolution. Jaffar et al. proved the soundness and completeness of a generalized resolution rule that unifies atoms *modulo* a separate set E of equational axioms. Furbach and Hölldobler obtained a similar result where the rôle of E is taken over by the equality interpretation in a fixed SIG-structure. Colmerauer implemented the Martelli-Montanari rules in Prolog II.

Chapter 6 The Relevance of Constructors

6.1 Introduction

Refinements of paramodulation (cf. Section 5.3) such as goal reduction (cf. Chapter 7) and narrowing (cf. Chapter 8) are complete only if certain requirements on <SIG,AX> are fulfilled, which, in turn, depend on the division of <SIG,AX> into a *base specification* <BSIG,BAX> and the rest of <SIG,AX>. The base signature BSIG contains all sorts, predicates and *sort-building* or *constructor* functions of SIG. Hence the remaining part of SIG consists of operation symbols called *non-constructor* or, with the name indicating their meaning, *destructor, inquiry, state-transition* or *value-returning* functions. Accordingly, BAX specifies the predicates, in particular the equality predicates, with the help of constructor functions. Non-base axioms must be conditional equations and should only be used to specify non-constructor functions.

This idea behind the base specification suggests that <SIG,AX> is *conservative* with respect to the base specification, i.e. that all ground base <SIG,AX>-theorems are already derivable from base axioms. In model-theoretic terms (cf. Sections 4.3 and 4.4), the restriction of I(SIG,AX) to BSIG is isomorphic to I(BSIG,BAX), i.e. the set of objects specified by <SIG,AX> is identified as the carrier of the initial base structure. Non-base axioms do not *confuse* this carrier. However, non-constructor functions may create new objects (terms) that are regarded as undefined *junk* (see Burstall and Goguen [2]). On the other hand, defined objects are all terms that have a *base representation*. This leads to the *partial inductive theory*, consisting of all atoms all base-representable ground instances of which are derivable from AX∪EAX (cf. Section 6.3). The outcome is the principle of *inductionless induction*: a goal γ is a partial inductive <SIG,AX>-theorem if <SIG,AX∪γ> is a conservative extension of <BSIG,BAX> (Theorem 6.3.2).

The following assumption summarizes syntactical notions related to the base specification. It applies to the whole rest of the book.

Base Assumption *BOP* is a subset of OP whose elements are called *base operations*. *BAX* is a subset of AX such that for all $q \Leftarrow \delta \in$ BAX the function symbols occurring in $q \Leftarrow \delta$ are base operations and, if q is an equation, say u≡u', then BAX (implicitly) includes u'≡u$\Leftarrow \delta$ as well. We say that *CE(BAX)*, the set of conditional equations of BAX, is *symmetric*.

BSIG = <S,BOP,PR> is called the *base signature*. <BSIG,BAX> is the *base specification*. Terms over BSIG, atoms over BSIG, BSIG-structures, clauses of

BAX, <BSIG,BAX>-theorems, etc. are called *base terms, base atoms, base structures, base axioms, base theorems,* etc.

BSIG is inhabited (and thus SIG is inhabited; cf. Section 4.1). The sets of non-base (or *new*) function symbols and axioms are denoted by *NOP* and *NAX*, respectively. NAX consists of conditional equations. Hence BAX includes all clauses of AX-CE(AX), i.e. all axioms that are not conditional equations. ∎

The symmetry of CE(BAX) is a technical requirement due to the refinements of paramodulation we are dealing with in Chapters 7-9: *goal reduction* and *narrowing* treat NAX as a set of *oriented* equations, while base equations remain applicable from both sides.

Definition <SIG,AX> is a *conservative extension* (of <BSIG,BAX>) if for all ground base atoms p

$$AX \cup EAX \vdash p \quad \text{implies} \quad BAX \cup EAX \vdash p. \blacksquare$$

For the purpose of proving that <SIG,AX> is a conservative extension it is often simpler to consider a subspecification of <BSIG,BAX> instead of the entire base specification:

Proposition 6.1.1 *Decomposition of the base specification*
Let $BOP' \subseteq BOP$ and $BAX' \subseteq BAX$ such that for all ground base terms t there is a ground term t' over BSIG' with $AX \cup EAX \vdash t \equiv t'$. If <SIG,AX> is a conservative extension of <BSIG',BAX'>, then <SIG,AX> is a conservative extension of <BSIG,BAX> as well. ∎

The base specification should not be confused with a specification of *visible sorts* (cf. Section 4.5). The former contains *all* sorts of SIG. Of course, one may divide <BSIG,BAX> into a *primitive specification* for the visible sorts and an extension that adds constructors, predicates and corresponding axioms for the non-visible sorts. The proof that <SIG,AX> is a conservative extension of the primitive specification should then proceed in two steps:

(1) <BSIG,BAX> is a conservative extension of the primitive specification.
(2) <SIG,AX> is a conservative extension of <BSIG,BAX>.

Methods to prove (2) are based upon Theorem 6.3.2 and Lemma 7.7.8. (1) is often trivial, at least if we can apply the following

Proposition 6.1.2 *Syntactical criterion for (1)*
Let <PSIG,PAX> be a subspecification of <BSIG,BAX>. <BSIG,BAX> is a conservative extension of <PSIG,PAX>, i.e. all ground <PSIG,BAX>-theorems are

<PSIG,PAX>-theorems, if
- for all operation symbols σ in BSIG-PSIG, sort(σ) is in BSIG-PSIG,
- for all Pt$\Leftarrow\delta \in$ BAX-PAX, P is in BSIG-PSIG.

Proof. First note that for all *equality* axioms Pt$\Leftarrow\delta$, which contain symbols of BSIG-PSIG, P is in BSIG-PSIG as well. This is obvious for reflexivity, symmetry, transitivity or PR-compatibility axioms. If Pt$\Leftarrow\delta$ is an OP-compatibility axiom, say $\sigma x \equiv \sigma y \Leftarrow x \equiv y$, then σ is in BSIG-PSIG. Hence by assumption, sort(σ) and thus P are in BSIG-PSIG as well.

Let γ be a ground base theorem over PSIG. By Theorem 5.2.4, there is a shortest resolving expansion $<d_1,...,d_n>$ of $<\gamma,id>$ to $<\emptyset,id>$ w.r.t. BAX∪EAX. We show by induction on n that γ is a <PSIG,PAX>-theorem.

If n = 1, then γ is empty and the proof is complete. Otherwise the Resolution Rule leads from $d_1 = <\gamma,id>$ to d_2, i.e. there are q$\Leftarrow\delta \in$ BAX∪EAX and δ,f such that $\gamma = \delta u\{q[f]\}$, $d_2 = <\delta u\delta[f],f>$ and f↾XG = id. By the induction hypothesis, δ is a <PSIG,PAX>-theorem. Hence it remains for us to show that q[f] is derivable from PAX∪EAX.

Since γ is a goal over PSIG, we have q = Pt for some predicate P in PSIG. Thus by assumption, q$\Leftarrow\delta \in$ PAX. Hence δ is a goal over PSIG. δ[f] is a goal over PSIG as well because, by assumption and a simple inductive argument, all terms t with sort(t) in PSIG are terms over PSIG. To sum up, δ[f] is a ground base theorem over PSIG, and thus by the induction hypothesis, a <PSIG,PAX>-theorem. Hence q[f] is is derivable from PAX∪EAX. ∎

Sample specifications where this proposition can be used are given in Sections 3.4, 3.7, 3.10, 3.11, 3.12, 3.14 and 3.15.

Definition A ground base term (sequence) u is a *base representation* of a term (sequence) t if t≡u is derivable from AX∪EAX. A ground base atom Pu is a base representation of an atom Pt if u is a base representation of t. t and Pt are called *base-representable*. <SIG,AX> is *sufficiently complete* if all ground terms are base-representable. ∎

Note that there may be base-representable, but non-ground, terms, e.g. a conditional function (cf. Section 4.8) leads to the term

$$\text{if true then 0 else y}$$

with base representation 0 if the equation

$$\text{if true then x else y} \equiv x$$

is derivable from AX∪EAX.

Sufficient completeness is sometimes included in the definition of a conservative extension (cf. Ehrig and Mahr, p. 152). Here we adopt the definition employed in mathematical logic (see Feferman). A useful criterion for sufficient completeness is given by

Proposition 6.1.3 Let A be a SIG-model of AX with initial representation function rep^A (cf. Section 4.4). If $rep^A(A)$ consists of base terms, then <SIG,AX> is sufficiently complete.

Proof. Let $t \in GT(SIG)$. By 4.4.5 (1), $nat \circ rep^A \circ eval^A = nat$. Thus the equation $t \equiv rep^A \circ eval^A(t)$ is derivable from $AX \cup EAX$. By assumption, $rep^A \circ eval^A(t)$ is a base term. Hence t has a base representation. ∎

6.2 Partial Semantics

Throughout this section let $A = I(SIG,AX)$ and let B be a BSIG-model of BAX with initial representation function rep^B. Remember that the latter is equivalent to the existence of an isomorphism between B and $I(BSIG,BAX)$ (cf. Theorems 4.4.3 and 4.4.5).

Definition Let *NBR* be the S-sorted set of all non-base-representable ground terms. An S-sorted function $eval : GT(BSIG) \cup NBR \to B \cup A$ is defined by

$$eval(t) = \begin{cases} eval^B(t) & \text{if } t \in GT(BSIG) \\ eval^A(t) & \text{if } t \in NBR. \end{cases}$$

The *initial SIG-extension of B*, denoted by $E(SIG,B)$, is given by
- $E(SIG,B)_s = \{eval(t) \mid t \in GT(BSIG)_s \cup NBR_s\}$ for all $s \in S$,

- $\sigma^{E(SIG,B)}(eval(t)) = \begin{cases} eval(u) & \text{if u is a base representation of } \sigma t \\ eval(\sigma t) & \text{otherwise} \end{cases}$

  for all $\sigma \in OP$,

- $p^{E(SIG,B)} = p^B \cup \{eval(t) \mid AX \cup EAX \vdash Pt, t \in (GT(BSIG) \cup NBR)^* - GT(BSIG)^*\}$
  for all $P \in PR$. ∎

Provided that this construction is well-defined it yields a SIG-structure whose base part coincides with B, i.e. for all $w \in S^*$, $s \in S$, $\sigma \in BOP_{ws}$ and $P \in PR_w$,

$$\sigma^{E(SIG,B)} \restriction B_w = \sigma^B \quad \text{and} \quad p^{E(SIG,B)} \cap B_w = p^B.$$

In accordance with regarding non-base-representable ground terms as undefined elements let us call E(SIG,B) the *partial semantics* of <SIG,AX>. It turns out that

(1) E(SIG,B) is a well-defined SIG-model of AX iff <SIG,AX> is a conservative extension (cf. Corollary 6.2.4),
(2) <SIG,AX> is a conservative extension iff E(SIG,B) and I(SIG,AX) are isomorphic SIG-structures (Corollary 6.2.5).

By (1), the conservative extension property of <SIG,AX> is the only guarantee that there is a SIG-model of AX which *preserves* the initial semantics of the *base* specification. By (2), this property is equivalent to the coincidence of the partial and the initial semantics of <SIG,AX>.

Lemma 6.2.1 Suppose that <SIG,AX> is a conservative extension. Then E(SIG,B) is well-defined. If in addition, <SIG,AX> is sufficiently complete, then E(SIG,B) = B.

Proof. Let $w \in S^*$ and $t,t' \in GT(BSIG)_w \cup NBR_w$ such that eval(t) = eval(t'). Since BAX and AX are initially correct w.r.t. B and A, respectively (cf. Lemma 4.4.1), Corollary 4.4.5 (2) implies that $t \equiv t'$ is derivable from AX∪EAX.

Let $s \in S$ and $\sigma \in OP_{ws}$. Then AX∪EAX $\vdash \sigma t \equiv \sigma t'$.

Case 1. σt and $\sigma t'$ have base representations, say u (u'). Then $u \equiv u'$ is derivable from AX∪EAX. Since <SIG,AX> is a conservative extension, $u \equiv u'$ is a base theorem. Thus by definition of E(SIG,B),

$$\sigma^{E(SIG,B)}(eval(t)) = eval^B(u) = eval^B(u') = \sigma^{E(SIG,B)}(eval(t')).$$

Case 2. Neither σt nor $\sigma t'$ has a base representation. Again, by definition of E(SIG,B),

$$\sigma^{E(SIG,B)}(eval(t)) = eval^A(\sigma t) = eval^A(\sigma t') = \sigma^{E(SIG,B)}(eval(t')).$$

Therefore, $\sigma^{E(SIG,B)}$ is well-defined.

Let $P \in PR$ and $t,t' \in (GT(BSIG) \cup NBR)^* - GT(BSIG)^*$ such that Pt is derivable from AX∪EAX. Since $t \equiv t'$ is derivable from AX∪EAX, Pt' is a <SIG,AX>-theorem as well, and we conclude that $P^{E(SIG,B)}$ is well-defined.

It is an immediate consequence of the definition of E(SIG,B) that it agrees with B if <SIG,AX> is sufficiently complete. ∎

The evaluation mapping of E(SIG,B) assigns to each base-representable (ground) term t the B-value of base representations of t, while non-base-representable terms are interpreted as in A:

Lemma 6.2.2 Let E(SIG,B) be well-defined. Then for all ground terms t,

$$\text{eval}^{E(SIG,B)}(t) = \begin{cases} \text{eval}(u) & \text{if u is a base representation of t} \\ \text{eval}(t) & \text{otherwise.} \end{cases}$$

Proof by induction on size(t):
Case 1. t is a constant.
Case 1.1. t has a base representation, say u. Then

$$\text{eval}^{E(SIG,B)}(t) = t^{E(SIG,B)} = \text{eval}(u).$$

Case 1.2. t is not base-representable. Then

$$\text{eval}^{E(SIG,B)}(t) = t^{E(SIG,B)} = \text{eval}(t).$$

Case 2. $t = \sigma\langle t_1,...,t_n\rangle$. W.l.o.g. there is $0 \le k \le n$ such that for all $1 \le j \le k$, t_j has a base representation, say u_j, and for all $k < j \le n$, t_j is not base-representable. By the induction hypothesis, for all $1 \le j \le k$,

$$\text{eval}^{E(SIG,B)}(t_j) = \text{eval}(u_j),$$

and for all $k < j \le n$

$$\text{eval}^{E(SIG,B)}(t_j) = \text{eval}(t_j),$$

Let $t' = \langle u_1,...,u_k,t_{k+1},...,t_n\rangle$. Hence

(1) $\quad \text{eval}^{E(SIG,B)}(t) = \sigma^{E(SIG,B)}(\text{eval}^{E(SIG,B)}(t_1),...,\text{eval}^{E(SIG,B)}(t_n))$
$= \sigma^{E(SIG,B)}(\text{eval}(t')).$

Case 2.1. t has a base representation, say u. Since $t \equiv \sigma t'$ is derivable from AX∪EAX, $\sigma t'$ has the base representation u as well. Thus by definition of E(SIG,B),

(2) $\quad\quad\quad\quad \sigma^{E(SIG,B)}(\text{eval}(t')) = \text{eval}(u).$

(1) and (2) imply $\text{eval}^{E(SIG,B)}(t) = \text{eval}(u)$.
Case 2.2. t is not base-representable. Since $t \equiv \sigma t'$ is derivable from AX∪EAX, $\sigma t'$ is not base-representable either. Again by definition of E(SIG,B),

(3) $\quad\sigma^{E(SIG,B)}(eval(t')) = eval^A(\sigma t') = eval^A(t)$.

(1) and (3) imply $eval^{E(SIG,B)}(t) = eval(t)$. ∎

A base-representable ground term t is evaluated in B even if t has non-base-representable subterms. For instance, given a conditional function as in Section 4.8 and t ∈ GT(BSIG), Lemma 6.2.2 implies

$$eval^{E(SIG,B)}(\text{if true then t else t'}) = eval^B(t)$$

for *all* ground terms t' provided that

(1) $\quad$ **if true then x else y ≡ x**

is derivable from AX∪EAX.

For a similar example, let <BSIG,BAX> = AGENT and <SIG,AX> = REC-AGENT (cf. Section 3.15). Whereas t' = (let x0 be (call x0)) is not base-representable, Lemma 6.2.2 implies

$$eval^{E(SIG,B)}(\text{head (evalAgent ε (write (val 0); t'))}) = eval^B(0)$$

because 0 is a base representation of (head (evalAgent ε (write (val 0); t'))). The crucial equation that corresponds to (1) in the first example is

(2) $\quad$ **head n&s ≡ n.**

By (1) and (2), one intends to interpret if-then-else and head as *non-strict* functions. (A strict interpretation would forbid non-base-representable arguments.) This is exactly what E(SIG,B) does.

Next we show that E(SIG,B) satisfies AX and has an initial representation function.

Theorem 6.2.3 *E(SIG,B) and I(SIG,AX) are isomorphic*

Suppose that <SIG,AX> is a conservative extension. Then E(SIG,B) satisfies AX. Moreover, E(SIG,B) has an initial representation function rep (cf. Section 4.4) that is defined by

$$rep(a) = \begin{cases} rep^B(a) & \text{if } a \in B \\ rep^A(a) & \text{otherwise} \end{cases}$$

where rep^A is an initial representation function for A. (Hence by Theorems 4.4.3 and 4.4.5, E(SIG,B) and I(SIG,AX) are isomorphic.)

Proof. Let $Pt \Leftarrow P_1t_1,...,P_nt_n \in AX$ and $b \in E(SIG,B)^X$ such that for all $1 \le i \le n$, $b*t_i \in P_i^{E(SIG,B)}$. Since $b = eval^{E(SIG,B)} \cdot f$ for some ground substitution f, Lemma 6.2.2 implies

(*) $\quad b*v = eval^{E(SIG,B)}(v[f]) = \begin{cases} eval(u) & \text{if } u \text{ is a base representation} \\ & \text{of } v[f] \\ eval(v[f]) & \text{otherwise} \end{cases}$

for all $v \in T(SIG)$.

Let $1 \le i \le n$ and $t_i = \langle u_1,...,u_m \rangle$. There is $0 \le k \le m$ such that w.l.o.g. for all $1 \le j \le k$, $u_j[f]$ has some base representation u_j', and for all $k<j \le n$, $u_j[f]$ is not base-representable. Let $t_i' = \langle u_1',...,u_k',u_{k+1}[f],...,u_n[f] \rangle$. Since $b*t_i \in P_i^{E(SIG,B)}$, (*) implies $eval(t_i') \in P_i^{E(SIG,B)}$.

If $eval(t_i') \in P_i^B$, we have $eval(t_i') = eval^B(t_i')$. Hence B satisfies $P_i t_i'$, and thus by Corollary 4.4.5 (2), $P_i t_i'$ is a base theorem.

Otherwise by definition of $P^{E(SIG,B)}$, $P_i t_i'$ is derivable from $AX \cup EAX$.

Hence in both cases, $AX \cup EAX \vdash P_i t_i'$. Hence $P_i t_i[f]$ is derivable as well because for all $k<j \le n$, $AX \cup EAX \vdash u_j[f] \equiv u_j'$.

Thus $\{P_1 t_1[f],...,P_n t_n[f]\}$ is a $\langle SIG,AX \rangle$-theorem, and we conclude that $Pt[f]$ is also a $\langle SIG,AX \rangle$-theorem. Let $t = \langle u_1,...,u_m \rangle$. There is $0 \le k \le m$ such that w.l.o.g. for all $1 \le j \le k$, $u_j[f]$ has some base representation u_j', and for all $k<j \le n$, $u_j[f]$ is not base-representable. Let $t' = \langle u_1',...,u_k',u_{k+1}[f],...,u_n[f] \rangle$. Since $Pt[f]$ is derivable from $AX \cup EAX$, Pt' is derivable as well because for all $k<j \le n$, $AX \cup EAX \vdash u_j[f] \equiv u_j'$.

If $k = n$, i.e. $t' \in GT(BSIG)^*$, the conservative extension property implies that Pt' is a base theorem. Hence B satisfies Pt' and thus $eval(t') = eval^B(t') \in P^B \subseteq P^{E(SIG,B)}$.

Otherwise by definition of $P^{E(SIG,B)}$, $eval(t') \in P^{E(SIG,B)}$.

Hence by (*), both cases imply $b*t \in P^{E(SIG,B)}$.

Therefore B satisfies $Pt \Leftarrow P_1 t_1,...,P_n t_n$.

It remains for us to show that rep is a coretraction of $eval^{E(SIG,B)}$ that satisfies the representation condition (cf. Section 4.4).

Let $a \in E(SIG,B)$. For the coretraction property, we consider two cases:

Case 1. $a \in B$. Then $rep^B(a) \in GT(BSIG)$ and by Lemma 6.2.2,

(1) $\quad eval^{E(SIG,B)} \cdot rep(a) = eval^{E(SIG,B)}(rep^B(a)) = eval^B(rep^B(a))$.

Since rep^B is a coretraction w.r.t. $eval^B$, (1) implies $eval^{E(SIG,B)} \cdot rep(a) = a$.

Case 2. $a \notin B$. Then $a = eval^A(t)$ for some non-base-representable ground term t. Since rep^A is an initial representation function for A, the equation $rep^A(eval^A(t)) \equiv t$ is derivable from $AX \cup EAX$ (cf. Corollary 4.4.5 (1)). Hence $rep^A(a)$ is not base-representable either. By Lemma 6.2.2,

(2) $\text{eval}^{E(SIG,B)} \cdot \text{rep}(a) = \text{eval}^{E(SIG,B)}(\text{rep}^A(a)) = \text{eval}^A(\text{rep}^A(a))$.

Since rep^A is a coretraction w.r.t. eval^A, (2) implies $\text{eval}^{E(SIG,B)} \cdot \text{rep}(a) = a$.

For the representation condition of rep, let $w \in S^*$, $s \in S$, $\sigma \in OP_{ws}$ and $a \in E(SIG,B)_w$. Of course, $a = \text{eval}(t)$ for some $t \in GT(BSIG)_w \cup UNBR_w$. Since rep^B and rep^A satisfy the representation condition, 4.4.5 (1) implies

(3) $AX \cup EAX \vdash \text{rep}(a) \equiv t$.

Case 1. σt has a base representation, say u. Then

$$\text{rep} \cdot \sigma^{E(SIG,B)}(a) = \text{rep}(\text{eval}(u)) = \text{rep}^B(\text{eval}^B(u)),$$

and thus by Corollary 4.4.5 (1),

$$AX \cup EAX \vdash \text{rep} \cdot \sigma^{E(SIG,B)}(a) \equiv u.$$

By (3),

$$AX \cup EAX \vdash \sigma \text{rep}(a) \equiv \sigma t.$$

Hence

$$AX \cup EAX \vdash \sigma \text{rep}(a) \equiv \text{rep} \cdot \sigma^{E(SIG,B)}(a).$$

Case 2. σt is not base-representable. Then

$$\text{rep} \cdot \sigma^{E(SIG,B)}(a) = \text{rep}(\text{eval}(\sigma t)) = \text{rep}^A(\text{eval}^A(\sigma t)),$$

and thus by Corollary 4.4.5 (1),

$$AX \cup EAX \vdash \text{rep} \cdot \sigma^{E(SIG,B)}(a) \equiv \sigma t.$$

By (3),

$$AX \cup EAX \vdash \sigma \text{rep}(a) \equiv \sigma t.$$

Hence

$$AX \cup EAX \vdash \sigma \text{rep}(a) \equiv \text{rep} \cdot \sigma^{E(SIG,B)}(a).$$

Let $P \in PR$ and $a \in P^{E(SIG,B)}$. Again, $a = \text{eval}(t)$ for some t. If $a \in P^B$, then $t \in GT(BSIG)^*$ and $\text{eval}(t) = \text{eval}^B(t)$. By Corollary 4.4.5 (2), $BAX \cup EAX \vdash Pt$. Otherwise by definition of $P^{E(SIG,B)}$, $AX \cup EAX \vdash Pt$. Hence in both cases, (3) implies $AX \cup EAX \vdash P\text{rep}(a)$. ∎

The conservative extension property can now be *characterized* by the existence of an isomorphism between $E(SIG,B)$ and $I(SIG,AX)$:

Corollary 6.2.4 <SIG,AX> is a conservative extension of the base specification iff E(SIG,B) is a SIG-model of AX.

Proof. The only-if part is given by Theorem 6.2.3. Conversely, let E(SIG,B) be a SIG-model of AX and let Pt be a ground base atom Pt that is derivable from AX∪EAX. By Theorem 4.2.2, Pt is valid in E(SIG,B), i.e. $eval^{E(SIG,B)}(t) \in p^{E(SIG,B)}$. Since t consists of base terms, Lemma 6.2.2 implies $eval^{E(SIG,B)}(t) = eval(t)$ and thus $eval(t) \in p^{E(SIG,B)}$. Since $t \in GT(BSIG)^*$, we obtain $eval^B(t) = eval(t) \in P^B$ and conclude from Corollary 4.4.5 (2) that Pt is a base theorem. ∎

Corollary 6.2.5 <SIG,AX> is a conservative extension of the base specification iff E(SIG,B) and I(SIG,AX) are isomorphic SIG-structures.

Proof. Again, the only-if part is given by Theorem 6.2.3. Conversely, let E(SIG,B) and I(SIG,AX) be isomorphic SIG-structures. By Theorem 4.3.2, I(SIG,AX) satisfies AX and thus by Theorems 4.4.3 and 4.4.4, E(SIG,B) satisfies AX as well. Hence Corollary 6.2.5 implies the if part. ∎

Proposition 6.2.6 *Inductive theory criterion using the initial representation function for B*

Suppose that <SIG,AX> is sufficiently complete (cf. Section 6.1). An atom p is an inductive <SIG,AX>-theorem iff for all $f \in rep^B(B)^X$, p[f] is derivable from AX∪EAX.

Proof. Let f be a ground substitution. Since <SIG,AX> is sufficiently complete, there is a ground base substitution g such that f≡g is a <SIG,AX>-theorem. By Corollary 4.4.5 (1), $rep^B \cdot eval^B \cdot g \equiv g$ is a <SIG,AX>-theorem as well. By assumption, $p[rep^B \cdot eval^B \cdot g]$ and thus p[f] are derivable from AX∪EAX. ∎

6.3 Inductionless Induction

Theorem 4.4.6 and Corollary 6.2.6 restrict the number of substitutions to be taken into account for inductive proofs. Nevertheless, we need appropriate induction hypotheses in order to manage infinitely many ground instances. The approach known as *inductionless induction* reduces inductive proofs to conservative extension proofs. It often presumes that <SIG,AX> is sufficiently complete. In order to avoid this assumption we adapt the inductive theory to partial semantics. Since we want to apply inductionless induction to non-atomic clauses, too, the appropriate notion reads as follows (see the remark that precedes Example 4.3.4).

Definition The *partial inductive theory of* ⟨SIG,AX⟩, *PITh(SIG,AX)*, consists of all clauses p⇐γ such that for all ground substitutions f with base-representable instance of p by f,

$$AX \cup EAX \vdash \gamma[f] \quad \text{implies} \quad AX \cup EAX \vdash p[f].$$

Elements and subsets of PITh(SIG,AX) are called *partial inductive ⟨SIG,AX⟩-theorems*. ∎

The following property ensures that expansions of base-representable ground goals always produce base-representable goals.

Definition A set C of clauses *preserves base-representability* if for all q⇐ϑ ∈ C and ground substitutions f such that C∪EAX ⊢ ϑ[f], ϑ[f] is base-representable if q[f] is base-representable. ∎

Example 6.3.1 Let ⟨BSIG,BAX⟩ = STORE and ⟨SIG,AX⟩ = ACCESS-FUN (cf. Section 3.4). Each term of the form ω[t] is not base-representable. Nevertheless, all axioms preserve base-representability. Take, for instance,

$$xm \neq xn \Leftarrow m \neq n.$$

If we substitute ω[t] into m or n, the instantiated premise is base-representable if the instantiated conclusion is base-representable. ∎

As a further example, note that all equality axioms preserve base-representability.

Under the assumption that ⟨SIG,AX⟩ is *partially complete* (see Broy et al., p.160) a clause q⇐ϑ can be forced to preserve base-representability. Suppose that there are $P⟨t_1,...,t_n⟩ \in \vartheta$ and $1 \leq i \leq n$ such that for all $1 \leq j < i$ and all ground substitutions f, $t_j[f]$ is base-representable, while for all $i \leq j \leq n$ and some ground substitution f, $t_j[f]$ is not base-representable, even if q[f] is base-representable. Then we extend ϑ by an atom (Def t_j) for each $i \leq j \leq n$ and demand that all ground terms t with AX∪EAX ⊢ (Def t) are base-representable. Consequently, for all ground substitutions f such that q[f] is base-representable, $\vartheta[f] \cup \{(Def\ t_j[f]) \mid i \leq j \leq n\}$ is base-representable as well or not derivable from AX∪EAX, i.e. the modified clause

$$q \Leftarrow \vartheta \cup \{(Def\ t_j) \mid i \leq j \leq n\}$$

preserves base-representability.

Theorem 6.3.2 *Inductionless Induction*

Let $p \Leftarrow \gamma$ be a clause.

(1) $p \Leftarrow \gamma$ is a partial inductive $\langle SIG,AX \rangle$-theorem if $\langle SIG,AX \cup \{p \Leftarrow \gamma\} \rangle$ is a conservative extension.

(2)   Suppose that $\langle SIG,AX \rangle$ is a conservative extension and $AX \cup \{p \Leftarrow \gamma\}$ preserves base-representability. $p \Leftarrow \gamma$ is a partial inductive $\langle SIG,AX \rangle$-theorem iff $\langle SIG,AX \cup \{p \Leftarrow \gamma\} \rangle$ is a conservative extension.

Proof. (1) Let $\langle SIG,AX \cup \{p \Leftarrow \gamma\} \rangle$ be a conservative extension, $p = Pt$ and f be a ground substitution such that $\gamma[f]$ is derivable from $AX \cup EAX$ and $t[f]$ has a base representation, say u. Then Pu is derivable from $AX \cup EAX \cup \{p \Leftarrow \gamma\}$. By assumption, we conclude that Pu is a base theorem. Therefore $AX \cup EAX \vdash p[f]$.

We conclude that $p \Leftarrow \gamma$ is a partial inductive $\langle SIG,AX \rangle$-theorem.

(2) By (1), it remains for us to show the only-if part. So let $p \Leftarrow \gamma \in PITh(SIG,AX)$ and Pt be a ground base atom that is derivable from $AX \cup EAX \cup \{p \Leftarrow \gamma\}$.

Suppose that Pt is derivable from $AX \cup EAX$. Since $\langle SIG,AX \rangle$ is a conservative extension, Pt is a base theorem, and we conclude that $\langle SIG,AX \cup \{p \Leftarrow \gamma\} \rangle$ is a conservative extension as well. Hence the proof is complete if Pt is derivable from $AX \cup EAX$ or, more generally, if for all ground goals δ that consist of base-representable atoms,

$$AX \cup EAX \cup \{p \Leftarrow \gamma\} \vdash \delta \quad \text{implies} \quad AX \cup EAX \vdash \delta.$$

So let δ be derivable from $AX \cup EAX \cup \{p \Leftarrow \gamma\}$. By Theorem 5.3.5, there is a shortest paramodulating expansion $\langle d_1,...,d_n \rangle$ of $\langle \delta, id \rangle$ to $\langle \emptyset, id \rangle$ w.r.t. $AX \cup \{p \Leftarrow \gamma\}$. We show by induction on n that δ is derivable from $AX \cup EAX$.

If $n = 1$, then δ is empty and the proof is complete. Otherwise one of the following two cases holds true:

Case 1. The Restricted Resolution Rule or the Unification Rule leads from $d_1 = \langle \delta, id \rangle$ to d_2, i.e. there are $q \Leftarrow \vartheta \in ((AX \cup \{p \Leftarrow \gamma\})-CE(AX \cup \{p \Leftarrow \gamma\})) \cup \{x \equiv x\}$, a ground goal φ and a ground substitution f such that $\delta = \varphi \cup \{q[f]\}$ and $d_2 = \langle \varphi \cup \vartheta[f], id \rangle$. Hence $\vartheta[f]$ is derivable from $AX \cup EAX \cup \{p \Leftarrow \gamma\}$. Since $q[f] \in \delta$, $q[f]$ and thus $\vartheta[f]$ are base-representable because $AX \cup \{p \Leftarrow \gamma\}$ preserves base-representability. Therefore $\varphi \cup \vartheta[f]$ is base-representable, and we conlude by the induction hypothesis that $\varphi \cup \vartheta[f]$ is derivable from $AX \cup EAX$. Hence $AX \cup EAX \vdash \delta$.

Case 2. The Paramodulation Rule leads from $d_1 = \langle \delta, id \rangle$ to d_2, i.e. there are a goal φ, $x \in single(\varphi)$, a ground substitution f and $u \equiv u' \Leftarrow \vartheta$ (or $u' \equiv u \Leftarrow \vartheta$) $\in AX \cup \{p \Leftarrow \gamma\}$ such that $\delta = \varphi[u[f]/x]$ and $d_2 = \langle \varphi[u'[f]/x] \cup \vartheta[f], id \rangle$.

As in case 1 we conclude that $\vartheta[f]$ is derivable from $AX \cup EAX$. Thus the base-representability of δ implies that $\varphi[u'[f]/x]$ is base-representable as well. Therefore $\varphi[u'[f]/x]u\vartheta[f]$ is base-representable, and we conclude by the induction hypothesis that $\varphi[u'[f]/x]u\vartheta[f]$ is derivable from AX∪EAX. Hence AX∪EAX ⊢ δ. ∎

6.4 Bibliographic Notes

The notion of sufficient completeness is due to Guttag. Criteria for the conservative extension property often include sufficient completeness (see, e.g. Consistency Theorem 3.5 in Padawitz [2]). Hence both properties were mostly treated together (see Goguen et al., Section 5.3.3). However, a specification formalism should not forbid *partial* function definitions.

Three approaches have been pursued to support the specification of partial functions. The first originates in recursive function theory and results in *fixpoint models* (see Lassez et al.): recursive function definitions are interpreted as limits of approximating total functions. So this approach is characterized by an order-theoretical treatment of partiality, while the second approach proceeds algebraically by employing notions of partial structures and partial homomorphisms (see Broy and Wirsing; Reichel).

The third concept stays within the framework of total functions. As the one we adopt here it refers to the partition of <SIG,AX> into a base part and an extension part and leads to *based* structures <B,A,h> consisting of a base model B, a model E of AX and a base homomorphism h from B to the base part of E (see Kreowski). The *undefined* elements are identified as the elements of E−h(B). In this chapter we have dealt with the case where B is isomorphic to the initial base structure, E is the initial SIG-extension of B (cf. Section 6.2) and h is the inclusion mapping inc from B to E. The *partial structure associated with* <B,E,inc> (see Kreowski), say P, is defined by

$$\sigma^P(\text{eval}(t)) = \begin{cases} \text{eval}(u) & \text{if t consists of base terms and u is a base representation of } \sigma t \\ \text{undefined} & \text{otherwise.} \end{cases}$$

(See Section 6.2 for the definition of eval.) Hence it represents *strict* partiality, while the partial structure derived from E(SIG,B), say P', is defined by

$$\sigma^{P'}(\text{eval}(t)) = \begin{cases} \text{eval}(u) & \text{if u is a base representation of } \sigma t \\ \text{undefined} & \text{otherwise} \end{cases}$$

and thus mirrors the specification with respect to definedness more closely than P. Furthermore, it is easy to see that <SIG,AX> is a conservative extension iff *there is* a based structure <B,I(SIG,AX),h> with injective h.

Corollary 6.2.4, moreover, provides a *construction*: <SIG,AX> is a conservative extension iff <B,E(SIG,B),inc> is a based structure.

Inductionless induction was invented by Musser, Goguen [1], and Huet and Hullot. Besides embedding the approach into Horn clause logic we have generalized it in several respects. First, instead of presuming sufficient completeness we are proving *partial* inductive theorems where validity is ensured only for base-representable instances. Secondly, base operations need not be *free*, i.e. there may be base axioms. Thirdly, Theorem 6.3.2 (2) states the general possibility of proving theorems by *stepwise* inductionless induction without referring to particular *termination* and *convergence* properties (cf. Chapter 9). For instance, Jouannaud and Kounalis presume such properties because they actually develop an *inductive completion procedure* (cf. Section 9.10), while, on the other hand, they get rid of Huet and Hullot's restriction to sufficiently complete specifications that only admit free constructors. On the whole, the assessment of an inductionless induction technique would be eased if its underlying idea were brought into a form like Theorem 6.3.2 and hence be separated from its implementation as an inductive completion procedure.

Chapter 7   Reduction

7.1 Introduction

In the previous chapter, we introduced the Base Assumption (cf. Section 6.1) that is fundamental for refinements of resolution and paramodulation such as *goal reduction* (handled in this chapter) and *narrowing* (treated in the next chapter). Both rules are specializations of the Paramodulation Rule (cf. Section 5.3). Goal reduction differs from paramodulation in the following respects.

First, goals are no longer instantiated before rules are applied. Consequently, goal reduction does not create solutions, but only serves as a *proof* rule.

Secondly, a term in a goal is rewritten only if it is a *left-hand* side instance of a conditional equation. Therefore the completeness of goal reduction can be guaranteed only if <SIG,AX> fulfils certain proof-theoretical requirements. To keep them as weak as possible we introduce goal reduction as a two-phased procedure. First, a goal is modified by *non-base* conditional equations (NAX) until an *irreducible* goal has been achieved, which, secondly, is subjected to the paramodulation calculus w.r.t. *base* axioms (BAX; cf. the Base Assumption given in Section 6.1).

A single goal reduction step takes a goal γ of the form $\delta[u[f]/x]$ and a NAX-axiom $u \equiv u' \Leftarrow \vartheta$ and transforms γ into the goal $\delta[u'[f]/x] \cup \vartheta[f]$. γ is *NAX-reducible* if a sequence of goal reduction steps leads from γ to a <SIG,BAX>-theorem. Of course, NAX-reducible goals are <SIG,AX>-theorems; but the converse, i.e. completeness of goal reduction w.r.t. deductive solutions, does not hold in general. To figure out sufficient conditions let us turn to the classical case of *equational* axioms and goals.

Given a set NAX of equations over SIG, the *term reduction relation* $\xrightarrow{NAX}$ is usually defined as the least reflexive, transitive and SIG-compatible relation on T(SIG) that includes all instances of NAX-equations. Given $t \xrightarrow{NAX} t'$, we say that t rewrites to t'. If NAX contains *conditional* equations, one has to remember the premises of all axiom instances that were applied to rewrite t to t'. This is the purpose of *conditional reductions* $t \xrightarrow{NAX} t' \Leftarrow \gamma$ that are defined inductively as follows:

- Let $u \equiv u' \Leftarrow \vartheta \in AX$, $t = v[u[f]/x]$ and $t' = v[u'[f]/x]$. Then $t \xrightarrow{NAX} t' \Leftarrow \vartheta[f]$.
- If $t \xrightarrow{NAX} t' \Leftarrow \gamma$ and $t' \xrightarrow{NAX} t'' \Leftarrow \gamma'$, then $t \xrightarrow{NAX} t'' \Leftarrow \gamma \cup \gamma'$.

Premises of conditional reductions are omitted only if they are NAX-reducible (see above): if $t\xrightarrow{NAX} t' \Leftarrow \gamma$ and γ is NAX-reducible or if $t = t'$, we write $t\xrightarrow{NAX} t'$ and call $t\xrightarrow{NAX} t'$ a *term reduction*.

Consequently, we are faced with three kinds of reduction: goal reduction, conditional reduction and term reduction, where the latter is defined in terms of the former.

In classical rewriting theory, one proves an equation $t \equiv t'$ by rewriting t and t' until both terms have been reduced to a common term v:

<SIG,AX> is called *Church-Rosser* if all <SIG,AX>-theorems are provable in this way. To extend this notion from the equational case to Horn clause logic, we rephrase the Church-Rosser property by saying that goal reduction is complete, i.e. *all <SIG,AX>-theorems are NAX-reducible*. Let us see how this notion agrees with the one used in equational rewriting theory.

An equation $t \equiv t'$ is NAX-reducible if, by definition, a sequence of goal reduction steps transforms $t \equiv t'$ into a <SIG,BAX>-theorem, say δ. In the classical case, NAX consists of unconditional equations and BAX has neither conditional nor unconditional equations. Hence δ is an equation, say $v \equiv v'$, and the goal reduction from $t \equiv t'$ to $v \equiv v'$ corresponds to two term reductions $t\xrightarrow{NAX} v$ and $t'\xrightarrow{NAX} v'$. Moreover, since $v \equiv v'$ is a <SIG,BAX>-theorem, Theorem 5.3.5 implies that there is a paramodulating expansion of <{v≡v'},id> to <∅,id> w.r.t. BAX. Since CE(BAX) is empty, $v \equiv v'$ can be eliminated only by the Unification Rule, i.e. $v = v'$. So we come up with (1) (cf. Corollary 7.7.6).

Thus in the case of equational specifications, the traditional Church-Rosser notion agrees with ours. On the other hand, we allow more general cases such as
- base axioms that are arbitrary clauses and
- non-base axioms that are conditional equations where the premises are arbitrary goals.

Traditional rewriting theory has accomplished a number of extensions of the original approach outlined above and subsequently referred to as the *Classical Approach*. These include the *Congruence Class Approach* as well as *Normal Form Approaches*. The concepts differ not only with respect to the general notions discussed above. They also bring about a variety of *confluence* criteria for the Church-Rosser property. Sections 7.2-7.5 sketch these approaches from the equational point of view. Section 7.6 provides their combination and generalization to Horn clause logic. The precise definitions as well as fundamental properties are summarized in Section 7.7. Section 7.8 presents confluence conditions and a general Church-Rosser criterion that lays down the foundation for local criteria (cf. Chapter 9). *Strategy-controlled* and *basic* reduction reduce the set of admissible goal reduction steps, although – under certain conditions – completeness is preserved.

In Sections 7.2-7.5, AX is assumed to be a set of equations.

7.2 The Classical Approach

Suppose that BAX is empty. A $\langle SIG, AX \rangle$-theorem $t \equiv t'$ is proved by constructing a reduction triangle of the form

$$\begin{array}{ccc} t & & t' \\ & \searrow_{NAX} \quad (*) \quad \swarrow_{NAX} & \\ & u & \end{array}$$

$\langle SIG, AX \rangle$ is called *Church-Rosser* if every $\langle SIG, AX \rangle$-theorem $t \equiv t'$ admits such a triangle.

A sufficient criterion for this Church-Rosser property is confluence: NAX is *confluent* if every branching

$$\begin{array}{c} \quad {}_{NAX}\nearrow u \\ t \\ \quad {}_{NAX}\searrow u' \end{array}$$

can be made *convergent,* i.e.

$$\begin{array}{c} u \searrow_{NAX} \\ \searrow t' \\ u' \nearrow^{NAX} \end{array}$$

for some t'.

Proposition 7.2.1 If NAX is confluent, then $\langle SIG, AX \rangle$ is Church-Rosser.

Proof. A $\langle SIG, AX \rangle$-theorem $t \equiv t'$ can be split into a sequence of reductions with alternating orientation, i.e.

$$t \xrightarrow{NAX} \xleftarrow{NAX} \cdots \xrightarrow{NAX} \xleftarrow{NAX} t'.$$

The result follows by induction on the length of this sequence.

Case 1. $t = t'$. Then the proof is complete.

Case 2. $t \neq t'$. Then there is a term t" such that $t'' \equiv t'$ is a $\langle SIG, AX \rangle$-theorem and either $t \xrightarrow{NAX} t''$ or $t \xleftarrow{NAX} t''$. The induction hypothesis yields a term u' with

$$\begin{array}{c} t'' \qquad\qquad t' \\ {}_{NAX}\searrow\quad\swarrow_{NAX} \\ u', \end{array}$$

and confluence of NAX implies

$$\begin{array}{c} t \qquad\qquad u' \\ {}_{NAX}\searrow\quad\swarrow_{NAX} \\ u \end{array}$$

for some u. ∎

There are two ways to *localize* the confluence property. The first is based on *Newman's Lemma* (cf. Huet [1], Lemma 2.4) and the *Superposition Theorem* (cf. Knuth and Bendix, Theorem 2.5), which reduces confluence to the convergence of *critical pairs* by employing Noetherian induction w.r.t. $\xrightarrow[NAX]{}$ (cf. Section 2.1). Hence this approach requires $\xrightarrow[NAX]{}$ to be a Noetherian relation.

The second way to localize confluence stems from the *Rule Schemata Theorem* (see Rosen, Theorem 6.5; O'Donnell [1], Theorem 17; or Raoult and Vuillemin, Proposition 10). Here $\xrightarrow[NAX]{}$ need not be Noetherian, but confluence is replaced by *strong confluence*, which almost forbids critical pairs entirely. Getting rid of the Noetherian property might be necessary when we are dealing with the specification of partial recursive functions such as language interpreters (cf. Section 3.15).

7.3 The Congruence Class Approach

Here BAX may be non-empty. The reduction relation $\xrightarrow[NAX]{}$ is replaced by the transitive closure of $\sim\!\xrightarrow[NAX]{} = (\xrightarrow[BAX]{} \circ \xrightarrow[NAX]{} - \xrightarrow[BAX]{})$, i.e. a reduction $t \sim\!\xrightarrow[NAX]{} t'$ consists of applications of BAX-equations, followed by at least one application of a NAX-equation. Thus a reduction step $t \sim\!\xrightarrow[NAX]{} t'$ can also be viewed as a non-empty NAX-step starting out from the *BAX-congruence class of t*.

In order to obtain a tractable confluence condition, $\sim\!\xrightarrow[NAX]{}$ is confined to a subrelation, denoted by $\xrightarrow[\sim NAX]{+}$, whose exact definition will be given in Section 7.7. For the moment it is only important to get an impression of properties of $\xrightarrow[\sim NAX]{+}$ that ensure the confluence of AX (defined analogously to the confluence of NAX; cf. Section 7.2). The reflexive closure of $\xrightarrow[\sim NAX]{+}$ is denoted by $\xrightarrow[\sim NAX]{}$.

$\xrightarrow[\sim NAX]{}$ *commutes with BAX* if for all terms t,u,u'

for some t'.

$\Rightarrow_{NAX}$ is *NAX-compatible* if for all terms t,u,u'

for some t'.

Proposition 7.3.1 If $\sim_{NAX}$ is Noetherian and $\Rightarrow_{NAX}$ is a NAX-compatible subrelation of $\sim_{NAX}$ that includes $\rightarrow_{NAX}$ and commutes with BAX, then AX is confluent.

Proof. Let

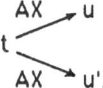

By Noetherian induction on t w.r.t. $\sim_{NAX}$ (cf. Section 2.1) we show

$$u \xleftarrow{AX} \atop u' \xrightarrow{AX} t'. \qquad (1)$$

for some t'.

Case 1. $t\underset{BAX}{\rightarrow}u$ or $t\underset{BAX}{\rightarrow}u'$. Then by symmetry of BAX, (1) follows from $u\underset{BAX}{\rightarrow}t\underset{AX}{\rightarrow}u'$ or $u'\underset{BAX}{\rightarrow}t\underset{AX}{\rightarrow}u$, respectively.

Case 2. $t\underset{AX}{\rightarrow}u$ and $t\underset{AX}{\rightarrow}u'$ contain applications of equations from NAX. Then there are terms v,v',w,w' such that

$$t \begin{array}{c} \xrightarrow{BAX} v \xrightarrow{NAX} w \xrightarrow{AX} u \\ \xrightarrow{BAX} v' \xrightarrow{NAX} w' \xrightarrow{AX} u'. \end{array}$$

Since $\Rightarrow_{NAX}$ includes $\rightarrow_{NAX}$ and commutes with BAX, we obtain a term v" with $v'\Rightarrow_{NAX} v''\underset{BAX}{\rightarrow} w$. Since $\Rightarrow_{NAX}$ is NAX-compatible, there is a term u" such that

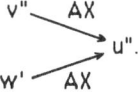

Since v" and w' are smaller than t w.r.t. $\sim_{NAX}$, the induction hypothesis

implies

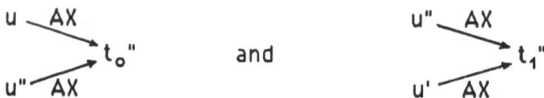

for some $t_0", t_1"$. Also $u"$ is smaller than t w.r.t. $\sim_{\overline{NAX}}$. Thus again by the induction hypothesis,

$$u \xrightarrow{\overline{AX}} t_0" \xrightarrow{AX} t'$$
$$u' \xrightarrow{\overline{AX}} t_1" \xrightarrow{AX}$$

for some t', and the proof is complete. ∎

The Noetherian property of $\sim_{\overline{NAX}}$ (presumed by Proposition 7.3.1) can be reduced to the Noetherian property of $\Rightarrow_{\overline{NAX}}$:

Proposition 7.3.2 (Jouannaud and Muñoz, Theorem 12) If $\Rightarrow_{\overline{NAX}}$ is a Noetherian subrelation of $\sim_{\overline{NAX}}$ that contains $\overline{NAX}$ and commutes with BAX, then $\sim_{\overline{NAX}}$ is Noetherian as well.

Proof. Let $t_0 \sim_{\overline{NAX}} t_1 \sim_{\overline{NAX}} t_2 \sim_{\overline{NAX}}$ ... By Noetherian induction on t_0 w.r.t. $\Rightarrow_{\overline{NAX}}$ we show that such a sequence is finite. Indeed, if $t_0 \Rightarrow_{\overline{NAX}} t_1$, then by the induction hypothesis, the sequence $t_1 \sim_{\overline{NAX}} t_2 \sim_{\overline{NAX}}$ ... is finite. Otherwise there is a term u such that $t_0 \overline{BAX} u \Rightarrow_{\overline{NAX}} t_1$. Since BAX is symmetric (cf. Section 6.1) and $\Rightarrow_{\overline{NAX}}$ commutes with BAX, we have $t_0 \Rightarrow_{\overline{NAX}} v \overline{BAX} t_1$ for some v. $v \overline{BAX} t_1 \sim_{\overline{NAX}} t_2$ implies $v \sim_{\overline{NAX}} t_2$. By the induction hypothesis, the sequence $v \sim_{\overline{NAX}} t_2 \sim_{\overline{NAX}} t_3 \sim_{\overline{NAX}}$ ... is finite.

Therefore, each sequence $t_0 \sim_{\overline{NAX}} t_1 \sim_{\overline{NAX}} t_2 \sim_{\overline{NAX}}$ ... is finite. ∎

Jouannaud and Kirchner have invented *BAX-coherence* and generalized the reduction $u \overline{BAX} t'$ in the definition of BAX-commutativity (see above) to a diagram of the form

$$u \Rightarrow_{\overline{NAX}} u"$$
$$\downarrow BAX$$
$$t' \Rightarrow_{\overline{NAX}} t".$$

But at the same time they have restricted the reduction $u' \Rightarrow_{\overline{NAX}} t'$ in that definition to $u' \Rightarrow_{\overline{NAX}}^+ t'$. Thus BAX-coherence is neither weaker nor stronger; it is incomparable with BAX-commutativity. In particular, it does not allow that u' and t' be equal.

When transferring the Congruence Class Approach to conditional equations we carry over BAX-commutativity and not BAX-coherence because it is simpler *and* valid under weak assumptions (cf. Lemma 9.7.1).

Roughly speaking, $\xrightarrow{\ne NAX}{}^+$ replaces a term that is *BAX-equivalent* to a left-hand side instance of a NAX-equation by its corresponding right-hand side instance. Given a decision procedure for BAX-equivalence, the set of $\xrightarrow{\ne NAX}$-redices is decidable as well. This does not apply to $\sim_{\overline{NAX}}$-redices! For a survey of such procedures, see Bürckert et al.

Huet [1], Theorem 3.3, returns from $\xrightarrow{\ne NAX}$ to $\xrightarrow{\overline{NAX}}$ by shifting all BAX-equivalences in $\xrightarrow{\ne NAX}$-reductions to the right. This idea leads us to the remaining two reduction approaches.

7.4 The Normal Form Approach

Again, we allow base equations. The Church-Rosser property defined in Section 7.2 is generalized as follows. A theorem t≡t' is provable by constructing a reduction triangle

$$
\begin{array}{ccc}
t & & t' \\
\text{NAX} \searrow (**) \swarrow \text{NAX} \\
& u \equiv u' &
\end{array}
$$

where u≡u' is an arbitrary <SIG,BAX>-theorem, while (*) demands identical terms u and u'. On the other hand, in the latter case it is easier to decide the equality of two terms than to show that the equation between them is derivable from BAX∪EAX. A reasonable restriction is to consider only *irreducible* terms u, i.e. for all terms v, $u \xrightarrow{\overline{NAX}} v$ implies u = v. So we suggest the following definition.

<SIG,AX> is *NAX-Church-Rosser* if every <SIG,AX>-theorem t≡t' admits a reduction triangle of the form (**) where u≡u' is a <SIG,BAX>-theorem with irreducible terms u and u'.

Besides confluence of NAX we need two further conditions to guarantee the NAX-Church-Rosser property:

NAX is *BAX-compatible* if for all terms t,u,u' with

$$
\begin{array}{c}
\text{NAX} \to u \\
t \\
\text{BAX} \to u'
\end{array}
$$

there are terms v,v' such that

$$
\begin{array}{c}
u \xrightarrow{\overline{NAX}} v \\
\downarrow \text{BAX} \\
u' \xrightarrow{\overline{NAX}} v'.
\end{array}
$$

NAX is *normalizing* if for each term t there is an irreducible term u with $t \xrightarrow{\overline{NAX}} u$.

Proposition 7.4.1 If NAX is confluent, BAX-compatible and normalizing, then <SIG,AX> is NAX-Church-Rosser.

Proof. A <SIG,AX>-theorem $t \equiv t'$ can be split into a sequence of reductions of the form

$$t \xrightarrow{NAX} \xleftarrow{NAX} \xrightarrow{BAX} \cdots \xrightarrow{NAX} \xleftarrow{NAX} \xrightarrow{BAX} t'.$$

The result follows by induction on the length of this sequence.

Case 1. $t = t'$. Then the proof is complete because NAX is normalizing.

Case 2. $t \neq t'$. Then there is a term t'' such that $t'' \equiv t'$ is a <SIG,AX>-theorem and either $t \xrightarrow{NAX} t''$ or $t \xleftarrow{NAX} t''$ or $t \xrightarrow{BAX} t''$. By the induction hypothesis,

$$\begin{array}{ccc} t'' & & t' \\ {\scriptstyle NAX}\searrow & & \swarrow{\scriptstyle NAX} \\ & u'' \equiv u' & \end{array}$$

for some <SIG,BAX>-theorem $u'' \equiv u'$.

Case 2.1. $t \xrightarrow{NAX} t''$. Then $t \xrightarrow{NAX} u''$, and we are done.

Case 2.2. $t \xleftarrow{NAX} t''$. Then by confluence of NAX, $t \xrightarrow{NAX} v$ and $u'' \xrightarrow{NAX} v$ for some v. Since v is irreducible, we have $u'' = v$. Hence $t \xrightarrow{NAX} u''$, and the proof is complete.

Case 2.3. $t \xrightarrow{BAX} t''$. Since BAX is symmetric (cf. Section 6.1) and NAX is BAX-compatible, there are terms v, v' such that

$$\begin{array}{c} t \xrightarrow{NAX} v \\ \downarrow BAX \\ u'' \xrightarrow{NAX} v'. \end{array}$$

Irreducibility of u'' implies $u'' = v'$. Since NAX is normalizing, there is an irreducible term u with $v' \xrightarrow{NAX} u$. BAX-compatibility of NAX leads to

$$\begin{array}{c} u \xrightarrow{NAX} v_0 \\ \downarrow BAX \\ v' \xrightarrow{NAX} v_1 \end{array}$$

for some v_0, v_1. Since u and v' are irreducible, we have $u = v_0$ and $v' = v_1$. Hence $u \xrightarrow{BAX} v' = u''$ and thus $u \equiv u'$ is a <SIG,BAX>-theorem. ∎

7.5 The Weak Normal Form Approach

Let us summarize. The Classical Approach rests either on the Noetherian property of $\xrightarrow{NAX}$ *and* confluence of NAX or on strong confluence. The

Congruence Class Approach is based upon the Noetherian reduction relation $\xrightarrow{\text{NAX}}$ and permits base equations. Confluence of NAX is replaced by compatibility conditions of $\xrightarrow{\text{NAX}}$ with BAX and NAX. The Normal Form Approach refers to confluence, BAX-compatibility and normalization of NAX, but does not depend on the Noetherian property of any reduction relation. However, the normalization property is not so far from the Noetherian property. In fact, the latter is often used as a criterion for the former. So let us see how to weaken the normalization property.

When tracing the proof of Proposition 7.4.1 one observes that only the terms of the equation $t \equiv t'$ to be proved need to be *normalizable*, i.e. $t \xrightarrow{\text{NAX}} v$ and $t' \xrightarrow{\text{NAX}} v'$ for some irreducible terms v, v'. Hence the Church-Rosser property is modified once more:

<SIG,AX> is *NAX-Church-Rosser* if each normalizable <SIG,AX>-theorem $t \equiv t'$ admits a reduction triangle of the form (∗∗) where $u \equiv u'$ is a <SIG,BAX>-theorem with irreducible terms u and u'.

This definition can be simplified.

Proposition 7.5.1 <SIG,AX> is NAX-Church-Rosser iff (1) for all normalizable <SIG,AX>-theorems $t \equiv t'$ with irreducible t' there is an irreducible term u such that $t \xrightarrow{\text{NAX}} u$ and $u \equiv t'$ is <SIG,BAX>-theorem.

Proof. Let (1) hold true and let $t \equiv t'$ be a normalizable <SIG,AX>-theorem. Then there is an irreducible term u' such that $t' \xrightarrow{\text{NAX}} u'$. Hence $t \equiv u'$ is a <SIG,AX>-theorem and thus by (1), there is an irreducible term u such that $t \xrightarrow{\text{NAX}} u$ and $u \equiv u'$ is a <SIG,BAX>-theorem. Therefore (∗∗) is satisfied, and we conclude that <SIG,AX> is NAX-Church-Rosser.

Conversely, let <SIG,AX> be NAX-Church-Rosser and let $t \equiv t'$ be a normalizable <SIG,AX>-theorem for some irreducible term t'. Then (∗∗) holds true with <SIG,BAX>-theorem $u \equiv u'$. Moreover, u' = t' because t' is irreducible. Hence $u \equiv t'$ is a <SIG,BAX>-theorem, and (1) holds true. ∎

Confluence and BAX-compatibility of NAX is not sufficient for the NAX-Church-Rosser property. We have to add the following requirement:

BAX respects normal forms if for all irreducible terms t, $t \xrightarrow{\text{BAX}} t'$ implies

for some irreducible t".

Then the analogue of Proposition 7.4.1 is

Proposition 7.5.2 If NAX is confluent and BAX-compatible and BAX respects normal forms, then ⟨SIG,AX⟩ is NAX-Church-Rosser.

Proof. By Proposition 7.5.1, it remains for us to show (1). So let $t \equiv t'$ be a ⟨SIG,AX⟩-theorem with irreducible term t'. We decompose $t \equiv t'$ into a sequence

$$t \xrightarrow{NAX} \xleftarrow{NAX} \xrightarrow{BAX} \ldots \xrightarrow{NAX} \xleftarrow{NAX} \xrightarrow{BAX} t'$$

and proceed by induction on the length of this sequence.

Case 1. $t = t'$. Then the proof is complete.

Case 2. $t \neq t'$. Then there is a term t'' such that $t'' \equiv t'$ is a ⟨SIG,AX⟩-theorem and either $t \xrightarrow{NAX} t''$ or $t \xleftarrow{NAX} t''$ or $t \xrightarrow{BAX} t''$. By the induction hypothesis, there is an irreducible term u'' such that $t'' \xrightarrow{NAX} u''$ and $u'' \equiv t'$ is a ⟨SIG,BAX⟩-theorem.

Case 2.1. $t \xrightarrow{NAX} t''$. Then $t \xrightarrow{NAX} u''$, and the proof is complete.

Case 2.2. $t \xleftarrow{NAX} t''$. Since NAX is confluent, $t \xrightarrow{NAX} u'$ and $u'' \xrightarrow{NAX} u'$ for some u'. Since u'' is irreducible, we have $u'' = u'$ and thus $t \xrightarrow{NAX} u''$.

Case 2.3. $t \xrightarrow{BAX} t''$. Since BAX is symmetric and NAX is BAX-compatible, there are terms u_0, u_1 such that

$$\begin{array}{c} u'' \xrightarrow{NAX} u_0 \\ \downarrow BAX \\ t \xrightarrow{NAX} u_1. \end{array}$$

Irreducibility of u'' implies $u'' = u_0$. Hence u_0 is irreducible. Since BAX respects normal forms,

$$\begin{array}{c} u_1 \searrow NAX \\   u' \\ u_0 \nearrow BAX \end{array}$$

for some irreducible u'. Hence $t \xrightarrow{NAX} u'$. The proof is complete because $u' \equiv u_0$, $u'' \equiv t'$ and thus $u' \equiv t'$ are ⟨SIG,BAX⟩-theorems. ∎

7.6 From Equations to Horn Clauses

To forbid base axioms would be too restrictive for a number of data type specifications (cf. Chapter 3). Hence the Classical Approach will not be generalized to Horn clauses. Instead, our concept of goal reduction will take into account the Congruence Class Approach *and* the Weak Normal Form Approach. More precisely, we take the schema of the latter and consider two instantiations: one with $\xrightarrow{NAX}$ and the other with $\xrightarrow{\sim NAX}$. Indeed, confluence conditions can be formulated so as to guarantee the Church-Rosser property with either $\xrightarrow{NAX}$ or $\xrightarrow{\sim NAX}$ being the underlying reduction relation (cf. Section 7.8). However, *criteria* for these confluence conditions will bring about essential differences between the two instantiations (cf. Chapter 9).

The generalization of $\xrightarrow[NAX]{}$ and $\xrightarrow[\sim NAX]{}$ to the three kinds of reduction outlined in Section 7.1 reads as follows. (More precise definitions will be given in the next section.)

Let AX' ∈ {NAX,~NAX}.

Conditional reduction
- Let $u \equiv u' \Leftarrow \vartheta \in NAX$, $t_o \in T(SIG)$ and $x \in var(t_o)$. Then
  $t_o[u[f]/x] \xrightarrow[NAX]{} t_o[u'[f]/x] \Leftarrow \vartheta[f]$.
- Let $u \equiv u' \Leftarrow \vartheta \in NAX$, $t_o, v \in T(SIG)$ and $x \in var(t_o)$. Then
  $BAX \cup EAX \vdash v \equiv u[f]$ implies $t_o[v/x] \xrightarrow[\sim NAX]{} t_o[u'[f]/x] \Leftarrow \vartheta[f]$.
- $t \xrightarrow[AX']{} t' \Leftarrow \gamma$ and $t' \xrightarrow[AX']{} t'' \Leftarrow \gamma'$ imply $t \xrightarrow[AX']{} t'' \Leftarrow \gamma \cup \gamma'$.

Goal reduction
- Let $u \equiv u' \Leftarrow \vartheta \in NAX$, $\delta \in Goal(SIG)$ and $x \in var(\delta)$. Then
  $\delta[u[f]/x] \xrightarrow[NAX]{RD} \delta[u'[f]/x] \cup \vartheta[f]$.
- Let $u \equiv u' \Leftarrow \vartheta \in NAX$, $\delta \in Goal(SIG)$, $x \in var(\delta)$ and $v \in T(SIG)$. Then
  $BAX \cup EAX \vdash v \equiv u[f]$ implies $\delta[v/x] \xrightarrow[\sim NAX]{RD} \delta[u'[f]/x] \cup \vartheta[f]$.
- $\gamma \xrightarrow[AX']{RD} \gamma'$ and $\gamma' \xrightarrow[AX']{RD} \gamma''$ imply $\gamma \xrightarrow[AX']{RD} \gamma''$.
- If $\gamma \xrightarrow[AX']{RD} \gamma'$ and γ' is an irreducible <SIG,BAX>-theorem, then γ is called *AX'-reducible*.

Term reduction
- If $t = t'$ or $t \xrightarrow[AX']{} t' \Leftarrow \gamma$ such that γ is AX'-reducible, then $t \xrightarrow[AX']{} t'$.

These definitions generalize the Weak Normal Form Approach. Indeed, an equation $t \equiv t'$ is AX'-reducible iff there is a reduction triangle of the form (∗∗) (with AX' instead of NAX) such that $u \equiv u'$ is an AX'-normalized <SIG,BAX>-theorem. Accordingly, we obtain two Church-Rosser notions (depending on whether AX' is NAX or ~NAX):

- <SIG,AX> is *AX'-Church-Rosser* if all normalizable <SIG,AX>-theorems are AX'-reducible.

Can proof arguments employed in Sections 7.2-7.5 be transferred to the Horn clause case? For instance, we have split an equational theorem $t \equiv t'$ into a sequence of reductions steps of the form

(∗) $\qquad t \xrightarrow[NAX]{} \xleftarrow[NAX]{} \xrightarrow[BAX]{} \ldots \xrightarrow[NAX]{} \xleftarrow[NAX]{} \xrightarrow[BAX]{} t'$.

On the other hand, we conclude from Theorem 5.3.5 that there is a paramodulating expansion of $\langle\{t \equiv t'\}, id\rangle$ to $\langle \emptyset, id \rangle$ w.r.t. AX. Indeed, the expansion induces a reduction sequence like (∗). However, if equations *with premises* are applied in the sequence, the reductions of (∗) can only be regarded as *conditional* ones. Of course, the premises are <SIG,AX>-theorems. But in order to eliminate them, i.e. to consider (∗) as a sequence of unconditional term reductions, all premises must be NAX-reducible. Actually, this condition can be weakened to normalizability (cf. Section 7.5), and induction on the length of (∗) is replaced by induction on the length of the paramodulating expansion. This proof method is used for the general Church-Rosser criterion Theorem 7.8.2.

7.7 Term and Goal Reduction

Following the presentation of the Horn clause, resolution and paramodulation calculi (cf. Sections 4.2, 5.2 and 5.3, respectively), conditional, goal and term reduction are expressed as inference rules. Conditional reductions are first defined for NAX (and BAX) and later for ~NAX, while goal and term reductions will be introduced for NAX and ~NAX at the same time.

Definition Let AX' ∈ {NAX,BAX}. The *conditional reduction calculus* (w.r.t. AX') consists of the following inference rules:

Single Reduction Rule Let t be a term, $x \in single(t)$ (cf. Section 2.2), $u \equiv u' \Leftarrow \delta \in AX'$ and f be a substitution. Then

$$t[u[f]/x] \xrightarrow{\overline{AX'}} t[u'[f]/x] \Leftarrow \delta[f].$$

Parallel Reduction Rule Let t be a term, $x \in single(t)^*$, $u = \langle u_1,...,u_n \rangle$, $u' = \langle u_1',...,u_n' \rangle$, $\delta = \delta_1 \cup ... \cup \delta_n$ and f be a substitution such that $u_1 \equiv u_1' \Leftarrow \delta_1,..., u_n \equiv u_n' \Leftarrow \delta_n \in AX'$. Then

$$t[u[f]/x] \xrightarrow{\overline{AX'}} t[u'[f]/x] \Leftarrow \delta[f].$$

Composition Rule Let t,t',t" be terms and γ,γ' be goals. Then

$$\frac{t \xrightarrow{\overline{AX'}} t' \Leftarrow \gamma, \ t' \xrightarrow{\overline{AX'}} t" \Leftarrow \gamma'}{t \xrightarrow{\overline{AX'}} t" \Leftarrow \gamma \cup \gamma'}.$$

Let t,t' be terms and let γ be a goal. If there is a derivation of $t \xrightarrow{\overline{AX'}} t' \Leftarrow \gamma$ via the conditional reduction calculus, then $t \xrightarrow{\overline{AX'}} t' \Leftarrow \gamma$ is called a *conditional reduction with premise* γ.

A sequence of conditional reductions $t_1 \xrightarrow{\overline{AX'}} t_1' \Leftarrow \gamma_1,..., t_n \xrightarrow{\overline{AX'}} t_n' \Leftarrow \gamma_n$ is abbreviated to $\langle t_1,...,t_n \rangle \xrightarrow{\overline{AX'}} \langle t_1',...,t_n' \rangle \Leftarrow \gamma_1 \cup ... \cup \gamma_n$.

Let f,g be two substitutions such that for some $x_1,\ldots,x_n \in X$ and all $1 \le i \le n$ there is a conditional reduction $fx_i \xrightarrow{AX} gx_i \Leftarrow \gamma_i$, while $x \in X-\{x_1,\ldots,x_n\}$ implies $fx = gx$. Then we write $f \xrightarrow{AX} g \Leftarrow \gamma_1 \cup \ldots \cup \gamma_n$.

We distinguish between two cost functions for conditional reductions: $|t \xrightarrow{AX} t' \Leftarrow \gamma|$ denotes the *simple length* of $t \xrightarrow{AX} t' \Leftarrow \gamma$, i.e. the least number of Single Reduction Rule applications needed to derive $t \xrightarrow{AX} t' \Leftarrow \gamma$. If t and t' are sequences of terms, say $t = \langle t_1,\ldots,t_n \rangle$ and $t' = \langle t_1',\ldots,t_n' \rangle$, then

$$|t \xrightarrow{AX} t' \Leftarrow \gamma| = \max\{|t_i \xrightarrow{AX} t_i' \Leftarrow \gamma| \mid 1 \le i \le n\}.$$

The *parallel length* of $t \xrightarrow{AX} t' \Leftarrow \gamma$, denoted by $\|t \xrightarrow{AX} t' \Leftarrow \gamma\|$, is defined in the same way except that the Single Reduction Rule is replaced by the Parallel Reduction Rule. ∎

Example 7.7.1 Let ⟨BSIG,BAX⟩ = NAT (cf. Section 3.2) and ⟨SIG,AX⟩ = SEQ-OF-NAT (cf. Section 3.7). A derivation of the conditional reduction

$$(\max 1\&(3\&(2\&\varepsilon))) \xrightarrow{NAX} 3 \Leftarrow \{1 \le 3, 2 < 3\}$$

is given by:

$(\max 1\&(3\&(2\&\varepsilon))) \xrightarrow{NAX} (\max 3\&(2\&\varepsilon)) \Leftarrow \{1 \le 3\}$
                                                                                (Single Reduction Rule)
$(\max (3\&(2\&\varepsilon))) \xrightarrow{NAX} (\max 3\&\varepsilon) \Leftarrow \{2 < 3\}$ (Single Reduction Rule)
$(\max 1\&(3\&(2\&\varepsilon))) \xrightarrow{NAX} (\max 3\&\varepsilon) \Leftarrow \{1 \le 3, 2 < 3\}$
                                                                                (Composition Rule)
$(\max 3\&\varepsilon) \xrightarrow{NAX} 3$ (Single Reduction Rule)
$(\max 1\&(3\&(2\&\varepsilon))) \xrightarrow{NAX} 3 \Leftarrow \{1 \le 3, 2 < 3\}$ (Composition Rule). ∎

Conditional reductions induce equational theorems provided that their premises are derivable.

Proposition 7.7.2 *Soundness of conditional reduction*
(1)   Let $AX' \in \{NAX, BAX\}$.
        If $t \xrightarrow{AX} t' \Leftarrow \gamma$ and $AX \cup EAX \vdash \gamma$, then $AX \cup EAX \vdash t \equiv t'$.
(2)   If $t \xrightarrow{BAX} t' \Leftarrow \gamma$ and $BAX \cup EAX \vdash \gamma$, then $BAX \cup EAX \vdash t \equiv t'$.

Proof. We show (1) by induction on $|t \xrightarrow{AX} t' \Leftarrow \gamma|$. (2) can be proved analogously.

Case 1. There are $u \equiv u' \Leftarrow \delta \in AX'$, a term v, $x \in var(v)$ and a substitution f such that $t = v[u[f]/x]$, $t' = v[u'[f]/x]$ and $\gamma = \delta[f]$. Using the Substitution Rule, $u[f] \equiv u'[f] \Leftarrow \delta[f]$ is derivable via the Horn Clause calculus (cf. Section 4.2). By the Cut Rule, $AX \cup EAX \vdash \delta[f]$ implies $AX \cup EAX \vdash u[f] \equiv u'[f]$. Thus by equality axioms, $AX \cup EAX \vdash t \equiv t'$.

Case 2. There are a term t" and goals δ,δ' such that $\delta \cup \delta' = \gamma$ and

$$|t \xrightarrow[AX']{} t'' \Leftarrow \delta|, |t'' \xrightarrow[AX']{} t' \Leftarrow \delta'| < |t \xrightarrow[AX']{} t' \Leftarrow \gamma|.$$

By the induction hypothesis, $t \equiv t''$ and $t'' \equiv t'$ are <SIG,AX>-theorems. Therefore $t \equiv t'$ is a <SIG,AX>-theorem as well. ∎

Definition The *conditional reduction calculus w.r.t. ~NAX* consists of the Composition Rule given above with ~NAX instead of AX' and corresponding reduction rules:

Single Reduction Rule Let t be a term, $x \in single(t)$, $u \equiv u' \Leftarrow \delta \in NAX$ and $v \xrightarrow[BAX]{} u[f] \Leftarrow \gamma$ be a conditional reduction with ~NAX-reduced γ (see below). Then

$$t[v/x] \xrightarrow[\sim NAX]{} t[u'[f]/x] \Leftarrow \delta[f].$$

Parallel Reduction Rule Let t be a term, $x \in single(t)^*$, $v = \langle v_1,...,v_n \rangle$, $u = \langle u_1,...,u_n \rangle$, $u' = \langle u_1',...,u_n' \rangle$, $\delta = \delta_1 \cup ... \cup \delta_n$ and for all $1 \leq i \leq n$, $v_i \xrightarrow[BAX]{} u_i[f] \Leftarrow \gamma_i$ be a conditional reduction with ~NAX-reduced γ_i, such that $u_1 \equiv u_1' \Leftarrow \delta_1,..., u_n \equiv u_n' \Leftarrow \delta_n \in NAX$. Then

$$t[v/x] \xrightarrow[\sim NAX]{} t[u'[f]/x] \Leftarrow \delta[f]. \blacksquare$$

An application of the Single Reduction Rule for ~NAX consists of a (possibly empty) BAX-step, followed by a NAX-step:

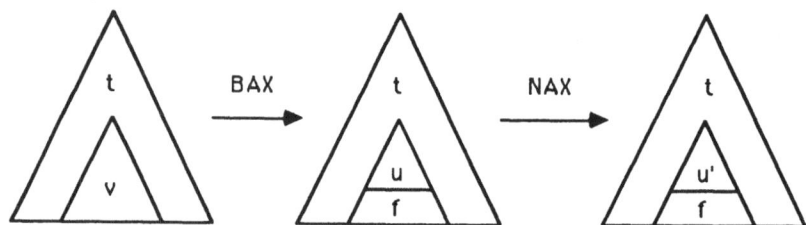

Of course, Proposition 7.7.2 (1) holds true for $\xrightarrow[\sim NAX]{}$ as well. If BAX does not contain conditional equations, then $\xrightarrow[\sim NAX]{}$ agrees with $\xrightarrow[NAX]{}$.

Definition Let $AX' \in \{NAX, \sim NAX\}$. A term t is *AX'-irreducible* or an *AX'-normal form* if there is no conditional reduction $t \xrightarrow[AX']{} t' \Leftarrow \gamma$. A substitution f is AX'-irreducible if for all $x \in X$, fx is AX'-irreducible. An atom Pt is AX'-irreducible if t is a sequence of AX'-normal forms. A goal γ is AX'-irreducible if all $p \in \gamma$ are AX'-irreducible. γ is *AX'-reduced* if, in addition, γ is a <SIG,BAX>-theorem. ∎

Note that a reduced goal may contain non-base function symbols and thus needs not be a base theorem.

Definition Let AX' ∈ {NAX,~NAX}. The *goal reduction calculus* (w.r.t. AX') consists of the following inference rules:

Success Rule Let γ be an AX'-reduced goal. Then

$$\frac{\gamma}{\emptyset}.$$

Single Reduction Rule Let δ be a goal, $x \in single(\delta)$, f be a substitution, $u \equiv u' \Leftarrow \vartheta \in$ NAX and
- either AX' = NAX and t = u[f]
- or AX' = ~NAX and $t \overline{_{BAX}} u[f] \Leftarrow \gamma$ for some ~NAX-reduced γ.

Then

$$\frac{\delta[t/x]}{\delta[u'[f]/x] \cup \vartheta[f]}.$$

Parallel Reduction Rule Let δ be a goal, $x \in single(\delta)^*$, $t = \langle t_1,...,t_n \rangle$, $u = \langle u_1,...,u_n \rangle$, $u' = \langle u_1',...,u_n' \rangle$, $\vartheta = \vartheta_1 \cup ... \cup \vartheta_n$ and f be a substitution such that $u_1 \equiv u_1' \Leftarrow \vartheta_1,...,u_n \equiv u_n' \Leftarrow \vartheta_n \in$ NAX and
- either AX' = NAX and t = u[f]
- or AX' = ~NAX and for all $1 \le i \le n$, $t_i \overline{_{BAX}} u_i[f] \Leftarrow \gamma_i$ for some ~NAX-reduced γ_i.

Then

$$\frac{\delta[t/x]}{\delta[u'[f]/x] \cup \vartheta[f]}.$$

Let γ,γ' be goals. A derivation of γ' from γ via the goal reduction calculus is called a *goal reduction* of γ to γ' (w.r.t. AX').

The corresponding inference relation is denoted by $\vdash^{RD}_{AX'}$ and called the AX'-*reduction relation*. If $\gamma \vdash^{RD}_{AX'} \emptyset$, then γ is AX'-*reducible*. ∎

Definition Let AX' ∈ {NAX,~NAX,} and t,t' be terms. The expression $t \overline{_{AX'}} t'$ is called a *term reduction* if t = t' or if there is a conditional reduction $t \overline{_{AX'}} t' \Leftarrow \gamma$ such that γ is AX'-reducible.

Let CAX ∈ {BAX,~BAX}. $t \overline{_{CAX}} t'$ is called a term reduction if t = t' or if there is a conditional reduction $t \overline{_{BAX}} t' \Leftarrow \gamma$ such that either CAX = BAX and γ is NAX-reduced or CAX = ~BAX and γ is ~NAX-reduced. ∎

As in the case of conditional reductions we distinguish between several cost functions of goal and term reductions.

Definition Let $AX' \in \{NAX, \sim NAX\}$. $|\gamma \models^{RD}_{AX'} \gamma'|$ ($\|\gamma \models^{RD}_{AX'} \gamma'\|$, respectively) denotes the least number of Single (Parallel) Reduction Rule applications needed to derive γ' from γ.

The *simple (parallel) length* of $t \twoheadrightarrow_{AX'} t'$, denoted by $|t \twoheadrightarrow_{AX'} t'|$ ($\|t \twoheadrightarrow_{AX'} t'\|$, respectively) is the minimum of sums

$$|t \twoheadrightarrow_{AX'} t' \Leftarrow \gamma| + |\gamma \models^{RD}_{AX'} \varnothing|, \quad \|t \twoheadrightarrow_{AX'} t' \Leftarrow \gamma\| + \|\gamma \models^{RD}_{AX'} \varnothing\|$$

over all conditional reductions $t \twoheadrightarrow_{AX'} t' \Leftarrow \gamma$.

$|t \twoheadrightarrow_{BAX'} t'|$ denotes the minimum of $|t \twoheadrightarrow_{BAX'} t' \Leftarrow \gamma|$ over all conditional reductions $t \twoheadrightarrow_{BAX'} t' \Leftarrow \gamma$ with $\sim$NAX-reduced γ. ∎

Lemma 7.7.3 *Soundness of goal reduction w.r.t. deductive theorems*
Let $AX' \in \{NAX, \sim NAX\}$.
(1) If $\gamma \models^{RD}_{AX'} \gamma'$ and $AX \cup EAX \vdash \gamma'$, then $AX \cup EAX \vdash \gamma$.
(2) AX'-reducible goals are $\langle SIG, AX \rangle$-theorems.

Proof. (2) follows from a special case of (1), namely $\gamma' = \varnothing$. We show (1) by induction on $|\gamma \models^{RD}_{AX'} \gamma'|$. If $\gamma = \gamma'$, the proof is complete. Otherwise there are $u \equiv u' \Leftarrow \delta \in NAX$, a goal δ, $x \in \text{single}(\delta)$, a substitution f and a term reduction $t \twoheadrightarrow_{BAX'} u[f]$ such that $\gamma = \delta[t/x]$ and $|\gamma \models^{RD}_{AX'} \gamma'| > |\varphi \models^{RD}_{AX'} \gamma'|$ where $\varphi = \delta[u'[f]/x] \cup \delta[f]$. By the induction hypothesis, $AX \cup EAX \vdash \varphi$. In particular, $AX \cup EAX \vdash \delta[f]$. Using the Substitution Rule, $u[f] \equiv u'[f] \Leftarrow \delta[f]$ is derivable via the Horn clause calculus (cf. Section 4.2). By the Cut Rule, $AX \cup EAX \vdash u[f] \equiv u'[f]$. Since $\delta[u'[f]/x]$ is a $\langle SIG, AX \rangle$-theorem, equality axioms imply that $\gamma = \delta[t/x]$ is a $\langle SIG, AX \rangle$-theorem as well. ∎

Lemma 7.7.4 *From term reduction to goal reduction*
Let $AX' \in \{NAX, \sim NAX\}$.
(1) If $t \twoheadrightarrow_{AX'} t' \Leftarrow \delta$, then for all goals γ and $x \in \text{var}(\gamma)$,

$$(*) \qquad |\gamma[t/x] \models^{RD}_{AX'} \gamma[t'/x] \cup \delta| \le |t \twoheadrightarrow_{AX'} t' \Leftarrow \delta|.$$

(2) If $t \twoheadrightarrow_{AX'} t'$ and $\gamma[t'/x] \models^{RD}_{AX'} \varnothing$, then $\gamma[t/x] \models^{RD}_{AX'} \varnothing$.

(3) If $t \twoheadrightarrow_{AX'} u$ und Pu is AX'-reduced, then $|\{Pt\} \models^{RD}_{AX'} \varnothing| \le |t \twoheadrightarrow_{AX'} u|$.

Proof. (1) Let $t \twoheadrightarrow_{AX'} t' \Leftarrow \delta$ and $x \in \text{var}(\gamma)$. We show (*) by induction on $|t \twoheadrightarrow_{AX'} t' \Leftarrow \delta|$. If $t \twoheadrightarrow_{AX'} t' \Leftarrow \delta$ is obtained by a single application of the Single (term) Reduction Rule, then the Single (goal) Reduction Rule implies (*).

Otherwise there are a term t" and goals φ,φ' such that $\varphi \cup \varphi' = \vartheta$ and

$$|t \xrightarrow{}_{\overline{AX'}} t" \Leftarrow \varphi| + |t" \xrightarrow{}_{\overline{AX'}} t' \Leftarrow \varphi'| = |t \xrightarrow{}_{\overline{AX'}} t' \Leftarrow \vartheta|.$$

By the induction hypothesis,

$$|\gamma[t/x] \vdash^{RD}_{AX'} \gamma[t"/x] \cup \varphi| \le |t \xrightarrow{}_{\overline{AX'}} t" \Leftarrow \varphi|$$

and

$$|\gamma[t"/x] \vdash^{RD}_{AX'} \gamma[t'/x] \cup \varphi'| \le |t" \xrightarrow{}_{\overline{AX'}} t' \Leftarrow \varphi'|.$$

Hence

$$|\gamma[t/x] \vdash^{RD}_{AX'} \gamma[t'/x] \cup \vartheta| \le |\gamma[t/x] \vdash^{RD}_{AX'} \gamma[t"/x] \cup \varphi| + |\gamma[t"/x] \vdash^{RD}_{AX'} \gamma[t'/x] \cup \varphi'|$$
$$\le |t \xrightarrow{}_{\overline{AX'}} t" \Leftarrow \varphi| + |t" \xrightarrow{}_{\overline{AX'}} t' \Leftarrow \varphi'|$$
$$= |t \xrightarrow{}_{\overline{AX'}} t' \Leftarrow \vartheta|.$$

(2) Let $t \xrightarrow{}_{\overline{AX'}} t'$ and $\gamma[t'/x]$ be AX'-reducible. Then there is a conditional reduction $t \xrightarrow{}_{\overline{AX'}} t' \Leftarrow \vartheta$ with AX'-reducible ϑ. Hence (1) implies

$$\gamma[t/x] \vdash^{RD}_{AX'} \gamma[t'/x] \cup \vartheta.$$

Since $\gamma[t'/x] \cup \vartheta$ is AX'-reducible, $\gamma[t/x]$ is AX'-reducible as well.

(3) Let $t \xrightarrow{}_{\overline{AX'}} u$ und Pu be AX'-reduced. If $t = u$, the proof is complete. Otherwise

$$|t \xrightarrow{}_{\overline{AX'}} u| = |t \xrightarrow{}_{\overline{AX'}} u \Leftarrow \vartheta| + |\vartheta \vdash^{RD}_{AX'} \emptyset|$$

for some ϑ. Since $t \xrightarrow{}_{\overline{AX'}} u \Leftarrow \vartheta$, Pu is AX'-reduced and ϑ is AX'-reducible, there is a goal reduction from {Pt} to the empty goal that passes the goal {Pu}$\cup \vartheta$. Thus by (1),

$$|\{Pt\} \vdash^{RD}_{AX'} \emptyset| \le |\{Pt\} \vdash^{RD}_{AX'} \{Pu\} \cup \vartheta| + |\vartheta \vdash^{RD}_{AX'} \emptyset|$$
$$\le |t \xrightarrow{}_{\overline{AX'}} u \Leftarrow \vartheta| + |\vartheta \vdash^{RD}_{AX'} \emptyset|$$
$$= |t \xrightarrow{}_{\overline{AX'}} u|. \blacksquare$$

Of course, Lemma 7.7.4 (1) can be shown analogously for the parallel length instead of the simple length.

Conversely, if γ is reducible, there are term reductions leading from γ to a reduced goal.

Lemma 7.7.5 *From goal reduction to term reduction*
Let AX' $\in$ {NAX,~NAX}. If the atom Pt is AX'-reducible, then there is a sequence u of terms such that $t \xrightarrow{}_{\overline{AX'}} u$, Pu is AX'-reduced,

(1) $$|t \xrightarrow{}_{\overline{AX'}} u| = |\{Pt\} \vdash^{RD}_{AX'} \emptyset|,$$

(2) $$\|t\underset{\overline{AX'}}{\to}u\| = \|(Pt) \vdash^{RD}_{\overline{AX'}} \emptyset\|.$$

Proof. We proceed by induction on $|(Pt) \vdash^{RD}_{\overline{AX'}} \emptyset|$. If Pt is AX'-reduced, we have
$$|t\underset{\overline{AX'}}{\to}t| = 0 = |(Pt) \vdash^{RD}_{\overline{AX'}} \emptyset|.$$

Hence (1) holds true for $u = t$.

Otherwise there are an atom Pv and a goal ϑ such that the Single (goal) Reduction Rule leads from {Pt} to {Pv}∪ϑ and

(3) $$|(Pt) \vdash^{RD}_{\overline{AX'}} \emptyset| = 1 + |(Pv) \vdash^{RD}_{\overline{AX'}} \emptyset| + |\vartheta \vdash^{RD}_{\overline{AX'}} \emptyset|.$$

Hence $t\underset{\overline{AX'}}{\to}v \Leftarrow \vartheta$ is a conditional reduction and thus

(4) $$|t\underset{\overline{AX'}}{\to}v| \leq 1 + |\vartheta \vdash^{RD}_{\overline{AX'}} \emptyset|.$$

By the induction hypothesis, there is an AX'-reduced atom Pu such that

(5) $$|v\underset{\overline{AX'}}{\to}u| = |(Pv) \vdash^{RD}_{\overline{AX'}} \emptyset|.$$

Therefore $t\underset{\overline{AX'}}{\to}u$. By Lemma 7.7.4 (3),

(6) $$|(Pt) \vdash^{RD}_{\overline{AX'}} \emptyset| \leq |t\underset{\overline{AX'}}{\to}u|.$$

(3)-(6) imply

$$\begin{aligned}|(Pt) \vdash^{RD}_{\overline{AX'}} \emptyset| &\leq |t\underset{\overline{AX'}}{\to}u| \\ &\leq |t\underset{\overline{AX'}}{\to}v| + |v\underset{\overline{AX'}}{\to}u| \\ &\leq 1 + |\vartheta \vdash^{RD}_{\overline{AX'}} \emptyset| + |(Pv) \vdash^{RD}_{\overline{AX'}} \emptyset| \\ &= |(Pt) \vdash^{RD}_{\overline{AX'}} \emptyset|.\end{aligned}$$

Therefore (1) holds true. (2) can be shown analogously. ∎

If there are no conditional base equations, an equation is reducible if and only if both sides have a common normal form.

Corollary 7.7.6 Let CE(BAX) be empty and $t \equiv t'$ be an equation. $t \equiv t'$ is NAX-reducible iff there is a NAX-irreducible term u such that

$$|(t \equiv t') \vdash^{RD}_{\overline{NAX}} \emptyset| = |t\underset{\overline{NAX}}{\to}u| + |t'\underset{\overline{NAX}}{\to}u|.$$

Proof. Let $t \equiv t'$ be NAX-reducible. By Lemma 7.7.5, there is a NAX-reduced equation u≡u' such that

$$|t \xrightarrow{NAX} u| + |t' \xrightarrow{NAX} u'| = |\langle t,t' \rangle \xrightarrow{NAX} \langle u,u' \rangle| = |(t≡t') \xrightarrow{RD}_{NAX} \emptyset|.$$

Since u≡u' is a <SIG,BAX>-theorem, Theorem 5.3.5 implies that there is a paramodulating expansion of <{u≡u'},id> to <∅,id> w.r.t. BAX. Since CE(BAX) is empty, u≡u' can be eliminated only by the Unification Rule, i.e. u = u'.

Conversely, let $t \xrightarrow{NAX} u$ and $t' \xrightarrow{NAX} u$ for some NAX-irreducible term u. Then u≡u is a NAX-reduced equation, and we conclude from Lemma 7.7.4 (2) that t≡t' is NAX-reducible. ∎

Example 7.7.7 Let <BSIG,BAX> = NAT (cf. Section 3.2) and <SIG,AX> = SEQ-OF-NAT (cf. Section 3.7). In Example 7.7.1 we derived the conditional reduction

$$(\max\ 1\&(3\&(2\&\varepsilon))) \xrightarrow{NAX} 3 \Leftarrow \{1 \le 3,\ 2 < 3\}.$$

Of course, its premise $\gamma = \{1\le 3, 2<3\}$ is NAX-irreducible. Moreover, γ is a <SIG,BAX>-theorem because we obtain a paramodulating expansion of <γ,id> to <∅,id>:

<γ, id>	
<{1 < 3, 2 < 3}, id>	(resolution with m ≤ n ⇐ m < n)
<{0| < 2|, 2 < 3}, id>	(paramodulation)
<{0 < 2, 2 < 3}, id>	(resolution with m| < n| ⇐ m < n)
<{0 < 1|, 2 < 3}, id>	(paramodulation)
<{2 < 3}, id>	(resolution with 0 < n|)
<{0|| < 1||}, id>	(paramodulation)
<{0| < 1|}, id>	(resolution with m| < n| ⇐ m < n)
<{0 < 1}, id>	(resolution with m| < n| ⇐ m < n)
<{0 < 0|}, id>	(paramodulation)
<∅, id>	(resolution with 0 < n|).

Hence γ is NAX-reduced and thus NAX-reducible. Therefore

(∗) $(\max\ 1\&(3\&(2\&\varepsilon))) \xrightarrow{NAX} 3$

is a term reduction. Moreover, Lemma 7.7.4 (2), (∗) and NAX-reducibility of γ imply that the goal

$$\{1 \le (\max\ 1\&(3\&(2\&\varepsilon))),\ 2 < 3\}$$

is NAX-reducible as well. ∎

Definition Let AX' ∈ {NAX,~NAX}. A goal γ is *AX'-normalizable* if for all Pt ∈ γ there is an AX'-irreducible atom Pu such that $t \xrightarrow{AX'} u$. AX' is *normalizing* if all goals are AX'-normalizable.

⟨SIG,AX⟩ is *(ground) AX'-Church-Rosser* if all (ground) AX'-normalizable ⟨SIG,AX⟩-theorems are AX'-reducible. ∎

Definition A set CE of conditional equations is *variable-preserving* if for all u≡u'⇐ϑ ∈ CE, var(u) = var(u'). ∎

Lemma 7.7.8 *Church-Rosser properties as conservative extension and inductive theory criteria*
(1) Let AX' ∈ {NAX,~NAX}. Suppose that ⟨SIG,AX⟩ is ground AX'-Church-Rosser, for all u≡u'⇐ϑ ∈ NAX, u is not a base term, and, if AX' = ~NAX, CE(BAX) is variable-preserving.
Then ⟨SIG,AX⟩ is a conservative extension (cf. Section 6.1).
(2) Let e be a conditional equation and let AX' be NAX∪{e} or ~(NAX∪{e}). Suppose that ⟨SIG,AX∪{e}⟩ is ground AX'-Church-Rosser, for all u≡u'⇐ϑ ∈ NAX∪{e}, u is not a base term, and, if AX' = ~(NAX∪{e}), CE(BAX) is variable-preserving.
Then e is a partial inductive ⟨SIG,AX⟩-theorem (cf. Section 6.3).

Proof. (1) Let γ be a ground ⟨BSIG,AX⟩-theorem. By assumption, γ is AX'-irreducible and thus AX'-normalizable. Hence γ is AX'-reducible because ⟨SIG,AX⟩ is ground AX'-Church-Rosser. Since γ is AX'-irreducible, γ is even AX'-reduced and thus a ⟨SIG,BAX⟩-theorem. By assumption, γ consists of base symbols. Therefore γ is a base theorem.
 (2) follows from (1) and Theorem 6.3.2 (1). ∎

The Base Assumption (cf. Section 6.1) banishes all predicates, which are not equality predicates, into the base specification. This forbids specifying non-equality predicates with the help of function symbols of the extension. But we always have the possibility to introduce a predicate as a Boolean function. Then it must be guaranteed that the equation **true≡false** does not come up as a ⟨SIG,AX⟩-theorem (cf. Section 4.8). In other words, ⟨SIG,AX⟩ must be a conservative extension of BOOL (cf. Section 3.1). By Lemma 7.7.8 (1), this would follow from the ground Church-Rosser property of ⟨SIG,AX⟩, provided that the *base* specification is a conservative extension of BOOL.

Hence, if ⟨SIG,AX⟩ is ground Church-Rosser, then the exclusion of non-equality predicates from the extension part of ⟨SIG,AX⟩ is actually no restriction.

7.8 Confluence Properties

Definition A pair of terms ⟨t,t'⟩ is *NAX-convergent* if

$$t \xrightarrow{NAX} u \xleftarrow{NAX} t'$$

for some u.

NAX is *(ground) confluent* if for all (ground) terms t,u,u' such that

$$u \xleftarrow{NAX} t \xrightarrow{NAX} u',$$

⟨u,u'⟩ is NAX-convergent.

Let AX' ∈ {NAX,~NAX} and CAX ∈ {BAX,~BAX}. A pair of terms ⟨t,t'⟩ is *AX'-convergent modulo CAX* if

$$\begin{array}{c} t \xrightarrow{AX'} u \\ \qquad \downarrow CAX \\ t' \xrightarrow{AX'} u' \end{array}$$

for some u,u'.

AX' is *(ground) confluent modulo CAX* if for all (ground) terms t,u,u' such that

$$u \xleftarrow{AX'} t \xrightarrow{AX'} u',$$

⟨u,u'⟩ is AX'-convergent modulo CAX.

AX' is *(ground) CAX-compatible* if for all (ground) terms t,u,u' and AX'-reduced goals γ such that t$\xrightarrow{AX'}$u and |t$\xrightarrow{CAX}$u'⇐γ| = 1, ⟨u,u'⟩ is AX'-convergent modulo CAX.

CAX *respects (ground) AX'-normal forms* if for all (ground) AX'-normal forms t and (ground) terms t', t$\xrightarrow{CAX}$t' implies

$$t' \xrightarrow{AX'} u \xleftarrow{CAX} t$$

for some AX'-normal form u. ∎

Criteria for confluence properties are presented in Chapter 9. The purpose of this section is to provide a general criterion (Theorem 7.8.2) stating that confluence conditions are sufficient for the two Church-Rosser properties defined at the end of the previous section. In some cases, confluence is accompanied by syntactical conditions like the ban on isolated variables (cf. Section 7.7) or the following requirements.

Definition Let CE be a set of conditional equations. CE satisfies the *Definition Principle* if for all $u \equiv u' \Leftarrow \delta \in$ CE, root(u) is neither a base operation nor a variable.

CE is *left-linear (linear)* if for all $u \equiv u' \Leftarrow \delta \in$ CE, u is linear (u and u' are linear, respectively; cf. Section 2.2).

CE *has isolated variables* if there is $u \equiv u' \Leftarrow \delta \in$ CE such that u or u' is a variable. ∎

The Definition Principle will be applied to NAX where, in any case, we assume that each conditional equation $u \equiv u' \Leftarrow \delta$ contributes to the specification of a non-constructor function and thus u is not a base term (cf. Lemma 7.7.8). The additional requirement of the Definition Principle is that one of these non-constructor functions is given by the leftmost symbol of u. Conversely, the axioms for a non-constructor function, say σ, cannot take into account the context in which σ may occur unless the context includes another non-constructor function or a further occurrence of σ as in the associativity axiom for +:

$$(k+m)+n \equiv k+(m+n).$$

The Definition Principle of NAX and confluence modulo CAX imply that goal reductions w.r.t. NAX do not affect base prefixes.

Lemma 7.8.1 *From goal reduction to term reduction*

Let either AX' = NAX and CAX = BAX or AX' = ~NAX and CAX = ~BAX. Suppose that AX' is (ground) confluent modulo CAX. Let γ be a base goal and let f be a (ground) substitution such that $\gamma[f]$ is AX'-normalizable and
- γ has no operation symbols
- or NAX satisfies the Definition Principle and, if AX' = ~NAX, then CE(BAX) has no isolated variables.

Then there is a substitution g such that $f \xrightarrow{}_{\overline{AX}} g$ and $\gamma[g]$ is AX'-irreducible. Moreover, if $\gamma[f]$ is AX'-reducible, then $\gamma[g]$ is AX'-reduced and thus

$$\|f \xrightarrow{}_{\overline{AX}} g\| = \|\gamma[f] \vdash^{RD}_{\overline{AX}} \emptyset\|.$$

Proof. For all $x \in var(\gamma)$, we introduce a set $occ(x,\gamma)$ of variables such that for each occurrence of x in γ there is a unique variable z in $occ(x,\gamma)$. The purpose is to obtain a *linear* base goal γ' with

$$\text{var}(\gamma') = \cup \{\text{occ}(x,\gamma) \mid x \in \text{var}(\gamma)\}$$

and

$$\gamma'[x/z \mid z \in \text{occ}(x,\gamma),\ x \in \text{var}(\gamma)] = \gamma.$$

Let

$$f' = [x/z \mid z \in \text{occ}(x,\gamma),\ x \in \text{var}(\gamma)][f].$$

Then $\gamma'[f'] = \gamma[f]$. Either since γ has no operation symbols or since NAX satisfies the Definition Principle and, if AX' = ~NAX, CE(BAX) has no isolated variables, goal reductions of $\gamma'[f']$ do not affect the function symbol occurrences of γ'. Since $\gamma[f]$ is AX'-normalizable, there is a substitution g' such that $f' \xrightarrow{\overline{AX'}} g'$ and $\gamma'[g']$ is AX'-irreducible.

Let $x \in \text{var}(\gamma)$ and $\text{occ}(x,\gamma) = \{z_1,...,z_n\}$. $fx = f'z_1 =...= f'z_n$ implies

$$f'z_i \begin{array}{c} \xrightarrow{AX'} g'z_i \\ \xrightarrow{AX'} g'z_{i+1} \end{array}$$

for all $1 \leq i < n$. Since AX' is confluent modulo CAX, there are t_i, u_i such that

$$\begin{array}{c} g'z_i \xrightarrow{\overline{AX'}} t_i \\ \downarrow \text{CAX} \\ g'z_{i+1} \xrightarrow{\overline{AX'}} u_i. \end{array}$$

Since $\gamma'[g']$ is AX'-reduced, $g'z_i$ is AX'-irreducible for all $1 \leq i \leq n$. Hence for all $1 \leq i < n$, $g'z_i = t_i$, $u_i = t_{i+1}$ and thus $g'z_i \overline{\text{CAX}} g'z_{i+1}$. We define a substitution g by

$$gx = \begin{cases} g'z & \text{if } x \in \text{var}(\gamma) \text{ and } z \text{ is some} \\ & \text{element of } \text{occ}(x,\gamma) \\ g'x & \text{otherwise.} \end{cases}$$

Since $\gamma'[g']$ is AX'-irreducible, $\gamma[g]$ is AX'-irreducible as well. Moreover,

$$\|f \xrightarrow{\overline{AX'}} g\| = \|f' \xrightarrow{\overline{AX'}} g'\|.$$

If $\gamma[f]$ is AX'-reducible, we proceed as above: Lemma 7.7.5 supplies a substitution g' such that $\|f' \xrightarrow{\overline{AX'}} g'\| = \|\gamma'[f'] \xrightarrow{\overline{AX'}}^{RD} \emptyset\|$ and $\gamma'[g']$ is AX'-reduced. With g defined as above we conclude that for all $x \in \text{var}(\gamma)$ and $z \in \text{occ}(x)$, $gx \overline{\text{CAX}} g'z$, gx and g'z are AX'-normal forms and $\gamma'[g']$ is AX'-reduced. Hence $\gamma[g]$ is AX'-reduced as well and

$$\|f \xrightarrow{\overline{AX'}} g\| = \|f' \xrightarrow{\overline{AX'}} g'\| = \|\gamma'[f'] \xrightarrow{\overline{AX'}}^{RD} \emptyset\| = \|\gamma[f] \xrightarrow{\overline{AX'}}^{RD} \emptyset\|. \blacksquare$$

Lemmata 7.7.5 and 7.8.1 allows us to infer term reductions from goal reductions. This step is essential for the derivation of Church-Rosser properties from confluence conditions.

Definition Let AX' ∈ {NAX,~NAX}. A set C of clauses *preserves (ground) AX'-normalizability* if for all q⇐ϑ ∈ C, terms t, x ∈ var(t) and (ground) substitutions f such that C∪EAX ⊢ ϑ[f], ϑ[f] is AX'-normalizable if
- q[f] is AX'-normalizable
- or q is an equation, say u≡u', and t[u/x][f] or t[u'/x][f] is AX'-normalizeable. ∎

Theorem 7.8.2 *General Church-Rosser criterion*
Let either AX' = NAX and CAX = BAX or AX' = ~NAX and CAX = ~BAX. Suppose that
- AX' is (ground) confluent modulo CAX,
- AX' is (ground) CAX-compatible,
- CAX respects (ground) AX'-normal forms,
- NAX satisfies the Definition Principle or for all Pu⇐ϑ ∈ BAX, ϑ does not contain function symbols and P is an equality predicate or u does not contain function symbols either,
- AX' = ~NAX implies that CE(BAX) has no isolated variables,
- AX preserves (ground) AX'-normalizability.

Then <SIG,AX> is (ground) AX'-Church-Rosser.

Proof. Let γ be an AX'-normalizable (ground) <SIG,AX>-theorem. By Theorem 5.3.5, there is a shortest paramodulating expansion <$d_1,...,d_n$> of <γ,id> to <$\varnothing$,id> w.r.t. AX. We show the AX'-reducibility of γ by induction on n. If n = 1, then γ is empty and the proof is complete. Otherwise one of the following two cases holds true.

Case 1. The Restricted Resolution Rule or the Unification Rule leads from d_1 = <γ,id> to d_2, i.e. there are q⇐ϑ ∈ (AX-CE(AX))∪{x≡x}, a (ground) goal φ and a (ground) substitution f such that γ = φ∪{q[f]} and d_2 = <φ∪ϑ[f],id>.

By Theorem 5.3.5, φ∪ϑ[f] is a <SIG,AX>-theorem. Since φ ⊆ γ, φ is AX'-normalizable. By assumption, ϑ[f] is AX'-normalizable. Hence by the induction hypothesis, φ∪ϑ[f] is AX'-reducible. It remains for us to show that q[f] is AX'-reducible as well. By the Base Assumption (cf. Section 6.1), q⇐ϑ ∈ BAX∪{x≡x}. Since ((q)∪ϑ)[f] is AX'-normalizable, Lemma 7.8.1 implies f $\overrightarrow{ax}$ f' for some f' such that ((q)∪ϑ)[f'] are AX'-irreducible.

As to ϑ, we have two subcases:

Case 1.1. ϑ is empty. Then q and thus q[f'] is a <SIG,BAX>-theorem. Moreover, all terms of q[f'] are AX'-irreducible. Hence q[f'] is AX'-reduced, and we conclude that q[f] is AX'-reducible.

Case 1.2. ϑ is not empty. Since ϑ is a base goal, Lemma 7.8.1 implies that there is a substitution g such that $f\xrightarrow[\overline{AX}]{}g$ and $\vartheta[g]$ is AX'-reduced. Since all terms in $\vartheta[f']$ and $\vartheta[g]$ are AX'-irreducible, confluence of AX' modulo CAX implies $f'x\xrightarrow[\overline{CAX}]{}gx$ for all $x \in var(\vartheta)$. Thus $\vartheta[f']$ is a $\langle SIG,BAX\rangle$-theorem. Since $q\Leftarrow\vartheta \in BAX$, $q[f']$ is a $\langle SIG,BAX\rangle$-theorem, too. But $q[f']$ is AX'-irreducible. Therefore $q[f']$ is AX'-reduced, and we conclude that $q[f]$ is AX'-reducible.

Case 2. The Paramodulation Rule leads from $d_1 = \langle\gamma,id\rangle$ to d_2, i.e. there are a (ground) goal φ, an atom p, $x \in single(p)$, a (ground) substitution f and $u\equiv u'\Leftarrow\vartheta$ or $u'\equiv u\Leftarrow\vartheta \in AX$ such that $\gamma = \varphi \cup \{p[u[f]/x]\}$ and

$$d_2 = \langle\varphi \cup \{p[u'[f]/x]\} \cup \vartheta[f], id\rangle.$$

By Theorem 5.3.5, φ, $p[u'[f]/x]$ and $\vartheta[f]$ are $\langle SIG,AX\rangle$-theorems. By assumption, $\vartheta[f]$ is AX'-normalizable. Hence by the induction hypothesis, $\varphi\cup\vartheta[f]$ is AX'-reducible. It remains for us to show that $p[u[f]/x]$ is AX'-reducible as well.

Let $p = P\langle t_1,...,t_n\rangle$. Then there is $1\le i\le n$ such that

$$p[u[f]/x] = P\langle t_1,...,t_i[u[f]/x],...,t_n\rangle$$

and

$$p[u'[f]/x] = P\langle t_1,...,t_i[u'[f]/x],...,t_n\rangle.$$

Since $p[u[f]/x]$ is AX'-normalizable, there is an AX'-normal form t with $t_i[u[f]/x]\xrightarrow[\overline{AX}]{}t$.

Case 2.1. $u\equiv u'\Leftarrow\vartheta \in NAX$. Then $u[f]\xrightarrow[\overline{NAX}]{}u'[f]$. Since AX' is confluent modulo CAX and t is AX'-irreducible, $t_i[u[f]/x]\xrightarrow[\overline{AX}]{}t$ implies $t_i[u'[f]/x]\xrightarrow[\overline{AX}]{}t'$ and $t\xrightarrow[\overline{CAX}]{}t'$ for some t'. Since CAX respects AX'-normal forms, there is an AX'-normal form t" such that $t'\xrightarrow[\overline{AX}]{}t"$. Therefore $t_i[u'[f]/x]$ and thus $p[u'[f]/x]$ are AX'-normalizable (via t'), and we conclude by induction hypothesis that $p[u'[f]/x]$ is AX'-reducible. Consequently, $p[u[f]/x]$ is AX'-reducible, too.

Case 2.2. $u'\equiv u\Leftarrow\vartheta \in NAX$. Then $u'[f]\xrightarrow[\overline{NAX}]{}u[f]$. Since $t_i[u[f]/x]\xrightarrow[\overline{AX}]{}t$, we obtain $t_i[u'[f]/x]\xrightarrow[\overline{AX}]{}t$. Therefore $p[u'[f]/x]$ is AX'-normalizable, and we conclude by the induction hypothesis that $p[u'[f]/x]$ is AX'-reducible.

By Lemma 7.7.5, there are terms $u_1,...,u_n$ such that $P\langle u_1,...,u_n\rangle$ is AX'-reduced, $t_i[u'[f]/x]\xrightarrow[\overline{AX}]{}u_i$ and $t_j\xrightarrow[\overline{AX}]{}u_j$ for all $1\le j\le n$ with $j\ne i$. Since AX' is confluent modulo CAX and u_i is AX'-irreducible, $t_i[u'[f]/x]\xrightarrow[\overline{AX}]{}t_i[u[f]/x]$ implies $t_i[u[f]/x]\xrightarrow[\overline{AX}]{}v_i$ and $u_i\xrightarrow[\overline{CAX}]{}v_i$ for some v_i. Since CAX respects AX'-normal forms, there is an AX'-normal form t' such that $v_i\xrightarrow[\overline{AX}]{}t'$ and $u_i\xrightarrow[\overline{CAX}]{}t'$. Hence $P\langle u_1,...,t',...,u_n\rangle$ is AX'-reduced. Since $t_i[u[f]/x]\xrightarrow[\overline{AX}]{}v_i\xrightarrow[\overline{AX}]{}t'$ and $P\langle u_1,...,u_n\rangle$ is AX'-reduced, we conclude that $p[u[f]/x]$ is AX'-reducible.

Case 2.3. $u\equiv u'\Leftarrow\vartheta \in BAX$. By Lemma 7.8.1, AX'-reducibility of $\vartheta[f]$ implies $f\xrightarrow[\overline{AX}]{}f'$ for some f' such that $\vartheta[f']$ is AX'-reduced.

Since AX' is confluent modulo CAX and t is an AX'-normal form, $t_i[u[f]/x] \overline{\overline{AX'}} t$ implies $t_i[u[f']/x] \overline{\overline{AX'}} t'$ and $t \overline{\overline{CAX}} t'$ for some t'. Since CAX respects AX'-normal forms, there is an AX'-normal form t" such that $t' \overline{\overline{AX'}} t"$. Therefore $t_i[u[f']/x] \overline{\overline{AX'}} t"$, while $u[f'] \overline{\overline{CAX}} u'[f'] \Leftarrow \vartheta[f']$ is a conditional reduction with simple length 1 and AX'-reduced $\vartheta[f']$. Hence CAX-compatibility of AX' implies $t_i[u'[f']/x] \overline{\overline{AX'}} u"$ and $t" \overline{\overline{CAX}} u"$ for some u". Since CAX respects AX'-normal forms, there is an AX'-normal form u_o such that $u" \overline{\overline{AX'}} u_o$. Therefore

$$t_i[u'[f]/x] \overline{\overline{AX'}} t_i[u'[f']/x] \overline{\overline{AX'}} u" \overline{\overline{AX'}} u_o$$

and thus $p[u'[f]/x]$ is AX'-normalizable. By the induction hypothesis, $p[u'[f]/x]$ is AX'-reducible.

By Lemma 7.7.5, there are terms $u_1,...,u_n$ such that $P\langle u_1,...,u_n \rangle$ is AX'-reduced, $t_i[u'[f]/x] \overline{\overline{AX'}} u_i$ and $t_j \overline{\overline{AX'}} u_j$ for all $1 \leq j \leq n$ with $j \neq i$. Since AX' is confluent modulo CAX and u_i is AX'-irreducible, $t_i[u'[f]/x] \overline{\overline{AX'}} u_i$ implies $t_i[u'[f']/x] \overline{\overline{AX'}} v_i$ and $u_i \overline{\overline{CAX}} v_i$ for some v_i. Since CAX respects AX'-normal forms, there is an AX'-normal form v_i' such that $v_i \overline{\overline{AX'}} v_i'$ and $u_i \overline{\overline{CAX}} v_i'$. Therefore $t_i[u'[f']/x] \overline{\overline{AX'}} v_i'$.

By the Base Assumption (cf. Section 6.1), BAX is symmetric. Hence $u'[f'] \overline{\overline{CAX}} u[f'] \Leftarrow \vartheta[f']$ is also a conditional reduction with simple length 1 and AX'-reduced $\vartheta[f']$. Thus by CAX-compatibility of AX' and AX'- irreducibility of v_i', $t_i[u'[f']/x] \overline{\overline{AX'}} v_i'$ implies $t_i[u[f']/x] \overline{\overline{AX'}} u_i'$ and $v_i' \overline{\overline{CAX}} u_i'$ for some u_i'. Since CAX respects AX'-normal forms, there is an AX'-normal form u_o such that $u_i' \overline{\overline{AX'}} u_o$ and $v_i' \overline{\overline{CAX}} u_o$. Therefore $u_i \overline{\overline{CAX}} u_o$, and thus $P\langle u_1,...,u_o,...,u_n \rangle$ is AX'-reduced. Since

$$t_i[u[f]/x] \overline{\overline{AX'}} t_i[u[f']/x] \overline{\overline{AX'}} u_i' \overline{\overline{AX'}} u_o,$$

we conclude that $p[u[f]/x]$ is AX'-reducible.

Case 2.4. $u' \equiv u \Leftarrow \vartheta \in BAX$. Analogous to Case 2.3. ∎

Though the preceding theorem establishes analogous criteria for both Church-Rosser properties, Chapter 9 will reveal trade-offs between both conditions (cf. Section 9.9), which Jouannaud attempts to overcome by breaking down NAX into a set NAXL of linear equations and a set NAXN of non-linear equations and to use the *union* of the NAXL- and the ~NAXN-reduction relations instead of either $\vdash\!\!\frac{RD}{NAX}$ or $\vdash\!\!\frac{RD}{\sim NAX}$. Instead of introducing a further reduction relation we prefer to simulate this approach as follows. First, we augment the base specification by NOP and NAXN; secondly, we try to show that this extension is ~NAXN-Church-Rosser; if so, we regard it as the new base specification and attempt to prove that the entire specification ⟨SIG,AX⟩ is NAXL-Church-Rosser.

7.9 Strategy-controlled Reduction

Lemma 7.9.1 *Term reductions preserve reducibility*
Let either AX' = NAX and CAX = BAX or AX' = ~NAX and CAX = ~BAX. Suppose that AX' is confluent modulo CAX and CAX respects AX'-normal forms.
If $\gamma[f]$ is AX'-reducible and $f \xrightarrow{AX'} g$, then $\gamma[g]$ is AX'-reducible as well.

Proof. Let $\gamma = (P_1\langle t_{11},...,t_{1k_1}\rangle,...,P_n\langle t_{n1},...,t_{nk_n}\rangle)$. By Lemma 7.7.5, there are terms $u_{11},...,u_{1k_1},...,u_{n1},...,u_{nk_n}$ such that for all $1 \le i \le n$ and $1 \le j \le k_i$

$$t_{ij}[f] \xrightarrow{AX'} u_{ij} \quad \text{and} \quad P_i\langle u_{i1},...,u_{ik_i}\rangle \text{ is AX'-reduced.}$$

On the other hand, $t_{ij}[f] \xrightarrow{AX'} t_{ij}[g]$. Since u_{ij} is AX'-irreducible, confluence of AX' modulo CAX implies $t_{ij}[g] \xrightarrow{AX'} v_{ij}$ and $u_{ij} \xrightarrow{CAX} v_{ij}$ for some v_{ij}. Since CAX respects AX'-normal forms, there is an AX'-normal form v_{ij}' such that

$$v_{ij} \xrightarrow{AX'} v_{ij}'$$
$$u_{ij} \xrightarrow{CAX} v_{ij}'$$

Since $P_i\langle u_{i1},...,u_{ik_i}\rangle$ is a $\langle SIG,BAX\rangle$-theorem, $P_i\langle v_{i1}',...,v_{ik_i}'\rangle$ is a $\langle SIG,BAX\rangle$-theorem as well. Therefore $P_i\langle v_{i1}',...,v_{ik_i}'\rangle$ is AX'-reduced. Hence $P_i\langle v_{i1},...,v_{ik_i}\rangle$ and thus $P_i\langle t_{i1},...,t_{ik_i}\rangle[g]$ and $\gamma[g]$ are AX'-reducible. ∎

This lemma tells us that the order of AX'-reduction steps does not count provided that AX' is confluent. In other words, under the confluence assumption every strategy to select reduction redices is complete w.r.t. goal reducibility. Let us give a precise meaning to *strategy* and *strategy-controlled reduction* within the goal reduction framework.

Given a goal γ, a reduction strategy selects a subterm t of γ. The choice of t depends on its *position* in γ. We follow Broy, Section 6.2, and describe *positions of γ* as expressions of the form $\delta \bullet t$ where δ is a goal (or term) containing the fixed variable x_0 exactly once and t is a term such that $\delta[t/x_0] = \gamma$. The set of all positions $\delta \bullet t$ with $\delta \in \text{Goal}(SIG)$ and $t \in T(SIG)$ is denoted by *Pos(SIG)*.

Definition Let AX' ∈ {NAX,~NAX}, γ be a goal, $\delta \bullet t$ be a position of γ, e = $(u \equiv u' \Leftarrow \delta) \in$ NAX and f be a substitution such that

- either AX' = NAX and t = u[f]
- or AX' = ~NAX and $t \underset{BAX}{=\!\!\Rightarrow} u[f]$.

Then $\delta \bullet t$ is called an *AX'-reduction redex of γ induced by e*. $\delta \bullet t$ is *feasible* if, in addition, $\vartheta[f]$ is AX'-reducible.

If the precise location of x_o in δ does not matter, we also call the term t a redex of γ. ∎

Definition Let AX' ∈ {NAX,~NAX}. Given a function S : Goal(SIG)⟶Pos(SIG), the *S-controlled reduction calculus* consists of the Success Rule (cf. Section 7.7) and the

S-controlled Reduction Rule Let γ be a goal, f be a substitution and $S(\gamma) = \delta \bullet t$ be an AX'-reduction redex induced by $u \equiv u' \Leftarrow \vartheta \in$ NAX. Then

$$\frac{\gamma}{\delta[u'[f]/x_o] \cup \vartheta[f]}.$$

Let γ,γ' be goals. A derivation of γ' from γ via the S-controlled reduction calculus is called an *S-controlled reduction of γ to γ'* (w.r.t. AX').

The corresponding inference relation is denoted by $S\vdash^{RD}_{AX'}$ and called the *S-controlled AX'-reduction relation*. If $\gamma\ S\vdash^{RD}_{AX'}\ \varnothing$, then γ is *AX'-reducible by S*. S-controlled term reductions are defined analogously to *term reductions* (cf. Section 7.7). Properties 7.7.3-7.7.6 hold true for S-controlled reduction as well.

S is called a *(ground) AX'-reduction strategy* if for all (ground) goals γ, $S(\gamma)$ is a feasible AX'-reduction redex whenever γ has a feasible AX'-reduction redex. ∎

We are now in a position to formulate the fundamental criteria for reduction strategy independence.

Theorem 7.9.2 *Reduction strategy independence*
Let either AX' = NAX and CAX = BAX or AX' = ~NAX and CAX = ~BAX. Suppose that S is a (ground) AX'-reduction strategy, $S\vdash^{RD}_{AX'}$ is Noetherian (on ground goals), AX' is (ground) confluent modulo CAX and CAX respects (ground) AX'-normal forms.

If γ is an AX'-reducible (ground) goal, then γ is AX'-reducible by S.

Proof by Noetherian induction on γ with respect to $S\vdash^{RD}_{AX'}$. Let γ be AX'-reducible. If $S(\gamma)$ is not a feasible AX'-reduction redex, then γ has no feasible AX'-reduction redex. Hence γ is AX'-reduced, and the proof is complete.

Otherwise $S(\gamma)$ is a feasible AX'-reduction redex, say $S(\gamma) = \delta \bullet t$, induced by, say, $u \equiv u' \Leftarrow \vartheta \in $ NAX. Then for some f, $\gamma = \delta[u[f]/x_0]$ and $\vartheta[f]$ is AX'-reducible. Thus $u[f] \xrightarrow{}_{\overline{AX'}} u'[f]$, and Lemma 7.9.1 implies that $\gamma' = \delta[u'[f]/x_0]$ is AX'-reducible as well. Since $\gamma \, S\vdash^{RD}_{AX'} \gamma' \cup \vartheta[f]$, we conclude by the induction hypothesis that $\gamma' \cup \vartheta[f]$ and thus γ are AX'-reducible by S. ∎

7.10 Basic Reduction

Basic reduction rejects all reduction redices $\delta \bullet t$ where root(t) is located *below* the right-hand side of the equation that caused the *preceding* reduction step. To describe basic reduction formally we split a goal γ into a goal-substitution pair $\langle \gamma', f \rangle$ such that $\gamma'[f] = \gamma$ and restrict reduction redices of γ to those positions $\delta \bullet t$ where t *overlaps* γ' (cf. Section 2.2). A basic reduction step starting out from γ results in a goal φ, again represented as a goal-substitution pair, say $\langle \varphi', g \rangle$, where φ' includes the right-hand side, say u', of the equation applied to γ, while the terms substituted into variables of u are part of g. This ensures that the next reduction redex, which must be a position $\delta \bullet t$ of φ where t overlaps φ', is not located below u'.

Definition Let AX' ∈ {NAX,~NAX}. The *basic reduction calculus* (w.r.t AX') consists of the following inference rules:

Basic Success Rule Let γ be a goal and let f be a substitution such that $\gamma[f]$ is AX'-reduced. Then

$$\frac{\langle \gamma, f \rangle}{\langle \emptyset, id \rangle}.$$

Basic Reduction Rule Let δ be a goal, x ∈ single(δ)-dom(f), t ∈ T(SIG)-X, $u \equiv u' \Leftarrow \vartheta \in $ NAX and f,g be substitutions such that
- either AX' = NAX and t[f] = u[g]
- or AX' = ~NAX and $t[f] \xrightarrow{}_{\overline{BAX}} u[g]$.
Then

$$\frac{\langle \delta[t/x], f \rangle}{\langle \delta[(u'/x)+f] \cup \vartheta, \, g \upharpoonright var(u) \rangle}.$$

Let γ, γ' be goals and f,f' be substitutions. A derivation of $\langle \gamma', f' \rangle$ from $\langle \gamma, f \rangle$ via the basic reduction calculus is called a *basic reduction* of $\langle \gamma, f \rangle$ to $\langle \gamma', f' \rangle$ (w.r.t. AX').

The corresponding inference relation, denoted by $B \vdash^{RD}_{AX'}$, is called the *basic*

AX'-reduction relation. If $\langle \gamma, f \rangle \; B\vdash^{RD}_{AX'} \langle \emptyset, id \rangle$, then $\langle \gamma, f \rangle$ is *basically AX'-reducible*.

$|\langle \gamma, f \rangle \; B\vdash^{RD}_{AX'} \langle \gamma', f' \rangle|$ denotes the least number of Basic Reduction Rule applications needed to derive $\langle \gamma', f' \rangle$ from $\langle \gamma, f \rangle$. ∎

As in the case of resolution and paramodulation (cf. Chapter 5) we assume a renaming of variables as those of XG after each derivation step: given a derived pair $\langle \gamma, f \rangle$, the renaming is here applied to the goal $\gamma[f]$.

Lemma 7.10.1 *Soundness of basic reduction w.r.t. goal reduction*

Let $AX' \in \{NAX, \sim NAX\}$ and for all $u \equiv u' \Leftarrow \vartheta \in NAX$, let $var(u') \cup var(\vartheta) \subseteq var(u)$. If $\langle \gamma, f \rangle \; B\vdash^{RD}_{AX'} \langle \varphi, g \rangle$ and $var(\gamma[f]) \subseteq XG$, then $\gamma[f] \vdash^{RD}_{AX'} \varphi[g]$.

Proof. If $\langle \gamma, f \rangle \; B\vdash^{RD}_{AX'} \langle \varphi, g \rangle$ is obtained only by the Basic Success Rule, then $\gamma[f]$ is AX'-reduced, φ is empty and $g = id$. Hence the Success Rule (cf. Section 7.7) implies $\gamma[f] \vdash^{RD}_{AX'} \varphi[g]$. Let

$$\langle \delta[t/x], f \rangle \; B\vdash^{RD}_{AX'} \langle \delta[(u'/x)+f] \cup \vartheta, g\restriction var(u) \rangle$$

be an application of the Basic Reduction Rule such that

(1) $\qquad\qquad var(\delta[t/x][f]) \subseteq XG$.

W.l.o.g. $x \notin var(f(dom(f)))$. Hence

(2) $\qquad\qquad \delta[t/x][f] = \delta[f][t[f]/x]$

and

(3) $\qquad\qquad \delta[(u'[g]/x)+f] = \delta[f][u'[g]/x]$.

(1) implies $var(f(var(\delta)-\{x\})) \subseteq XG$. Since XG is disjoint from $var(u)$, we obtain

(4) $\qquad\qquad f(var(\delta)-\{x\})[g\restriction var(u)] = f(var(\delta)-\{x\})$.

From $var(u') \cup var(\vartheta) \subseteq var(u)$, (4) and (3) one concludes

(5) $(\delta[(u'/x)+f] \cup \vartheta)[g\restriction var(u)] = \delta[(u'[g]/x)+f] \cup \vartheta[g] = \delta[f][u'[g]/x] \cup \vartheta[g]$.

By (2) and (5), the Single Reduction Rule (cf. Section 7.7) implies

$$\delta[t/x][f] \vdash^{RD}_{AX'} (\delta[(u'/x)+f] \cup \vartheta)[g\restriction var(u)]. \quad \blacksquare$$

Conversely, reducible goals are basically reducible:

Lemma 7.10.2 *Completeness of basic reduction w.r.t goal reduction*
Let AX' ∈ {NAX,~NAX}. Suppose that the AX'-reduction relation is Noetherian and for all u≡u'⇐ϑ ∈ NAX, var(u') ∪ var(ϑ) ⊆ var(u).
Let γ be a goal and f be an AX'-irreducible substitution such that γ[f] is AX'-reducible and var(γ[f]) ⊆ XG. Then <γ,f> is basically AX'-reducible.

Proof by Noetherian induction on γ[f] w.r.t. $\vdash^{RD}_{AX'}$. If γ[f] is AX'-reduced, then the proof is complete. Otherwise there are goals δ and φ, x ∈ single(δ), u≡u'⇐ϑ ∈ NAX, a substitution g such that t = u[g] (t$=_{BAX}$u[g]) and

$$\gamma[f] = \delta[t/x] \vdash^{RD}_{AX'} \delta[u'[g]/x] \cup \vartheta[g] = \varphi.$$

Since f is AX'-irreducible, there are a goal δ' and a term t' ∉ X with δ'[t'/x] = γ, t'[f] = u[g] and δ'[f] = δ. W.l.o.g. x ∉ dom(f). Hence

(1) <γ,f> B$\vdash^{RD}_{AX'}$ <φ',g'>

where φ' = δ'[{u'/x}+f] ∪ ϑ and g' = g↾var(u). By assumption,

$$var(f(var(\delta')-\{x\})) \subseteq var(\delta'[t'/x][f]) = var(\gamma[f]) \subseteq XG.$$

Since XG is disjoint from var(u),

$$f(var(\delta')-\{x\})[g↾var(u)] = f(var(\delta')-\{x\}).$$

Since var(u') ∪ var(ϑ) ⊆ var(u) and w.l.o.g. x ∉ var(f(dom(f))), we conclude

$$\varphi = \delta[u'[g]/x] \cup \vartheta[g] = \delta'[f][u'[g]/x] \cup \vartheta[g] = \delta'[\{u'[g]/x\}+f] \cup \vartheta[g]$$
$$= (\delta'[\{u'/x\}+f] \cup \vartheta)[g↾var(u)] = \varphi'[g'].$$

Case 1. g' is AX'-irreducible. Then by the induction hypothesis (after variables have been renamed to satisfy var(φ'[g']) ⊆ XG) there are γ',f' such that <φ',g'> B$\vdash^{RD}_{AX'}$ <γ',f'> and γ'[f'] is AX'-reduced. Hence by (1),

$$<\gamma,f> B\vdash^{RD}_{AX'} <\gamma',f'>.$$

Case 2. g' is not AX'-irreducible. This is just the case where φ may have reduction redices located *below* the right-hand side u' of the conditional equation u≡u'⇐ϑ applied to <γ,f> and leading to <φ',g'>. However, these reduction redices already occur in γ[f]. Those which are located most deeply in $\gamma[f]$ allow us to transform $\langle\gamma,f\rangle$ by basic reduction into pairs $\langle\psi,h'\rangle$ with irreducible h'. We can apply the induction hypothesis to $\psi[h']$, which gives us a basic reduction from $\langle\psi,h'\rangle$ to some $\langle\gamma',f'\rangle$ such that $\gamma'[f']$ is reduced. So we compose this with the basic reduction from $\langle\gamma,f\rangle$ to $\langle\psi,h'\rangle$ and obtain a basic reduction from $\langle\gamma,f\rangle$ to $\langle\gamma',f'\rangle$. The detailed proof reads as follows.

Since g' is not AX'-irreducible, there are $y \in var(u)$, $u_1 \equiv u_1' \Leftarrow \delta_1 \in NAX$, a term v, $z \in single(v)$, an AX'-irreducible substitution h such that $t_1 = u_1[h]$ ($t_1 \Rightarrow_{BAX} u_1[h]$) and $gy = v[t_1[h]/z]$. Since $t'[f] = u[g]$ and f is AX'- irreducible, we have $t' = t''[v'/z]$ and $v'[f] = t_1[h]$ for some t'',v'.

W.l.o.g. $z \notin var(\delta') \cup dom(f)$. Hence

$$\gamma = \delta'[t'/x] = \delta'[t''[v'/z]/x] = \delta'[t''/x][v'/z]$$

and thus

(2) $\qquad\qquad\qquad \langle\gamma,f\rangle \; B\vert^{RD}_{AX'} \; \langle\psi,h'\rangle$

where $\psi = \delta'[t''/x][(u_1'/z)+f] \cup \delta_1$ and $h' = h\restriction var(u_1)$. By Lemma 7.10.1,

$$\gamma[f] \; \vert^{RD}_{AX'} \; \psi[h'].$$

Hence by the induction hypothesis (after variables have been renamed to satisfy $var(\psi[h']) \subseteq XG$), there are γ',f' such that $\langle\psi,h'\rangle \; B\vert^{RD}_{AX'} \; \langle\gamma',f'\rangle$ and $\gamma'[f']$ is AX'-reduced. By (2), $\langle\gamma,f\rangle \; B\vert^{RD}_{AX'} \; \langle\gamma',f'\rangle$. ∎

7.11 Bibliographic Notes

Huet and Oppen provide a summary of notions and results on equational rewriting obtained up to 1980. (A short, but illustrative introduction is given by Bundy, Section 9.) The main contributions to the Congruence Class Approach are due to Lankford and Ballantyne, Peterson and Stickel, and Jouannaud, who worked out the relationship between the version of Peterson and Stickel and that of Huet [1] (cf. Section 7.3).

The *termination* of rewrite systems deserves particular interest whenever a reduction relation must be Noetherian in order to employ induction on that relation (as in the proof of Theorem 7.9.2 or 7.10.2). We refer to Dershowitz [1,2,3] and the application of his results to abstract data types in Padawitz [1] (see also Section 9.4). Kaplan [2] invented the notion of *fairness* to denote sets of conditional equations that induce a Noetherian reduction relation.

The concepts of conditional term rewriting are manifold (see Bergstra and Klop; Kaplan [1]; Pletat et al.; and Zhang and Remy), differing with regard to their treatment of premises. The last two papers cited argue for a hierarchical treatment: the verification of premises is separated from term reduction by restricting them to conditions of *primitive types* in contrast to properties of the *type of interest,* which is embodied by <SIG,AX>. The approach outlined in this chapter should have shown that a hierarchical concept is not inherent to conditional rewriting. On the other hand, *proof-theoretical* demands sometimes impose restrictions on the form of premises that actually resemble hierarchy constraints (cf. Section 9.4).

The Definition Principle is adopted from Huet and Hullot's *Principle of Definition,* which, however, is considerably stronger: it requires that <SIG,AX> be a sufficiently complete conservative extension without base axioms (cf. Section 6.1).

Term convergence has been weakened to *subconnectedness,* a condition that was invented by Winkler and Buchberger, refined to a critical pair criterion by Küchlin and applied to ground confluence by Göbel. Instead of presuming a single diagram of the form

$$u \xrightarrow{AX'} v$$
$$\downarrow CAX$$
$$u' \xrightarrow{AX'} v'$$

(cf. Section 7.8) subconnectedness of u and u' admits a finite number of such diagrams. Given a triangle

$$t \xrightarrow{AX'} u$$
$$ \searrow_{AX'} u',$$

it is sufficient to have terms $u_1,...,u_n,v,v_1,...,v_n,v_1',...,v_n',v'$ such that

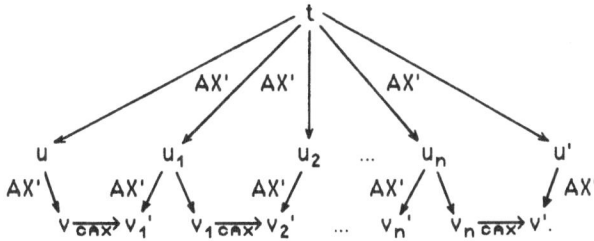

It might be a subject of further research to see how far the results of Sections 7.8 and 7.9, which depend on confluence properties, can be generalized to corresponding results where term convergence is replaced by sub- connectedness. Of course, this makes sense only after we have explored a number of sample specifications and found out that, indeed, subconnectedness works when term convergence does not hold.

Reduction strategies are known as *computation rules* (cf. Manna, Section 5.2, for the case of subterm selection, and Lloyd, Chapter 2, for the case of atom selection).

Basic reduction stems from Hullot, Section 4.

Chapter 8 Narrowing

8.1 Introduction

The Narrowing Rule is both a specialization of the Paramodulation Rule (cf. Section 5.3) and a generalization of the Single (goal) Reduction Rule (cf. Section 7.7). As a particular case of paramodulation narrowing applies conditional equations only from *left to right* and instantiates a goal only by *irreducible* substitutions. With regard to goal reduction, narrowing adds the possibility of substituting into the variables of a goal before reducing it. However, the restriction to irreducible substitutions implies that a goal, say γ, can be narrowed only if it already contains some *proper prefix* of a reduction redex. An instantiation of γ is to complete the prefix to the full redex. "Proper" means that the prefix must not be a variable. Therefore reduction redices cannot be generated arbitrarily, just by substituting left-hand sides of conditional equations into variables of γ. Consequently, the number of possible narrowing steps starting out from γ is considerably smaller than the number of paramodulants of γ, even if we confine ourselves to most general paramodulation.

Since paramodulation is complete w.r.t. deductive solutions (Theorem 5.3.5), we must pay for the specialization to narrowing by restrictions to the set of deducible solutions. We are faced with two restrictions. The first is that only NAX- (~NAX-) irreducible solutions can be obtained. Secondly, we are sure that *all* these solutions are computable only if <SIG,AX> is NAX- (~NAX-) Church-Rosser.

We inherit from goal reduction the splitting into NAX- and BAX-steps: beginning with a goal-substitution pair <γ,id>, applications of the Narrowing Rule should lead to a pair <φ,f> such that narrowing steps cannot be applied to φ. But a paramodulating expansion of φ w.r.t. base axioms may produce a solution g of φ. If so, we call f[g] a narrowing solution of γ.

Since the Church-Rosser property is synonymous with completeness of goal reduction, the proof that narrowing is complete w.r.t. deductive solutions reduces to a proof that narrowing is complete w.r.t. goal reduction (cf. Section 8.2). Afterwards, narrowing is lifted to most general narrowing, just as paramodulation was lifted to most general paramodulation (cf. Section 5.4). In both cases, forward lifting rests on backward lifting. However, the narrowing analogue of Lemma 5.3.2 is much easier to establish, since we are only concerned with irreducible substitutions. In fact, this restriction allows us to dispense with prefixed axioms (cf. Section 5.3).

Section 8.3 extends strategy-controlled reduction (cf. Section 7.9) to *strategy-controlled narrowing.* In Section 8.4, we develop a condition on NAX (and ~NAX) that is sufficient for *uniform* reduction strategies to serve as narrowing strategies as well. *Ground term generating term sets* and an inductive theory criterion based on narrowing are treated in Section 8.5.

Section 8.6 generalizes basic reduction (cf. Section 7.10) to *basic narrowing*. Section 8.7 deals with the alternation between narrowing and normalization called *reduced narrowing*. Section 8.8 combines both refinements and presents assumptions under which *reduced basic narrowing* is complete w.r.t. narrowing.

While strategy-controlled, basic and lazy narrowing restrict the set of admissible narrowing steps, *optimized narrowing* augments the calculus by permitting intermediate optimizations of subgoals (cf. Section 8.9). The result of applying an *optimizing function* to a goal, say γ, need not only depend on the immediate predecessor of γ. It may depend on the whole actual derivation tree bearing γ as a leaf. The *local correctness* of an optimizing function ensures that corresponding optimization steps do not violate the soundness and completeness of narrowing. Section 8.10 presents a number of locally correct optimizing functions that are built into implementations of the narrowing calculus.

A narrowing counterpart of lazy resolution (cf. Section 5.5) is presented in Section 8.11.

8.2 The Narrowing Calculus

Let AX' $\in$ {NAX,~NAX} (cf. Section 7.7). Remember the Variable Assumption of Chapter 5: given a goal-substitution pair $\langle\gamma,f\rangle$ with var(γ) $\subseteq$ XG and a derivation step from $\langle\gamma,f\rangle$ to $\langle\gamma',f'\rangle$, all x $\in$ var(γ')-XG are renamed as variables of XG before $\langle\gamma',f'\rangle$ is subjected to further deduction steps.

Definition The *narrowing calculus* (w.r.t. AX') consists of the following inference rules:

Success Rule Let γ be a goal and f,g be substitutions such that γ[g] is AX'-reduced. Then

$$\frac{\langle\gamma,f\rangle}{\langle\emptyset,f[g]\rangle}.$$

Narrowing Rule Let δ be a goal, x $\in$ single(δ) (cf. Section 2.2), t $\in$ T(SIG)-X, u$\equiv$u'$\Leftarrow\delta$ $\in$ NAX and f,g be substitutions such that
- either AX' = NAX and t[g] = u[g]
- or AX' = ~NAX and t[g]$\overrightarrow{\approx_{BAX}}$u[g].

Then
$$\frac{\langle \delta[t/x], f \rangle}{\langle (\delta[u'/x] \cup \vartheta)[g], f[g\restriction XG] \rangle}.$$

Let γ, γ' be goals and f, f' be substitutions. A derivation of $\langle \gamma', f' \rangle$ from $\langle \gamma, f \rangle$ via the narrowing calculus is called a *narrowing expansion* of $\langle \gamma, f \rangle$ to $\langle \gamma', f' \rangle$ (w.r.t. AX').

The corresponding inference relation is denoted by $\vdash_{AX'}^{N}$. If $\langle \gamma, id \rangle \vdash_{AX'}^{N} \langle \emptyset, f \rangle$, then f is an *N-solution* of γ (w.r.t. AX').

$|\langle \gamma, f \rangle \vdash_{AX'}^{N} \langle \gamma', f' \rangle|$ denotes the least number of Narrowing Rule applications needed to derive $\langle \gamma', f' \rangle$ from $\langle \gamma, f \rangle$. ∎

Example 8.2.1 Let $\langle BSIG, BAX \rangle =$ NAT and $\langle SIG, AX \rangle =$ NAT-ARITHMETIC (cf. Section 3.2). A narrowing expansion of

$$\gamma = \{y \equiv x + 1, x \equiv 2\}$$

is given by:

$\langle \gamma, id \rangle$
$\langle \{y \equiv x+0|, m \equiv 2\}, id \rangle$ (narrowing with $1 \equiv 0|$)
$\langle \{y \equiv (m+0)|, m \equiv 2\}, \{m/x\} \rangle$ (narrowing with $m + n| \equiv (m + n)|$)
$\langle \{y \equiv m'|, m' \equiv 2\}, \{m/x\}[m'/m] \rangle$ (narrowing with $m' + 0 \equiv m'$)
$\langle \{y \equiv m'|, m' \equiv 0||\}, \{m/x\}[m'/m] \rangle$ (narrowing with $2 \equiv 0||$)
$\langle \emptyset, \{m/x\}[m'/m][0|||/y, 0||/m'] \rangle$ (application of the Success Rule:
the goal $\{0||| \equiv 0|||, 0|| \equiv 0||\}$
is NAX-reduced.)

Hence $f = \{m/x\}[m'/m][m'|/y, 0||/m']$ is an N-solution of γ. In particular, $fx = 0||$ and $fy = 0|||$. ∎

Proposition 8.2.2 *Narrowing expansions simulate paramodulating expansions*

If $\langle \gamma, f \rangle \vdash_{AX'}^{N} \langle \varphi, g \rangle$, then $\langle \gamma, f \rangle \vdash_{AX}^{P} \langle \varphi, g \rangle$.

Proof. Suppose that $\langle \gamma, f \rangle \vdash_{AX'}^{N} \langle \varphi, g \rangle$. If φ is non-empty, then $\langle \gamma, f \rangle \vdash_{AX}^{P} \langle \varphi, g \rangle$ follows from the fact that the Narrowing Rule simulates one or more (if AX' is ~NAX) applications of the Paramodulation Rule. Let $\varphi = \emptyset$. Then there are a non-empty goal δ and substitutions h, h' such that $\langle \gamma, f \rangle \vdash_{AX'}^{N} \langle \delta, h \rangle$, $\delta[h']$ is AX'-reduced and $g = h[h']$. Hence $\delta[h']$ is a $\langle SIG, BAX \rangle$-theorem, and we conclude $\langle \delta, id \rangle \vdash_{AX}^{P} \langle \emptyset, h' \rangle$ and thus $\langle \delta, h \rangle \vdash_{AX}^{P} \langle \emptyset, h[h'] \rangle = \langle \emptyset, g \rangle$ from Theorem 5.3.5. Since δ is non-empty, $\langle \gamma, f \rangle \vdash_{AX'}^{N} \langle \delta, h \rangle$ implies $\langle \gamma, f \rangle \vdash_{AX}^{P} \langle \delta, h \rangle$ (cf. the first case of this proof). Therefore $\langle \gamma, f \rangle \vdash_{AX}^{P} \langle \emptyset, g \rangle = \langle \varphi, g \rangle$. ∎

Lemma 8.2.3 *Soundness of narrowing w.r.t. goal reduction*

(1) If $\langle \gamma, id \rangle \vdash^N_{AX'} \langle \varphi, h \rangle$, then

$$|\gamma[h] \vdash^{RD}_{AX'} \varphi| \leq |\langle \gamma, id \rangle \vdash^N_{AX'} \langle \varphi, h \rangle|.$$

(2) If $\langle \gamma, id \rangle \vdash^N_{AX'} \langle \emptyset, h \rangle$, then $\gamma[h]$ is AX'-reducible and

$$|\gamma[h] \vdash^{RD}_{AX'} \emptyset| \leq |\langle \gamma, id \rangle \vdash^N_{AX'} \langle \emptyset, h \rangle|.$$

Proof. (2) is a special case of (1). We show (1) by induction on $|\langle \gamma, id \rangle \vdash^N_{AX'} \langle \varphi, h \rangle|$.

Case 1. $\langle \gamma, id \rangle$ expands to $\langle \varphi, h \rangle$ by applying only the Success Rule. Then φ is empty, $\gamma[h]$ is AX'-reduced and thus

$$|\gamma[h] \vdash^{RD}_{AX'} \varphi| \leq 1 = |\langle \gamma, id \rangle \vdash^N_{AX'} \langle \varphi, h \rangle|.$$

Case 2. $\langle \gamma, id \rangle$ expands to $\langle \varphi, h \rangle$ by a single application of the Narrowing Rule. Then there are a goal δ, $x \in single(\delta)$, $u \equiv u' \Leftarrow \vartheta \in NAX$ and $t \in T(SIG)$-X such that $t[h] = u[h]$ (or $t[h] \xrightarrow{}_{BAX} u[h]$), $\gamma = \delta[t/x]$ and $\varphi = (\delta[u'/x] \cup \vartheta)[h]$. By the Single Reduction Rule (cf. Section 7.7), $\gamma[h] \vdash^{RD}_{AX'} \varphi$. Moreover,

$$|\gamma[h] \vdash^{RD}_{AX'} \varphi| \leq 1 = |\langle \gamma, id \rangle \vdash^N_{AX'} \langle \varphi, h \rangle|.$$

Case 3. There are δ, h', h'' with $h'[h''] = h$ and

$$|\langle \gamma, id \rangle \vdash^N_{AX'} \langle \varphi, h \rangle| = |\langle \gamma, id \rangle \vdash^N_{AX'} \langle \delta, h' \rangle| + |\langle \delta, id \rangle \vdash^N_{AX'} \langle \varphi, h'' \rangle|.$$

Of course,

$$|\langle \gamma, id \rangle \vdash^N_{AX'} \langle \delta[h''], h \rangle| \leq |\langle \gamma, id \rangle \vdash^N_{AX'} \langle \delta, h' \rangle|.$$

Thus by the induction hypothesis,

$$|\gamma[h] \vdash^{RD}_{AX'} \delta[h'']| \leq |\langle \gamma, id \rangle \vdash^N_{AX'} \langle \delta[h''], h \rangle|$$

and

$$|\delta[h''] \vdash^{RD}_{AX'} \varphi| \leq |\langle \delta, id \rangle \vdash^N_{AX'} \langle \varphi, h'' \rangle|.$$

Hence

$$|\gamma[h] \vdash^{RD}_{AX'} \varphi|$$
$$\leq |\gamma[h] \vdash^{RD}_{AX'} \delta[h'']| + |\delta[h''] \vdash^{RD}_{AX'} \varphi|$$
$$\leq |\langle \gamma, id \rangle \vdash^N_{AX'} \langle \delta[h''], h \rangle| + |\langle \delta, id \rangle \vdash^N_{AX'} \langle \varphi, h'' \rangle|$$
$$\leq |\langle \gamma, id \rangle \vdash^N_{AX'} \langle \delta, h' \rangle| + |\langle \delta, id \rangle \vdash^N_{AX'} \langle \varphi, h'' \rangle|$$
$$= |\langle \gamma, id \rangle \vdash^N_{AX'} \langle \varphi, h \rangle|. \blacksquare$$

Completeness of narrowing is guaranteed only for *irreducible* substitutions:

Lemma 8.2.4 *Completeness of narrowing w.r.t. goal reduction*
Let γ, φ be goals and let h be an AX'-irreducible substitution such that $\gamma[h]$ $\vdash^{RD}_{AX'} \varphi$ and $\text{var}(\gamma) \cup \text{dom}(h) \subseteq XG$. Then

$$|\langle \gamma, id\rangle \vdash^{N}_{AX'} \langle \varphi, h\rangle| = |\gamma[h] \vdash^{RD}_{AX'} \varphi|.$$

Proof. We show the statement by induction on $|\gamma[h] \vdash^{RD}_{AX'} \varphi|$.

Case 1. $\gamma[h]$ reduces to φ by applying only the Success Rule. Then $\gamma[h]$ is AX'-reduced, and the proof is complete by the Success Rule of the narrowing calculus.

Case 2. $\gamma[h]$ reduces to φ by a single application of the Goal Reduction Rule. Then there are a goal δ, $x \in \text{single}(\delta)$, $u \equiv u' \Leftarrow \vartheta \in NAX$ and a substitution g such that $t = u[g]$ (or $t \xrightarrow{}_{BAX} u[g]$),

(1) $\qquad \gamma[h] = \delta[t/x] \quad \text{and} \quad \varphi = \delta[u'[g]/x] \cup \vartheta[g].$

Since $\gamma[h] = \delta[t/x]$ and h is AX'-irreducible, t overlaps γ in $\gamma[h]$, i.e. there are a goal γ' and a term $t' \notin X$ such that

(2) $\qquad \gamma = \gamma'[t'/x], \ t'[h] = t \ \text{and} \ \gamma'[h\upharpoonright(X-\{x\})] = \delta.$

By (1) and (2),

$$\varphi = \delta[u'[g]/x] \cup \vartheta[g] = \gamma'[h\upharpoonright(X-\{x\})][u'[g]/x] \cup \vartheta[g] = \gamma'[h'] \cup \vartheta[g]$$

where $h' = h\upharpoonright(X-\{x\}) + (u'[g]/x)$. Let $h'' = h + g\upharpoonright(X-XG)$. W.l.o.g. $x \in XG$. Hence by assumption and (2), $\text{var}(\gamma') \subseteq XG$ and thus

$$\varphi = (\gamma'[u'/x] \cup \vartheta)[h''].$$

By (2), the Narrowing Rule implies $\langle \gamma, id\rangle \vdash^{N}_{AX'} \langle \varphi, h\upharpoonright XG\rangle = \langle \varphi, h\rangle$ and

$$|\langle \gamma, id\rangle \vdash^{N}_{AX'} \langle \varphi, h\rangle| = |\gamma[h] \vdash^{RD}_{AX'} \varphi|.$$

Case 3. $|\gamma[h] \vdash^{RD}_{AX'} \varphi| = |\gamma[h] \vdash^{RD}_{AX'} \varphi'| + |\varphi' \vdash^{RD}_{AX'} \varphi|$ for some goal φ'. By the induction hypothesis,
$$|\langle \gamma, id\rangle \vdash^{N}_{AX'} \langle \varphi', h\rangle| = |\gamma[h] \vdash^{RD}_{AX'} \varphi'|$$
and
$$|\langle \varphi', h\rangle \vdash^{N}_{AX'} \langle \varphi, h\rangle| = |\langle \varphi', id\rangle \vdash^{N}_{AX'} \langle \varphi, id\rangle| = |\varphi' \vdash^{RD}_{AX'} \varphi|.$$

By composition, $\langle \gamma, id\rangle \vdash^{N}_{AX'} \langle \varphi, h\rangle$. Hence Lemma 8.2.3 (1) yields

$$|\gamma[h] \vdash^{RD}_{AX} \varphi| \le |\langle\gamma,id\rangle \vdash^{N}_{AX} \langle\emptyset,h\rangle| \le |\langle\gamma,id\rangle \vdash^{N}_{AX} \langle\varphi',h\rangle| + |\langle\varphi',h\rangle \vdash^{N}_{AX} \langle\varphi,h\rangle|$$
$$= |\gamma[h] \vdash^{RD}_{AX} \varphi'| + |\varphi' \vdash^{RD}_{AX} \varphi| = |\gamma[h] \vdash^{RD}_{AX} \varphi|. \blacksquare$$

As a consequence of Lemma 8.2.4, we may compute normal forms of ground terms by narrowing without losing the efficiency of term reduction. Let t be a ground term, let t' be a NAX-normal form with $t \xrightarrow{NAX} t'$, and let $x \in XG_{sort(t)}$. Then by Corollary 7.7.6 and Lemma 8.2.4,

$$|t \xrightarrow{NAX} t'| = |\langle\{t\equiv x\},id\rangle \vdash^{N}_{AX} \langle\emptyset,\{t'/x\}\rangle|$$

where AX' is NAX.

Example 8.2.5 Trivial examples show that narrowing is incomplete for reducible solutions:

```
<SIG,AX>
   base :  NAT (cf. Section 3.2)
   opns :  c : nat
           f_ : nat⟶nat
   axms :  c ≡ 0
```

Of course, the goal {fn≡f0} has the deductive solution {c/n}. But {c/n} is not derivable via the narrowing calculus: the Narrowing Rule cannot be applied to {fn≡f0} and the axiom c≡0 because c does not overlap fn.

On the other hand, note that {fn≡f0}[c/n] is AX-reducible. Hence we conclude from this example that the irreducibility assumption of Lemma 8.2.4 cannot be omitted. ∎

Analogously to paramodulation, narrowing expansions are confined to most general ones (cf. Section 5.4).

Definition A narrowing expansion $\langle d_1,...,d_n \rangle$ is *most general* if for all $1 \le i < n$ the step from d_i to d_{i+1} is performed by a rule of the narrowing calculus where the respective substitution g is minimal w.r.t. the subsumption ordering (cf. Section 2.2).

The corresponding inference relation is denoted by $\vdash^{GN}_{AX}$. If $\langle\gamma,id\rangle \vdash^{GN}_{AX} \langle\emptyset,f\rangle$, then f is a *GN-solution* of γ (w.r.t. AX'). ∎

Lemma 8.2.6 *Forward lifting of narrowing expansions*
Let f be an AX'-irreducible substitution and $\langle\gamma,id\rangle \vdash^{N}_{AX} \langle\varphi,f\rangle$. Then there are φ',f',h such that $\langle\gamma,id\rangle \vdash^{GN}_{AX} \langle\varphi',f'\rangle$, $\varphi'[h] = \varphi$, $f'[h] = f$ and

$$|\langle\gamma,id\rangle \vdash^{GN}_{AX'} \langle\varphi',f'\rangle| \le |\langle\gamma,id\rangle \vdash^{N}_{AX'} \langle\varphi,f\rangle|.$$

In particular, if f is an N-solution of γ w.r.t. AX', then there are a GN-solution f' of γ w.r.t. AX' such that f' subsumes f and

$$|\langle\gamma,id\rangle \vdash^{GN}_{AX'} \langle\emptyset,f'\rangle| \le |\langle\gamma,id\rangle \vdash^{N}_{AX'} \langle\emptyset,f\rangle|.$$

Proof by induction on $n = |\langle\gamma,id\rangle \vdash^{N}_{AX'} \langle\varphi,f\rangle|$. If $n \le 1$, then the result follows immediately. Otherwise there are δ,g,h such that $g[h] = f$,

$$|\langle\gamma,id\rangle \vdash^{N}_{AX'} \langle\varphi,f\rangle| = |\langle\gamma,id\rangle \vdash^{N}_{AX'} \langle\delta,g\rangle| + |\langle\delta,id\rangle \vdash^{N}_{AX'} \langle\varphi,h\rangle|$$

and $\langle\varphi,h\rangle$ is obtained from $\langle\delta,id\rangle$ by applying the Narrowing Rule exactly once. By the induction hypothesis, there are δ',g',h' such that

(1) $\quad |\langle\gamma,id\rangle \vdash^{GN}_{AX'} \langle\delta',g'\rangle| \le |\langle\gamma,id\rangle \vdash^{N}_{AX'} \langle\delta,g\rangle|,\ \delta'[h'] = \delta$ and $g'[h'] = g$.

Since $g'[h'][h] = g[h] = f$ is AX'-irreducible, we may assume that h' is AX'-irreducible as well. Since $\delta'[h'] = \delta$, the left-hand side of the axiom applied to δ overlaps δ' (cf. Section 2.2). Hence

$$\langle\delta,id\rangle \vdash^{N}_{AX'} \langle\varphi,h\rangle$$

can be lifted to

$$\langle\delta',id\rangle \vdash^{N}_{AX'} \langle\varphi,h'[h]\rangle$$

such that

$$|\langle\delta',id\rangle \vdash^{N}_{AX'} \langle\varphi,h'[h]\rangle| \le |\langle\delta,id\rangle \vdash^{N}_{AX'} \langle\varphi,h\rangle|.$$

Once more, by the induction hypothesis,

(2) $\quad |\langle\delta',id\rangle \vdash^{GN}_{AX'} \langle\varphi',g''\rangle| \le |\langle\delta',id\rangle \vdash^{N}_{AX'} \langle\varphi,h'[h]\rangle|,$
$\varphi'[h''] = \varphi$ and $g''[h''] = h'[h]$

for some φ',g'',h''. (1) and (2) yield

$$\langle\gamma,id\rangle \vdash^{GN}_{AX'} \langle\varphi',g'[g'']\rangle,\ \varphi'[h''] = \varphi,\ g'[g''][h''] = g'[h'][h] = g[h] = f$$

and

$$|\langle\gamma,id\rangle \vdash^{GN}_{AX'} \langle\varphi',g'[g'']\rangle|$$
$$\le\ |\langle\gamma,id\rangle \vdash^{GN}_{AX'} \langle\delta',g'\rangle| + |\langle\delta',id\rangle \vdash^{GN}_{AX'} \langle\varphi',g''\rangle|$$
$$\le\ |\langle\gamma,id\rangle \vdash^{N}_{AX'} \langle\delta,g\rangle| + |\langle\delta',id\rangle \vdash^{N}_{AX'} \langle\varphi,h'[h]\rangle|$$
$$\le\ |\langle\gamma,id\rangle \vdash^{N}_{AX'} \langle\delta,g\rangle| + |\langle\delta,id\rangle \vdash^{N}_{AX'} \langle\varphi,h\rangle|$$
$$=\ |\langle\gamma,id\rangle \vdash^{N}_{AX'} \langle\varphi,f\rangle|.\ \blacksquare$$

In contrast to paramodulating expansions (cf. Lemma 5.3.2), the *backward lifting* of $\langle\delta'[h'],id\rangle \vdash^N_{AX} \langle\varphi,h\rangle$ to $\langle\delta',id\rangle \vdash^N_{AX} \langle\varphi,h'[h]\rangle$ can be concluded from the fact that h' is AX'-irreducible: each narrowing redex of $\delta'[h']$ is the instance of a narrowing redex of δ' by h'.

Lemmata 8.2.3, 8.2.4 and 8.2.6 result in

Theorem 8.2.7 *Soundness and completeness of most general narrowing w.r.t. deductive solutions*

Suppose that $\langle SIG,AX\rangle$ is (ground) AX'-Church-Rosser (cf. Section 7.7).

Let γ be a goal and let f be an AX'-irreducible substitution such that $\gamma[f]$ is an AX'-normalizable (ground) goal. f is a deductive $\langle SIG,AX\rangle$-solution of γ iff γ has a GN-solution w.r.t. AX', which subsumes f. ∎

8.3 Strategy-controlled Narrowing

Given a substitution f, we define the instance of a position $\delta \bullet t$ by f as

$$(\delta \bullet t)[f] = \delta[f\uparrow(X-\{x_o\})] \bullet t[f]$$

(cf. Section 7.9). Thus, instantiating $\delta \bullet t$ by f means substituting f into the variables of δ and t, leaving out the occurrence of x_o in δ. Consequently, two positions of the same goal are equal if and only if they are unifiable:

Proposition 8.3.1 For all goals γ, positions $\delta \bullet t$, $\varphi \bullet u$ in γ and substitutions f, $(\delta \bullet t)[f] = (\varphi \bullet u)[f]$ implies $\delta \bullet t = \varphi \bullet u$.

Proof. Let $(\delta \bullet t)[f] = (\varphi \bullet u)[f]$. Then $\delta[f\uparrow(X-\{x_o\})] = \varphi[f\uparrow(X-\{x_o\})]$ and $t[f] = u[f]$. Hence $\delta = \lambda[g\uparrow(X-\{x_o\})]$, $\varphi = \lambda[h\uparrow(X-\{x_o\})]$, $t = v[g]$ and $u = v[h]$ for some λ,v,g,h. Thus $\lambda[v/x_o][g] = \delta[t/x_o] = \gamma = \varphi[u/x_o] = \lambda[v/x_o][h]$. Hence $gx = hx$ for all $x \in (var(\lambda)-\{x_o\}) \cup var(v)$. Therefore $\delta = \varphi$ and $t = u$. ∎

Definition Let γ be a goal, $\delta \bullet t$ be a position of γ, $t \in T(SIG)-X$, $e = (u \equiv u' \Leftarrow \vartheta) \in NAX$ and f be a substitution such that
- either AX' = NAX and $t[f] = u[f]$
- or AX' = ~NAX and $t[f] \xrightarrow{\sim BAX} u[f]$.

Then $\delta \bullet t$ is called an *AX'-narrowing redex of γ induced by e and f*.

If the precise location of x_o in δ does not matter, we also call the term t a redex of γ. ∎

Definition Given a function S : Goal(SIG)→Pos(SIG), the *S-controlled narrowing calculus* consists of the Success Rule (cf. Section 8.2) and the

S-controlled Narrowing Rule Let γ be a goal, f,g be substitutions and $S(\gamma) = \delta \bullet t$ be an AX'-narrowing redex induced by $u \equiv u' \Leftarrow \vartheta \in $ NAX and g. Then

$$\frac{\langle \gamma, f \rangle}{\langle (\delta[u'/x_o]u\vartheta)[g], f[g\restriction XG] \rangle}.$$

Let γ, γ' be goals and f, f' be substitutions. A derivation of $\langle \gamma', f' \rangle$ from $\langle \gamma, f \rangle$ via the S-controlled narrowing calculus is called an *S-controlled (most general) narrowing expansion* of $\langle \gamma, f \rangle$ to $\langle \gamma', f' \rangle$ (w.r.t. AX').

The corresponding inference relation is denoted by $S\vdash^N_{AX'}$ ($S\vdash^{GN}_{AX'}$). If $\langle \gamma, id \rangle$ $S\vdash^{GN}_{AX'} \langle \emptyset, f \rangle$, then f is an *S-controlled N- (GN-) solution* of γ (w.r.t. AX').

$|\langle \gamma, f \rangle\ S\vdash^N_{AX'}\ \langle \gamma', f' \rangle|$ denotes the least number of S-controlled Narrowing Rule applications needed to derive $\langle \gamma', f' \rangle$ from $\langle \gamma, f \rangle$. ∎

NF-Assumption (for the present and the following section) S is a function from Goal(SIG) to Pos(SIG). NF is a set of AX'-irreducible substitutions such that for all $f, g \in T(SIG)^X$, $f[g] \in NF$ implies $f, g \in NF$. (Hence the identity substitution id is always included in NF.) ∎

Of course, the NF-Assumption is satisfied by the set of *all* AX'-irreducible substitutions. However, the following requirements on a narrowing strategy may enforce the restriction to a smaller set of substitutions. Then the usual candidate for NF is the set of all *base* substitutions. In the sequel, *AX'-narrowing redex* always means AX'-narrowing redex induced by some $f \in NF$.

Definition S is an *AX'-narrowing strategy* if for all goals γ the following conditions hold true:
- $S(\gamma)$ is an AX'-narrowing redex of γ whenever γ has an AX'-narrowing redex.
- If $S(\gamma)$ is an AX'-narrowing redex of γ, then for all $f \in NF$, $S(\gamma[f]) = S(\gamma)[f]$.
∎

The last condition implies that the root location of the redex selected by S in γ is the same for *all* NF-instances of γ. We attend to this consequence in Section 8.4 where narrowing strategies are discussed in detail.

The proofs of soundness and completeness of S-controlled narrowing w.r.t. S-controlled reduction proceed analoguously to Lemmata 8.2.3 and 8.2.4, respectively. However, both results are restricted to substitutions taken from NF.

Lemma 8.3.2 *Soundness of strategy-controlled narrowing w.r.t. strategy-controlled reduction*

Suppose that S is an AX'-narrowing strategy and $h \in NF$.
(1) If $\langle \gamma, id \rangle\ S\vdash^N_{AX'} \langle \varphi, h \rangle$, then $\gamma[h]\ S\vdash^{RD}_{AX'} \varphi$.

(2) If $\langle\gamma,\text{id}\rangle S\vdash^N_{AX'} \langle\emptyset,h\rangle$, then $\gamma[h]$ is AX'-reducible by S.

Proof. (2) is a special case of (1). We show (1) by induction on $|\langle\gamma,\text{id}\rangle S\vdash^N_{AX'} \langle\varphi,h\rangle|$.

Case 1. $\langle\gamma,\text{id}\rangle$ expands to $\langle\varphi,h\rangle$ by applying only the Success Rule. Then φ is empty, $\gamma[h]$ is AX'-reduced and thus $\gamma[h] S\vdash^{RD}_{AX'} \varphi$.

Case 2. $\langle\gamma,\text{id}\rangle$ expands to $\langle\varphi,h\rangle$ by a single application of the S-controlled Narrowing Rule. Then there are a goal δ, $x \in \text{single}(\delta)$, $u \equiv u' \Leftarrow \vartheta \in \text{NAX}$ and $t \in T(\text{SIG})$-X such that $t[h] = u[h]$ (or $t[h] \xrightarrow{}_{BAX} u[h]$), $S(\gamma) = \delta \bullet t$ and $\varphi = (\delta[u'/x_0]u\vartheta)[h]$. Since S is a narrowing strategy,

$$S(\gamma[h]) = S(\gamma)[h] = (\delta \bullet t)[h] = \delta[h\Gamma(X-\{x_0\})] \bullet t[h].$$

Therefore $S(\gamma[h])$ is a reduction redex, and the S-controlled Reduction Rule (cf. Section 7.9) implies

$$\gamma[h] S\vdash^{RD}_{AX'} \delta[h\Gamma(X-\{x_0\})][u'[h]/x_0] \cup \vartheta[h] = \varphi.$$

Case 3. There are δ,h',h'' with $h'[h''] = h$ and

$$|\langle\gamma,\text{id}\rangle S\vdash^N_{AX'} \langle\varphi,h\rangle| = |\langle\gamma,\text{id}\rangle S\vdash^N_{AX'} \langle\delta,h'\rangle| + |\langle\delta,\text{id}\rangle S\vdash^N_{AX'} \langle\varphi,h''\rangle|.$$

Of course,

$$|\langle\gamma,\text{id}\rangle S\vdash^N_{AX'} \langle\delta[h''],h\rangle| \le |\langle\gamma,\text{id}\rangle S\vdash^N_{AX'} \langle\delta,h'\rangle|.$$

Thus by the induction hypothesis, $\gamma[h] S\vdash^{RD}_{AX'} \delta[h'']$ and $\delta[h''] S\vdash^{RD}_{AX'} \varphi$. Hence

$$\gamma[h] S\vdash^{RD}_{AX'} \varphi. \blacksquare$$

Lemma 8.3.3 *Completeness of strategy-controlled narrowing w.r.t. strategy-controlled reduction*

Suppose that S is an AX'-narrowing strategy. Let γ,φ be goals and $h \in \text{NF}$ such that $\gamma[h] S\vdash^{RD}_{AX'} \varphi$ and $\text{var}(\gamma) \cup \text{dom}(h) \subseteq XG$. Then

$$\langle\gamma,\text{id}\rangle S\vdash^N_{AX'} \langle\varphi,h\rangle.$$

Proof. We show the statement by induction on $|\gamma[h] S\vdash^{RD}_{AX'} \varphi|$.

Case 1. $\gamma[h]$ reduces to φ by applying only the Success Rule. Then $\gamma[h]$ is AX'- reduced, and the proof is complete by the Success Rule of the narrowing calculus (cf. Section 8.2).

Case 2. $\gamma[h]$ reduces to φ by a single application of the S-controlled Reduction Rule. Then there are a goal δ, $x \in \text{single}(\delta)$, $u \equiv u' \Leftarrow \vartheta \in \text{NAX}$ and a substitution g such that $t = u[g]$ (or $t \xrightarrow{}_{BAX} u[g]$),

(1) $\quad\quad\quad S(\gamma[h]) = \delta \bullet t \quad \text{and} \quad \varphi = \delta[u'[g]/x_o] \cup \vartheta[g].$

Since $\gamma[h] = \delta[t/x_o]$ and h is AX'-irreducible, t overlaps γ in $\gamma[h]$, i.e. there are a goal γ' and a term $t' \notin X$ such that

(2) $\quad\quad\quad \gamma = \gamma'[t'/x_o], \; t'[h] = t \; \text{and} \; \gamma'[h\restriction(X-\{x_o\})] = \delta.$

By (1) and (2),

(3) $\varphi = \delta[u'[g]/x_o] \cup \vartheta[g] = \gamma'[h\restriction(X-\{x_o\})][u'[g]/x_o] \cup \vartheta[g] = \gamma'[h'] \cup \vartheta[g]$

where $h' = h\restriction(X-\{x_o\})+(u'[g]/x_o)$. Let $h'' = h+g\restriction(X-XG)$. W.l.o.g. $x_o \in XG$. Hence by assumption and (2), $var(\gamma') \subseteq XG$ and thus by (3),

$$\varphi = (\gamma'[u'/x_o] \cup \vartheta)[h''].$$

(2) implies $\delta \bullet t = (\gamma' \bullet t')[h]$. Since $\delta \bullet t$ is a reduction redex of $\gamma[h]$, $\gamma' \bullet t'$ is a narrowing redex of γ. Therefore $S(\gamma)$ is a narrowing redex and $S(\gamma)[h] = S(\gamma[h]) = \delta \bullet t$. By Proposition 8.3.1, $S(\gamma) = \gamma' \bullet t'$. Hence by (2), the S-controlled Narrowing Rule implies $\langle\gamma,id\rangle \; S\vdash^N_{AX'} \; \langle\varphi,h''\restriction XG\rangle = \langle\varphi,h\rangle$.

Case 3. There is a goal φ' such that the S-controlled reduction of $\gamma[h]$ to φ breaks down into S-controlled reductions of $\gamma[h]$ to φ' and of φ' to φ. By the induction hypothesis, $\langle\gamma,id\rangle \; S\vdash^N_{AX'} \; \langle\varphi',h\rangle$ and $\langle\varphi',id\rangle \; S\vdash^N_{AX'} \; \langle\varphi,id\rangle$. The latter holds true because $id \in NF$. Hence $\langle\gamma,id\rangle \; S\vdash^N_{AX'} \; \langle\varphi,h\rangle$. ∎

Lemma 8.3.4 *Forward lifting of S-controlled narrowing expansions*
Suppose that S is an AX'-narrowing strategy, $f \in NF$ and $\langle\gamma,id\rangle \; S\vdash^N_{AX'} \; \langle\varphi,f'\rangle$. Then there are φ',f',h such that $\langle\gamma,id\rangle \; S\vdash^{GN}_{AX'} \; \langle\varphi',f'\rangle$, $\varphi'[h] = \varphi$ and $f'[h] = f$.

Proof by induction on $n = |\langle\gamma,id\rangle \; S\vdash^N_{AX'} \; \langle\varphi,f\rangle|$. If $n \leq 1$, then the result follows immediately. Otherwise there are δ,g,h such that $g[h] = f$,

$$|\langle\gamma,id\rangle \; S\vdash^N_{AX'} \; \langle\varphi,f\rangle| = |\langle\gamma,id\rangle \; S\vdash^N_{AX'} \; \langle\delta,g\rangle| + |\langle\delta,id\rangle \; S\vdash^N_{AX'} \; \langle\varphi,h\rangle|$$

and $\langle\varphi,h\rangle$ is obtained from $\langle\delta,id\rangle$ by applying the Narrowing Rule exactly once. By the induction hypothesis, there are δ',g',h' such that

(1) $\quad\quad\quad \langle\gamma,id\rangle \; S\vdash^{GN}_{AX'} \; \langle\delta',g'\rangle, \; \delta'[h'] = \delta \text{ and } g'[h'] = g.$

From $g'[h'][h] = g[h] = f$ one concludes $h' \in NF$. Since $\delta'[h'] = \delta$ and h' is AX'-irreducible, u overlaps δ' in δ. Hence δ' has a narrowing redex. Thus $S(\delta')$ is a narrowing redex. Let $S(\delta) = \lambda \bullet u$. Since S is a narrowing strategy, $S(\delta')[h'] =$

$S(\delta'[h']) = S(\delta)$. Therefore

$$\langle \delta, id \rangle \; S \vdash^{N}_{AX'} \langle \varphi, h \rangle$$

can be lifted to

$$\langle \delta', id \rangle \; S \vdash^{N}_{AX'} \langle \varphi, h'[h] \rangle.$$

Once more, by the induction hypothesis,

(2) $\langle \delta', id \rangle \; S \vdash^{GN}_{AX'} \langle \varphi', g'' \rangle$, $\varphi'[h''] = \varphi$ and $g''[h''] = h'[h]$

for some φ', g'', h''. (1) and (2) yield $\langle \gamma, id \rangle \; S \vdash^{GN}_{AX'} \langle \varphi', g'[g''] \rangle$, $\varphi'[h''] = \varphi$ and $g'[g''][h''] = g'[h'][h] = g[h] = f$. ∎

Lemmata 8.3.2, 8.3.3, 8.3.4 and Theorem 7.9.2 (reduction strategy independence) amount to

Theorem 8.3.5 *Soundness and completeness of strategy-controlled narrowing w.r.t. deductive solutions*

Let either AX' = NAX and CAX = BAX or AX' = ~NAX and CAX = ~BAX. Suppose that ⟨SIG,AX⟩ is (ground) AX'-Church-Rosser, AX' is (ground) confluent modulo CAX, CAX respects (ground) AX'-normal forms and S is both a (ground) AX'-reduction strategy and an AX'-narrowing strategy such that $S \vdash^{RD}_{AX'}$ is Noetherian (on ground goals).

Let γ be a goal and $f \in NF$ such that $\gamma[f]$ is an AX'-normalizable (ground) goal. f is a deductive ⟨SIG,AX⟩-solution of γ iff γ has an S-controlled GN-solution w.r.t. AX' that subsumes f. ∎

Note that S is required to be a narrowing strategy *and* a reduction strategy. Therefore, the narrowing redex selected by S must be a feasible reduction redex (cf. Section 7.9) whenever the goal to be narrowed has a feasible reduction redex (see the end of the following section).

8.4   Narrowing Strategies

Let us have a closer look at the second condition on a narrowing strategy demanding that for all goals γ and $f \in NF$, $S(\gamma[f]) = S(\gamma)[f]$. The usual *computation rules* (see Manna, p. 375 ff.) do not satisfy this "uniformity" requirement automatically.

Example 8.4.1 Let ⟨BSIG,BAX⟩ = NAT (cf. Section 3.2),

⟨SIG,AX⟩
   base : NAT-ARITHMETIC

opns : c : nat
        h _ : nat→nat
vars : m : nat
axms : c ≡ 0
        h m| ≡ h m   (E)

and AX' = NAX. Suppose that S works *leftmost-outermost* and selects a narrowing redex of γ = {hn*c≡0}. Though {0/n} is an N-solution of γ (because of the axiom m*0≡0), {0/n} is not found by S. Instead, S will substitute m| into n, apply (E) and come up with a variant of γ, namely {hm*c≡0}. This follows from the fact that S is not uniform. On one hand, we have

(*)   S(γ) = S({hn*c≡0}) = {x_o*c≡0}•hn.

On the other hand,

$$S(\gamma[0/n]) = S(\{h0*c≡0\}) = \{h0*x_o≡0\}•c$$

because h0 is not a narrowing redex. (*) implies

$$S(\gamma)[0/n] = \{x_o*c≡0\}•h0,$$

but this position is different from S(γ[0/n]). ∎

The previous example suggests the conjecture that S is not uniform because f has not been specified completely: an axiom for h0 is missing. Therefore, we must go deeper into the structure of goals.

Definition The *label* of a *location* w ∈ $\mathbb{N}^*$ in a term t or in an atom p is inductively defined as follows:

$$\text{label}(w,t) = \begin{cases} \text{root}(t) & \text{if } w = \varepsilon \\ \text{label}(v,t_i) & \text{if } t = \sigma \langle t_1,...,t_n \rangle, w = iv, 1 \leq i \leq n \\ \perp & \text{otherwise} \end{cases}$$

$$\text{label}(w,p) = \begin{cases} \perp & \text{if } w = \varepsilon \\ \text{label}(v,t_i) & \text{if } p = P \langle t_1,...,t_n \rangle, w = iv, 1 \leq i \leq n \\ \perp & \text{otherwise.} \end{cases}$$

Conversely, the set of *occurrences* of σ ∈ OPuX in a term or atom t is defined as

$$\text{Occ}(\sigma,t) = \{w \in \mathbb{N}^* \mid \text{label}(w,t) = \sigma\}.$$

If Occ(σ,t) is a singleton, say {w}, we write *occ*(σ,t). ∎

Definition S is a *uniform strategy* if for all unifiable atoms p and p', S(p) = q•t and S(p') = q'•t' imply
- $occ(x_o, q) = occ(x_o, q')$,
- $S(\gamma u(p)) = (\gamma u(q)) \cdot t$ for all goals γ. ∎

Definition AX' is *redex stable w.r.t. S* if for all AX'-narrowing redices p•t in the range of S and all f ∈ NF, (p•t)[f] is an AX'-narrowing redex as well. ∎

Lemma 8.4.2 Suppose that S is uniform, AX' is redex stable w.r.t. S and for all goals γ, $S(\gamma)$ is an AX'-narrowing redex of γ whenever γ has an AX'-narrowing redex. Then S is an AX'-narrowing strategy.

Proof. Let γ be a goal, $S(\gamma) = \delta \cdot t$ be an AX'-narrowing redex of γ and f ∈ NF. We must show that $S(\gamma[f]) = S(\gamma)[f]$.

Of course, there are a goal λ and atoms p,q such that $\gamma = \lambda u(p)$, $\delta = \lambda u(q)$, $x_o \notin var(\lambda)$ and S(p) = q•t is a narrowing redex of p. Since AX' is redex stable w.r.t. S, $(q \cdot t)[f] = q[f\restriction(X-\{x_o\})] \cdot t[f]$ is a narrowing redex of p[f]. Hence p[f] has a narrowing redex and thus by assumption there is a position q'•t' such that S(p[f]) = q'•t' is a narrowing redex of p[f] as well. Therefore

(1) $\qquad q[f\restriction(X-\{x_o\})][t[f]/x_o] = p[f] = q'[t'/x_o]$.

Since p and p[f] are unifiable and S is uniform, S(p) = q•t and S(p[f]) = q'•t' imply

(2) $\qquad occ(x_o, q) = occ(x_o, q')$.

From (1) and (2) we conclude $q[f\restriction(X-\{x_o\})] = q'$ and $t[f] = t'$. Hence

$$S(p[f]) = q' \cdot t' = q[f\restriction(X-\{x_o\})] \cdot t[f].$$

Uniformity of S leads to

$S(\gamma[f]) = S(\lambda[f]u(p[f])) = (\lambda[f]u(q[f\restriction(X-\{x_o\})])) \cdot t[f] = ((\lambda u(q)) \cdot t)[f]$
$= (\delta \cdot t)[f] = S(\gamma)[f]$. ∎

Redex stability of AX' w.r.t. S can be reduced to a *local* condition on axiom instances.

INF-Assumption (for the present section) *INF* is a set of substitutions such that for all f ∈ NF there is g with f[g] ∈ INF. ∎

INF stands for *instances of NF*. Typical candidates for INF are the set of all ground instances of NF or - provided that AX' is normalizing (cf. Section 7.7) - the set of all ground and irreducible instances of NF. If NF consists of base substitutions (cf. Section 8.3), we may restrict INF to base substitutions as well.

Definition *NAX is locally redex stable* w.r.t. S if for all NAX-narrowing redices p•t in the range of S and all g ∈ INF there is a NAX-axiom instance t[g]≡u⇐𝛿.
~NAX *is locally redex stable* w.r.t. S if for all ~NAX-narrowing redices p•t in the range of S and all g ∈ INF there are a reduction t[g]$\xrightarrow{BAX}$v and a NAX-axiom instance v≡u⇐𝛿. ∎

Proposition 8.4.3 If AX' is locally redex stable w.r.t. S, then AX' is redex stable w.r.t. S.

Proof. W.l.o.g. suppose that AX' is NAX. Let p•t be an AX'-narrowing redex in the range of S and f ∈ NF. By assumption, f[g] ∈ INF for some g. Since AX' is locally redex stable w.r.t. S, there is a NAX-axiom instance t[f][g]≡u⇐𝛿. Therefore (p•t)[f] is an AX'-narrowing redex as well. ∎

Definition NAX is *ground term reducing* if all ground NAX-normal forms are base terms (or, vice versa, non-base ground terms are not NAX-irreducible).
A term t is an *innermost* term if root(t) ∈ NOP and all other symbols of t are base symbols. A set CE of conditional equations is *innermost* if for all u≡u'⇐𝛿 ∈ CE,
- u is an innermost term,
- var(u') ∪ var(𝛿) ⊆ var(u),
- for all v≡v' ∈ 𝛿, v' is a base term. ∎

Example 8.4.4 Let NF = T(BSIG)^X, INF = GT(BSIG)^X and S be an *innermost* strategy, i.e. if q•t and q'•t' are two narrowing redices of the same atom p and occ(x_o,q) < occ(x_o,q') (w.r.t. the lexicographic ordering on ℕ*), then S(p) ≠ q'•t'. Suppose that NAX is ground term reducing.
Of course, S is uniform. Moreover, NAX is locally redex stable w.r.t. S. Let q•t be a NAX-narrowing redex in the range of S, i.e. S(p) = q•t for some atom p. Since S is an innermost strategy and NAX is ground term reducing, we conclude that t is an innermost term. Hence for all ground base substitutions g, t[g] is an innermost term as well. There is a NAX-axiom instance t[g]≡u⇐𝛿 because NAX is ground term reducing. Hence NAX is locally redex stable w.r.t. S and thus by Proposition 8.4.3 and Lemma 8.4.2, S is a NAX-narrowing strategy. ∎

What about other strategies? Let us keep the assumptions of Example 8.4.4 as far as they do not concern S to find out weak requirements to S such that NAX is locally redex stable w.r.t. S. Let q•t be a NAX-narrowing redex in the range of S, i.e. S(p) = q•t for some atom p, and let g be a ground base substitution. How can we guarantee the existence of a NAX-axiom instance t[g]≡u⇐ϑ?

Example 8.4.5 (due to Echahed) Let S be an *outermost* strategy, <BSIG,BAX> = NAT (cf. Section 3.2),

<SIG,AX>
   base : NAT-ARITHMETIC
   opns : f _ _ : nat,nat→nat
   vars : m,n : nat
   axms : f 0 0 ≡ 0
           f m| 0 ≡ 1
           f m n| ≡ 2   (E)

and let p be the equation (f(fxy)z)≡0. p has the deductive solution {0/x,0/y,0/z}. However, S does not find this solution because it applies (E) to p:

$$\langle\{p\}, id\rangle \; S\vdash^{N}_{AX} \; \langle\{2\equiv 0\}, \{(fxy)/m, n|/z\}\rangle.$$

Indeed, NAX is not locally redex stable w.r.t. S: although the term (f(fxy)z) may be a narrowing redex selected by S and 0/z ∈ INF, the instance (f(fxy)0) is not a narrowing redex. The situation can be remedied by exchanging the single axiom (f m n| ≡ 2) for two axioms (f 0 n| ≡ 2) and (f m| n| ≡ 2). This change of the specification modifies the deductive, but not the inductive theory of <SIG,AX>: the two new axioms cover all ground base instances of the replaced axiom. ∎

The idea of Example 8.4.5 can be generalized with the help of the following notion.

Definition A set E of equations is *non-sub-unifiable* if for all $\sigma \in$ NOP, $\sigma u \equiv u'$, $\sigma v \equiv v' \in E$ and $w \in \mathbb{N}^+$, label(w,σu) is a variable whenever label(w,σv) is a variable and for all w' < w, label(w',σu) = label(w',σv). ∎

The axiom modification in Example 8.4.5 ensures that NAX becomes non-sub-unifiable. In general, we have

Proposition 8.4.6 Let NAX be non-sub-unifiable, ground term reducing and innermost. Then NAX is locally redex stable w.r.t. *every* S.

Proof. Let σt be a narrowing redex and g be a ground base substitution. We have to show that $\sigma t[g]$ is the lefthand side of a NAX-axiom instance. At first, σt is broken down into an innermost term $\sigma t'$ and a substitution h such that $\sigma t'[h] = \sigma t$, $\text{dom}(h) \subseteq \text{var}(t')$ and for all $x \in \text{dom}(h)$, $\text{root}(hx) \in \text{NOP}$. Let

$$\text{LOC} = \{\text{occ}(x,\sigma t') \mid x \in \text{dom}(h)\}.$$

Since σt is a narrowing redex, there are $\sigma u \equiv u' \in \text{NAX}$ and a substitution g' such that $\sigma t[g'] = \sigma u[g']$. Thus $\sigma t'[h][g'] = \sigma u[g']$. Since σu is innermost and for all $x \in \text{dom}(h)$, $\text{root}(hx) \in \text{NOP}$, σu is a prefix of $\sigma t'[g'\restriction(X-\text{dom}(h))]$. Hence for all $w \in \text{LOC}$ there is $w' \leq w$ such that $\text{label}(w',\sigma u)$ is a variable.

Since NAX is ground term reducing, there are $\sigma v \equiv v' \in \text{NAX}$ and a ground base substitution g' such that

(1) $\qquad \sigma t'[g'\restriction(X-\text{dom}(h))+g'\restriction\text{dom}(h)] = \sigma v[g'].$

Let $w'' \in \mathbb{N}^*$ such that $\text{label}(w'',\sigma v) \neq \perp$ and $w'' \geq w$ for some $w \in \text{LOC}$. Then there is $w' \leq w''$ such that $\text{label}(w',\sigma u)$ is a variable. Since NAX is non-sub-unifiable, $\text{label}(w',\sigma u)$ is a variable as well. Hence $w' = w$ and thus $w'' = w$. Therefore $g'\restriction\text{dom}(h)$ does not overlap σv in $\sigma v[g']$, i.e. by (1),

(2) $\qquad \sigma t'[g'\restriction(X-\text{dom}(h))] = \sigma v[g'']$

for some g''. Hence $\sigma t[g] = \sigma t'[h][g] = \sigma t'[g'\restriction(X-\text{dom}(h))][h] = \sigma v[g''][h]$, i.e. the equation $\sigma t[g] \equiv v'[g''][h]$ is a NAX-axiom instance. ∎

Instead of modifying the specification one may also change the strategy S such that NAX becomes locally redex stable w.r.t. S. The symbols of an atom might be visited in leftmost-outermost order, but if a redex, say t, has been found, t is selected for a narrowing step only if local redex stability is guaranteed, i.e. if for all ground base substitutions g there is an axiom instance $t[g] \equiv u \Leftarrow \vartheta$. This can be checked by verifying that the set

$$\text{ARG}(t) = \{\langle gx_1,...,gx_n\rangle \mid \exists u,\vartheta : t[g] \equiv u \Leftarrow \vartheta \in \text{NAX}\}$$

is *ground term generating* (cf. Section 8.5). ($x_1,...,x_n$ are supposed to be the variables of t.) For instance, if this strategy visits the atom $(f(fxy)z) \equiv 0$ of Example 8.4.5 and encounters the redex $(f(fxy)z)$, it will find out that $\text{ARG}(f(fxy)z)$ is not ground term generating because there is no axiom instance of the form $(f(fgxgy)0) \equiv u \Leftarrow \vartheta$. So it proceeds to the next redex of $(f(fxy)z) \equiv 0$ in leftmost-outermost order, that is (fxy). Since $\text{ARG}(fxy)$ is ground term generating, (fxy) will be selected for an application of the

Narrowing Rule. Finally, we obtain the solution $\{0/x, 0/y, 0/z\}$ of $(f(fxy)z) \equiv 0$, which the strict leftmost-outermost strategy was unable to achieve.

Note that other definitions of NF or INF might work as well. Remember the conditions NF and INF must satisfy:
- NF is a set of irreducible substitutions.
- For all substitutions f, g, $f[g] \in$ NF implies $f, g \in$ NF.
- For all $f \in$ NF there is g with $f[g] \in$ INF.

A general trick to ensure local redex stability by changing the specification is to add a *bottom* constant $\bot$ and a *grounding* equation $t[g] \equiv \bot$ whenever t is a narrowing redex in the range of S and $g \in$ INF, but NAX lacks an axiom instance of the form $t[g] \equiv u \Leftarrow \vartheta$.

Example 8.4.7 Let $\langle$SIG,AX$\rangle$ be as in Example 8.4.1, AX' = NAX and S be a leftmost-outermost strategy. Local redex stability of NAX w.r.t. S is guaranteed if the first two axioms for subtraction:

$$n - 0 \equiv n$$
$$0 - n \equiv 0$$

are replaced by

$$0 - 0 \equiv 0$$
$$n| - 0 \equiv n|$$
$$0 - n| \equiv 0$$

and the axiom $h0 \equiv \bot$ is added to NAX.

Without the first modification we would be faced with, e.g., the narrowing redex 1-n, although there is no axiom instance of the form $1-0 \equiv u \Leftarrow \vartheta$. (The original set of subtraction axioms is not non-sub-unifiable!) By the second modification, S is now able to compute the solution $\{0/n\}$ of $\{hn*c \equiv 0\}$ (cf. Example 8.4.1). Indeed, an S-controlled narrowing expansion reads as follows:

$\langle\{hn*c \equiv 0\}, id\rangle \; S \vdash^N_{AX'} \; \langle\{\bot * c \equiv 0\}, \{0/n\}\rangle \; S \vdash^N_{AX'} \; \langle\{\bot * 0 \equiv 0\}, \{0/n\}\rangle$
$S \vdash^N_{AX'} \; \langle\{0 \equiv 0\}, \{0/n\}\rangle \; S \vdash^N_{AX'} \; \langle\varnothing, \{0/n\}\rangle$. ∎

Definition Let GNF $\subseteq$ T(SIG) such that
- for all terms t, substitutions h and $u \in$ GNF, $t = u$ (or $t \xrightarrow{}_{BAX} u$) implies $t[h] \in$ GNF,
- for all AX'-irreducible terms t, $x \in$ var(t) and $u \in$ GNF, $t[u/x]$ is AX'-irreducible, too.

Given $t \in$ GNF, $t \equiv \bot$ is called a *grounding equation*. ∎

Grounding equations do not create new reducible goals.

Proposition 8.4.8 Let γ be a goal (without $\perp$), let $t \equiv \perp$ be a grounding equation and
- either $AX' = NAX$ and $AX" = NAX \cup \{t \equiv \perp\}$
- or $AX' = \sim NAX$ and $AX" = \sim(NAX \cup \{t \equiv \perp\})$.

If a goal γ is $AX"$-reducible by S, then γ is AX'-reducible by S.

Proof. Let $w \in S^+$ and $z = \langle z_1,...,z_n \rangle \in X_w$. For all $u = \langle u_1,...,u_n \rangle \in T(SIG \cup \{\perp\})_w$, we write u/z for the substitution $\{u_i/z_i \mid 1 \leq i \leq n\}$. Suppose that $\gamma[\perp/z]$ is $AX"$-reducible.

We show by induction on $|\gamma[\perp/z] \, S \underset{AX"}{\overset{RD}{\vdash}} \, \emptyset|$ that for all $u \in GNF_w$, $\gamma[u/z]$ is AX'-reducible. Then the statement of the lemma follows as a special case.

So let $u \in GNF_w$. If $\gamma[\perp/z]$ is $AX"$-reduced, then, of course, γ is AX'-reduced. The second assumption concerning GNF implies that $\gamma[u/z]$ is AX'-reduced as well.

Suppose that $\gamma[\perp/z]$ is not $AX"$-reduced. Then there are $u' \equiv u" \Leftarrow \vartheta \in NAX \cup \{t \equiv \perp\}$, $u_o \in T(SIG)$, $g \in T(SIG)^X$, $h \in T(SIG \cup \{\perp\})^X$ and a position $\varphi \cdot v[h]$ of $\gamma[\perp/z]$ such that $S(\gamma[\perp/z]) = \varphi \cdot v[h]$, $v = u'[g]$ (or $v \underset{\sim BAX}{\rightarrow} u'[g]$). Moreover, the S-controlled Reduction Rule transforms $\gamma[\perp/z]$ into

$$\delta = \varphi[u"[g][h]/x_o] \cup \vartheta[g][h]$$

and

$$|\gamma[\perp/z] \, S\underset{AX"}{\overset{RD}{\vdash}} \, \emptyset| = 1 + |\delta \, S\underset{AX"}{\overset{RD}{\vdash}} \, \emptyset|.$$

Case 1. $u' \equiv u" \Leftarrow \vartheta \in NAX$. There are $\delta', \varphi' \in Goal(SIG)$ and $h' \in T(SIG)^X$ such that $\delta'[\perp/z] = \delta$, $\varphi'[\perp/z] = \varphi$ and $h'[\perp/z] = h$. Since $\perp$ occurs neither in $u' \equiv u" \Leftarrow \vartheta$ nor in the range of g, all $\perp$-occurrences of δ are either in φ or in the range of h. Hence

$$\delta' = \varphi'[u"[g][h']/x_o] \cup \vartheta[g][h'].$$

Let $\varphi" = \varphi'[u/z]$ and $h" = h'[u/z]$. W.l.o.g. $x_o \notin var(u)$. Thus

$$\delta'[u/z] = \varphi"[u"[g][h"]/x_o] \cup \vartheta[g][h"].$$

By the induction hypothesis, $\delta'[u/z]$ is AX'-reducible by S. Since $\gamma[\perp/z] = \varphi'[u[g][h']/x_o]$ and $\gamma[u/z] = \varphi"[u[g][h"]/x_o]$, $S(\gamma[\perp/z]) = \varphi \cdot v[h]$ implies $S(\gamma[u/z]) = \varphi" \cdot v[h"]$. Therefore

$$\gamma[u/z] \, S\underset{AX'}{\overset{RD}{\vdash}} \, \delta'[u/z],$$

and we conclude that $\gamma[u/z]$ is AX'-reducible by S.

Case 2. $(u \equiv u' \Leftarrow \vartheta) = (t \equiv \perp)$. Then $v = t[g]$ (or $v \underset{\sim BAX}{\rightarrow} t[g]$) and $\delta = \varphi[\perp/x_o]$.

Again, there are $\varphi' \in \text{Goal(SIG)}$ and $h' \in T(\text{SIG})^X$ such that $\varphi = \varphi'[\bot/z]$ and $h = h'[\bot/z]$. Therefore $\gamma[\bot/z] = \varphi[v[h]/x_o] = \varphi'[\bot/z][v[h]/x_o]$. Since $\bot$ does not occur in γ or v, we obtain $\gamma = \varphi'[v[h']/x_o]$. Let $\varphi'' = \varphi'[u/z]$ and $h'' = h'[u/z]$. W.l.o.g. $x_o \notin \text{var}(u)$. Hence

(1) $\qquad \gamma[u/z] = \varphi'[v[h']/x_o][u/z] = \varphi''[v[h'']/x_o]$.

By assumption, $t[g] \in \text{GNF}$ and thus $v[h''] \in \text{GNF}$. Since $\delta = \varphi'[\bot/z, \bot/x_o]$ and $u, v[h''] \in \text{GNF}$, the induction hypothesis implies that $\varphi''[v[h'']/x_o] = \varphi'[u/z, v[h'']/x_o]$ is AX'-reducible by S. Hence by (1), $\gamma[u/z]$ is AX'-reducible by S as well. ∎

Of course, grounding equations should not violate the Church-Rosser property of $\langle \text{SIG}, \text{AX} \rangle$. Otherwise the completeness of S-controlled narrowing w.r.t. deductive solutions might get lost (cf. Theorem 8.3.5). Consequently, $t \equiv \bot$ should not be added if some instance of t has a base representation (cf. Section 6.1), say t', since otherwise $t' \equiv \bot$ would be derivable, although $t' \equiv \bot$ is not a base theorem. In such a case $\langle \text{SIG}, \text{AX} \cup \{t \equiv \bot\} \rangle$ is not a conservative extension and, by Lemma 7.7.8 (1), $\langle \text{SIG}, \text{AX} \cup \{t \equiv \bot\} \rangle$ is not Church-Rosser. For instance, if we used the grounding equation $fm0 \equiv \bot$ in Example 8.4.5 to accomplish local redex stability, we would be able to deduce the *inconsistent* equation $0 \equiv \bot$.

Let us combine Theorem 8.3.5 with Lemma 8.4.2 and Proposition 8.4.3.

Theorem 8.4.9 *Soundness and completeness of strategy-controlled narrowing w.r.t. deductive solutions under local redex stability*

Let either AX' = NAX and CAX = BAX or AX' = ~NAX and CAX = ~BAX. Suppose that $\langle \text{SIG}, \text{AX} \rangle$ is (ground) AX'-Church-Rosser, AX' is (ground) confluent modulo CAX, CAX respects (ground) AX'-normal forms and S is a (ground) uniform AX'-reduction strategy such that $S \vdash_{AX'}^{RD}$ is Noetherian (on ground goals), AX' is locally redex stable w.r.t. S and for all goals γ, $S(\gamma)$ is an AX'-narrowing redex whenever γ has an AX'-narrowing redex.

Let γ be a goal and $f \in \text{NF}$ such that $\gamma[f]$ is an AX'-normalizable (ground) goal. f is a deductive $\langle \text{SIG}, \text{AX} \rangle$-solution of γ iff γ has an S-controlled GN-solution w.r.t. AX' that subsumes f. ∎

We are left with the question as to when uniform strategies are (ground) reduction strategies (cf. Section 7.9). Consulting Example 8.4.1 again, we see that the goal $\gamma = \{hn*c \equiv 0\}$ has a further N-solution, namely the identity substitution:

$$\langle \gamma, \text{id} \rangle \vdash_{AX'}^{N} \langle \{hn*0 \equiv 0\}, \text{id} \rangle \vdash_{AX'}^{N} \langle \{0 \equiv 0\}, \text{id} \rangle \vdash_{AX'}^{N} \langle \emptyset, \text{id} \rangle.$$

However, a leftmost-innermost *narrowing* strategy S will not find this solution even if NAX is extended by the grounding equation $h0 \equiv \bot$ (cf. Example 8.4.7). The reason for this is that S is not a *reduction* strategy: γ has the reduction redex c, while S returns the narrowing redex hn, which is not a reduction redex.

Is S a *ground* reduction strategy? Of course, since, with respect to ground goals, every narrowing redex is a reduction redex as well. One problem remains: the selected narrowing redex need not be *feasible,* i.e. the premise of a corresponding axiom instance need not be reducible (cf. Section 7.9).

8.5 Ground Term Generating Term Sets

This section aims at an inductive theory criterion that makes use of narrowing expansions (Theorem 8.5.4): a goal γ is an inductive theorem if there is a set M of N-solutions of γ, which *generates* all ground instances of γ.

Definition A set M of linear base term sequences is *ground term generating* if there is $w \in S^*$ such that $M \subseteq T(BSIG)_w$ and for all $t \in GT(BSIG)_w$ some $t' \in M$ subsumes t.

Let *FSL* be the S^*-sorted set of sets of term sequences defined by

$$FSL_w = \begin{cases} \{\{\varepsilon\}\} & \text{if } w = \varepsilon \\ \{M \subseteq T(BSIG)_w \mid M \text{ is finite and consists} \\ \text{of linear term sequences}\} & \text{if } w \neq \varepsilon. \end{cases}$$

To determine the ground term generating elements of FSL_w effectively we define an S^*-sorted subset GEN of FSL inductively as follows:

- $GEN_\varepsilon = \{\{\varepsilon\}\}$.
- For all $s \in S$, $w \in S^*$, $M \subseteq X_s$, $x \in M$ and $M(x) \in FSL_w$,
  $\{xt \mid x \in M, t \in M(x)\} \in GEN_{sw}$
  iff $\{t \mid x \in M, t \in M(x)\} \in GEN_w$.
- For all $s \in S$, $w \in S^*$, $M \subseteq FSL_s - X_s$, $u \in M$ and $M(u) \in FSL_w$
  $\{ut \mid u \in M, t \in M(u)\} \in GEN_{sw}$
  iff for all $v \in S^*$ and $\sigma \in BOP_{vs}$,
  $\{z_t t \mid x \in M \cap X, t \in M(x)\} \cup \{u't \mid \sigma u' \in M, t \in M(\sigma u')\} \in GEN_{vw}$
  where $z_t \in X_v$ is chosen such that $z_t t$ is linear. ∎

Padawitz [1], Theorem 7.3, shows that an element of FSL is ground term reducing iff it belongs to GEN. Therefore, the inductive definition of GEN supplies a decision algorithm for ground term generating sets.

Example 8.5.1 (due to Huet and Hullot) Let ⟨BSIG,BAX⟩ = NAT (cf. Section 3.2) and

$$M = \{\langle n,0\rangle, \langle 0,n|\rangle, \langle m|,0|\rangle, \langle m|,n||\rangle\}.$$

By unfolding the assertion $M \in GEN$ with respect to the definition of GEN we see that M is ground term generating:

$$
\begin{array}{rl}
M \in GEN & \text{iff } \{(0,n|\}, \{\langle z,0\rangle, \langle m,0|\rangle, \langle m,n||\rangle\} \in GEN \\
& \text{iff } \{(\varepsilon)\}, \{n\}, \{0,0|,n||\} \in GEN \\
& \text{iff } \{n\}, \{0,0|,n||\} \in GEN \\
& \text{iff } \{\varepsilon\}, \{0,n|\} \in GEN \\
& \text{iff } \{0,n|\} \in GEN \\
& \text{iff } \{\varepsilon\}, \{n\} \in GEN \\
& \text{iff } \{n\} \in GEN \\
& \text{iff } \{\varepsilon\} \in GEN. \ \blacksquare
\end{array}
$$

Ground term generating sets allows us to decide whether NAX is ground term reducing (cf. Section 8.4):

Proposition 8.5.2 If for all $\sigma \in NOP$ the set

$$ARG(\sigma) = \{v \in T(SIG)^* \mid v \text{ is linear}, \exists u' : \sigma v \equiv u' \in NAX\}$$

is ground term generating, then NAX is ground term reducing. The converse holds true under the assumption that NAX is a left-linear set of unconditional equations u≡u' where u is not a base term.

Proof. Suppose that for all $\sigma \in NOP$, the set $ARG(\sigma)$ is ground term generating. Let t be a non-base ground term. Of course, t has an innermost subterm t', i.e. t' = $\sigma v'$ for some $\sigma \in NOP$ and v' $\in GT(BSIG)^*$. Since $ARG(\sigma)$ is ground term generating, some $v \in ARG(\sigma)$ subsumes v'. Therefore, t is not NAX-normal.

Conversely, suppose that NAX is ground term reducing. Let $w \in S^*$, $s \in S$, $\sigma \in NOP_{ws}$ and $t \in GT(BSIG)_w$. Then there is t' with $\sigma t \overline{_{NAX}} t'$ and $t' \neq \sigma t$. By assumption, the only NAX-reduction redex of σt is σt itself. Hence there is $\sigma v \equiv u' \in NAX$ such that v is linear and subsumes t. Thus $v \in ARG(\sigma)$, and we conclude that $ARG(\sigma)$ is ground term generating. $\blacksquare$

Since the inductive theory criterion presented below presumes that ⟨SIG,AX⟩ is sufficiently complete (cf. Section 6.1), let us turn to the close relationship between that condition and the ground-term-reducing property. Of course, ⟨SIG,AX⟩ is sufficiently complete if NAX is ground term reducing and normalizing (cf. Section 7.7). Conversely, one obtains

Proposition 8.5.3 Suppose that ⟨SIG,AX⟩ is ground NAX-Church-Rosser, NAX is normalizing, BAX is variable-preserving and for all $u\equiv u'\Leftarrow\delta\in$ NAX, u is not a base term. Let ⟨SIG,AX⟩ be sufficiently complete. Then NAX is ground term reducing.

Proof. Let t be a non-base ground term. By sufficient completeness, t has a base representation, say t'. Hence t≡t' is a ground ⟨SIG,AX⟩-theorem. t≡t' is NAX-normalizable because NAX is normalizing. Since ⟨SIG,AX⟩ is ground NAX-Church-Rosser, t≡t' is NAX-reducible. By Lemma 7.7.5, there is a NAX-reduced equation v≡v' such that $t\xrightarrow{\overline{NAX}}v$ and $t'\xrightarrow{\overline{NAX}}v'$. t' is a base term, but for all $u\equiv u'\Leftarrow\delta\in$ NAX, u is not a base term. Hence t' = v' and thus v≡t' is a ⟨SIG,BAX⟩-theorem. By Theorem 5.3.5, there is a shortest paramodulating expansion of ⟨{v≡t'},id⟩ to ⟨∅,f⟩ w.r.t. BAX for some f with f↾XG = id. Since t' is a base term and for all $u\equiv u'\Leftarrow\delta\in$ BAX, var(u) = var(u'), we conclude from a simple induction on the length of this expansion that v is a base term as well. Therefore t is not equal to v. ∎

By Propositions 8.5.2 and 8.5.3, the decision algorithm for ground term generating sets can be used to determine the sufficient completeness of ⟨SIG,AX⟩ provided that
- ⟨SIG,AX⟩ is ground NAX-Church-Rosser,
- BAX is variable-preserving,
- NAX is a left-linear and normalizing set of unconditional equations u≡u' where u is not a base term.

Theorem 8.5.4 *Soundness of narrowing w.r.t. inductive theorems*
Let ⟨SIG,AX⟩ be sufficiently complete and AX' ∈ (NAX,~NAX). A goal γ is an inductive ⟨SIG,AX⟩-theorem if there is a set SOL of N-solutions of γ w.r.t. AX' such that the set SOL(γ) = {⟨$gx_1,...,gx_n$⟩ | g ∈ SOL} is ground term generating where {$x_1,...,x_n$} = var(γ).

Proof Since ⟨SIG,AX⟩ is sufficiently complete, the proof is complete if for all ground base substitutions f, γ[f] is a ⟨SIG,AX⟩-theorem. So let f ∈ GT(BSIG)^X. If SOL(γ) is ground term generating, γ has an N-solution g w.r.t. AX' such that g↾var(γ) subsumes f. By Lemmata 8.2.3 (3) and 7.7.3 (2), γ[g] and thus γ[f] are ⟨SIG,AX⟩-theorems. ∎

8.6 Basic Narrowing

Recall from Section 7.10 that basic reduction rejects a reduction redex δ•t if root(t) is located *below* the right-hand side of the equation that caused the preceding reduction step. To keep track of such locations we broke down a goal γ into a goal γ' and a substitution f and described basic reduction steps as transformations of goal-substitution pairs. As goal reduction was extended to narrowing, basic narrowing is the generalization of basic reduction to a calculus that allows us to deduce goal solutions. Consequently, basic narrowing transforms *triples* consisting of a goal and two substitutions, the first of which represents a part of the goal to be narrowed, while the second corresponds to the substitution component of goal-substitution pairs subjected to the Narrowing Rule (cf. Section 8.2).

Definition Let AX' ∈ {NAX, ~NAX}. The *basic narrowing calculus* (w.r.t. AX') consists of the following inference rules:

Basic Success Rule Let γ be a goal and f,h,h' be substitutions such that γ[f][h'] is AX'-reduced. Then

$$\frac{\langle \gamma, f, h \rangle}{\langle \emptyset, id, h[h'] \rangle}.$$

Basic Narrowing Rule Let δ be a goal, x ∈ single(δ)-dom(f[h']), u≡u'⇐ϑ ∈ NAX, t ∈ T(SIG)-X, f,h,h',g be substitutions and
- either AX' = NAX and t[f][h'] = u[g]
- or AX' = ~NAX and t[f][h'] $\Rightarrow_{BAX}$ u[g].

Then

$$\frac{\langle \delta[t/x], f, h \rangle}{\langle \delta[(u'/x)+f[h']] \cup \vartheta, g|var(u), h[h'↑XG] \rangle}.$$

Let γ,γ' be goals and f,g,f',g' be substitutions. A derivation of $\langle \gamma',f',g' \rangle$ from $\langle \gamma,f,g \rangle$ via the basic narrowing calculus is called a *basic narrowing expansion* of $\langle \gamma,f,g \rangle$ to $\langle \gamma',f',g' \rangle$ (w.r.t. AX').

The corresponding inference relation is denoted by $B\vdash^N_{AX'}$. If $\langle \gamma,f,id \rangle$ $B\vdash^N_{AX'}$ $\langle \emptyset,id,g \rangle$, then g is called a *basic N-solution of γ[f]* (w.r.t. AX').

|$\langle \gamma,f,g \rangle$ $B\vdash^N_{AX'}$ $\langle \gamma',f',g' \rangle$| denotes the least number of Basic Narrowing Rule applications needed to derive $\langle \gamma',f',g' \rangle$ from $\langle \gamma,f,g \rangle$. ∎

Lemma 8.6.1 *Soundness of basic narrowing w.r.t. narrowing*
Suppose that for all u≡u'⇐ϑ ∈ NAX, var(u') ∪ var(ϑ) ⊆ var(u).
If $\langle \gamma,f,id \rangle$ $B\vdash^N_{AX'}$ $\langle \varphi,f',h \rangle$ and var(γ[f]) ⊆ XG, then $\langle \gamma[f],id \rangle$ $\vdash^N_{AX'}$ $\langle \varphi[f'],h \rangle$.

Proof (analogous to the proof of Lemma 7.10.1). If

$$\langle\gamma,f,id\rangle \; B\vdash^N_{AX'} \; \langle\varphi,f',h\rangle$$

is obtained by the Basic Success Rule only, then $\gamma[f][h]$ is AX'-reduced, φ is empty and $f' = id$. Hence the Success Rule of the narrowing calculus (cf. Section 8.2) implies

$$\langle\gamma[f],id\rangle \vdash^N_{AX'} \langle\varphi[f'],h\rangle.$$

Let
$$\langle\delta[t/x], f, id\rangle \; B\vdash^N_{AX'} \; \langle\delta[\{u'/x\}+f[h]] \cup \vartheta, \; g\upharpoonright var(u), \; h\upharpoonright XG\rangle$$

be an application of the Basic Narrowing Rule such that

(1) $\qquad var(\delta[t/x][f]) \subseteq XG.$

W.l.o.g. $x \notin var(f(dom(f)))$. Hence

(2) $\qquad \delta[t/x][f] = \delta[f][t[f]/x]$

and

(3) $\qquad \delta[\{u'[g]/x\}+f] = \delta[f][u'[g]/x].$

(1) implies $var(f(var(\delta)-\{x\})) \subseteq XG$. Since XG is disjoint from $var(u)$, we obtain

(4) $\qquad f(var(\delta)-\{x\})[g\upharpoonright var(u)] = f(var(\delta)-\{x\}).$

From $var(u') \cup var(\vartheta) \subseteq var(u)$, (4) and (3) one concludes

(5) $(\delta[\{u'/x\}+f]\cup\vartheta)[g\upharpoonright var(u)] = \delta[\{u'[g]/x\}+f] \cup \vartheta[g] = \delta[f][u'[g]/x] \cup \vartheta[g].$

By (2) and (5), the Narrowing Rule (cf. Section 8.2) implies

$$\langle\delta[t/x][f], id\rangle \; \vdash^N_{AX'} \; \langle(\delta[\{u'/x\}+f]\cup\vartheta)[g\upharpoonright var(u)], h\upharpoonright XG\rangle. \blacksquare$$

Of course, basic reductions correspond to basic narrowing expansions with the identity substitution:

Proposition 8.6.2 If $\langle\gamma,f\rangle \; B\vdash^{RD}_{AX'} \; \langle\gamma',f'\rangle$, then $\langle\gamma,f,id\rangle \; B\vdash^N_{AX'} \; \langle\gamma',f',id\rangle. \blacksquare$

Lemma 8.6.3 *Completeness of basic narrowing w.r.t. basic reduction*
Suppose that for all $u\equiv u' \Leftarrow \vartheta \in NAX$, $var(u') \cup var(\vartheta) \subseteq var(u)$. Let h be an AX'-irreducible substitution. If $\langle\gamma[h],f\rangle$ is basically AX'-reducible, then for all substitutions h_0 and h_1, $h_0[h_1] = h$ implies

(*) $\quad\quad\quad\quad\quad\quad\quad \langle \gamma, h_o, id \rangle \; B\vdash^N_{AX'} \; \langle \varnothing, id, h_1[f]\restriction XG \rangle.$

Proof. We show the statement by induction on $|\langle \gamma[h],f \rangle \; B\vdash^{RD}_{AX'} \; \langle \varnothing,id \rangle|$ (cf. Section 7.9). Let $h = h_o[h_1]$.

Case 1. $\langle \gamma[h],f \rangle$ reduces to $\langle \varnothing,id \rangle$ by applying only the Basic Success Rule. Then $\gamma[h][f] = \gamma[h_o][h_1][f]$ is AX'-reduced, and the Basic Success Rule of the basic narrowing calculus implies (*).

Case 2. $\langle \gamma[h],f \rangle$ reduces to $\langle \varnothing,id \rangle$ only by first applying the Basic Reduction Rule. Then there are a goal δ, a substitution g, $x \in single(\delta)\text{-dom}(f)$, $t \in T(SIG)\text{-}X$, $u \equiv u' \Leftarrow \vartheta \in NAX$ and $t[f] = u[g]$ (or $t[f] \Rightarrow_{BAX} u[g]$) such that $\gamma[h] = \delta[t/x]$ and

(1) $\quad\quad |\langle \gamma[h],f \rangle \; B\vdash^{RD}_{AX'} \; \langle \varnothing,id \rangle| = 1 + |\langle \varphi, gfvar(u) \rangle \; B\vdash^{RD}_{AX'} \; \langle \varnothing,id \rangle|$

where $\varphi = \delta[\{u'/x\}+f]u\vartheta$. Since $\gamma[h] = \delta[t/x]$ and h is AX'-irreducible, t overlaps γ in $\gamma[h]$, i.e. there are a goal γ' and a term $t' \notin X$ such that

(2) $\quad\quad\quad\quad \gamma = \gamma'[t'/x], \; t'[h] = t$ and $\gamma'[h\restriction(X-\{x\})] = \delta.$

W.l.o.g. $x \notin var(h(X-\{x\}))$. Therefore

(3) $\quad\quad \varphi = \gamma'[h\restriction(X-\{x\})][\{u'/x\}+f] \cup \vartheta = \gamma'[\{u'/x\}+h[f]\restriction(X-\{x\})] \cup \vartheta$
$\quad\quad\quad = \gamma'[\{u'/x\}+h_o[h_1][f]\restriction(X-\{x\})] \cup \vartheta.$

By (2), we have

(4) $\quad\quad\quad\quad t'[h_o][h_1][f] = t'[h][f] = t[f] = u[g]$

(or $t'[h_o][h_1][f] \Rightarrow_{BAX} u[g]$). W.l.o.g. $x \notin dom(h)$. Hence $x \notin dom(h[f])$, and by (2)-(4), the Basic Narrowing Rule implies

$\quad\quad\quad\quad \langle \gamma,h_o,id \rangle \; B\vdash^N_{AX'} \; \langle \varphi, gfvar(u), h_1[f]\restriction XG \rangle.$

By Proposition 8.6.2, (1) yields

$\quad\quad\quad\quad \langle \varphi, gfvar(u), h_1[f] \rangle \; B\vdash^N_{AX'} \; \langle \varnothing, id, h_1[f]\restriction XG \rangle,$

and we conclude

$\quad\quad\quad\quad \langle \gamma,h_o,id \rangle \; B\vdash^N_{AX'} \; \langle \varnothing, id, h_1[f]\restriction XG \rangle.$ ∎

Definition A basic narrowing expansion $\langle d_1,...,d_n \rangle$ is *most general* if for all $1 \leq i < n$ the step from d_i to d_{i+1} is performed by a rule of the basic narrowing calculus where the respective substitution h' is minimal w.r.t. the subsumption ordering (cf. Section 2.2).

The corresponding inference relation is denoted by $B\vdash^{GN}_{AX'}$. If

$$\langle \gamma, id, id \rangle \; B\vdash^{GN}_{AX'} \; \langle \emptyset, id, f \rangle,$$

then f is a *basic GN-solution* of γ (w.r.t. AX'). ∎

Lemma 8.6.4 *Forward lifting of basic narrowing expansions*
Let f be an AX'-irreducible substitution and $\langle \gamma, h_o, f \rangle \; B\vdash^N_{AX'} \; \langle \varphi, h_1, f \rangle$. Then there are φ', f', h_1', h such that $\varphi'[h] = \varphi$, $h_1'[h] = h_1$, $f'[h] = f$ and

$$\langle \gamma, h_o, id \rangle \; B\vdash^{GN}_{AX'} \; \langle \varphi', h_1', f' \rangle.$$

In particular, if f is a basic N-solution of γ w.r.t. AX', then there are a basic GN-solution f' of γ w.r.t. AX', which subsumes f.

Proof by induction on $n = |\langle \gamma, h_o, id \rangle \; B\vdash^N_{AX'} \; \langle \varphi, h_1, f \rangle|$. If $n \leq 1$, then the result follows immediately. Otherwise there are δ, g_o, g, h such that $g[h] = f$ and

$$|\langle \gamma, h_o, id \rangle \; B\vdash^N_{AX'} \; \langle \varphi, h_1, f \rangle| = |\langle \gamma, h_o, id \rangle \; B\vdash^N_{AX'} \; \langle \delta, g_o, g \rangle| + |\langle \delta, g_o, id \rangle \; B\vdash^N_{AX'} \; \langle \varphi, h_1, h \rangle|$$

and $\langle \varphi, h_1, h \rangle$ is obtained from $\langle \delta, g_o, id \rangle$ by applying the Basic Narrowing Rule exactly once. By the induction hypothesis, there are δ', g', g_1, h' such that

(1) $\quad \langle \gamma, h_o, id \rangle \; B\vdash^{GN}_{AX'} \; \langle \delta', g_1, g' \rangle, \quad \delta'[h'] = \delta, \quad g_1[h'] = g_o \text{ and } g'[h'] = g.$

Since $g'[h'][h] = g[h] = f$ is AX'-irreducible, we may assume that h' is AX'-irreducible as well. Since $\delta'[h'] = \delta$, the left-hand side of the axiom applied to δ overlaps δ'. Hence

$$\langle \delta, g_o, id \rangle \; B\vdash^N_{AX'} \; \langle \varphi, h_1, h \rangle$$

can be lifted to

$$\langle \delta', g_1, id \rangle \; B\vdash^N_{AX'} \; \langle \varphi, h_1, h'[h] \rangle.$$

Once more, by the induction hypothesis,

(2) $\quad \langle \delta', g_1, id \rangle \; B\vdash^{GN}_{AX'} \; \langle \varphi', h_1', g'' \rangle, \quad \varphi'[h''] = \varphi, \quad h_1'[h''] = h_1 \text{ and } g''[h''] = h'[h]$

for some φ', g'', h_1', h''. (1) and (2) yield $\langle \gamma, h_o, id \rangle \; B\vdash^{GN}_{AX'} \; \langle \varphi', h_1', g'[g''] \rangle$, $\varphi'[h''] = \varphi$, $h_1'[h''] = h_1$ and $g'[g''][h''] = g'[h'][h] = g[h] = f$. ∎

Theorem 8.6.5 *Completeness of most general basic narrowing w.r.t. narrowing*
Suppose that the AX'-reduction relation is Noetherian and for all $u \equiv u' \Leftarrow \delta \in$ NAX, $var(u') \cup var(\delta) \subseteq var(u)$.

Let γ be a goal and let f be an AX'-irreducible N-solution of γ w.r.t. AX' such that var(γ[f]) ⊆ XG. Then there is a basic GN-solution g of γ w.r.t. AX', which subsumes f.

Proof. By Lemma 8.2.3 (2), γ[f] is AX'-reducible. Hence by Lemma 7.10.2, <γ,f> is basically AX'-reducible. By Lemma 8.6.3, <γ,id,id> B$\xrightarrow{N}_{AX}$ <∅,id,f>, i.e. f is a basic N-solution of γ w.r.t. AX'. Finally, by Lemma 8.6.4, there is a basic GN-solution f' of γ w.r.t. AX', which subsumes f. ∎

8.7 Reduced Narrowing

Another refinement of the Narrowing Rule works as follows. Variables in the goal to be narrowed are not instantiated as long as the goal has *reduction redices*. Since reduction redices are particular narrowing redices, this refinement does not modify the inference rules. Instead, it may be regarded as a strategy that prefers narrowing steps with identity substitution to narrowing steps with non-identity substitution. (In contrast to the strategies discussed in Sections 8.3 and 8.4 the location of the redex does not matter.) Reduced narrowing is based on a *reduction mapping* R : T(SIG)⟶T(SIG), which assigns to each term t a term t' with t$\xrightarrow{}_{AX'}$t'. R is extended to goals γ and substitutions f by:

$$R(\gamma) = \{P<R(t_1),...,R(t_n)> \mid P<t_1,...,t_n> \in \gamma\} \quad \text{and} \quad R(f)(x) = R(fx).$$

This definition implies that for all goals γ there is an AX'-reducible goal ϑ such that γ $\xrightarrow{RD}_{AX'}$ R(γ)∪ϑ and var(R(γ)) ∩ var(ϑ) = ∅.

Definition Given a reduction mapping R, the *reduced narrowing calculus* consists of the Success Rule (cf. Section 8.2) and the

Reduced Narrowing Rule Let δ be a goal, x ∈ single(δ), u≡u'⇐ϑ ∈ NAX, t ∈ T(SIG)-X, f,g be substitutions and
- either AX' = NAX and t[g] = u[g]
- or AX' = ~NAX and t[g]$\xrightarrow{}_{BAX}$u[g].

Then

$$\frac{<\delta[t/x], f>}{<R((\delta[u'/x]\cup\vartheta)[g]), f[g\upharpoonright XG]>}.$$

Let γ,γ' be goals and f,f' be substitutions. A derivation of <γ',f'> from <γ,f> via the reduced narrowing calculus is called a *reduced narrowing expansion* of <γ,f> to <γ',f'> (w.r.t. AX').

The corresponding inference relation is denoted by $\vdash_{AX'}^{RN}$.

$|\langle\gamma,f\rangle\ R\vdash_{AX'}^{N}\ \langle\gamma',f'\rangle|$ denotes the least number of Reduced Narrowing Rule applications needed to derive $\langle\gamma',f'\rangle$ from $\langle\gamma,f\rangle$. ∎

Lemma 8.7.1 *Soundness of reduced narrowing w.r.t. narrowing*
Let $\langle\gamma,id\rangle\ R\vdash_{AX'}^{N}\ \langle\emptyset,f\rangle$ and $var(\gamma)\subseteq XG$. Then $\langle\gamma,id\rangle\vdash_{AX'}^{N}\langle\emptyset,f\rangle$.

Proof by induction on $|\langle\gamma,id\rangle\ R\vdash_{AX'}^{N}\langle\emptyset,f\rangle|$. If $\langle\emptyset,f\rangle$ is obtained from $\langle\gamma,id\rangle$ by applying only the Success Rule, the proof is complete. Otherwise $\langle\gamma,id\rangle$ expands to $\langle\emptyset,f\rangle$ only by first applying the Reduced Narrowing Rule. Then there are a single application of the Narrowing Rule from $\langle\gamma,id\rangle$ to some $\langle\psi,g\rangle$ and a substitution h such that g[h] = f and

$$|\langle\gamma,id\rangle\ R\vdash_{AX'}^{N}\langle\emptyset,f\rangle|\ =\ 1\ +\ |\langle R(\psi),id\rangle\ R\vdash_{AX'}^{N}\langle\emptyset,h\rangle|.$$

$var(\gamma)\subseteq XG$ implies $var(\psi)\subseteq XG$ and thus w.l.o.g. $var(R(\psi))\subseteq XG$. Since $\psi\vdash_{AX'}^{RD}R(\psi)\cup\vartheta'$ for some AX'-reducible ϑ', completeness of narrowing w.r.t. goal reduction (Lemma 8.2.4) implies $\langle\psi,id\rangle\vdash_{AX'}^{N}\langle R(\psi)\cup\vartheta',id\rangle$ and thus

(3) $\qquad\qquad\langle\psi,g\rangle\vdash_{AX'}^{N}\langle R(\psi)\cup\vartheta',g\rangle.$

By the induction hypothesis, $\langle R(\psi),id\rangle\vdash_{AX'}^{N}\langle\emptyset,h\rangle$. Since $var(R(\psi))$ is disjoint from $var(\vartheta')$, we conclude

(4) $\qquad\qquad\langle R(\psi)\cup\vartheta',g\rangle\vdash_{AX'}^{N}\langle\vartheta',g[h]\rangle.$

Since ϑ' is AX'-reducible, Lemma 8.2.4 implies $\langle\vartheta',id\rangle\vdash_{AX'}^{N}\langle\emptyset,id\rangle$. Thus by (3) and (4), $\langle\gamma,id\rangle\vdash_{AX'}^{N}\langle\emptyset,f\rangle$. ∎

For completeness of reduced narrowing we employ Noetherian induction and refer to Lemma 7.9.1, which presumes confluence properties.

Lemma 8.7.2 *Completeness of reduced narrowing w.r.t. narrowing*
Let either AX' = NAX and CAX = BAX or AX' = ~NAX and CAX = ~BAX. Suppose that $\vdash_{AX'}^{RD}$ is Noetherian, AX' is confluent modulo CAX and that CAX respects AX'-normal forms (cf. Section 7.8).

If $\langle\gamma,id\rangle\vdash_{AX'}^{N}\langle\emptyset,f\rangle$ for some AX'-irreducible f such that $var(\gamma)\cup dom(f)\subseteq XG$, then $\langle\gamma,id\rangle\ R\vdash_{AX'}^{N}\langle\emptyset,f\rangle$.

Proof by Noetherian induction on $\gamma[f]$ w.r.t. $\vdash_{AX'}^{RD}$. The proof is complete if $\langle\gamma,id\rangle$ expands to $\langle\emptyset,f\rangle$ by applying only the Success Rule. Otherwise $\langle\gamma,id\rangle$ expands to some $\langle\delta,g\rangle$ by a single application of the Narrowing Rule, $\langle\delta,id\rangle\vdash_{AX'}^{N}$

$\langle \emptyset, g' \rangle$ and $f = g[g']$ for some g' with $dom(g') \subseteq XG$. Hence

(∗) $\qquad\qquad \langle \gamma, id \rangle \; R\vdash^N_{AX'} \; \langle R(\delta), g \rangle$,

and by Lemma 8.2.3 (2), $\delta[g']$ is AX'-reducible.

By Lemma 7.9.1, $\delta[g'] \vdash^{RD}_{AX'} \emptyset$ implies $R(\delta)[g'] \vdash^{RD}_{AX'} \emptyset$. By (∗), $var(R(\delta)) \subseteq XG$. Hence by Lemma 8.2.4, $\langle R(\delta), id \rangle \vdash^N_{AX'} \langle \emptyset, g' \rangle$.

The narrowing step from $\langle \gamma, id \rangle$ to $\langle \delta, g \rangle$ extends to a narrowing step from $\langle \gamma, id \rangle$ to $\langle \delta[g'], g[g'] \rangle = \langle \delta[g'], f \rangle$. Thus by Lemma 8.2.3 (1),

$$\gamma[f] \vdash^{RD}_{AX'} \delta[g'] \vdash^{RD}_{AX'} R(\delta)[g']\cup\vartheta$$

for some AX'-reducible ϑ. Therefore $R(\delta)[g']$ is less than $\gamma[f]$ w.r.t. $\vdash^{RD}_{AX'}$. Hence by the induction hypothesis, $\langle R(\delta), id \rangle \; R\vdash^N_{AX'} \; \langle \emptyset, g' \rangle$, and composition with (∗) yields

$$\langle \gamma, id \rangle \; R\vdash^N_{AX'} \; \langle \emptyset, g[g'] \rangle = \langle \emptyset, f \rangle. \blacksquare$$

Of course, Lemma 8.7.2 holds true for *most general* narrowing as well.

Lemmata 8.7.1 and 8.7.2 imply

Theorem 8.7.3 *Soundness and completeness of reduced narrowing w.r.t. narrowing*

Let either AX' = NAX and CAX = BAX or AX' = ~NAX and CAX = ~BAX. Suppose that $\vdash^{RD}_{AX'}$ is Noetherian, AX' is confluent modulo CAX and that CAX respects AX'-normal forms. Let g be a goal and let f be an AX'-irreducible substitution such that $var(\gamma) \cup dom(f) \subseteq XG$.

Then $\langle \gamma, id \rangle \vdash^N_{AX'} \langle \emptyset, f \rangle$ iff $\langle \gamma, id \rangle \; R\vdash^N_{AX'} \; \langle \emptyset, f \rangle$. $\blacksquare$

The following section combines reduced with basic narrowing.

8.8 Reduced Basic Narrowing

Definition Given a reduction mapping R, the *reduced basic narrowing calculus* consists of the Basic Success Rule (cf. Section 8.6) and the

Reduced Basic Narrowing Rule Let δ be a goal, $x \in single(\delta) - dom(f[h'])$, $t \in T(SIG)-X$, $u \equiv u' \Leftarrow \vartheta \in NAX$, f,h,h',g be substitutions and
- either AX' = NAX and $t[f][h'] = u[g]$
- or AX' = ~NAX and $t[f][h'] \overline{=_{BAX}} u[g]$.

Then

$$\frac{\langle\delta[t/x], f, h\rangle}{\langle R(\delta[\{u'/x\}+f[h']] \cup \vartheta), R(g\uparrow var(u)), h[h'\uparrow XG]\rangle.}$$

Let γ,γ' be goals and f,g,f',g' be substitutions. A derivation of $\langle\gamma',f',g'\rangle$ from $\langle\gamma,f,g\rangle$ via the reduced basic narrowing calculus is called a *reduced basic narrowing expansion* of $\langle\gamma,f,g\rangle$ to $\langle\gamma',f',g'\rangle$ (w.r.t. AX').

The corresponding inference relation is denoted by $RB\vdash^N_{AX'}$.

$|\langle\gamma,f,g\rangle \; RB\vdash^N_{AX'} \; \langle\gamma',f',g'\rangle|$ denotes the least number of Reduced Basic Narrowing Rule applications needed to derive $\langle\gamma',f',g'\rangle$ from $\langle\gamma,f,g\rangle$. ∎

Lemma 8.8.1 *Soundness of reduced basic narrowing w.r.t. narrowing*
Suppose that for all $u \equiv u' \Leftarrow \vartheta \in NAX$, $var(u') \cup var(\vartheta) \subseteq var(u)$.
Let $\langle\gamma,g,id\rangle \; RB\vdash^N_{AX'} \; \langle\varnothing,id,f\rangle$ and $var(\gamma[g]) \subseteq XG$. Then $\langle\gamma[g],id\rangle \vdash^N_{AX'} \langle\varnothing,f\rangle$.

Proof (1) is shown by induction on $|\langle\gamma,g,id\rangle \; R\vdash^N_{AX'} \; \langle\varnothing,id,f\rangle|$. If $\langle\varnothing,id,f\rangle$ is obtained from $\langle\gamma,g,id\rangle$ by applying only the Basic Success Rule, the proof is complete. Otherwise $\langle\gamma,g,id\rangle$ expands to $\langle\varnothing,id,f\rangle$ only by first applying the Reduced Basic Narrowing Rule. Then there are a single application of the Basic Narrowing Rule from $\langle\gamma,g,id\rangle$ to some $\langle\psi,g',f'\rangle$ and a substitution f" such that f'[f"] = f and

$$|\langle\gamma,g,id\rangle \; RB\vdash^N_{AX'} \; \langle\varnothing,id,f\rangle| \; = \; 1 + |\langle R(\psi),R(g'),id\rangle \; RB\vdash^N_{AX'} \; \langle\varnothing,id,f''\rangle|.$$

$var(\gamma[g]) \subseteq XG$ implies $var(\psi[g']) \subseteq XG$ and thus w.l.o.g. $var(R(\psi)[R(g')]) \subseteq XG$. Since $\psi[g'] \vdash^{RD}_{AX'} R(\psi)[R(g')]\cup\vartheta'$ for some AX'-reducible ϑ', completeness of narrowing w.r.t. goal reduction (Lemma 8.2.4) implies

$$\langle\psi[g'], id\rangle \vdash^N_{AX'} \langle R(\psi)[R(g')]\cup\vartheta', id\rangle$$

and thus

(3) $\langle\psi[g'], f'\rangle \vdash^N_{AX'} \langle R(\psi)[R(g')]\cup\vartheta', f'\rangle.$

By Lemma 8.6.1, the basic narrowing step from $\langle\gamma,g,id\rangle$ to $\langle\psi,g',f'\rangle$ corresponds to a narrowing step from $\langle\gamma[g],id\rangle$ to $\langle\psi[g'],f'\rangle$.

By the induction hypothesis, $\langle R(\psi)[R(g')],id\rangle \; B\vdash^N_{AX'} \; \langle\varnothing,f''\rangle$. Since $var(\vartheta')$ is disjoint from $var(R(\psi)[R[g']))$, we conclude

(4) $\langle R(\psi)[R(g')]\cup\vartheta', f'\rangle \; B\vdash^N_{AX'} \; \langle\vartheta', f'[f'']\rangle.$

Since ϑ' is AX'-reducible, Lemma 8.2.4 implies $\langle\vartheta',id\rangle \vdash^N_{AX'} \langle\varnothing,id\rangle$. Thus by (3) and (4), $\langle\gamma,id\rangle \vdash^N_{AX'} \langle\varnothing,f\rangle$. ∎

The proof of completeness of reduced basic narrowing w.r.t. basic narrowing refers to Lemma 7.9.1 (term reductions preserve reducibility), Lemma 7.10.2 (completeness of basic reduction w.r.t. goal reduction) and Lemma 8.6.3 (completeness of basic narrowing w.r.t. basic reduction). In addition to the assumptions of those results, the reduction mapping is supposed to return normal forms. The proof proceeds along the lines of the proof of Lemma 8.7.2 that stated completeness of reduced narrowing w.r.t. narrowing.

Lemma 8.8.2 *Completeness of reduced basic narrowing w.r.t. basic narrowing*

Let either AX' = NAX and CAX = BAX or AX' = ~NAX and CAX = ~BAX. Suppose that
- for all terms t, R(t) is AX'-irreducible,
- for all u≡u'⇐ϑ ∈ NAX, var(u') ∪ var(ϑ) ⊆ var(u),
- $\vdash^{RD}_{AX'}$ is Noetherian,
- AX' is confluent modulo CAX,
- CAX respects AX'-normal forms.

If $\langle \gamma, f, id \rangle$ B$\vdash^{N}_{AX'}$ $\langle \varnothing, id, g \rangle$ for some AX'-irreducible g such that var($\gamma[f]$) ⊆ XG, then $\langle \gamma, f, id \rangle$ RB$\vdash^{N}_{AX'}$ $\langle \varnothing, id, g \rangle$.

Proof by Noetherian induction on $\gamma[f][g]$ w.r.t. $\vdash^{RD}_{AX'}$. The proof is complete if $\langle \gamma, f, id \rangle$ expands to $\langle \varnothing, id, g \rangle$ by applying only the Basic Success Rule. Otherwise $\langle \gamma, f, id \rangle$ expands to some $\langle \delta, f', g' \rangle$ by a single application of the Basic Narrowing Rule, $\langle \delta, f', id \rangle$ B$\vdash^{N}_{AX'}$ $\langle \varnothing, id, g" \rangle$ and g = g'[g"] for some g" with dom(g") ⊆ XG. By Lemma 8.6.1,

$$\langle \gamma[f], id \rangle \vdash^{N}_{AX'} \langle \delta[f'], g' \rangle \quad \text{and} \quad \langle \delta[f'], id \rangle \vdash^{N}_{AX'} \langle \varnothing, g" \rangle.$$

Hence by Lemma 8.2.3 (2), $\delta[f'][g"]$ is AX'-reducible.

By Lemma 7.9.1, $\delta[f'][g"] \vdash^{RD}_{AX'} \varnothing$ implies $R(\delta)[R(f')][g"] \vdash^{RD}_{AX'} \varnothing$. Since g" is AX'-irreducible and w.l.o.g. var(R(δ)[R(f')][g"]) ⊆ XG, Lemma 7.10.2 implies $\langle R(\delta)[R(f')], g" \rangle$ B$\vdash^{RD}_{AX'}$ $\langle \varnothing, id \rangle$. By assumption, R(f') is AX'-irreducible. Hence by Lemma 8.6.3,

(1) $\qquad \langle R(\delta), R(f'), id \rangle$ B$\vdash^{N}_{AX'}$ $\langle \varnothing, id, g" \rangle$.

The narrowing step from $\langle \gamma[f], id \rangle$ to $\langle \delta[f'], g' \rangle$ extends to a narrowing step from $\langle \gamma[f], id \rangle$ to $\langle \delta[f'][g"], g'[g"] \rangle$ = $\langle \delta[f'][g"], g \rangle$. Thus by Lemma 8.2.3 (1),

$$\gamma[f][g] \vdash^{RD}_{AX'} \delta[f'][g"] \vdash^{RD}_{AX'} R(\delta)[R(f')][g"] \cup \vartheta$$

for some AX'-reducible ϑ. Therefore R(δ)[R(f')][g"] is less than $\gamma[f][g]$ w.r.t.

$\vdash^{RD}_{AX'}$. Hence by (1) and the induction hypothesis,

(2) $\qquad\qquad$ ⟨R(δ), R(f'), id⟩ RB$\vdash^{N}_{AX'}$ ⟨∅, id, g"⟩.

The basic narrowing step from ⟨γ,f,id⟩ to ⟨δ,f',g'⟩ extends to a reduced basic narrowing step from ⟨γ,f,id⟩ to ⟨R(δ),R(f'),g'⟩. Therefore composition with (2) implies

$\qquad\qquad$ ⟨γ, f, id⟩ RB$\vdash^{N}_{AX'}$ ⟨∅, id, g'[g"]⟩ = ⟨∅, id, g⟩. ∎

Of course, Lemma 8.8.2 holds true for *most general* basic narrowing as well.

The way from narrowing to reduced basic narrowing passes goal reduction (Lemma 8.2.3), basic reduction (Lemma 7.10.2) and basic narrowing (Lemma 8.6.3). Hence Lemmata 8.8.1 and 8.8.2 lead to

Theorem 8.8.3 *Soundness and completeness of reduced basic narrowing w.r.t. narrowing*

Let either AX' = NAX and CAX = BAX or AX' = ~NAX and CAX = ~BAX. Suppose that
- for all terms t, R(t) is AX'-irreducible,
- for all u≡u'⇐δ ∈ NAX, var(u') ∪ var(δ) ⊆ var(u),
- $\vdash^{RD}_{AX'}$ is Noetherian,
- AX' is confluent modulo CAX,
- CAX respects AX'-normal forms.

Let γ be a goal and f,g be substitutions such that f[g] is AX'-irreducible and var(γ[f]) ⊆ XG. Then ⟨γ,f,id⟩ RB$\vdash^{N}_{AX'}$ ⟨∅,id,g⟩ iff ⟨γ[f],id⟩ $\vdash^{N}_{AX'}$ ⟨∅,g⟩.

Proof. The only-if part follows from Lemma 8.8.1.

Let ⟨γ[f],id⟩ $\vdash^{N}_{AX'}$ ⟨∅,g⟩. By Lemma 8.2.3 (2), γ[f][g] is AX'-reducible. W.l.o.g. var(γ[f][g]) ⊆ XG. Hence by Lemma 7.10.2, ⟨γ[f][g],id⟩ is basically AX'-reducible. Lemma 8.6.3 implies ⟨γ,f,id⟩ B$\vdash^{N}_{AX'}$ ⟨∅,id,g,⟩ and thus ⟨γ,f,id⟩ RB$\vdash^{N}_{AX'}$ ⟨∅,id,g⟩ follows from Lemma 8.8.2. ∎

8.9 Optimized Narrowing

Given a goal γ, solutions of γ are often attained faster if goal-substitution pairs are *optimized* before the Narrowing Rule is applied. The purpose of this section is to find out correctness conditions on *optimizing functions* to ensure that the completeness of narrowing is maintained. The result of an optimization step may depend not only on the actual pair ⟨φ,f⟩ to be optimized but also on the entire set of goal-substitution pairs ⟨δ,g⟩ derived from a predecessor of ⟨φ,f⟩ within a fixed number of narrowing steps.

Moreover, optimizations may cut off expansion branches which cannot lead to solutions of γ.

Let $GoalSub = Goal(SIG) \times T(SIG)^X$. An *optimizing function* is given by a family

$$Op = \{Op(M) \mid M \subseteq GoalSub\}$$

of partial functions $Op(M) : GoalSub \rightarrow GoalSub$ that are *compatible with substitution prefixes,* i.e. for all goals $\langle \delta, f \rangle \in GoalSub$ and substitutions g,

$$Op(M)(\delta,f) = \langle \delta_o, f_o \rangle \quad \text{implies} \quad Op(g[M])(\delta, g[f]) = \langle \delta_o, g[f_o] \rangle$$

where $g[M] = \{\langle \varphi, g[h] \rangle \mid \langle \varphi, h \rangle \in M\}$.

Actually, we are concerned with those sets M that consist of all goal-substitution pairs $\langle \varphi, f \rangle$ derived from the same pair $\langle \gamma, id \rangle$ within a fixed number of optimized narrowing steps. Hence, in contrast to previous inference rules, the result of an optimized narrowing step may depend on the entire derivation tree up to fixed depth.

Definition Given an optimizing function Op and a goal γ, a partial function

$$OpT : \mathbb{N}^* \longrightarrow GoalSub$$

is called an *optimized narrowing tree for γ* if
- $OpT(\varepsilon) = \langle \gamma, id \rangle$,
- for all $n \in \mathbb{N}$, $w \in \mathbb{N}^{\leq n}$ and $i \in \mathbb{N}$, $OpT(wi)$ is either undefined or for some δ, f and $M \subseteq OpT(\mathbb{N}^{\leq n})$, $OpT(wi) = Op(M)(\delta, f)$ and $OpT(w) \vdash_{Ax}^{N} \langle \delta, f \rangle$ by a single rule application.

Pairs on the same path of an optimized narrowing tree are related by the *optimized narrowing relation* $Op\vdash_{Ax}^{N}$, i.e.

$$\langle \gamma, f \rangle \; Op\vdash_{Ax}^{N} \; \langle \gamma', f' \rangle$$

iff there are an optimized narrowing tree OpT and $v, w \in \mathbb{N}^*$ such that

$$OpT(v) = \langle \gamma, f \rangle \quad \text{and} \quad OpT(vw) = \langle \gamma', f' \rangle. \blacksquare$$

Of course, the soundness and completeness of optimized narrowing depends on the optimizing function Op involved. Since Op modifies subgoals, certain solutions obtained by pure narrowing might not be derivable by optimized narrowing. Therefore we need a correctness criterion for optimizing functions to ensure that the N-solutions of $\langle \delta, f \rangle$ are subsumed by the N-solutions of $Op(M)(\delta, f)$. The following definition of such a criterion refers to the *N-solution ordering* $<$ on goal-solution pairs:

$\langle \gamma, f \rangle < \langle \delta, g \rangle$ iff $|\langle \gamma, id \rangle \vdash^N_{AX} \langle \emptyset, f \rangle| < |\langle \delta, id \rangle \vdash^N_{AX} \langle \emptyset, g \rangle|$.

Definition An optimizing function Op is *locally correct* if the following conditions hold true:

(i) Let f be a substitution and let δ be a goal with an AX'-irreducible N-solution g. Then $Op(\emptyset)(\delta, f)$ is defined, say $Op(\emptyset)(\delta, f) = \langle \delta_0, f_0 \rangle$, and there is an AX'-irreducible N-solution g_0 of δ_0 such that $\langle \delta_0, g_0 \rangle \leq \langle \delta, g \rangle$ and $f_0[g_0]$ subsumes $f[g]$.

(ii) Let $M \subseteq \text{GoalSub}$ and $Op(M)(\delta, f) = \langle \delta_0, f_0 \rangle$ such that δ_0 has a deductive solution, say g_0. Then there are $\langle \delta_1, f_1 \rangle \in Mu(\langle \delta, f \rangle)$ and a substitution g_1 such that g_0 is a deductive solution of $\delta_1[g_1]$ and $f_0 \equiv f_1[g_1]$ is a deductive theorem. ∎

To illustrate condition (i), imagine a narrowing expansion of the form

$$\langle \gamma, id \rangle \vdash^N_{AX} \langle \delta, f \rangle \vdash^N_{AX} \langle \emptyset, f[g] \rangle.$$

Hence $f[g]$ is a N-solution of γ, and by (i), $Op(\emptyset)(\langle \delta, f \rangle) = \langle \delta_0, f_0 \rangle$ and

$$\langle \delta_0, f_0 \rangle \vdash^N_{AX} \langle \emptyset, f_0[g_0] \rangle$$

for some δ_0, f_0 such that $f_0[g_0]$ subsumes $f[g]$. Roughly speaking, the solution $f[g]$ has survived the optimization step from $\langle \delta, f \rangle$ to $\langle \delta_0, f_0 \rangle$, and we conclude that optimized narrowing is *complete* w.r.t. narrowing.

Conversely, let $|\langle \gamma, id \rangle \vdash^N_{AX} \langle \delta, f \rangle| = n$ and suppose that M is the set of goal-substitution pairs obtained by expansions of $\langle \gamma, id \rangle$ within less than n steps. Let $Op(M)(\delta, f) = \langle \delta_0, f_0 \rangle$ and let g_0 be a deductive solution of δ_0. Soundness of optimized narrowing demands that $f_0[g_0]$ be a deductive solution of γ. In fact, by (ii), there are $\langle \delta_1, f_1 \rangle \in Mu(\langle \delta, f \rangle)$ and a substitution g_1 such that g_0 is a deductive solution of $\delta_1[g_1]$ and $f_0 \equiv f_1[g_1]$ is a deductive theorem. Since all elements of $Mu(\langle \delta, f \rangle)$, in particular $\langle \delta_1, f_1 \rangle$, are derived from $\langle \gamma, id \rangle$, $f_1[g_1][g_0]$ is a deductive solution of γ. Moreover, $f_1[g_1][g_0]$ agrees with $f_0[g_0]$ modulo AX, i.e. $f_1[g_1][g_0] \equiv f_0[g_0]$ is a deductive theorem. Moreover, note that

$$|\langle \gamma, id \rangle \vdash^N_{AX} \langle \delta_1, f_1 \rangle| \leq |\langle \gamma, id \rangle \vdash^N_{AX} \langle \delta, f \rangle|,$$

i.e. expansions of $\langle \gamma, id \rangle$ achieve $\langle \delta_1, f_1 \rangle$ not later than $\langle \delta, f \rangle$. This fact allows us to induce from single optimization steps within an expansion of $\langle \gamma, id \rangle$ – as outlined above – to optimized narrowing trees for γ.

Lemma 8.9.1 *Soundness of optimized narrowing w.r.t. deductive solutions*
Let Op be a locally correct optimizing function, γ be a goal and OpT be an optimized narrowing tree for γ. Then for all pairs $\langle\emptyset,f\rangle$ in the range of OpT, f is a deductive solution of γ.

Proof. More generally, we show the following for all goals φ.
(∗) If $\langle\varphi,f\rangle$ is in the range of OpT, then all deductive solutions h of φ are deductive solutions of $\gamma[f]$.

Let $\langle\varphi,f\rangle$ be in the range of OpT and $\varphi[h]$ be a deductive theorem. Then there is $w \in \mathbb{N}^*$ such that $\text{OpT}(w) = \langle\varphi,f\rangle$. We show (∗) by induction on $n = \text{length}(w)$. If $n = 0$, then $\langle\varphi,f\rangle = \langle\gamma,\text{id}\rangle$, and the proof is complete. Otherwise $w = vi$ for some $v \in \mathbb{N}^{<n}$ and $i \in \mathbb{N}$. Hence there are $\langle\delta,g\rangle$ and $M \subseteq \text{OpT}(\mathbb{N}^{<n})$ such that $\text{OpT}(v) \vdash^N_{AX'} \langle\delta,g\rangle$ by a single rule application and $\text{Op}(M)(\delta,g) = \langle\varphi,f\rangle$.

Let h be a deductive solution of φ. By (ii), there are $\langle\delta_1,f_1\rangle \in \text{Mu}(\langle\delta,g\rangle)$ and a substitution g_1 such that h is a deductive solution of $\delta_1[g_1]$ and $f \equiv f_1[g_1]$ is a deductive theorem.

Case 1. $\langle\delta_1,f_1\rangle \in M$. Then there is $v' \in \mathbb{N}^{<n}$ with $\text{OpT}(v') = \langle\delta_1,f_1\rangle$. Hence by the induction hypothesis, h is a deductive solution of $\gamma[f_1][g_1]$ and thus of $\gamma[f]$.

Case 2. $\langle\delta_1,f_1\rangle = \langle\delta,g\rangle$. Let $\text{OpT}(v) = \langle\delta_0,f_0\rangle$. Since $\text{OpT}(v) \vdash^N_{AX'} \langle\delta,g\rangle$, there is g' with $f_0[g'] = g$. Since h is a deductive solution of $\delta_1[g_1]$ and $\delta_1 = \delta$, h is a deductive solution of $\delta_0[g'][g_1]$ as well. In other words, $g'[g_1][h]$ is a deductive solution of δ_0. Since $v \in \mathbb{N}^{<n}$, the induction hypothesis implies that $g'[g_1][h]$ is a deductive solution of $\gamma[f_0]$. Since $f_0[g'][g_1] = g[g_1] = f_1[g_1]$ and $f_1[g_1] \equiv f$ is a deductive theorem, we conclude that h is a deductive solution of $\gamma[f]$.

Therefore (∗) holds true. ∎

Hence soundness of optimized narrowing is a consequence of (ii). On the other hand, completeness follows from (i):

Lemma 8.9.2 *Completeness of optimized narrowing w.r.t. narrowing*
Let Op be a locally correct optimizing function and let f be an AX'-irreducible N-solution of γ. Then there are an optimized narrowing tree OpT for γ and a substitution g such that $\langle\emptyset,g\rangle$ is in the range of OpT and g subsumes f.

Proof by induction on $\langle\gamma,f\rangle$ with respect to the N-solution ordering (see above). If $\langle\gamma,\text{id}\rangle = \langle\emptyset,f\rangle$, the proof is complete with the one-node narrowing tree OpT assigning $\langle\emptyset,f\rangle$ to ε. Otherwise there are δ,g,h such that $\langle\gamma,\text{id}\rangle \vdash^N_{AX'} \langle\delta,g\rangle$ by a single rule application,

(∗) $\qquad |\langle\gamma,\text{id}\rangle \vdash^N_{AX'} \langle\emptyset,f\rangle| = 1 + |\langle\delta,g\rangle \vdash^N_{AX'} \langle\emptyset,f\rangle|$

and $g[h] = f$. Thus h is an AX'-irreducible N-solution of δ, and (i) implies $Op(\emptyset)(\delta,g) = \langle\delta_0,f_0\rangle$ for some δ_0, f_0. Moreover, there is an AX'-irreducible N-solution g_0 of δ_0 such that $\langle\delta_0,g_0\rangle \leq \langle\delta,h\rangle$ and $f_0[g_0]$ subsumes f. By (∗), $\langle\delta,h\rangle \ll \langle\gamma,f\rangle$. Hence $\langle\delta_0,g_0\rangle \ll \langle\gamma,f\rangle$ and thus by the induction hypothesis, there are an optimized narrowing tree OpT' of δ_0 and a substitutions g_1 such that $\langle\emptyset,g_1\rangle$ is in the range of OpT' and g_1 subsumes g_0. In particular,

- $OpT'(\varepsilon) = \langle\delta_0, id\rangle$,
- for all $n \in \mathbb{N}$, $w \in \mathbb{N}^{\leq n}$ and $i \in \mathbb{N}$ such that $OpT'(wi)$ is either undefined or $OpT'(w) \vdash^N_{AX'} \langle\delta',f'\rangle$ by a single rule application and $Op(M')(\delta',f') = OpT'(wi)$ for some δ',f' and $M \subseteq OpT'(\mathbb{N}^{\leq n})$.

We define a further partial function OpT : $\mathbb{N}^* \to$ GoalSub as follows:

- $OpT(\varepsilon) = \langle\gamma, id\rangle$,
- for all $w \in \mathbb{N}^*$, $OpT(0w) = \langle\varphi, f_0[h_0]\rangle$ if $OpT'(w) = \langle\varphi, h_0\rangle$,
- for all $w \in \mathbb{N}^*$ and $i \geq 1$, $OpT(iw)$ is undefined.

Since $\langle\emptyset,g_1\rangle$ is in the range of OpT', we conclude $OpT(0w) = \langle\emptyset, f_0[g_1]\rangle$ for some w. Since $f_0[g_0]$ subsumes f and g_1 subsumes g_0, $f_0[g_1]$ subsumes f as well.

It remains for us to show that OpT is an optimized narrowing tree for γ.

Let $n \in \mathbb{N}$, $w \in \mathbb{N}^{\leq n}$ and $i \in \mathbb{N}$ such that $OpT(wi)$ is defined.

Case 1. $w = \varepsilon$. Then $i = 0$ and thus $OpT(wi) = OpT(0) = \langle\delta_0,f_0\rangle$ because $OpT'(\varepsilon) = \langle\delta_0, id\rangle$. Furthermore, $OpT(w) = \langle\gamma, id\rangle \vdash^N_{AX'} \langle\delta,g\rangle$ by a single rule application and $Op(\emptyset)(\delta,g) = \langle\delta_0,f_0\rangle = OpT(wi)$.

Case 2. $w \neq \varepsilon$. Then $w = 0w'$ for some $w' \in \mathbb{N}^{<n}$. Hence there are δ_1,f_1 such that $OpT'(w'i) = \langle\delta_1,f_1\rangle$ and $OpT(wi) = \langle\delta_1, f_0[f_1]\rangle$. Thus $OpT'(w') \vdash^N_{AX'} \langle\delta',f'\rangle$ by a single rule application and $Op(M')(\delta',f') = \langle\delta_1,f_1\rangle$ for some $M' \subseteq OpT'(\mathbb{N}^{<n})$.

Let $OpT'(w') = \langle\varphi,h_0\rangle$. Then $OpT(w) = \langle\varphi, f_0[h_0]\rangle$. Hence $OpT(w) \vdash^N_{AX'} \langle\delta', f_0[f']\rangle$ by a single rule application and, since Op is compatible with substitution prefixes, $Op(M)(\delta', f_0[f']) = \langle\delta_1, f_0[f_1]\rangle$ where $M = \{\langle\psi, f_0[h_1]\rangle \mid \langle\psi,h_1\rangle \in M'\}$. By definition of OpT, $M' \subseteq OpT'(\mathbb{N}^{<n})$ implies $M \subseteq OpT(\mathbb{N}^{\leq n})$. ∎

Theorem 8.2.7 and Lemmata 8.9.1 and 8.9.2 result in

Theorem 8.9.3 *Soundness and completeness of optimized narrowing w.r.t. deductive solutions*

Suppose that Op is a locally correct optimizing function and $\langle SIG, AX\rangle$ is (ground) AX'-Church-Rosser. Let γ be a goal and f be an AX'-irreducible substitution such that $\gamma[f]$ is an AX'-normalizable (ground) goal.

f is a deductive solution of γ iff there are an optimized narrowing tree OpT for γ and a substitution g such that $\langle\emptyset,g\rangle$ is in the range of OpT and g subsumes f. ∎

The reader is invited to combine optimized narrowing with strategy-controlled, basic and/or reduced narrowing and to compare the cost of corresponding expansions.

Before discussing concrete optimizing functions let us show that the local correctness of optimizing functions is preserved under their composition. This allows us to apply several optimizing functions sequentially without losing the completeness of optimized narrowing.

Proposition 8.9.4 The composition Op'•Op of two locally correct optimizing functions Op and Op', defined by

$$\text{Op'}\bullet\text{Op} = \{\text{Op'}(M)\bullet\text{Op}(M) \mid M \subseteq \text{GoalSub}\},$$

is locally correct.

Proof. Let f be a substitution and let δ be a goal with an irreducible N-solution g. Since Op is locally correct, there are δ_0, f_0 and an irreducible N-solution g_0 of δ_0 such that $\text{Op}(\emptyset)(\delta,f) = \langle\delta_0,f_0\rangle$, $\langle\delta_0,g_0\rangle \leq \langle\delta,g\rangle$ and $f_0[g_0]$ subsumes f[g]. Since Op' is locally correct, there are δ_1, f_1 and an irreducible N-solution g_1 of δ_1 such that $\text{Op'}(\emptyset)(\delta_0,f_0) = \langle\delta_1,f_1\rangle$, $\langle\delta_1,g_1\rangle \leq \langle\delta_0,g_0\rangle$ and $f_1[g_1]$ subsumes $f_0[g_0]$. Therefore $\langle\delta_1,g_1\rangle \leq \langle\delta,g\rangle$ and $f_1[g_1]$ subsumes f[g]. Hence Op'•Op satisfies condition (i) of local correctness. It remains to show condition (ii).

Let M be a set of goal-substitution pairs and Op•Op'(M)(δ,f) = $\langle\varphi,h\rangle$ such that φ has a deductive solution, say g_0. Then Op(M)(δ,f) = $\langle\delta_0,f_0\rangle$ and Op'(M)(δ_0,f_0) = $\langle\varphi,h\rangle$ for some δ_0,f_0. Since Op' is locally correct, there are $\langle\varphi_1,h_1\rangle \in Mu(\langle\delta_0,f_0\rangle)$ and a substitution h_0 such that g_0 is a deductive solution of $\varphi_1[h_0]$ and $h\equiv h_1[h_0]$ is a deductive theorem.

If $\langle\varphi_1,h_1\rangle \in M$, the proof is complete by condition (ii) of local correctness of Op'•Op.

Otherwise $\langle\varphi_1,h_1\rangle = \langle\delta_0,f_0\rangle$, and we conclude from local correctness of Op that there are $\langle\delta_1,f_1\rangle \in Mu(\langle\delta,f\rangle)$ and a substitution g_1 such that g_0 is a deductive solution of $\delta_1[g_1][h_0]$ and $h_1\equiv f_1[g_1]$ is a deductive theorem. Hence $h_1[h_0]\equiv f_1[g_1][h_0]$ and thus $h\equiv f_1[g_1][h_0]$ are deductive theorems as well. ∎

8.10 Optimizing Functions

Practical experience with optimized narrowing has been gained with the following optimizations:

(1) subsumption of goals,
(2) subsumption of solutions,
(3) expansion of variables,
(4) construction of substitutions,
(5) splitting of equations,
(6) absorption of equations,
(7) clash of equations,
(8) rejection of non-narrowable goals.

(1)-(6) are properties of *total* optimizing functions. (7) and (8) recognize *failing* expansions in which case they are not defined, while in other cases they return their argument without modification.

Definition Let Op be an optimizing function that consists of total functions. Let M ⊆ GoalSub and $\langle \delta, f \rangle, \langle \delta_o, f_o \rangle \in$ GoalSub such that $Op(M)(\delta, f) = \langle \delta_o, f_o \rangle \neq \langle \delta, f \rangle$.

(1) Op *subsumes goals* if $\langle \delta_o, f_o \rangle \in M$, $\delta = \delta_o[h]$ and $f = f_o[h]$ for some h such that for all AX'-irreducible N-solutions g of δ, h[g] is AX'-irreducible and dom(h) ⊆ XG.

(2) Op *subsumes solutions* if $\langle \delta_o, f_o \rangle \in M$, $\delta_o = \emptyset$ and $f = f_o[h]$ for some h.

(3) Op *expands variables* if there are a goal λ, a term t and x ∈ X-var(t) such that
$$\delta = \lambda \cup \{x \equiv t\}, \quad \delta_o = \lambda[t/x], \quad f_o = f[t/x]$$
and for all $u \equiv u' \Leftarrow \delta \in$ NAX, u does not overlap t.

(4) Op *constructs substitutions* if there are a goal λ, x ∈ X, a term σt and z ∈ (XG-var(δ))* such that
$$\delta = \lambda \cup \{x \equiv \sigma t\}, \quad \delta_o = (\lambda \cup \{z \equiv t\})[\sigma z/x], \quad f_o = f[\sigma z/x],$$
for all $u \equiv u' \Leftarrow \delta \in$ NAX, root(u) ≠ σ, and for all AX'-irreducible N-solutions g of δ, root(gx) = σ implies gx = σz[g]. (Remember that z≡t stands for the set of all equations between corresponding components of z and t.)

(5) Op *splits equations* if there are a goal λ and terms σt,σu such that
$$\delta = \lambda \cup \{\sigma t \equiv \sigma t'\}, \quad \delta_o = \lambda \cup \{t \equiv t'\}, \quad f_o = f$$
and for all $u \equiv u' \Leftarrow \delta \in$ NAX, root(u) ≠ σ.

(6) Op *absorbs equations* if there is a term t such that $\delta = \delta_o u\{t \equiv t\}$ and $f_o = f$. ∎

Of course, expansion and construction can also be applied to equations with isolated variables on the *right*-hand side.

An expansion step can be simulated by a sequence of construction steps and trivial expansion steps where the term t to be substituted for x is again a variable. In contrast to expansion, construction avoids checking whether x occurs in t or NAX overlaps t. On the other hand, if x does occur in t, then construction produces the subgoal $\{z \equiv t[\sigma z/x]\}$ with an occurrence of z in $t[\sigma z/x]$ and thus iterated construction will not terminate.

Definition Let Op be an optimizing function such that for all subsets M of GoalSub, Op(M) is a restriction of the identity on GoalSub. Let $M \subseteq$ GoalSub and $\langle \delta, f \rangle \in$ GoalSub such that $Op(M)(\delta, f)$ is undefined.

(7) Op *detects clashes* if there are $\lambda \in$ Goal(SIG) and $\sigma t, \tau t' \in$ T(SIG) such that $\delta = \lambda u(\sigma t \equiv \tau t')$, $\sigma \neq \tau$ and for all $u \equiv u' \Leftarrow \vartheta \in$ NAX, $\sigma \neq \text{root}(u) \neq \tau$.

(8) Op *rejects non-narrowable goals* if there are a goal λ and an atom p such that $\delta = \lambda u\{p\}$, var(p) $\subseteq$ XG and for all $u \equiv u' \Leftarrow \vartheta \in$ NAX and $q \Leftarrow \lambda \in$ (BAX−CE(BAX))u$\{x \equiv x\}$, u does not overlap p and p,q are not unifiable. ∎

The following lemmata establish the local correctness of (1)-(8).

Lemma 8.10.1 Each optimizing function that subsumes goals is locally correct.

Proof. Let Op be an optimizing function that subsumes goals, $Op(\emptyset)(\delta, f) = \langle \delta_o, f_o \rangle$, $\delta = \delta_o[h]$ and $f = f_o[h]$ for some h such that for all AX'-irreducible N-solutions g of δ, h[g] is AX'-irreducible and dom(h) $\subseteq$ XG.

Suppose that g is an AX'-irreducible N-solution of δ. By Lemma 8.2.3 (2),

(∗) $\qquad |\delta[g] \vdash^{RD}_{AX'} \emptyset| \leq |\langle \delta, \text{id} \rangle \vdash^{N}_{AX'} \langle \emptyset, g \rangle|$.

Since $h \in NF$, g is AX'-irreducible and dom(g) $\subseteq$ XG, the assumption implies that h[g] is AX'-irreducible as well. Hence by Lemma 8.2.4 and (∗),

$|\langle \delta_o, \text{id} \rangle \vdash^{N}_{AX'} \langle \emptyset, h[g] \rangle| = |\delta_o[h][g] \vdash^{RD}_{AX'} \emptyset| \leq |\langle \delta, \text{id} \rangle \vdash^{N}_{AX'} \langle \emptyset, g \rangle|$,

i.e. $\langle \delta_o, h[g] \rangle \leq \langle \delta, g \rangle$. Moreover, $f_o[h][g] = f[g]$. Thus condition (i) of local correctness holds true. Condition (ii) is trivially valid because for all $M \subseteq$ GoalSub and $\langle \delta, f \rangle \in$ GoalSub, $Op(M)(\delta, f) \in Mu\{\langle \delta, f \rangle\}$. ∎

Lemma 8.10.2 Each optimizing function that subsumes solutions is locally correct.

Proof. Let Op be an optimizing function that subsumes solutions, $Op(\emptyset)(\delta,f) = \langle \delta_o,f_o \rangle$, $\delta = \emptyset$ and $f = f_o[h]$ for some h. Suppose that g is an AX'-irreducible N-solution of δ. Since δ_o is empty, we have

$$|\langle \delta_o, id \rangle \vdash^N_{AX'} \langle \emptyset, id \rangle| = 0.$$

Hence $\langle \delta_o, id \rangle \leq \langle \delta, g \rangle$ and $f_o[id][h][g] = f_o[h][g] = f[g]$. Thus (i) is satisfied. (ii) is trivially valid because for all $M \subseteq$ GoalSub and $\langle \delta,f \rangle \in$ GoalSub, $Op(M)(\delta,f) \in Mu\{\langle \delta,f \rangle\}$. ∎

Lemma 8.10.3 If CE(BAX) is empty, then each optimizing function that expands variables is locally correct.

Proof. Let AX' = NAX, Op be an optimizing function that expands variables, $\delta = \lambda u \{x \equiv t\}$ with $x \in X\text{-var}(t)$, for all $u \equiv u' \Leftarrow \vartheta \in$ NAX, u does not overlap t,

$$Op(\emptyset)(\delta,f) = \langle \delta_o, f_o \rangle = \langle \lambda[t/x], f[t/x] \rangle$$

and let g be a NAX-irreducible N-solution of δ. By Lemma 8.2.3 (2),

(1) $\qquad |\delta[g] \vdash^{RD}_{AX'} \emptyset| \leq |\langle \delta, id \rangle \vdash^N_{AX'} \langle \emptyset, g \rangle|.$

In particular, $gx \equiv t[g]$ is a NAX-reducible equation. Since for all $u \equiv u' \Leftarrow \vartheta \in$ NAX, u does not overlap t, Corollary 7.7.6 implies $gx = t[g]$ and thus $\lambda[g] = \lambda[t/x][g] = \delta_o[g]$. Since $\lambda \subseteq \delta$, we obtain $\delta_o[g] \subseteq \delta[g]$ and by (1),

(2) $\qquad |\delta_o[g] \vdash^{RD}_{AX'} \emptyset| \leq |\langle \delta, id \rangle \vdash^N_{AX'} \langle \emptyset, g \rangle|.$

Since g is AX'-irreducible and dom(g) $\subseteq$ XG, Lemma 8.2.4 and (2) imply

$$|\langle \delta_o, id \rangle \vdash^N_{AX'} \langle \emptyset, g \rangle| = |\delta_o[g] \vdash^{RD}_{AX'} \emptyset| \leq |\langle \delta, id \rangle \vdash^N_{AX'} \langle \emptyset, g \rangle|,$$

i.e. $\langle \delta_o, g \rangle \leq \langle \delta, g \rangle$. Since $gx = t[g]$, we have $g = \{t/x\}[g]$. Therefore

$$f[g] = f[t/x][g] = f_o[g],$$

and (i) holds true.

For (ii), let $M \subseteq$ GoalSub, $\langle \delta,f \rangle \in$ GoalSub, $Op(M)(\delta,f) = \langle \delta_o, f_o \rangle$ and g_o be a deductive solution of δ_o. We have

(3) $\qquad \delta[t/x] = (\lambda u\{x \equiv t\})[t/x] = \lambda[t/x] \cup \{t \equiv t\}$

because x does not occur in t. Since $\lambda[t/x] = \delta_0$ and g_0 is a deductive solution of δ_0, we conclude from (3) that g_0 is a deductive solution of $\delta[t/x]$. Therefore $f_0 = f[t/x]$ implies (ii). ∎

Lemma 8.10.4 If CE(BAX) is empty, then each optimizing function that constructs substitutions is locally correct.

Proof. Let AX' = NAX, Op be an optimizing function that constructs substitutions, $\delta = \lambda u\{x \equiv \sigma t\}$, $z \in (XG\text{-var}(\delta))^*$, for all $u \equiv u' \Leftarrow \delta \in$ NAX, root(u) ≠ σ, for all NAX-irreducible N-solutions g of δ, root(gx) = σ implies gx = $\sigma z[g]$,

$$Op(\emptyset)(\delta, f) = \langle \delta_0, f_0 \rangle = \langle (\lambda u\{z \equiv t\})[\sigma z/x], f[\sigma z/x] \rangle$$

and let g be a NAX-irreducible N-solution of δ. By Lemma 8.2.3 (2),

(1) $\qquad |\delta[g] \vdash^{RD}_{NAX} \emptyset| \le |\langle \delta, id \rangle \vdash^{N}_{AX'} \langle \emptyset, g \rangle|$.

In particular, gx≡σt[g] is a NAX-reducible equation. Since for all u≡u'⇐δ ∈ NAX, σ ≠ root(u), Corollary 7.7.6 implies

(2) $\qquad |t[g]_{\overline{NAX}} t'| + 1 = |\sigma t[g]_{\overline{NAX}} \sigma t'| = |(gx \equiv \sigma t[g]) \vdash^{RD}_{NAX} \emptyset|$

for some NAX-irreducible $t' \in T(SIG)^*$ with $\sigma t' = gx$. Let $t' = \langle t_1,...,t_n \rangle$, $z = \langle z_1,...,z_n \rangle$ and $h = \{t_1/z_1,...,t_n/z_n\}$. By assumption, gx = σgz, i.e. gz = t'. Hence by (2), gz≡t[g] is NAX-reducible and thus by Corollary 7.7.6,

(3) $\qquad |t[g]_{\overline{NAX}} gz| = |(gz \equiv t[g]) \vdash^{RD}_{NAX} \emptyset|$.

gx = σz[g] implies g = {σz/x}[g] and thus $\delta_0[g] = (\lambda u\{z \equiv t\})[g]$. Hence by Lemma 8.2.4, (1), (2) and (3),

$\qquad |\langle \delta_0, id \rangle \vdash^{N}_{AX'} \langle \emptyset, g \rangle|$
$= |\delta_0[g] \vdash^{RD}_{NAX} \emptyset|$
$= |\lambda[g] \vdash^{RD}_{NAX} \emptyset| + |(gz \equiv t[g]) \vdash^{RD}_{NAX} \emptyset|$
$= |\lambda[g] \vdash^{RD}_{NAX} \emptyset| + |\sigma t[g]_{\overline{NAX}} \sigma t'|$
$= |\lambda[g] \vdash^{RD}_{NAX} \emptyset| + |(gx \equiv \sigma t[g]) \vdash^{RD}_{NAX} \emptyset|$
$= |\delta[g] \vdash^{RD}_{NAX} \emptyset|$
$\le |\langle \delta, id \rangle \vdash^{N}_{AX'} \langle \emptyset, g \rangle|$,

i.e. $\langle \delta_0, g \rangle \le \langle \delta, g \rangle$. Since $f[g] = f[\sigma z/x][g] = f_0[g]$, (i) holds true.

For (ii), let M ⊆ GoalSub, $\langle \delta, f \rangle \in$ GoalSub, Op(M)(δ,f) = $\langle \delta_0, f_0 \rangle$ and g_0 be a deductive solution of δ_o. We have $\delta_o = \lambda[\sigma z/x] \cup \{z \equiv t[\sigma z/x]\}$ and

$$\delta[\sigma z/x] = (\lambda u\{x \equiv \sigma t\})[\sigma z/x] = \lambda[\sigma z/x] \cup \{\sigma z \equiv \sigma t[\sigma z/x]\}.$$

Hence g_o is a deductive solution of $\delta[\sigma z/x]$. Therefore $\langle \delta_1, f_1 \rangle = \langle \delta, f \rangle$ and $g_1 = \{\sigma z/x\}$ imply $f_o = f_1[g_1]$, and (ii) holds true. ∎

Lemma 8.10.5 If AX' = ~NAX, suppose that for all $u \equiv u' \Leftarrow \delta \in$ NAX and $v \equiv v' \Leftarrow \lambda \in$ BAX, root(u) ∉ BOP and v ∉ X.

Each optimizing function that splits equations is locally correct.

Proof. Let Op be an optimizing function that splits equations, $\delta = \lambda u\{\sigma t \equiv \sigma t'\}$, for all $u \equiv u' \Leftarrow \delta \in$ NAX, root(u) ≠ σ,

$$Op(\emptyset)(\delta,f) = \langle \delta_o, f_o \rangle = \langle \lambda u\{t \equiv t'\}, f \rangle$$

and let g be an AX'-irreducible N-solution of δ. By Lemma 8.2.3 (2),

(1) $\qquad |\delta[g] \vdash^{RD}_{AX'} \emptyset| \leq |\langle \delta, id \rangle \vdash^{N}_{AX'} \langle \emptyset, g \rangle|.$

In particular, $\{\sigma t \equiv \sigma t'\}[g]$ is an AX'-reducible equation. Since for all $u \equiv u' \Leftarrow \delta \in$ NAX, σ ≠ root(u), we have

(2) $\qquad |\{t \equiv t'\}[g] \vdash^{RD}_{AX'} \emptyset| = |\{\sigma t \equiv \sigma t'\}[g] \vdash^{RD}_{AX'} \emptyset|.$

By (1) and (2),

$$|\delta_o[g] \vdash^{RD}_{AX'} \emptyset| = |\delta[g] \vdash^{RD}_{AX'} \emptyset| \leq |\langle \delta, id \rangle \vdash^{N}_{AX'} \langle \emptyset, g \rangle|.$$

Since g is AX'-irreducible and dom(g) ⊆ XG, Lemma 8.2.4 implies

$$|\langle \delta_o, id \rangle \vdash^{N}_{AX'} \langle \emptyset, g \rangle| = |\delta_o[g] \vdash^{RD}_{AX'} \emptyset| \leq |\langle \delta, id \rangle \vdash^{N}_{AX'} \langle \emptyset, g \rangle|,$$

i.e. $\langle \delta_o, g \rangle \leq \langle \delta, g \rangle$. Moreover, $f[g] = f_o[g]$. Thus (i) holds true.

For (ii), let M ⊆ GoalSub, $\langle \delta, f \rangle \in$ GoalSub, $Op(M)(\delta,f) = \langle \delta_o, f_o \rangle$ and g_o be a deductive solution of δ_o. Using the equality axiom

$$\sigma \langle x_1,...,x_n \rangle \equiv \sigma \langle y_1,...,y_n \rangle \Leftarrow x_1 \equiv y_1,...,x_n \equiv y_n$$

(cf. Section 4.2), we conclude that g_o is a deductive solution of δ as well. Hence $f_o = f$ implies (ii). ∎

Lemma 8.10.6 Each optimizing function that absorbs equations is locally correct.

Proof. Let Op be an optimizing function that splits equations, $\delta = \lambda u\{t \equiv t\}$,

$$Op(\emptyset)(\delta,f) = \langle \delta_o, f_o \rangle = \langle \lambda, f \rangle$$

and let g be an AX'-irreducible N-solution of δ. Since $\delta_o \subseteq \delta$, we have

$$|\langle \delta_o, id \rangle \overset{N}{\underset{AX'}{\mapsto}} \langle \emptyset, g \rangle| \le |\langle \delta, id \rangle \overset{N}{\underset{AX'}{\mapsto}} \langle \emptyset, g \rangle|,$$

i.e. $\langle \delta_o, g \rangle \le \langle \delta, g \rangle$. Moreover, $f[g] = f_o[g]$. Thus (i) holds true.

For (ii), let $M \subseteq$ GoalSub, $\langle \delta, f \rangle \in$ GoalSub, $Op(M)(\delta,f) = \langle \delta_o, f_o \rangle$ and g_o be a deductive solution of δ_o. Then g_o solves δ as well, and the proof is complete because $f_o = f$. ∎

Lemma 8.10.7 If CE(BAX) is empty, then each optimizing function that detects clashes is locally correct.

Proof. Let AX' = NAX, Op be an optimizing function that detects clashes, $\delta = \lambda u\{\sigma t \equiv \tau t'\}$, $\sigma \ne \tau$ and for all $u \equiv u' \Leftarrow \mathcal{S} \in$ NAX, $\sigma \ne root(u) \ne \tau$.

Let g be a NAX-irreducible N-solution of δ. By Lemma 8.2.3 (2), $\delta[g]$ is NAX-reducible. In particular, $(\sigma t \equiv \tau t')[g]$ is a NAX-reducible equation. Since for all $u \equiv u' \Leftarrow \mathcal{S} \in$ NAX, $\sigma \ne root(u)$, Corollary 7.7.6 implies $\sigma t[g] \overline{_{NAX}} \sigma v$ and $\tau t'[g] \overline{_{NAX}} \tau v'$ for some $\sigma v = \tau v'$. But this is impossible because $\sigma \ne \tau$. Therefore δ has no NAX-irreducible N-solution, and (i) holds true.

Since for all $M \subseteq$ GoalSub and $\langle \delta, f \rangle \subseteq$ GoalSub, $Op(M)(\delta,f)$ is defined iff $Op(M)(\delta,f) = \langle \delta,f \rangle$, (ii) is trivially valid. ∎

Lemma 8.10.8 If CE(BAX) is empty, then each optimizing function that rejects non-narrowable goals is locally correct.

Proof. Let AX' = NAX, Op be an optimizing function that rejects non-narrowable goals, $\delta = \lambda u\{Pt\}$, $var(Pt) \subseteq XG$, $\sigma \ne \tau$ and for all $u \equiv u' \Leftarrow \mathcal{S} \in$ NAX and $q \Leftarrow \lambda \in$ BAX$\cup\{x \equiv x\}$, u does not overlap Pt and Pt and q are not unifiable.

Let g be a NAX-irreducible N-solution of δ. By Lemma 8.2.3 (2), $\delta[g]$ is NAX-reducible. Since for all $u \equiv u' \Leftarrow \mathcal{S} \in$ NAX, u does not overlap Pt, Lemma 7.7.5 implies that Pt[g] is NAX-reduced. Since CE(BAX) is empty, Pt[g] must be unifiable with the conclusion q of some clause in BAX$\cup\{x \equiv x\}$, i.e. Pt[g][h] = q[h] for some h. Since $var(Pt) \subseteq XG$, the variables of Pt are disjoint from the variables of q, and we may assume g[h] = h. Thus, contrary to our assumption, Pt and q are unifiable, and we conclude that δ has no NAX-irreducible N-solution. Hence (i) holds true.

Since for all $M \subseteq$ GoalSub and $\langle \delta, f \rangle \subseteq$ GoalSub, $Op(M)(\delta,f)$ is defined iff $Op(M)(\delta,f) = \langle \delta,f \rangle$, (ii) is trivially valid. ∎

Recall that the set of locally correct optimizing functions is closed under composition (Proposition 8.9.4). Hence subsumption of goals, expansion of variables, etc., can be iterated and performed sequentially without losing the completeness of optimized narrowing (cf. Theorem 8.9.3).

8.11 Lazy Narrowing

The reader may have noted the similarity between certain narrowing optimizations on one hand and the Martelli-Montanari rules on the other hand (cf. Section 5.5). However, lazy resolution and unification provide a complete calculus for deductive solutions (Theorem 5.5.6), while variable expansion, equation splitting, etc., are used *in addition* to the narrowing calculus, which is complete already, without these additional transformations. Nevertheless, the question arises whether narrowing can be *replaced* by a calculus that employs Martelli-Montanari rules and a narrowing counterpart of the Lazy Resolution Rule (cf. Section 5.5).

Analogously to lazy resolution the attribute "lazy" concerns the way in which axioms are applied to a goal. Given a conditional equation e, a lazy narrowing rule creates a subgoal that *demands* a narrowing redex for e. On the other hand, *eager* narrowing as handled in the previous sections is *data-driven* in that it applies an axiom only if such a redex is already present in the given goal.

A lazy narrowing calculus does not work without additional assumptions. Remember the restrictions involved in its "predecessors":
- the completeness of narrowing is guaranteed only w.r.t. irreducible solutions,
- the local correctness of variable expansion, equation splitting, etc., presumes certain non-overlapping conditions.

The rules presented here are tailored to goals consisting of equations with one side being a base term. (W.l.o.g., we put the base term on the right-hand side.) Moreover, CE(BAX) is supposed to be empty and NAX to be innermost (cf. Section 8.4).

Definition The *lazy narrowing calculus* (w.r.t. AX') consists of the Success Rule (cf. Section 8.2) and the following rules:

Lazy Narrowing Rule Let γ be a goal, $\sigma t \equiv u$ be an equation and $\sigma u' \equiv t' \Leftarrow \vartheta \in$ NAX. Then

$$\frac{\langle \gamma \cup \{\sigma t \equiv u\}, f \rangle}{\langle \gamma \cup \{t \equiv u', t' \equiv u\} \cup \delta, f \rangle.}$$

Splitting Rule Let γ be a goal and $\sigma t \equiv \sigma u$ be an equation. Then

$$\frac{\langle \gamma \cup \{\sigma t \equiv \sigma u\}, f \rangle}{\langle \gamma \cup \{t \equiv u\}, f \rangle.}$$

Construction Rule Let γ be a goal, $x \in X$, $\sigma t \equiv x$ be an equation and u be a term such that the variables of u do not occur in $\gamma \cup \{\sigma t \equiv x\}$ and
- $\sigma \in BOP$ and $u \in X^*$ or
- $\sigma \in NOP$ and σu is an AX'-irreducible ground term.

Then

$$\frac{\langle \gamma \cup \{\sigma t \equiv x\}, f \rangle}{\langle (\gamma \cup \{t \equiv u\})[\sigma u/x], f[\sigma u/x] \rangle.}$$

Let γ, γ' be goals and f, f' be substitutions. A derivation of $\langle \gamma', f' \rangle$ from $\langle \gamma, f \rangle$ via the lazy narrowing calculus is called a *lazy narrowing expansion* of $\langle \gamma, f \rangle$ to $\langle \gamma', f' \rangle$ (w.r.t. AX').

The corresponding inference relation is denoted by $\vdash^N_{AX'}$. If $\langle \gamma, id \rangle \vdash^N_{AX'} \langle \emptyset, f \rangle$, then f is an *LN-solution* of γ (w.r.t. AX').

$|\langle \gamma, f \rangle \vdash^N_{AX'} \langle \gamma', f' \rangle|$ denotes the length of a shortest lazy narrowing expansion of $\langle \gamma, f \rangle$ to $\langle \gamma', f' \rangle$. ∎

If NAX is ground term reducing, then NAX-irreducible ground terms of the form σu with $\sigma \in NOP$ do not exist. Hence, in this case, the Construction Rule can only be applied to equations $\sigma t \equiv x$ where σ is a base symbol.

Example 8.11.1 Let

<BSIG,BAX>
  base : NAT
  sorts : seq
  opns :   ε : seq
         _&_ : nat,seq→seq

<SIG,AX> = SEQ-OF-NAT (cf. Section 3.7) and AX' = NAX. Here NAX is not ground term reducing. For instance, the equation (head tail 0&ε)≡x has the *irreducible* solution {(head ε)/x}. Nevertheless, {(head ε)/x} is obtained by lazy narrowing:

$$
\begin{array}{ll}
& \langle\{\text{head tail } 0\&\varepsilon \equiv x\}, \text{id}\rangle \\
L\vdash^N_{AX'} & \langle\{\text{head tail } 0\&\varepsilon \equiv \text{head } \varepsilon\}, \{(\text{head } \varepsilon)/x\}\rangle \quad \text{(Construction Rule)} \\
L\vdash^N_{AX'} & \langle\{\text{tail } 0\&\varepsilon \equiv \varepsilon\}, \{(\text{head } \varepsilon)/x\}\rangle \quad \text{(Splitting Rule)} \\
L\vdash^N_{AX'} & \langle\{0\&\varepsilon \equiv n\&s, s \equiv \varepsilon\}, \{(\text{head } \varepsilon)/x\}\rangle \quad \text{(Lazy Narrowing Rule)} \\
L\vdash^N_{AX'} & \langle\emptyset, \{(\text{head } \varepsilon)/x\}\rangle \quad \text{(Unification Rule).} \blacksquare
\end{array}
$$

Example 8.11.2 Let ⟨BSIG,BAX⟩ and ⟨SIG,AX⟩ be as in Example 8.4.5 and AX' = NAX. A lazy narrowing expansion of the equation (f(fxy)z)≡0 leads to the solution {0/x, 0/y, 0/z}:

$$
\begin{array}{ll}
& \langle\{(f(fxy)z)\equiv 0\}, \text{id}\rangle \\
L\vdash^N_{AX'} & \langle\{fxy\equiv 0, z\equiv 0, 0\equiv 0\}, \text{id}\rangle \quad \text{(Lazy Narrowing Rule)} \\
L\vdash^N_{AX'} & \langle\{x\equiv 0, y\equiv 0, z\equiv 0, 0\equiv 0\}, \text{id}\rangle \quad \text{(Lazy Narrowing Rule)} \\
L\vdash^N_{AX'} & \langle\emptyset, \{0/x, 0/y, 0/z\}\rangle \quad \text{(Success Rule).} \blacksquare
\end{array}
$$

Example 8.11.3 (due to You) Let ⟨BSIG,BAX⟩ = NAT (cf. Section 3.2) and

⟨SIG,AX⟩
  base : NAT
  opns : f _ _ : nat,nat→nat
         g _ : nat→nat
  vars : m,n : nat
  axms : f m 0 ≡ 0
        f 0 n| ≡ 0
        g n| ≡ 0

We immediately see that {0/x} and {n|/x} are deductive solutions of the equation (f(gx)x)≡0. Both can be derived by lazy narrowing:

$$
\begin{array}{ll}
& \langle\{(f(gx)x)\equiv 0\}, \text{id}\rangle \\
L\vdash^N_{AX'} & \langle\{gx\equiv m, x\equiv 0, 0\equiv 0\}, \text{id}\rangle \quad \text{(Lazy Narrowing Rule)} \\
L\vdash^N_{AX'} & \langle\emptyset, \{0/x, g0/m\}\rangle \quad \text{(Success Rule).}
\end{array}
$$

$$
\begin{array}{ll}
& \langle\{(f(gx)x)\equiv 0\}, \text{id}\rangle \\
L\vdash^N_{AX'} & \langle\{gx\equiv 0, x\equiv n|, 0\equiv 0\}, \text{id}\rangle \quad \text{(Lazy Narrowing Rule)} \\
L\vdash^N_{AX'} & \langle\{x\equiv n|, 0\equiv 0\}, \text{id}\rangle \quad \text{(Lazy Narrowing Rule)} \\
L\vdash^N_{AX'} & \langle\emptyset, \{n|/x\}\rangle \quad \text{(Success Rule).} \blacksquare
\end{array}
$$

Lemma 8.11.4 *Soundness of lazy narrowing w.r.t. deductive solutions*
(1) If ⟨γ,id⟩ $L\vdash^N_{AX'}$ ⟨φ,g⟩ and h is a deductive solution of φ, then g[h] is a deductive solution of γ.
(2) All LN-solutions of a goal γ are deductive solutions of γ.

Proof. (2) is a special case of (1). We show (1) by induction on $|\langle\gamma,\text{id}\rangle \vdash^N_{\text{AX}} \langle\varphi,g\rangle|$. Suppose that $AX \cup EAX \vdash \varphi[h]$.

Case 1. $\langle\gamma,\text{id}\rangle$ expands to $\langle\varphi,g\rangle$ by applying only the Success Rule. Then φ is empty and $\gamma[g]$ is AX'-reduced. Hence $BAX \cup EAX \vdash \gamma[g]$, and we conclude that $g[h]$ is a deductive solution of γ.

Case 2. $\langle\gamma,\text{id}\rangle$ expands to $\langle\varphi,g\rangle$ by a single application of the Lazy Narrowing Rule. Then $g = \text{id}$ and there are a goal δ, an equation $\sigma t \equiv u$ and $\sigma u' \equiv t' \Leftarrow \vartheta \in NAX$ such that $\gamma = \delta \cup \{\sigma t \equiv u\}$ and $\varphi = \delta \cup \{t \equiv u', t' \equiv u\} \cup \vartheta$. By assumption,

$$AX \cup EAX \vdash (\delta \cup \{t \equiv u', t' \equiv u\} \cup \vartheta)[h].$$

Hence

$$AX \cup EAX \vdash (\delta \cup \{\sigma t \equiv \sigma u', \sigma u' \equiv t', t' \equiv u\})[h]$$

and thus

$$AX \cup EAX \vdash (\delta \cup \{\sigma t \equiv u\})[h].$$

Therefore $g[h]$ is a deductive solution of γ.

Case 3. $\langle\gamma,\text{id}\rangle$ expands to $\langle\varphi,g\rangle$ by a single application of the Splitting Rule.
Then $g = \text{id}$ and there are a goal δ and equation $\sigma t \equiv \sigma u$ such that $\gamma = \delta \cup \{\sigma t \equiv \sigma u\}$ and $\varphi = \delta \cup \{t \equiv u\}$. We immediately see that $AX \cup EAX \vdash \varphi[h]$ implies $AX \cup EAX \vdash \gamma[g][h]$.

Case 4. $\langle\gamma,\text{id}\rangle$ expands to $\langle\varphi,g\rangle$ by a single application of the Construction Rule. Then there are a goal δ, $x \in X$, an equation $\sigma t \equiv x$ and a term σu such that $\gamma = \delta \cup \{\sigma t \equiv x\}$, $\varphi = (\delta \cup \{t \equiv u\})[\sigma u/x]$, $g = \{\sigma u/x\}$ and $x \notin \text{var}(\sigma u)$. By assumption,

$$AX \cup EAX \vdash (\delta \cup \{t \equiv u\})[\sigma u/x][h].$$

Hence

$$AX \cup EAX \vdash (\delta \cup \{\sigma t \equiv \sigma u\})[\sigma u/x][h]$$

and thus

$$AX \cup EAX \vdash (\delta \cup \{\sigma t \equiv x\})[\sigma u/x][h].$$

Therefore $g[h]$ is a deductive solution of γ.

Case 5. There are δ, g', g'' with $g'[g''] = g$ and

$$|\langle\gamma,\text{id}\rangle \vdash^N_{\text{AX}} \langle\varphi,g\rangle| = |\langle\gamma,\text{id}\rangle \vdash^N_{\text{AX}} \langle\delta,g'\rangle| + |\langle\delta,\text{id}\rangle \vdash^N_{\text{AX}} \langle\varphi,g''\rangle|.$$

Of course,

$$|\langle\gamma,\text{id}\rangle \vdash^N_{\text{AX}} \langle\delta[g''],g\rangle| \leq |\langle\gamma,\text{id}\rangle \vdash^N_{\text{AX}} \langle\delta,g'\rangle|.$$

Thus by the induction hypothesis, $g''[h]$ is a deductive solution of δ. In other words, h is a deductive solution of $\delta[g'']$. Hence again by the induction hypothesis, $g[h]$ is a deductive solution of γ. ∎

For completeness we need additional assumptions. We said above that goals are confined to sets of equations t≡u with u being a base term. Actually, this would be too restrictive: the Construction Rule may produce equations which are not of this form unless we restrict it to base operations σ. But then one is forced to assume that only base substitutions are irreducible. So we introduce the following notion relating *base term* and *irreducible term*.

Definition A NAX-irreducible term t is *strongly irreducible* if the root of every non-ground subterm of t is a base symbol. *SNF* denotes the set of strongly irreducible terms. An equation is *SNF-based* if its right-hand side is strongly irreducible. ∎

Of course, all base terms are strongly irreducible. On the other hand, SNF is closed under composition: if t,t' ∈ SNF, then for all x ∈ X, t[t'/x] ∈ SNF as well. SNF shares this property with T(BSIG), but not with the set of all NAX-irreducible terms.

The completeness of lazy narrowing is shown for SNF-based equations. The inductive argument of the proof rests on the fact that every rule of the lazy-narrowing calculus transforms SNF-based equations into SNF-based equations. To ensure this for the Lazy Narrowing Rule we must assume that NAX is innermost (cf. Section 8.4). As far as the Construction Rule is concerned, the closure property of SNF mentioned above guarantees that SNF-based equations are turned into SNF-based equations.

Note that SNF-based equations of the form t≡x can be handled by the Unification, the Lazy Narrowing or the Construction Rule, while an SNF-based equation x≡u can always be eliminated by the Unification Rule because each ground instance of the strongly irreducible term u by an irreducible substitution is irreducible as well.

Lemma 8.11.5 *Completeness of lazy narrowing w.r.t. innermost goal reduction*

Suppose that CE(BAX) is empty, NAX is innermost (cf. section 8.4), γ is a goal consisting of SNF-based equations and S is an innermost reduction strategy (cf. Section 7.9 and Example 8.4.4).

Let g be a NAX-irreducible substitution such that $\gamma[g]$ is ground and NAX-reducible by S. Then g↾var(γ) = f↾var(γ) for some LN-solution f of γ.

Proof. For all goals δ, let size(δ) be the number of function symbol occurrences of δ. Let AX' = NAX. We show $\langle\gamma,\text{id}\rangle \vdash^{N}_{AX'} \langle\emptyset,f\rangle$ for some f with f↾var(γ) = g↾var(γ) by induction on the pair

$$\langle |\gamma[g] \text{ S}\xrightarrow[\text{NAX}]{\text{RD}} \emptyset|, \text{size}(\gamma[g])\rangle$$

w.r.t. the lexicographic extension of > to an ordering on $\mathbb{N} \times \mathbb{N}$.

Case 1. $\gamma[g]$ reduces to $\emptyset$ by applying only the Success Rule (cf. Section 7.7). Then $\gamma[g]$ is NAX-reduced, and the proof is complete by the Success Rule of the lazy narrowing calculus.

Case 2. There are a goal δ and an equation $t \equiv u$ such that $\gamma = \delta u\{t \equiv u\}$ and $t[g] \equiv u[g]$ reduces to $\emptyset$ only by first applying the S-controlled Reduction Rule (cf. Section 7.9). Since $u \in$ SNF, g is irreducible and NAX is innermost, $u[g]$ is irreducible, too. Since CE(BAX) is empty, we obtain

(1) $\qquad |\gamma[g] \text{ S}\xrightarrow[\text{NAX}]{\text{RD}} \emptyset| = |\delta[g] \text{ S}\xrightarrow[\text{NAX}]{\text{RD}} \emptyset| + |t[g] \text{ S}\xrightarrow[\text{NAX}]{} u[g]|.$

Case 2.1. A shortest S-controlled reduction from $t[g]$ to $u[g]$ includes a step $t'' \xrightarrow[\text{NAX}]{} u''$ with the whole term t'' as reduction redex. Then there are $\sigma \in$ NOP, $v \in T(SIG)^*$ and $\sigma u' \equiv t' \Leftarrow \delta \in$ NAX such that $t = \sigma v$ and

(2) $\qquad |t[g] \text{ S}\xrightarrow[\text{NAX}]{} u[g]|$
$= |v[g] \text{ S}\xrightarrow[\text{NAX}]{} u'[h]| + |t'[h] \text{ S}\xrightarrow[\text{NAX}]{} u[g]| + 1 + |\delta[h] \text{ S}\xrightarrow[\text{NAX}]{\text{RD}} \emptyset|$

for some ground substitution h. Here the "1" is the cost of the conditional reduction

$$\sigma u'[h] \text{ S}\xrightarrow[\text{NAX}]{} t'[h] \Leftarrow \delta[h]$$

that is induced by the axiom $\sigma u' \equiv t' \Leftarrow \delta$. Since this is an innermost step, $u'[h]$ is irreducible. W.l.o.g. var(u') is disjoint from var(γ). Let

$$\varphi = \delta u\{v \equiv u', t' \equiv u\} u \delta \quad \text{and} \quad g' = g\restriction\text{var}(\gamma) + h\restriction\text{var}(u').$$

By the Lazy Narrowing Rule,

(3) $\qquad\qquad\qquad \langle\gamma,\text{id}\rangle \text{ L}\xrightarrow[\text{AX}]{\text{N}} \langle\varphi,\text{id}\rangle.$

Since var(t')∪var(δ) ⊆ var(u'), we obtain

$$\varphi[g'] = \delta[g] \cup \{v[g] \equiv u'[h], t'[h] \equiv u[g]\} \cup \delta[h].$$

$u'[h]$ and $u[g]$ are irreducible. Therefore

(4) $\qquad |\varphi[g'] \text{ S}\xrightarrow[\text{NAX}]{\text{RD}} \emptyset|$
$= |\delta[g] \text{ S}\xrightarrow[\text{NAX}]{\text{RD}} \emptyset| + |v[g] \text{ S}\xrightarrow[\text{NAX}]{} u'[h]| + |t'[h] \text{ S}\xrightarrow[\text{NAX}]{} u[g]| + |\delta[h] \text{ S}\xrightarrow[\text{NAX}]{\text{RD}} \emptyset|.$

By (1), (2) and (4),

$$|\varphi[g'] \; S\vdash^{RD}_{\overline{NAX}} \; \emptyset| < |\gamma[g] \; S\vdash^{RD}_{\overline{NAX}} \; \emptyset|.$$

Since NAX is innermost, all equations of φ have a strongly irreducible term on their right-hand side. Moreover, g' is irreducible and $\varphi[g']$ is a ground goal because $var(\varphi) = var(\gamma) \cup var(u')$. Thus by the induction hypothesis,

$$\langle \varphi, id \rangle \; L\vdash^{N}_{AX} \; \langle \emptyset, f \rangle$$

for some f with $f\upharpoonright var(\varphi) = g'\upharpoonright var(\varphi)$. Hence by (3), $\langle \gamma, id \rangle \; L\vdash^{N}_{AX} \; \langle \emptyset, f \rangle$. The proof is complete because $var(\gamma) \subseteq var(\varphi)$ and thus $f\upharpoonright var(\gamma) = g'\upharpoonright var(\gamma) = g\upharpoonright var(\gamma)$.

Case 2.2. A shortest S-controlled reduction from $t[g]$ to $u[g]$ does not include a step "$t"_{\overline{NAX}} u$" with the whole term t" as reduction redex. Then $t[g] = \sigma t'$ and $u[g] = \sigma u'$ for some $\sigma \in OP$ and $t', u' \in T(SIG)^*$. Moreover,

(5) $$|t[g] \; S_{\overline{NAX}} \; u[g]| = |t' \; S_{\overline{NAX}} \; u'|.$$

Case 2.2.1. $t = \sigma v$ and $u = \sigma v'$ for some $v, v' \in T(SIG)^*$. Let $\varphi = \delta \cup \{v \equiv v'\}$. By the Splitting Rule

(6) $$\langle \gamma, id \rangle \; L\vdash^{N}_{AX} \; \langle \varphi, id \rangle.$$

Since $v'[g]$ is irreducible,

(7) $$|\varphi[g] \; S\vdash^{RD}_{\overline{NAX}} \; \emptyset| = |\delta[g] \; S\vdash^{RD}_{\overline{NAX}} \; \emptyset| + |v[g] \; S_{\overline{NAX}} \; v'[g]|.$$

Since $t' = v[g]$ and $u' = v'[g]$, (1), (5) and (7) imply

$$|\varphi[g] \; S\vdash^{RD}_{\overline{NAX}} \; \emptyset| \leq |\gamma[g] \; S\vdash^{RD}_{\overline{NAX}} \; \emptyset|.$$

Since $var(\varphi) = var(\gamma)$, $\varphi[g]$ is ground. Of course, all equations of φ have a strongly irreducible term on their right-hand side. Since $size(\varphi[g]) < size(\gamma[g])$, the induction hypothesis implies

$$\langle \varphi, id \rangle \; L\vdash^{N}_{AX} \; \langle \emptyset, f \rangle$$

for some f with $f\upharpoonright var(\varphi) = g\upharpoonright var(\varphi)$. Hence by (6), $\langle \gamma, id \rangle \; L\vdash^{N}_{AX} \; \langle \emptyset, f \rangle$. The proof is complete because $var(\gamma) = var(\varphi)$.

Case 2.2.2. t is a variable. Then $t[g] \equiv u[g]$ is irreducible, which contradicts the assumption of case 2.

Case 2.2.3. $t = \sigma v$ for some $\sigma \in OP$ and $v \in T(SIG)^*$, and u is a variable, say x. Then $gx = \sigma u'$.

If $\sigma \in$ BOP, let $\sigma v'$ be a term where v' is a sequence of variables that do not occur in γ. Of course, $\sigma v' \in$ SNF.

If $\sigma \in$ NOP, let $v' = u'$. Hence $\sigma v' = \sigma u' = gx$ is ground and thus $\sigma v' \in$ SNF as well.

In both cases, there is a ground substitution h such that $gx = \sigma u' = \sigma v'[h]$. Let

$$\varphi = (\delta \cup (v \equiv v'))[\sigma v'/x] \quad \text{and} \quad g' = g\lceil var(\gamma) + h \lceil var(v').$$

By the Construction Rule,

(8) $\qquad \langle \gamma, id \rangle \vdash^{N}_{AX} \langle \varphi, \{\sigma v'/x\} \rangle.$

Since $g'x = gx = \sigma v'[h] = \sigma v'[g']$, we have $g' = \{\sigma v'/x\}[g']$. Moreover,

$$\varphi[g'] = (\delta \cup (v \equiv v'))[g'] = \delta[g] \cup \{v[g] \equiv u'\}.$$

Since u' is irreducible,

(9) $\qquad |\varphi[g'] S^{RD}_{NAX} \emptyset| = |\delta[g] S^{RD}_{NAX} \emptyset| + |v[g] S_{NAX} u'|.$

Since $v[g] = t'$, (1), (5) and (9) imply

$$|\varphi[g'] S^{RD}_{NAX} \emptyset| \leq |\gamma[g] S^{RD}_{NAX} \emptyset|.$$

Moreover, size($\varphi[g']$) < size($\gamma[g]$). Since g is irreducible and $v'[h]$ is a subterm of gx, g' is irreducible as well. $\varphi[g']$ is ground because var(φ) $\subseteq$ var(γ)$\cup$var(v'). To apply the induction hypothesis to $\varphi[g']$ it remains for us to show that all equations of φ are SNF-based. $x \in$ var(γ) implies $x \notin$ var(v'). Hence

$$\varphi = \delta[\sigma v'/x] \cup \{v[\sigma v'/x] \equiv v'\}.$$

$\delta[\sigma v'/x]$ is SNF-based because all equations of $\delta \subseteq \gamma$ are SNF-based and $\sigma v' \in$ SNF. (Here we need the property that SNF is closed under composition.) Moreover, v' is a sequence of strongly irreducible terms and thus $v[\sigma v'/x] \equiv v'$ is SNF-based as well.

So the induction hypothesis implies $\langle \varphi, id \rangle \vdash^{N}_{AX} \langle \emptyset, f \rangle$ for some f with $f \lceil var(\varphi) = g' \lceil var(\varphi)$. Hence by (8),

$$\langle \gamma, id \rangle \vdash^{N}_{AX} \langle \emptyset, \{\sigma v'/x\}[f] \rangle.$$

Let $f' = \{\sigma v'/x\}[f]$. Thus $f'x = \sigma v'[f] = \sigma v'[g'] = \sigma v'[h] = gx$.

Since var(γ) $\subseteq$ var(φ)$\cup\{x\}$, we have $f'y = fy = g'y = gy$ for all $y \in$ var(γ)$-\{x\}$. Therefore $f' \lceil var(\gamma) = g \lceil var(\gamma)$. ∎

Theorem 8.11.6 *Soundness and completeness of lazy narrowing w.r.t. deductive solutions*

Suppose that <SIG,AX> is ground NAX-Church-Rosser, CE(BAX) is empty, NAX is innermost and ground confluent (cf. Section 7.8), γ is a goal consisting of SNF-based equations and S is an innermost reduction strategy such that $S\vdash_{NAX}^{RD}$ is Noetherian on ground goals.

Let g be a NAX-irreducible substitution such that $\gamma[g]$ is a NAX-normalizable ground goal. g is a deductive solution of γ iff f↾var(γ) = g↾var(γ) for some LN-solution f of γ.

Proof. Let g be a deductive solution of γ. Since <SIG,AX> is ground NAX-Church-Rosser, $\gamma[g]$ is NAX-reducible. Since NAX is ground confluent and $S\vdash_{NAX}^{RD}$ is Noetherian on ground goals, Theorem 7.9.2 implies that $\gamma[g]$ is NAX-reducible by S. Hence by Lemma 8.11.5, f↾var(γ) = g↾var(γ) for some LN-solution f of γ.

The converse follows from Lemma 8.11.4 (2). ∎

8.12 Bibliographic Notes

Narrowing was invented by Lankford and Slagle. Closely related is the concept of *demodulation* (see Wos et al.): instead of explicitly referring to *oriented* equations, demodulation rules out symmetric applications of equations by restricting the set of substitutions.

A narrowing algorithm for solving equations under the assumption of confluence was given by Fay and improved by Hullot. Fay worked with reduced narrowing, Hullot introduced basic narrowing, and Réty combined basic with reduced narrowing (also called normal narrowing). However, all these approaches are restricted to equational axioms and an empty set of base axioms. Only Kaplan [2] formulated the Narrowing Rule for (fair) sets of conditional equations (cf. Section 7.11). Hußmann presented a completeness proof for narrowing with arbitrary conditional equations (but without base axioms).

The *innermost* case of strategy-controlled narrowing (cf. Example 8.4.4) was employed by Fribourg [1]. Uniformity and local redex stability as crucial conditions on reduction strategies that induce complete narrowing strategies stem from Padawitz [4]. Echahed provided Example 8.4.5, which is not locally redex stable w.r.t. outermost narrowing. He invented *non-sub-unifiability* as a condition on the left-hand sides of equational axioms, which we have shown to be sufficient for local redex stability w.r.t. arbitrary strategies (cf. Proposition 8.4.6).

Ground term generating term sets are called *complete* sets of term tuples in Section 2 of Huet and Hullot. In essence, the conditions for decidability of sufficient completeness presented in Section 8.5 are due to Nipkow and Weikum.

Theorem-provers based on narrowing were designed by Geser and Hußmann, Fribourg [2], Réty et al., and Josephson and Dershowitz. They do not allow base axioms, but employ one or more of the refinements presented in this chapter: strategy-controlled, basic, reduced and/or optimized narrowing. In particular, the optimizations proved correct in Section 8.10 are used by Réty et al. (subsumption of goals), Hußmann (subsumption of solutions, expansion of variables, splitting and clash of equations, rejection of non-narrowable goals) and Fribourg [2] (construction of substitutions).

Lazy narrowing stems from Reddy. The calculus presented in Section 8.11 combines *lazy paramodulation* as it appears in Gallier and Snyder and in Hölldobler with You's *outer narrowing*. The main idea adopted from You is to confine oneself to innermost axioms and, accordingly, to goal equations with a base term on one side. Martelli et al. introduced a more general lazy narrowing rule: given an axiom $\sigma u' \equiv t'$, it turns an equational goal of the form $v[\sigma t/x] \equiv u$ into the goal $(v[t'/x] \equiv u, t \equiv u')$. Our narrowing rule only admits the case $v = x$. In other cases we would apply the Splitting or the Construction Rule.

Conditions on a specification that guarantee the completeness of narrowing with respect to non-irreducible solutions were given by You and Subrahmanyam. We have not pursued this approach because our attention concentrates on *finite* objects, which are usually represented by irreducible terms. However, this does not entail that we only consider axioms with a Noetherian reduction relation. Actually, some results depend on $\xrightarrow{AX}$ being Noetherian or NAX being ground term reducing. But many other conclusions can be drawn without assuming these properties and thus can be applied to specifications with *partial* functions, too.

Chapter 9 Church-Rosser Criteria

9.1 Introduction

We saw in Chapters 7 and 8 that Church-Rosser properties are crucial for the completeness of reduction and narrowing. Our general Church-Rosser criterion (Theorem 7.8.2) presumes confluence and BAX- (or ~BAX-) compatibility of NAX (or ~NAX, respectively). This chapter is mainly devoted to confluence and compatibility criteria based upon the *convergence of critical pairs*.

Let AX' ∈ {NAX,~NAX}. Remember that the definition of confluence starts out from reduction triangles of the form

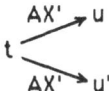

(cf. Section 7.8). The term pair ⟨u,u'⟩ is *critical* if the diagram above results from two conditional reductions $t_{\overline{AX'}} u \Leftarrow \gamma$ and $t_{\overline{AX'}} u' \Leftarrow \gamma'$ with simple length 1 such that the left-hand side of the axiom underlying $t_{\overline{AX'}} u' \Leftarrow \gamma'$ overlaps in t the left-hand side of the axiom underlying $t_{\overline{AX'}} u \Leftarrow \gamma$. Given that v is the left-hand side of the latter axiom, we call the reduction $t_{\overline{AX'}} u' \Leftarrow \gamma'$ *v-overlapping*. Inference rules which generate all *overlapping* reductions are presented in Section 9.2. This section also introduces *fully parallel reductions* that allow us to formulate "balanced" - not too weak and not strong - BAX-compatibility criteria (cf. Section 7.8). Section 9.3 collects three technical lemmata, which establish convergence properties and which are used in the proofs of confluence criteria given in Sections 9.5-9.8. Section 9.4 defines several variants of critical pairs and their respective convergence conditions. Again, there are three technical lemmata needed in proofs of confluence criteria. The section closes with two non-trivial examples of how one verifies critical pair convergence.

The technical results of Sections 9.2-9.4 give rise to a variety of confluence criteria. If the NAX-reduction relation is Noetherian, critical pair convergence is sufficient for confluence of NAX (cf. Section 9.5). *Strong convergence* implies *strong* confluence and makes it possible to avoid the Noetherian property (cf. Section 9.6). The corresponding criterion for confluence of ~NAX presumes the Noetherian property of the ~NAX-reduction relation (cf. Section 9.7). BAX-compatibility criteria are presented in Section 9.8. The main results of Sections 7.8 and 9.5-9.8 culminate in three

Church-Rosser criteria, which are combined into a heuristic procedure for Church-Rosser proofs (cf. Section 9.9).

9.2 Fully Parallel and Overlapping Reductions

Both the conditional and the goal reduction calculus supply us with a Parallel Reduction Rule that admits the application of several axioms at the same time (cf. Section 7.7). So far, only Lemmata 7.7.5 and 7.8.1 have referred to these rules, actually by establishing statements about the parallel length of reductions. This is the crucial number one induces on when deriving strong confluence from strong critical pair convergence (cf. Theorem 9.6.1). Redices of the same parallel reduction step are always *distinct* subterms of the term (or goal) the Parallel Reduction Rule rule is applied to. We call this kind of parallelism *horizontal* parallelism because one can draw a tree-like picture of the term such that the roots of all redices to be replaced in parallel are connected by a horizontal line. On the other hand, *vertical* parallelism allows the joint replacement of many redices, some of which may be embedded in others. This defines fully parallel reduction steps, which are referred to in Section 9.8 where BAX-compatibility criteria are presented. Hence we confine this notion to BAX-reductions.

Definition The *fully parallel reduction calculus* consists of the following inference rules:

Reflexivity Rule For all terms t,

$$t \xrightarrow{BAX} t \Leftarrow \emptyset.$$

Abstraction Rule Let f and g be substitutions and let $\{\gamma_x \mid x \in X\}$ be a set of goals. Then

$$\frac{\forall x \in X : fx \xrightarrow{BAX} gx \Leftarrow \gamma_x}{f \xrightarrow{BAX} g \Leftarrow \cup\{\gamma_x \mid x \in X\}}.$$

Fully Parallel Reduction Rule Let t be a term and $x \in single(t)^*$, $u = \langle u_1,...,u_n \rangle$, $u' = \langle u_1',...,u_n' \rangle$ and $\vartheta = \vartheta_1 \cup ... \cup \vartheta_n$ such that $u_1 \equiv u_1' \Leftarrow \vartheta_1, ..., u_n \equiv u_n' \Leftarrow \vartheta_n \in BAX$. Then

$$\frac{f \xrightarrow{BAX} g \Leftarrow \gamma}{t[u[f]/x] \xrightarrow{BAX} t[u'[g]/x] \Leftarrow \vartheta[f]u\gamma}.$$

Let t,t' be terms and γ be a goal. If there is a derivation of $t \xrightarrow{BAX} t' \Leftarrow \gamma$ via the fully parallel reduction calculus, then $t \overset{}{\underset{BAX}{\Longrightarrow}} t' \Leftarrow \gamma$ is called a (conditional) *fully parallel reduction*. If γ is NAX-reduced, we write $t \overset{}{\underset{BAX}{\Longrightarrow}} t'$.

$\|t \overset{}{\underset{BAX}{\Longrightarrow}} t' \Leftarrow \gamma\|$ denotes the *length* of $t \overset{}{\underset{BAX}{\Longrightarrow}} t' \Leftarrow \gamma$, i.e. the least number of Fully Parallel Reduction Rule applications needed to derive $t \overset{}{\underset{BAX}{\Longrightarrow}} t' \Leftarrow \gamma$.

$\|t \overset{}{\underset{BAX}{\Longrightarrow}} t'\|$ denotes the minimum of $\|t \overset{}{\underset{BAX}{\Longrightarrow}} t' \Leftarrow \gamma\|$ over all NAX-reduced goals γ. ∎

A fully parallel BAX-reduction is sketched in the following picture. The inner triangles represent the left- and right-hand sides of the equations that generate the reduction step.

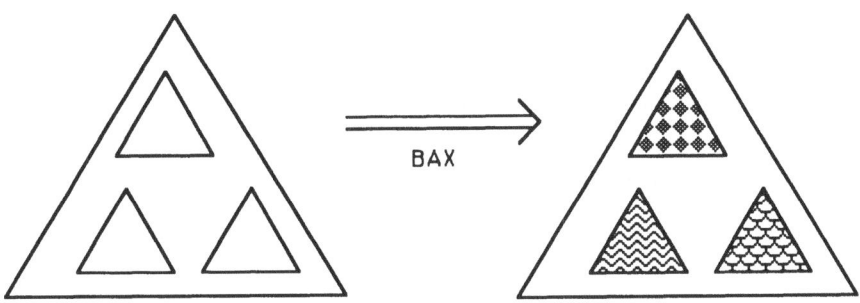

Note that we did not provide a composition rule for fully parallel reductions. This is because in all situations where these reductions occur they are needed as *single* steps.

Of course, $\overset{}{\underset{BAX}{\Longrightarrow}}$ is included in $\overset{}{\underset{BAX}{\longrightarrow}}$, but the converse is false: a sequence of BAX-applications cannot always be expressed as a $\overset{}{\underset{BAX}{\Longrightarrow}}$-step. Compare the following definitions with their $\overset{}{\underset{BAX}{\longrightarrow}}$-counterparts given in Section 7.8:

Definition A pair of terms $\langle t, t'\rangle$ *strongly NAX-convergent modulo BAX* if

$$t \overset{}{\underset{NAX}{\Longrightarrow}} u$$
$$\Downarrow BAX$$
$$t \overset{}{\underset{NAX}{\Longrightarrow}} u'$$

for some u, u'.

BAX is *strongly (ground) BAX-compatible* if for all (ground) terms t, u, u' such that

$$t \overset{NAX}{\underset{BAX}{\diagdown}} \overset{u}{\underset{u'}{,}}$$

$\langle u, u'\rangle$ is strongly NAX-convergent modulo BAX.

BAX *weakly respects (ground) NAX-normal forms* if for all (ground) NAX-normal forms t and all (ground) terms t', $t \overset{}{\underset{BAX}{\Longrightarrow}} t'$ implies

for some NAX-normal form u. ∎

Clearly, if NAX is strongly BAX-compatible, then NAX is BAX-compatible. The converse does not hold because the reduction $v \xRightarrow{BAX} v'$ need not be fully parallel. On the other hand, strong BAX-compatibility is the appropriate induction hypothesis for deriving BAX-compatibility from critical pair convergence (cf. Section 9.8).

Furthermore, we have

Lemma 9.2.1 Suppose that BAX weakly respects (ground) NAX-normal forms and NAX is strongly (ground) BAX-compatible. Then BAX respects (ground) NAX-normal forms.

Proof. Let t be a (ground) NAX-normal form such that $t \xRightarrow{BAX} t'$ for some (ground) term t'. There is a conditional reduction $t \xRightarrow{BAX} t' \Leftarrow \gamma$ with NAX-reduced goal γ. We establish a NAX-normal form u with

(∗)

$$t' \xrightarrow{NAX} u \qquad t \xrightarrow{BAX} u$$

by induction on $n = |t \xRightarrow{BAX} t' \Leftarrow \gamma|$.

Case 1. n = 0. Then t = t' and the proof is complete with u = t'.

Case 2. n > 0. Then $|t \xRightarrow{BAX} t'' \Leftarrow \gamma'| < n$ and $|t'' \xRightarrow{BAX} t' \Leftarrow \gamma''| = 1$ for some NAX-reduced goals γ', γ'' with $\gamma' \cup \gamma'' = \gamma$. By the induction hypothesis, there is a NAX-normal form u' such that $t'' \xrightarrow{NAX} u'$ and $t \xRightarrow{BAX} u'$. Since NAX is strongly (ground) BAX-compatible and u' is NAX-irreducible, $u' \xRightarrow{BAX} v$ and $t' \xrightarrow{NAX} v$ for some v. Since BAX weakly respects (ground) NAX-normal forms, there is a NAX-normal form u such that $v \xrightarrow{NAX} u$ and $u' \xRightarrow{BAX} u$. Hence (∗) holds true. ∎

Given a conditional equation $u \equiv u' \Leftarrow \delta$ and a reduction step $t \to t'$ such that u subsumes t, we call $t \to t'$ a *u-overlapping* reduction if the reduction redices of t (w.r.t. $t \to t'$) overlap u. Supposing that $t \to t'$ is induced by two equations, say $u_0 \equiv u_0'$ and $u_1 \equiv u_1'$, the situation looks as follows.

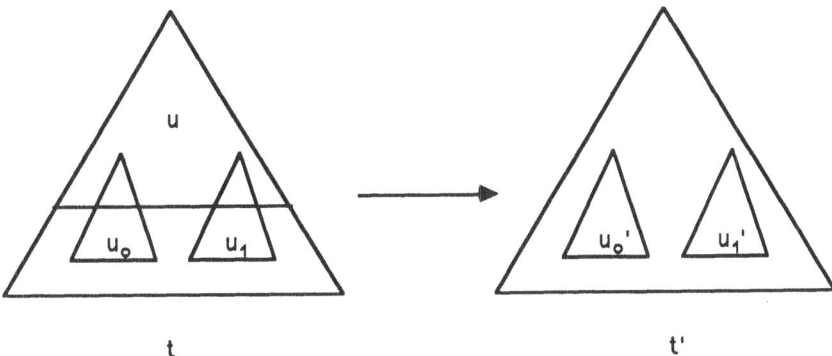

Overlapping reductions are created by *superposition rules*:

Definition Let t be a term, f be a substitution, $x \in X^*$, $u = \langle u_1,...,u_n \rangle$, $u' = \langle u_1',...,u_n' \rangle$, $v \in T(SIG)^*$ and $\vartheta = \vartheta_1 \cup ... \cup \vartheta_n$ such that $u_1 \equiv u_1' \Leftarrow \vartheta_1, ..., u_n \equiv u_n' \Leftarrow \vartheta_n \in$ NAX.

$\overrightarrow{NAX}$-*Superposition Rule*   If f unifies v and u, then

$$t[v[f]/x] \;{}^{t[v/x]}\!\!\overrightarrow{NAX}\; t[u'[f]/x] \Leftarrow \vartheta[f].$$

$\overrightarrow{=NAX}$-*Superposition Rule*   If $v[f] \overrightarrow{=BAX} u[f]$, then

$$t[v[f]/x] \;{}^{t[v/x]}\!\!\overrightarrow{=NAX}\; t[u'[f]/x] \Leftarrow \vartheta[f].$$

$\overrightarrow{BAX}$-*Superposition Rule*   If f unifies v and u, then

$$\dfrac{f \overrightarrow{BAX} g \Leftarrow \gamma}{t[v[f]/x] \;{}^{t[v/x]}\!\!\overrightarrow{BAX}\; t[u'[g]/x] \Leftarrow \vartheta[f] \cup \gamma.}$$

Let $\rightarrow \in \{\overrightarrow{NAX}, \overrightarrow{=NAX}, \overrightarrow{BAX}\}$ and $t \rightarrow t' \Leftarrow \gamma$ be a conditional reduction such that $t^u \rightarrow t' \Leftarrow \gamma$ is an instance of the $\rightarrow$-Superposition Rule. Then $t \rightarrow t' \Leftarrow \gamma$ is called *u-overlapping*.

$t^u \rightarrow t' \Leftarrow \gamma$ is *most general* if $t^u \rightarrow t' \Leftarrow \gamma$ is obtained by a $\rightarrow$-Superposition Rule instance where the substitution f is minimal w.r.t. the *subsumption ordering* $\leq$, which is defined by: $f \leq g$ if f subsumes g (cf. Section 2.2).

A conditional reduction of the form $u[f] \rightarrow t \Leftarrow \gamma$ *affects* u if there are conditional reductions $u[f'] \rightarrow t' \Leftarrow \delta$ and $f'' \rightarrow g \Leftarrow \varphi$ such that $u[f'] \rightarrow t' \Leftarrow \delta$ is u-overlapping, $f'+f'' = f$, $\|f'' \rightarrow g \Leftarrow \varphi\| \leq \|u[f] \rightarrow t \Leftarrow \gamma\|$, $t = t'[g]$ and $\gamma = \delta[f''] \cup \varphi$.

Pictorially:

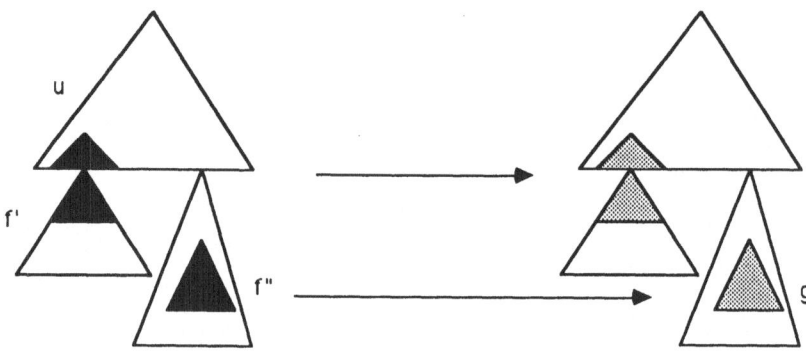

Here $u[f] \rightarrow t$ is generated by two equations whose left- and right-hand sides are denoted by black and dotted areas, respectively. In general, there may be an arbitrary number of conditional equations to induce the reduction $u[f] \rightarrow t$. The important point is that at least one of their left-hand sides overlaps u. ∎

A reduction of the form $v[f] \rightarrow t$ that does *not* affect v can be decomposed as follows.

Lemma 9.2.2 Let $\rightarrow \in \{\overrightarrow{NAX}, \overrightarrow{\approx NAX}, \overrightarrow{BAX}\}$ and $v[f] \rightarrow t \Leftarrow \gamma$ be a conditional reduction with parallel length 1 (cf. Section 7.7) that does not affect v. Then there is a substitution g such that $\|f \rightarrow g \Leftarrow \gamma\| = 1$ and
(1) $t = v[g]$ if v is linear,
(2) $t \rightarrow v[g]$ if $\rightarrow \in \{\overrightarrow{NAX}, \overrightarrow{\approx NAX}\}$ and $|v[f] \rightarrow t \Leftarrow \gamma| = 1$.

Proof. We show the statement by induction on size(v).

Case 1. There is $u \equiv u' \Leftarrow \delta \in$ NAX (or BAX) such that $v[f] = u[f]$ (or $v[f] \approx_{\overrightarrow{BAX}} u[f]$), $u'[f] = t$ and $\delta[f] = \gamma$. Since $v[f] \rightarrow t \Leftarrow \gamma$ does not affect v, we conclude that v is a variable. Hence the proof is complete with g defined by $gv = t$ and $gx = fx$ for all $x \in X - \{v\}$.

Case 2. $v = \sigma \langle v_1, ..., v_n \rangle$, $t = \sigma \langle t_1, ..., t_n \rangle$ for some $\sigma \in$ OP, $\gamma = \gamma_1 \cup ... \cup \gamma_n$ and $v_i[f] \rightarrow t_i \Leftarrow \gamma_i$ for all $1 \leq i \leq n$. Since $v[f] \rightarrow t \Leftarrow \gamma$ does not affect v, we conclude that for all $1 \leq i \leq n$, $v_i[f] \rightarrow t_i \Leftarrow \gamma_i$ does not affect v_i. By the induction hypothesis, $\|f \rightarrow g_i \Leftarrow \gamma_i\| = 1$ for some g_i.

Case 2.1. v is linear. Then all v_i are linear and thus by the induction hypothesis, $v_i[g_i] = t_i$. Moreover, we may assume that all g_i have disjoint domains. Hence (1) and thus (2) hold true for $g = g_1 + ... + g_n$.

Case 2.2. $|v[f] \rightarrow t \Leftarrow \gamma| = 1$, i.e. $v[f] \rightarrow t \Leftarrow \gamma$ is obtained by one application of the Single Reduction Rule. Then w.l.o.g. $v_1[f] \rightarrow t_1 \Leftarrow \gamma$ and for all $2 \leq i \leq n$, $v_i[f] = t_i$. By the induction hypothesis, $\|f \rightarrow g \Leftarrow \gamma\| = 1$ and $t_1 \rightarrow v_1[g]$ for some g. Hence

$$t = \sigma \langle t_1, t_2, ..., t_n \rangle \rightarrow \sigma \langle v_1[g], v_2[g], ..., v_n[g] \rangle = v[g]. \blacksquare$$

9.3 Convergence Properties

The following lemma, which is a consequence of the previous one, will be used in the proof of Theorem 9.6.1 (strong confluence criterion).

Lemma 9.3.1 Let $u \equiv u' \Leftarrow \vartheta \in NAX$ be left-linear and let the conditional reduction $u[f] \xrightarrow{NAX} t \Leftarrow \gamma$ be obtained by one application of the Parallel Reduction Rule such that $u[f] \xrightarrow{NAX} t \Leftarrow \gamma$ does not affect u, $\vartheta[f]u\gamma$ is NAX-reducible,

$$\|u[f]\xrightarrow{NAX} t\| = 1 + \|\gamma \xrightarrow{NAX}^{RD} \vartheta\|, \quad \|u[f]\xrightarrow{NAX} u'[f]\| = 1 + \|\vartheta[f] \xrightarrow{NAX}^{RD} \vartheta\|$$

and for all subterms v of $\vartheta[f]$ and terms v', v'',

$$\|v \xrightarrow{NAX} v'\| + \|v \xrightarrow{NAX} v''\| < \|u[f] \xrightarrow{NAX} t\| + \|u[f] \xrightarrow{NAX} u'[f]\|$$

implies

$$\|v' \xrightarrow{NAX} t'\| \le \|v \xrightarrow{NAX} v''\| \quad \text{and} \quad \|v'' \xrightarrow{NAX} t'\| \le \|v \xrightarrow{NAX} v'\|$$

for some t'. Then

$$\|u'[f] \xrightarrow{NAX} t'\| \le \|u[f] \xrightarrow{NAX} t\| \quad \text{and} \quad \|t \xrightarrow{NAX} t'\| \le \|u[f] \xrightarrow{NAX} u'[f]\|$$

for some t'.

Proof. By Lemma 9.2.2 (1), $\|f \xrightarrow{NAX} g \Leftarrow \gamma\| = 1$ and $t = u[g]$ for some g. Of course, there is a linear goal φ without operation symbols such that $\varphi[f'] = \vartheta[f]$, $\|f' \xrightarrow{NAX} g' \Leftarrow \gamma\| = 1$ and $\varphi[g'] = \vartheta[g]$ for some f', g'. Thus $\varphi[f']$ is NAX-reducible. By Lemma 7.7.5, there is a substitution h' such that $f' \xrightarrow{NAX} h'$, $\varphi[h']$ is NAX-reduced and

$$\|f' \xrightarrow{NAX} h'\| = \|\varphi[f'] \xrightarrow{NAX}^{RD} \vartheta\|.$$

Hence for all $x \in var(\varphi)$, $h'x$ is NAX-irreducible. Since $\varphi[f'] = \vartheta[f]$, $f'x$ is a subterm of $\vartheta[f]$ and

$$\|f'x \xrightarrow{NAX} g'x\| + \|f'x \xrightarrow{NAX} h'x\| \le 1 + \|\gamma \xrightarrow{NAX}^{RD} \vartheta\| + \|\vartheta[f] \xrightarrow{NAX}^{RD} \vartheta\|$$
$$< \|u[f] \xrightarrow{NAX} t\| + \|u[f] \xrightarrow{NAX} u'[f]\|.$$

Thus by assumption, $\|g'x \xrightarrow{NAX} h'x\| \le \|f'x \xrightarrow{NAX} h'x\|$ because $h'x$ is NAX-irreducible. Let $g'' = g'\uparrow var(\varphi)$ and $h'' = h'\uparrow var(\varphi)$. Since $g'' \xrightarrow{NAX} h''$ and $\varphi[h']$ is NAX-reduced, Lemma 7.7.4 (3) (with the parallel instead of the simple length) implies

$$\|\varphi[g'] \xrightarrow{NAX}^{RD} \vartheta\| \le \|g'' \xrightarrow{NAX} h''\|.$$

Therefore

$$\|u'[f]\xrightarrow{\overline{NAX}} u'[g]\| \leq \|f\xrightarrow{\overline{NAX}} g\|$$
$$\leq \|f\xrightarrow{\overline{NAX}} g\Leftarrow \gamma\| + \|\gamma \xrightarrow{RD}_{\overline{NAX}} \emptyset\|$$
$$\leq 1 + \|\gamma \xrightarrow{RD}_{\overline{NAX}} \emptyset\| = \|u[f]\xrightarrow{\overline{NAX}} t\|$$

and

$$\|t\xrightarrow{\overline{NAX}} u'[g]\| = \|u[g]\xrightarrow{\overline{NAX}} u'[g]\|$$
$$\leq 1 + \|\delta[g] \xrightarrow{RD}_{\overline{NAX}} \emptyset\|$$
$$= 1 + \|\varphi[g'] \xrightarrow{RD}_{\overline{NAX}} \emptyset\|$$
$$\leq 1 + \|g''\xrightarrow{\overline{NAX}} h''\|$$
$$\leq 1 + \|f'\uparrow var(\varphi)\xrightarrow{\overline{NAX}} h''\|$$
$$\leq 1 + \|\varphi[f'] \xrightarrow{RD}_{\overline{NAX}} \emptyset\|$$
$$= 1 + \|\delta[f] \xrightarrow{RD}_{\overline{NAX}} \emptyset\|$$
$$= \|u[f]\xrightarrow{\overline{NAX}} u'[f]\|. \blacksquare$$

The following lemma is needed for inductive arguments in the proofs of Theorems 9.5.1, 9.7.2 (confluence criteria) and Theorems 9.8.1, 9.8.2 (BAX-compatibility criteria).

Lemma 9.3.2 Let $\rightarrow \in \{\xrightarrow{\overline{NAX}}, \xrightarrow{\sim NAX}, \xrightarrow{\overline{BAX}}\}$, $u\equiv u'\Leftarrow \delta \in$ NAX and $\delta[f]$ be a (ground) goal. Suppose that the (ground) conditional reduction $u[f]\rightarrow t\Leftarrow \gamma$ has parallel length 1 and does not affect u.

(1) If $\rightarrow = \xrightarrow{\overline{NAX}}$, $\delta[f]u\gamma$ is NAX-reducible, $u[f]\xrightarrow{\overline{NAX}} t'\Leftarrow \gamma$ is obtained by one application of the Single Reduction Rule and for all subterms v of $\delta[f]$, $v\xrightarrow{\overline{NAX}} v'$ and $v\xrightarrow{\overline{NAX}} v''$ imply that $\langle v',v''\rangle$ is NAX-convergent, then $\langle u'[f],t\rangle$ is NAX-convergent.

(2) If $\rightarrow = \xrightarrow{\sim NAX}$, $\delta[f]u\gamma$ is ~NAX-reducible, $u[f]\xrightarrow{\sim NAX} t'\Leftarrow \gamma$ is obtained by one application of the Single Reduction Rule, ~BAX respects (ground) ~NAX-normal forms (cf. Section 7.8) and for all subterms v of $\delta[f]$, $v\xrightarrow{\sim NAX} v'$ and $v\xrightarrow{\sim NAX} v''$ imply that $\langle v',v''\rangle$ is ~NAX-convergent modulo ~BAX, then $\langle u'[f],t\rangle$ is ~NAX-convergent modulo ~BAX.

(3) If $\rightarrow = \xrightarrow{\overline{BAX}}$, u is linear, $\delta[f]$ is NAX-reducible, γ is NAX-reduced, BAX weakly respects (ground) NAX-normal forms (cf. Section 9.2) and for all subterms v of $\delta[f]$, $\|v\xrightarrow{\overline{NAX}} v'\| \leq \|\delta[f]\xrightarrow{RD}_{\overline{NAX}} \emptyset\|$ and $v\xrightarrow{\overline{BAX}} v''$ imply that $\langle v,v'\rangle$ is strongly NAX-convergent modulo BAX, then $\langle u'[f],t\rangle$ is strongly NAX-convergent modulo BAX.

Proof. (1)&(2) Let AX' $\in$ {NAX,~NAX}. By Lemma 9.2.2 (2), $f\xrightarrow{\overline{AX'}} g\Leftarrow \gamma$ and $t\xrightarrow{\overline{AX'}} u[g]$ for some g. There is a linear goal φ without operation symbols such that $\varphi[f'] = \delta[f]$, $f'\xrightarrow{\overline{AX'}} g'$ and $\varphi[g'] = \delta[g]$ for some f',g'. Thus $\varphi[f']$ is AX'-reducible. By Lemma 7.7.5, there is a substitution h' such that $f'\xrightarrow{\overline{AX'}} h'$ and $\varphi[h']$ is AX'-reduced. Hence for all $x \in var(\varphi)$, h'x is AX'-irreducible.

Since $\varphi[f'] = \delta[f]$, f'x is a subterm of $\delta[f]$. Thus by assumption, $\langle g'x,h'x\rangle$

is AX'-convergent (modulo ~BAX), i.e. there is a substitution h such that g'x $\xrightarrow{AX'}$ hx and h'x = hx (or h'x $\xrightarrow{\sim BAX}$ hx. Since ~BAX respects ~NAX-normal forms, there is an AX'-irreducible substitution h" with hx $\xrightarrow{\sim NAX}$ h"x and h'x $\xrightarrow{\sim BAX}$ h"x). Since φ[h'] is AX'-reduced, φ[h] (φ[h"]) is AX'-reduced as well. Therefore ϑ[g] = φ[g'] is AX'-reducible, and we obtain

$$\begin{array}{c} u'[f] \xrightarrow{AX'} \\ \hspace{2em} \searrow u'[g]. \\ t \xrightarrow{AX'} u[g] \xrightarrow{AX'} \end{array}$$

(3) By Lemma 9.2.2 (1), f $\xrightarrow{BAX}$ g $\Leftarrow$ γ and t = u[g] for some g. There is a linear goal φ without operation symbols such that φ[f'] = ϑ[f], f' $\xrightarrow{BAX}$ g' and φ[g'] = ϑ[g] for some f',g'. Thus φ[f'] is NAX-reducible. By Lemma 7.7.5, there is a substitution h' such that ||f' $\xrightarrow{NAX}$ h'|| = ||φ[f']$\xrightarrow{RD}_{NAX}$ ∅|| and φ[h'] is NAX-reduced. Hence for all x ∈ var(φ), h'x is NAX-irreducible.

Since φ[f'] = ϑ[f], f'x is a subterm of ϑ[f]. Thus by assumption, ⟨g'x,h'x⟩ is strongly NAX-convergent modulo BAX, i.e. there is a substitution h such that g'x $\xrightarrow{NAX}$ hx and h'x $\xrightarrow{BAX}$ hx. Since BAX weakly respects NAX-normal forms, there is a NAX-irreducible substitution h" with hx $\xrightarrow{NAX}$ h"x and h'x $\xrightarrow{BAX}$ h"x. Since φ[h'] is NAX-reduced, φ[h"] is NAX-reduced as well. Therefore φ[h] and thus ϑ[g] = φ[g'] are NAX-reducible, and we obtain

$$\begin{array}{c} u'[f] \xrightarrow{BAX} \\ \hspace{2em} \searrow u'[g]. \blacksquare \\ t = u[g] \xrightarrow{NAX} \end{array}$$

The following lemma is used for inductive arguments in the proofs of Theorems 9.8.1 and 9.8.2 (BAX-compatibility criteria).

Lemma 9.3.3 Suppose that CE(BAX) is non-empty and that NAX is (ground) confluent and satisfies the Definition Principle (cf. Section 7.8). Let u≡u' $\Leftarrow$ ϑ ∈ BAX and f,g be (ground) substitutions such that f $\xrightarrow{BAX}$ g, u[f] $\xrightarrow{NAX}$ t and ϑ[f] is NAX-reduced.

Then there is a substitution h with f $\xrightarrow{NAX}$ h and t $\xrightarrow{NAX}$ u[h]. If u is linear, then ||f $\xrightarrow{NAX}$ h|| = ||u[f] $\xrightarrow{NAX}$ u[h]|| and u[h] = t. If for all x ∈ var(u), ⟨hx,gx⟩ is NAX-convergent modulo BAX, then ⟨t,u'[g]⟩ is strongly NAX-convergent modulo BAX as well.

Proof. We show the statement by induction on size(u). If u is a constant or a variable, then choose h = f (or h = f[t/u]). Otherwise u = σ⟨u_1,...,u_n⟩ for some σ,u_1,...,u_n. Since u[f] $\xrightarrow{NAX}$ t and NAX satisfies the Definition Principle, there are t_1,...,t_n with t = σ⟨t_1,...,t_n⟩. By the induction hypothesis, there are substitutions h_1,...,h_n such that f $\xrightarrow{NAX}$ h_i and t_i $\xrightarrow{NAX}$ u_i[h_i] or ||f $\xrightarrow{NAX}$ h_i|| =

$\|u_i[f]_{\overrightarrow{NAX}} u_i[h_i]\|$ and $u_i[h_i] = t_i$, respectively. Since NAX is confluent, some h satisfies $h_i \overrightarrow{NAX} h$ for all $1 \le i \le n$. If u is linear, we do not need the confluence of NAX. Instead, we may assume $h_i = h$ for all $1 \le i \le n$. Hence

or
$$f \overrightarrow{NAX} h \text{ and } t \overrightarrow{NAX} \sigma\langle u_1[h_1],\dots,u_n[h_n]\rangle \overrightarrow{NAX} u[h]$$

$$\|f \overrightarrow{NAX} h\| = \|u[f] \overrightarrow{NAX} u[h]\| \text{ and } t = \sigma\langle u_1[h_1],\dots,u_n[h_n]\rangle = u[h],$$

respectively. By assumption, $f \overrightarrow{BAX} g$. Suppose that for all $x \in var(u)$, $\langle gx, hx \rangle$ is strongly NAX-convergent modulo BAX, i.e.

$$\begin{array}{c} hx \overrightarrow{NAX} h'x \\ \Downarrow BAX \\ gx \overrightarrow{NAX} g'x \end{array}$$

for some h',g'. Since $\vartheta[f]$ is NAX-reduced, we have $\vartheta[f] = \vartheta[h] = \vartheta[h']$. Therefore

$$\begin{array}{c} t \overrightarrow{NAX} u[h] \overrightarrow{NAX} u[h'] \\ \Downarrow BAX \\ u'[g] \overrightarrow{NAX} u'[g''] \end{array}$$

where $g'' = g'\restriction var(u) + g\restriction(X-var(u))$. ∎

9.4 Critical Pairs

The three reduction relations $\overrightarrow{NAX}$, $\overrightarrow{\sim NAX}$ and $\overrightarrow{BAX}$ give rise to three kinds of critical pairs.

Definition Let $\rightarrow \in \{\overrightarrow{NAX}, \overrightarrow{\sim NAX}, \overrightarrow{BAX}\}$, $u \equiv u' \Leftarrow \vartheta \in NAX$ and $u[f] \rightarrow t \Leftarrow \gamma$ be a u-overlapping conditional reduction. Then

$$cp = \langle u'[f] \Leftarrow \vartheta[f], t \Leftarrow \gamma \rangle$$

is a *critical pair* of $\rightarrow$ into NAX with premises $\vartheta[f]$ and γ. (If $\vartheta[f]$ or γ is empty, we simply write u'[f] or t instead of $u'[f] \Leftarrow \vartheta[f]$ or $t \Leftarrow \gamma$.)
    cp is *feasible* if $\vartheta[f][g]$ is NAX-reducible for some g and
- $\gamma[g]$ is AX'-reducible if $\rightarrow = \overrightarrow{AX'}$ (where AX' is NAX or ~NAX),
- $\gamma[g]$ is NAX-reduced if $\rightarrow = \overrightarrow{BAX}$.

cp is *most general* if $u[f]^u \rightarrow t \Leftarrow \gamma$ is most general (cf. Section 9.2). ∎

A critical pair results from two conditional reductions

$$u[f] \xrightarrow{NAX} u'[f] \Leftarrow \delta[f] \quad \text{and} \quad u[f]^u \rightarrow t \Leftarrow \gamma$$

that start out from the same term u[f]. It consists of the "reduced" terms u'[f] and t, each of them equipped with the corresponding reduction premise. The critical pair is feasible if both premises have a common "reductive" solution, for instance an N-solution (cf. Lemma 8.2.3).

Example 9.4.1 Let <BSIG,BAX> = BINARY and <SIG,AX> = BINARY-ADD-MULT (cf. Section 3.5). The following reductions are (a*b0)-overlapping.

(1)   a*00 $\xrightarrow{NAX}$ (a*0)0
      is generated by the NAX-axiom a*b0 ≡ (a*b)0.

(2)   a*00 $\xrightarrow{\sim NAX}$ 0
      is generated by the reduction a*00 $\xrightarrow{\sim BAX}$ a*0, followed by the NAX-axiom a*0 ≡ 0.

(3)   a*00 $\xrightarrow{BAX}$ a*0
      is generated by the base axiom 00 ≡ 0.

Since a*b0≡(a*b)0 ∈ NAX, (1) results in the critical pair <(a*0)0, (a*0)0> of $\xrightarrow{NAX}$ into NAX, (2) generates the critical pair <(a*0)0, 0> of $\xrightarrow{\sim NAX}$ into NAX, and (3) leads to the critical pair <(a*0)0, a*0> of $\xrightarrow{BAX}$ into NAX.

Since we assume that conditional base equations are symmetric (cf. Section 6.1), the base axiom 0≡00 must be considered as well. Indeed, it generates the following (a*0)-overlapping reductions.

(4)   a*0 $\xrightarrow{\sim NAX}$ (a*0)0
      consists of a*0 $\xrightarrow{\sim BAX}$ a*00, followed by the NAX-axiom
      a*00 ≡ (a*0)0.

(5)   a*0 $\xrightarrow{BAX}$ a*00
      is induced by the base axiom 0 ≡ 00.

Since a*0≡0 ∈ NAX, (4) generates the critical pair <0, (a*0)0> of $\xrightarrow{\sim NAX}$ into NAX, and (5) leads to the critical pair <0, a*00> of $\xrightarrow{BAX}$ into NAX. ■

We distinguish between five convergence conditions on critical pairs.

Definition Let cp = <t⇐γ,t'⇐γ'> be a critical pair.
cp is *(ground) NAX-convergent* if for all NAX-irreducible (ground) substitutions f such that (γuγ')[f] is NAX-reducible, <t[f],t'[f]> is NAX-convergent.
cp is *(ground) ~NAX-convergent modulo ~BAX* if for all ~NAX-irreducible (ground) substitutions f such that (γuγ')[f] is ~NAX-reducible, <t[f],t'[f]> is ~NAX-convergent modulo ~BAX.

cp is *weakly (ground) NAX-convergent modulo BAX* if for all NAX-irreducible (ground) substitutions f such that γ[f] is NAX-reducible and γ'[f] is NAX-reduced, there are goals ψ, λ and terms u,u' such that var(u) ⊆ var(t), ψ[f] is NAX-reducible, λ[f] is NAX-reduced,

$$t \xrightarrow[NAX]{} u \Leftarrow \psi, \quad t' \xrightarrow[NAX]{} u' \Leftarrow \gamma \cup \psi \quad \text{and} \quad u \xrightarrow[BAX]{} u' \Leftarrow \lambda.$$

cp is *strongly (ground) NAX-convergent modulo BAX* if γ is a base goal and for all (ground) substitutions f such that $(\gamma \cup \gamma')$[f] is NAX-reduced, there are goals ψ, λ and terms u,u' such that $(\psi \cup \lambda)$[f] is NAX-reduced,

$$t \xrightarrow[NAX]{} u \Leftarrow \psi, \quad t' \xrightarrow[NAX]{} u' \Leftarrow \gamma \cup \psi \quad \text{and} \quad u \xrightarrow[BAX]{} u' \Leftarrow \lambda.$$

cp is *(ground) NAX-convergent modulo BAX* if cp is both weakly and strongly (ground) NAX-convergent modulo BAX. ∎

Example 9.4.2 (cf. Example 9.4.1) Since (a*0)0 = (a*0)0, the critical pair ⟨(a*0)0,(a*0)0⟩ is NAX-convergent. Since

$$(a*0)0 \xrightarrow{NAX} 00$$
$$0 \xrightarrow{\sim BAX}$$

the critical pair ⟨(a*0)0,0⟩ is ~NAX-convergent modulo ~BAX. Since

$$(a*0)0 \xrightarrow[NAX]{} 00$$
$$\Downarrow BAX$$
$$a*0 \xrightarrow[NAX]{} 0$$

the critical pair ⟨(a*0)0,a*0⟩ is NAX-convergent modulo BAX. Since

$$0 \xrightarrow{\sim BAX} 00$$
$$(a*0)0 \xrightarrow{NAX}$$

the critical pair ⟨0,(a*0)0⟩ is ~NAX-convergent modulo ~BAX. Since

$$0 \xrightarrow[BAX]{} 00$$
$$\uparrow NAX$$
$$a*00 \xrightarrow[NAX]{} (a*0)0$$

the critical pair ⟨0,a*00⟩ is NAX-convergent modulo BAX. Further convergence proofs are given at the end of this section. ∎

Note the difference between the convergence of arbitrary term pairs (as defined in Section 7.8) and the convergence of critical pairs. While the former only concerns the terms themselves, the latter takes into account their instances. Lemmata 9.4.4 and 9.4.6 given below provide the link between both notions by reducing the convergence of arbitrary term pairs to the convergence of most general critical pairs.

When AX is finite, there are only finitely many most general critical pairs. Nevertheless, given such a critical pair, say cp = $\langle t \Leftarrow \gamma, t' \Leftarrow \gamma' \rangle$, the convergence proof for cp might fail when each instance of cp by an irreducible substitution needs its own converging diagram. In practice, one starts out from t and t' (regardless of the substitutions) and constructs converging diagrams, say $D_1,...,D_n$, consisting of conditional reductions with premises, say $\delta_1,...,\delta_n$. Then the remaining task is to check that $D_1,...,D_n$ cover all cases, i.e. that the *covering formula*

(∗) $(\delta_1$ or δ_2 or ... or $\delta_n) \Leftarrow \gamma \cup \gamma'$

holds true. If so, the proof is complete because for each instance of cp, e.g. cp[f], there will be some $1 \le i \le n$ such that the corresponding premise instance $\delta_i[f]$ is a $\langle SIG, AX \rangle$-theorem. However, this does not necessarily mean that $\delta_i[f]$ is reducible. (Otherwise we would *presume* the Church-Rosser property which we are just going to *prove* by showing that critical pairs are convergent!) Thus we need additional knowledge about $\langle SIG, AX \rangle$ that allows us to establish the reducibility of $\delta_i[f]$. A further problem is that (∗) is not a Horn clause. Thus we must employ non-Horn deduction or some meta-reasoning in order to verify (∗).

Zhang and Remy circumvent these problems by admitting only base premises in conditional reductions, thereby turning (∗) into a conjecture of the base theory. The drawback of this approach is that the Church-Rosser property, which follows from critical pair convergence, no longer "decides" the theory of Mod(SIG,AX). Instead, the theory of Zhang and Remy's *contextual reductions* is complete for a proper subclass of Mod(SIG,AX) where the premises of axioms are interpreted in a particular base domain. In practice, one's knowledge about the given specification mostly suffices in order to solve the problems mentioned, without changing the model-theoretic background.

We continue the series of technical lemmata with a statement that will be used in the proofs of Lemmata 9.4.4 and 9.4.6 (1) where convergence is reduced from arbitrary term pairs to most general critical pairs.

Lemma 9.4.3 Let AX' ∈ {NAX,~NAX} be normalizing (on ground terms; cf.

Section 7.7) and f be a (ground) substitution such that $\gamma[f]$ is AX'-reducible. Suppose that for all subterms v of $\gamma[f]$, if $v \xrightarrow{AX'} u$ and $v \xrightarrow{AX'} u'$, then $\langle u,u' \rangle$ is AX'-convergent. If AX' = ~NAX, suppose that ~BAX respects (ground) ~NAX-normal forms (cf. Section 7.8).

Then there is an AX'-irreducible substitution g such that $f \xrightarrow{AX'} g$ and $\gamma[g]$ is AX'-reducible.

Proof. Since AX' is normalizing, we have $f \xrightarrow{AX'} g$ for some AX'-irreducible g. There is a linear goal φ without operation symbols such that $\varphi[f'] = \gamma[f]$, $f' \xrightarrow{AX'} g'$ and $\varphi[g'] = \gamma[g]$ for some f',g'. Thus $\varphi[f']$ is AX'-reducible. By Lemma 7.7.5, there is a substitution h' such that $f' \xrightarrow{AX'} h'$ and $\varphi[h']$ is AX'-reduced. Hence for all $x \in var(\varphi)$, h'x is AX'-irreducible.

Since $\varphi[f'] = \vartheta[f]$, f'x is a subterm of $\gamma[f]$. Thus by assumption, $\langle g'x,h'x \rangle$ is AX'-convergent, i.e. there is a substitution h such that $g'x \xrightarrow{AX'} hx$ and $h'x = hx$ (or $h'x \xrightarrow{BAX} hx$. Since ~BAX respects ~NAX-normal forms, there is an AX'-irreducible substitution h" with $hx \xrightarrow{NAX} h"x$ and $h'x \xrightarrow{BAX} h"x$). $\varphi[h']$ is AX'-reduced and thus $\varphi[h]$ (resp. $\varphi[h"]$) is AX'-reduced as well. Therefore $\gamma[g] = \varphi[g']$ is AX'-reducible. ∎

The first lemma for reducing a convergence property from arbitrary to most general critical pairs is needed in the proofs of Theorems 9.5.1 and 9.7.2 (confluence criteria).

Lemma 9.4.4 Let AX' $\in$ {NAX,~NAX} be normalizing (on ground terms) and $\langle t \Leftarrow \gamma, t' \Leftarrow \gamma' \rangle$ be a (ground) critical pair of $\xrightarrow{AX'}$ into NAX with AX'-reducible γ and γ'.

Suppose that all feasible most general critical pairs of $\xrightarrow{AX'}$ into NAX are (ground) AX'-convergent (modulo ~BAX) and for all subterms v of $\gamma \cup \gamma'$, if $v \xrightarrow{AX'} u$ and $v \xrightarrow{AX'} u'$, then $\langle u,u' \rangle$ is AX'-convergent (modulo ~BAX). If AX' = ~NAX, suppose that ~BAX respects (ground) ~NAX-normal forms.

Then $\langle t,t' \rangle$ is AX'-convergent (modulo ~BAX).

Proof. Of course, there is a most general critical pair cp = $\langle v \Leftarrow \delta, v' \Leftarrow \delta' \rangle$ of $\xrightarrow{AX'}$ into NAX such that $v[f] = t$, $v'[f] = t'$ and $(\delta \cup \delta')[f] = \gamma \cup \gamma'$ for some (ground) substitution f. By assumption, cp is (ground) AX'-convergent (modulo ~BAX). By Lemma 9.4.3, there is an AX'-irreducible substitution g such that $(f+f_0) \xrightarrow{AX'} g$ and $(\delta \cup \delta')[g]$ is AX'-reducible. Since cp is (ground) AX'-convergent (modulo ~BAX), we conclude that $\langle v[g],v'[g] \rangle$ and thus $\langle t,t' \rangle$ are AX'-convergent (modulo ~BAX) as well. ∎

Our second lemma for reducing a convergence property from arbitrary to most general critical pairs (Lemma 9.4.6) refers to the reduction relation $\xrightarrow[AX']{RD}$ as a relation on *terms*, which is defined as the transitive closure of

$\{\langle t,t_i\rangle \mid 0\le i\le n \text{ and } \exists\ t\xrightarrow{}_{\overline{AX}} t_o \Leftarrow (P\langle t_1,\ldots,t_n\rangle)\cup\delta\}.$

In contrast to $\xrightarrow{}_{\overline{AX}}$, $\vdash^{RD}_{AX}$ is in general not reflexive. Moreover, $\vdash^{RD}_{AX}$ is not OP-compatible (cf. Section 2.3), but *weakly* OP-compatible:

Definition A binary term relation $>$ is *weakly OP-compatible* if for all terms u and $x \in var(u)$,

$$t > t' \quad \text{implies} \quad u[t/x] > u[t'/x] \text{ or } u[t/x] > t'. \ \blacksquare$$

Of course, if NAX consists of *unconditional* equations, then $\vdash^{RD}_{AX}$ is OP-compatible and agrees with $\xrightarrow{}_{\overline{AX}}$.

The *term* relation $\vdash^{RD}_{AX}$ can be imagined as a set of trees where a direct successor of a node is either the right-hand side or a (maximal) term in the premise of a conditional reduction. If $\vdash^{RD}_{AX}$ is Noetherian, then all these trees are finite and thus all conditional reductions have finite length. By Lemma 7.7.4 (1), the *goal* relation $\vdash^{RD}_{AX}$ would also be Noetherian. The converse holds true as well. In fact, the Noetherian property of $\vdash^{RD}_{AX}$ is usually shown by reference to the *term* relation $\vdash^{RD}_{AX}$. For instance, $\vdash^{RD}_{NAX}$ is Noetherian if the *generating set* of $\vdash^{RD}_{NAX}$, i.e.

$$\{\langle t,t_i\rangle \mid 0\le i\le n \text{ and } \exists\ t\equiv t_o \Leftarrow (P\langle t_1,\ldots,t_n\rangle)\cup\delta \in NAX\}$$

can be embedded into a *recursive path ordering*. Let us take a quick look at such orderings.

Definition The set

$$\{\langle t[u/x],u\rangle \mid t \in T(SIG)-X, u \in T(SIG), x \in var(u)\}$$

is called the *proper-subterm relation* and is denoted by $\supset$.

Let $\ge$ be a transitive ordering on OP and let R_{lex} be the lexicographic extension of a binary term relation to a binary relation on term *sequences*.

The *recursive path ordering induced by* $\ge$, $RPO(\ge)$, is defined as the least binary term relation that includes $\supset$ and satisfies the following closure properties:
- If $t \supset u$ and $\langle u,v\rangle \in RPO(\ge)$, then $\langle t,v\rangle \in RPO(\ge)$.
- Let σt and $\tau u = \langle u_1,\ldots,u_n\rangle$ be terms such that $\sigma \ge \tau$ and for all $1\le i\le n$, $\langle \sigma t, u_i\rangle \in RPO(\ge)$.
  If $\tau \ge \sigma$ does not hold or $\langle t,u\rangle \in RPO(\ge)_{lex}$, then $\langle \sigma t, \tau u\rangle \in RPO(\ge)$. $\blacksquare$

A suitable ordering $\ge$ on OP is mostly given by:

$\sigma \geq \tau$ iff $\exists \; \sigma t \equiv t' \Leftarrow \vartheta \in$ NAX such that τ occurs in t' or ϑ.

Recursive path orderings are irreflexive, transitive, OP-compatible, closed under instantiation and include the proper-subterm relation. In short, they are *simplification orderings* (cf. Dershowitz [2], Theorem 3, or Padawitz [1], Theorem 6.5). In turn, simplification orderings are Noetherian, which is a consequence of Kruskal's Tree Theorem stating that every infinite term sequence $\{t_i \mid i \in \mathbb{N}\}$ contains two terms t_i, t_j with $i < j$ such that $\langle t_j, t_i \rangle$ belongs to the reflexive, transitive and OP-compatible closure of $\supset$ (cf. Dershowitz [1], p. 3 ff., or Padawitz [1], Lemma 5.1).

This way of showing the Noetherian property of $\vdash^{RD}_{AX}$ is important for our purposes because in some subsequent proofs, Noetherian induction often refers to the union of $\supset$ and $\vdash^{RD}_{AX}$. Hence the embedding of $\vdash^{RD}_{AX}$ into a Noetherian relation that includes $\supset$ would provide us with the relation we actually need. Nevertheless, in the case when the Noetherian property of $\vdash^{RD}_{AX}$ has been proved in another way, we obtain the necessary relation as well:

Lemma 9.4.5 If R is a Noetherian and weakly OP-compatible (ground) term relation, then the union of R and the proper-subterm relation, denoted by $\supset R$, is Noetherian (on ground terms) as well.

Proof. Let $t_0 \supset R \; t_1 \supset R \; t_2 \supset R \ldots$ By Noetherian induction on t_0 w.r.t. R one concludes that such a sequence is finite: if $t_0 \; R \; t_1$, then by the induction hypothesis, the sequence $t_1 \supset R \; t_2 \supset R \ldots$ is finite and the proof is complete. Otherwise there is $i \geq 1$ such that $t_0 \supset t_i \; R \; t_{i+1}$. Hence $t_0 = u[t_i/x]$ for some $u \in T(SIG)-X$ and $x \in var(u)$. Since R is weakly OP-compatible, we obtain

$$t_0 \; R \; u[t_{i+1}/x] \supset t_{i+1} \quad \text{or} \quad t_0 \supset t_{i+1}.$$

By the induction hypothesis, the sequence $u[t_{i+1}/x] \supset R \; t_{i+1} \supset R \; t_{i+2} \supset R \ldots$ is finite and the proof is complete as well. ∎

The second lemma for reducing a convergence property from arbitrary term pairs to most general critical pairs will be used in the proofs of Theorems 9.8.1 and 9.8.2 (BAX-compatibility criteria).

Lemma 9.4.6 Let NAX be (ground) confluent and let $\langle t \Leftarrow \gamma, t' \Leftarrow \gamma' \rangle$ be a (ground) critical pair of $\xrightarrow{BAX}$ into NAX with NAX-reducible γ and NAX-reduced γ'. Suppose that BAX weakly respects (ground) NAX-normal forms (cf. Section 9.2) and one of the following conditions (1) and (2) holds true:

(1) NAX is normalizing, all feasible most general critical pairs of $\xrightarrow{BAX}$ into NAX are weakly (ground) NAX-convergent modulo BAX and for all $v \xrightarrow{NAX} u$ and $v \xrightarrow{BAX} u'$ such that v is a subterm of γ or $t \supset \vdash^{RD}_{NAX} v$, $\langle u, u' \rangle$ is strongly NAX-convergent modulo BAX.

(2) All feasible most general critical pairs of $\xrightarrow[BAX]{}$ into NAX are strongly (ground) NAX-convergent modulo BAX, and for all $v\xrightarrow[NAX]{}u$ and $v\xrightarrow[BAX]{}u'$ such that $\|v\xrightarrow[NAX]{}u\| \le \|\gamma\xrightarrow[NAX]{RD}\varnothing\|$, $\langle u,u'\rangle$ is strongly NAX-convergent modulo BAX.

Then $\langle t,t'\rangle$ is strongly NAX-convergent modulo BAX.

Proof. (1) Of course, there is a most general critical pair cp = $\langle v\Leftarrow\delta, v'\Leftarrow\delta'\rangle$ of $\xrightarrow[BAX]{}$ into NAX such that $v[f+f_o] = t$, $f_o\xrightarrow[BAX]{}g_o$, $v'[f+g_o] = t'$, $\delta[f+f_o] = \gamma$ and $\delta'[f+f_o] = \gamma'$ for some (ground) substitutions f,f_o. By (ground) confluence of NAX and Lemma 9.4.3, there are NAX-irreducible substitutions g,g_1 such that $f\xrightarrow[NAX]{}g$, $f_o\xrightarrow[NAX]{}g_1$ and $\delta[g+g_1]$ is NAX-reducible. By assumption, cp is weakly (ground) NAX-convergent modulo BAX. Hence there are goals ψ,λ and terms u,u' such that $var(u) \subseteq var(v)$, $\psi[g+g_1]$ is NAX-reducible, $\lambda[g+g_1]$ is NAX-reduced,

(*) $\qquad\qquad v\xrightarrow[NAX]{}u\Leftarrow\psi,\quad v'\xrightarrow[NAX]{}u'\Leftarrow\delta u\psi\quad\text{and}\quad u\xrightarrow[BAX]{}u'\Leftarrow\lambda.$

Let φ be a linear goal without operation symbols such that $\varphi[f'] = (\delta u\psi)[f+f_o]$, $f'\xrightarrow[BAX]{}g'$ and $\varphi[g'] = (\delta u\psi)[f+g_o]$. Since $(\delta u\psi)[g+g_1]$ is NAX-reducible and $(f+f_o)\xrightarrow[NAX]{}(g+g_1)$, $\varphi[f']$ is NAX-reducible as well. Thus by Lemma 7.7.5, there is a substitution h' such that $f'\xrightarrow[NAX]{}h'$ and $\varphi[h']$ is NAX-reduced. Hence for all $x \in var(\varphi)$, $h'x$ is NAX-irreducible.

Since $\varphi[f'] = (\delta u\psi)[f+f_o]$, for all $x \in var(\varphi)$, either $f'x$ is a subterm of $\gamma = \delta[f+f_o]$ or $f'x$ is a subterm of $\psi[f+f_o]$ and thus by (*), $t = v[f+f_o] \supset\xrightarrow[NAX]{RD} f'x$. By assumption, $f'\xrightarrow[NAX]{}h'$ and $f'\xrightarrow[BAX]{}g'$ imply that $\langle h'x, g'x\rangle$ is strongly NAX-convergent modulo BAX, i.e. $h'x\xrightarrow[BAX]{}hx$ and $g'x\xrightarrow[NAX]{}hx$ for some h because $h'x$ is NAX-irreducible. Since BAX weakly respects NAX-normal forms, there is a NAX-irreducible substitution h'' with $hx\xrightarrow[NAX]{}h''x$ and $h'x\xrightarrow[BAX]{}h''x$. Since $\varphi[h']$ is NAX-reduced, $\varphi[h'']$ is NAX-reduced as well. Hence $\varphi[h]$ and thus $(\delta u\psi)[f+g_o] = \varphi[g']$ are NAX-reducible, and we conclude $v'[f+g_o]\xrightarrow[NAX]{}u'[f+g_o]$ from (*).

Since $var(u) \subseteq var(v)$, for all $x \in var(u)$, $f_o x$ is a subterm of $v[f+f_o] = t$. Thus by assumption, $f_o\xrightarrow[NAX]{}g_1$ and $f_o\xrightarrow[BAX]{}g_o$ imply that for all $x \in var(u)$, $\langle g_1 x, g_o x\rangle$ is strongly NAX-convergent modulo BAX, i.e. $g_1 x\xrightarrow[BAX]{}h_o x$ and $g_o x\xrightarrow[NAX]{}h_o x$ for some h_o because $g_1 x$ is NAX-irreducible.

Let $h_1 = h_o\restriction var(u) + g_o\restriction(X-var(u))$. We obtain

$$t = v[f+f_o] \xrightarrow[NAX]{} v[g+g_1] \xrightarrow[NAX]{} u[g+g_1]$$
$$\Downarrow BAX$$
$$t' = v'[f+g_o] \xrightarrow[NAX]{} u'[f+g_o] \xrightarrow[NAX]{} u'[g+h_1]$$

and conclude that $\langle t,t'\rangle$ is strongly NAX-convergent modulo BAX.

(2) Of course, there is a most general critical pair cp = $\langle v\Leftarrow\delta, v'\Leftarrow\delta'\rangle$ of

$\xrightarrow{BAX}$ into NAX such that $v[f+f_o] = t$, $f_o \xrightarrow{BAX} g_o$, $v'[f+g_o] = t'$, $\delta[f+f_o] = \gamma$ and $\delta'[f+f_o] = \gamma'$ for some (ground) substitutions f, f_o. By assumption, cp is strongly (ground) NAX-convergent modulo BAX. In particular, δ is a base goal. By (ground) confluence of NAX and Lemma 7.8.1, there are substitutions g, g_1 such that $f \xrightarrow{NAX} g$, $f_o \xrightarrow{NAX} g_1$, $\|(f+f_o)\xrightarrow{NAX}(g+g_1)\| = \|\delta[f+f_o]\vdash^{RD}_{NAX} \emptyset\|$ and $\delta[g+g_1]$ is NAX-reduced. Moreover, there are ψ, λ, u, u' such that $(\psi u \lambda)[g+g_1]$ is NAX-reduced,

$(**)$ $\qquad\qquad v \xrightarrow{NAX} u \Leftarrow \psi$, $v' \xrightarrow{NAX} u' \Leftarrow \delta u \psi$ and $u \xrightarrow{BAX} u' \Leftarrow \lambda$.

Let φ be a linear goal without operation symbols such that $\varphi[f'] = (\delta u \psi)[f+f_o]$, $f' \xrightarrow{BAX} g'$ and $\varphi[g'] = (\delta u \psi)[f+g_o]$. Since $(\delta u \psi)[g+g_1]$ is NAX-reduced and $(f+f_o)\xrightarrow{NAX}(g+g_1)$, $\varphi[f']$ is NAX-reducible. Thus by Lemma 7.7.5, there is a substitution h' such that $\|f' \xrightarrow{NAX} h'\| = \|\varphi[f']\vdash^{RD}_{NAX} \emptyset\|$ and $\varphi[h']$ is NAX-reduced. Hence for all $x \in \text{var}(\varphi)$, $h'x$ is NAX-irreducible.

Since $\varphi[f'] = \gamma$, $f' \xrightarrow{NAX} h'$ and $f' \xrightarrow{BAX} g'$, the assumption implies that for all $x \in \text{var}(\varphi)$, $\langle h'x, g'x \rangle$ is strongly NAX-convergent modulo BAX, i.e. $h'x \xrightarrow{BAX} hx$ and $g'x \xrightarrow{NAX} hx$ for some h because $h'x$ is NAX-irreducible. Since BAX weakly respects NAX-normal forms, there is a NAX-irreducible substitution h'' with $hx \xrightarrow{NAX} h''x$ and $h'x \xrightarrow{BAX} h''x$. Since $\varphi[h']$ is NAX-reduced, $\varphi[h'']$ is NAX-reduced as well. Hence $\varphi[h]$ and thus $(\delta u \psi)[f+g_o] = \varphi[g']$ are NAX-reducible, and we conclude $v'[f+g_o] \xrightarrow{NAX} u'[f+g_o]$ from $(**)$.

Since $\|f_o \xrightarrow{NAX} g_1\| \le \|\delta[f+f_o]\vdash^{RD}_{NAX} \emptyset\|$, $\delta[f+f_o] = \gamma$ and $f_o \xrightarrow{BAX} g_o$, the assumption implies that for all $x \in X$, $\langle g_1 x, g_o x \rangle$ is strongly NAX-convergent modulo BAX, i.e. $g_1 \xrightarrow{NAX} h_1 \xrightarrow{BAX} h_o$ and $g_o \xrightarrow{NAX} h_o$ for some h_o, h_1. We obtain

$$t = v[f+f_o] \xrightarrow{NAX} v[g+g_1] \xrightarrow{NAX} u[g+g_1] \xrightarrow{NAX} u[g+h_1]$$
$$\Downarrow \text{BAX}$$
$$t' = v'[f+g_o] \xrightarrow{NAX} u'[f+g_o] \xrightarrow{NAX} u'[g+h_o]$$

and conclude that $\langle t, t' \rangle$ is strongly NAX-convergent modulo BAX. ∎

We close the section with two sample proofs of critical pair convergence. The first deals with ACCESS-FUN (cf. Section 3.4), the second with FINSET-REMOVE (cf. Section 3.10). In Section 9.9, these results are embedded into a proof that both specifications are NAX-Church-Rosser.

Example 9.4.7 (cf. Section 3.4) Let $\langle BSIG, BAX \rangle = $ STORE and $\langle SIG, AX \rangle$ be a left-linear version of ACCESS-FUN, i.e. axiom (A3) is replaced by

(A3') $\qquad\qquad s[x \leftarrow n][y] \equiv n \Leftarrow x \equiv y$.

Besides (A3') we have the NAX-axiom

(A4) $\quad\quad\quad\quad s[x \leftarrow n][y] \equiv s[y] \Leftarrow x \not\equiv y$

and are confronted with six most general critical pairs of $\xrightarrow[BAX]{}$ into NAX, cp1-cp6.

Let $t = s'[x \leftarrow n][y]$. The base axiom $s[x \leftarrow m][x \leftarrow n] \equiv s[x \leftarrow n]$ generates the t-overlapping reduction

$$t[s[x \leftarrow m]/s'] \xrightarrow[BAX]{} s[x \leftarrow n][y].$$

Together with (A3') we obtain the critical pair

$$cp1 = \langle n \Leftarrow \{x \equiv y\}, s[x \leftarrow n][y] \rangle.$$

The right-hand term reduces to the left-hand term by the conditional reduction

$$s[x \leftarrow n][y] \xrightarrow[NAX]{} n \Leftarrow \{x \equiv y\}.$$

Hence cp1 is NAX-convergent modulo BAX, pictorially:

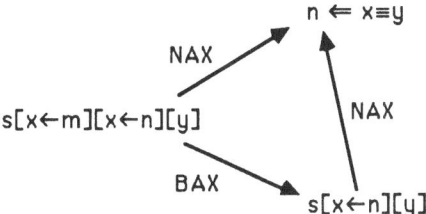

Together with (A4) we obtain the critical pair

$$cp2 = \langle s[x \leftarrow m][y] \Leftarrow \{x \not\equiv y\}, s[x \leftarrow n][y] \rangle.$$

Both terms have a common reduct:

$$s[x \leftarrow m][y] \xrightarrow[NAX]{} s[y] \Leftarrow \{x \not\equiv y\}$$
$$s[x \leftarrow n][y] \xrightarrow[NAX]{} s[y] \Leftarrow \{x \not\equiv y\}.$$

Hence cp2 is NAX-convergent modulo BAX, pictorially:

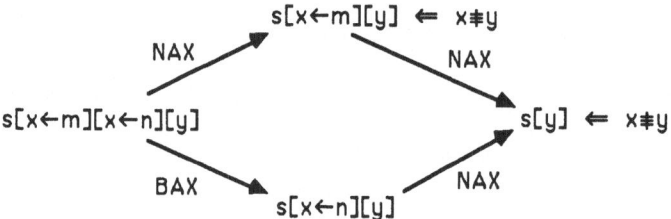

The base axiom $s[x \leftarrow n] = s[x \leftarrow m][x \leftarrow n]$ generates the t-overlapping reduction

$$t[s/s'] \xrightarrow{BAX} s[x \leftarrow m][x \leftarrow n][y].$$

Together with (A3') we obtain the critical pair

$$cp3 = \langle n \Leftarrow \{x \equiv y\}, s[x \leftarrow m][x \leftarrow n][y] \rangle.$$

The right-hand term reduces to the left-hand term:

$$s[x \leftarrow m][x \leftarrow n][y] \xrightarrow{NAX} n \Leftarrow \{x \equiv y\}.$$

Hence cp3 is NAX-convergent modulo BAX, pictorially:

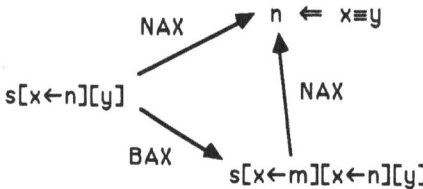

Together with (A4) we obtain the critical pair

$$cp4 = \langle s[y] \Leftarrow \{x \not\equiv y\}, s[x \leftarrow m][x \leftarrow n][y] \rangle.$$

The right-hand term reduces to the left-hand term:

$$s[x \leftarrow m][x \leftarrow n][y] \xrightarrow{NAX} s[x \leftarrow m][y] \xrightarrow{NAX} s[y] \Leftarrow \{x \not\equiv y\}.$$

Hence cp4 is NAX-convergent modulo BAX, pictorially:

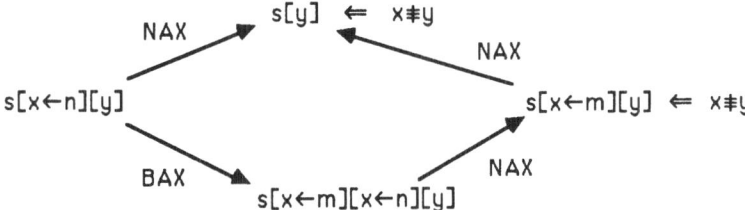

The base axiom $s[z \leftarrow m][x \leftarrow n] \equiv s[x \leftarrow n][z \leftarrow m] \Leftarrow z \not\equiv x$ generates the t-overlapping reduction

$$t[s[z \leftarrow m]/s'] \xrightarrow[BAX]{} s[x \leftarrow n][z \leftarrow m][y] \Leftarrow \{z \not\equiv x\}.$$

Together with (A3') we obtain the critical pair

$$cp5 = \langle n \Leftarrow \{x \equiv y\}, s[x \leftarrow n][z \leftarrow m][y] \Leftarrow \{z \not\equiv x\} \rangle.$$

The right-hand term reduces to the left-hand term:

$$s[x \leftarrow n][z \leftarrow m][y] \xrightarrow[NAX]{} s[x \leftarrow n][y] \xrightarrow[NAX]{} n \Leftarrow \{z \not\equiv y, x \equiv y\}.$$

Let f be a ground substitution such that $\{fx \equiv fy, fz \not\equiv fx\}$ is NAX-reduced. Then $fx \equiv fy$ and $fz \not\equiv fx$ are base theorems, and "meta-knowledge" about the base specification STORE implies that $fz \not\equiv fy$ is a base theorem as well. Therefore $\{fz \not\equiv fy, fx \equiv fy\}$ is NAX-reduced, and we conclude that cp5 is ground NAX-convergent modulo BAX. Pictorially:

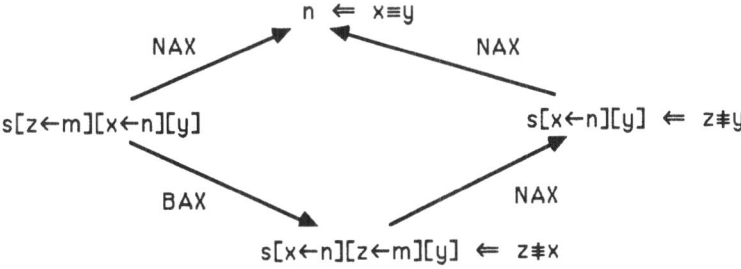

Together with (A4) we obtain the critical pair

$$cp6 = \langle s[z \leftarrow m][y] \Leftarrow \{x \not\equiv y\}, s[x \leftarrow n][z \leftarrow m][y] \Leftarrow \{z \not\equiv x\} \rangle.$$

The conditions $z \equiv y$ and $z \not\equiv y$ lead to common reducts of the terms of cp6:

(1) $\qquad s[z \leftarrow m][y] \xrightarrow[NAX]{} m \Leftarrow \{z \equiv y\}$

$$s[x \leftarrow n][z \leftarrow m][y] \xrightarrow{NAX} m \Leftarrow \{z \equiv y\}.$$

(2)
$$s[z \leftarrow m][y] \xrightarrow{NAX} s[y] \Leftarrow \{z \neq y\}$$
$$s[x \leftarrow n][z \leftarrow m][y] \xrightarrow{NAX} s[x \leftarrow n][y] \xrightarrow{NAX} s[y] \Leftarrow \{z \neq y, x \neq y\}.$$

Let f be a ground substitution such that $\{fx \neq fy, fz \neq fx\}$ is NAX-reduced. Then $fx \neq fy$ and $fz \neq fx$ are base theorems. Again, meta-knowledge about STORE implies that $fz \equiv fy$ *or* $fz \neq fy$ is a base theorem. Therefore $fz \equiv fy$ or $fz \neq fy$ is NAX-reduced, and we conclude from (1) and (2) that cp6 is ground NAX-convergent modulo BAX. Pictorially:

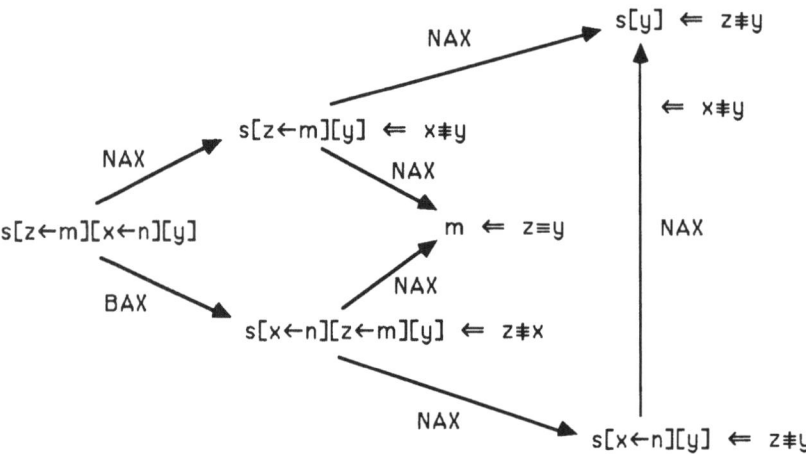

Thus all most general critical pairs of $\xrightarrow{BAX}$ into NAX are ground NAX-convergent modulo BAX. ∎

Example 9.4.8 (cf. Section 3.10) Let <BSIG,BAX> = FINSET and <SIG,AX> be a left-linear version of FINSET-REMOVE, i.e. axiom (A3) is replaced by

(A3')   remove m (insert n s) ≡ remove m s ⇐ m ≡ n.

Besides (A3') we have the NAX-axiom

(A4)   remove m (insert n s) ≡ remove m s ⇐ m ≢ n.

and are faced with six most general critical pairs of $\xrightarrow{BAX}$ into NAX, cp1-cp6.

Let t = (remove m (insert n s')) and t' = (remove m (insert n s')). The base axiom *insert n (insert n s) ≡ insert n s* generates the t-overlapping reduction
$$t[(insert\ n\ s)/s'] \xrightarrow{BAX} (remove\ m\ (insert\ n\ s)).$$

Together with (A3') we obtain the critical pair

cp1 = ⟨(remove m (insert n s)) ⇐ {m≡n}, (remove m (insert n s))⟩.

Since both terms are identical, cp1 is NAX-convergent modulo BAX.

Together with (A4) we obtain the critical pair

cp2 = ⟨t'[(insert n s)/s'] ⇐ {m≢n}, (remove m (insert n s))⟩.

The following reduction diagram shows that cp2 is NAX-convergent modulo BAX:

t'[(insert n s)/s'] $\overrightarrow{NAX}$ (insert n (insert n (remove m s))) ⇐ {m≢n}
$\Downarrow$ BAX
(remove m (insert n s)) $\overrightarrow{NAX}$ (insert n (remove m s)) ⇐ {m≢n}.

The base axiom *insert n ≡ insert n (insert n s)* generates the t-overlapping reduction

t[s/s'] $\overrightarrow{BAX}$ (remove m (insert n (insert n s))).

Together with (A3') we obtain the critical pair

cp3 = ⟨(remove m s) ⇐ {m≡n}, (remove m (insert n (insert n s)))⟩.

The right-hand term reduces to the left-hand term:

(remove m (insert n (insert n s))) $\overrightarrow{NAX}$ (remove m (insert n s))
$\overrightarrow{NAX}$ (remove m s) ⇐ {m≡n}.

Hence cp3 is NAX-convergent modulo BAX.

Together with (A4) we obtain the critical pair

cp4 = ⟨t'[s/s'] ⇐ {m≢n}, (remove m (insert n (insert n s)))⟩.

The following reduction diagram shows that cp4 is NAX-convergent modulo BAX:

t'[s/s'] $\overrightarrow{BAX}$ (insert n (insert n (remove m s)))
$\uparrow$ NAX ⇐ {m≢n}
(remove m (insert n (insert n s))) $\overrightarrow{NAX}$ (insert n (remove m (insert n s)))
⇐ {m≢n}.

The base axiom *insert n (insert k s) ≡ insert k (insert n s)*
generates the t-overlapping reduction

$$t[(insert\ k\ s)/s'] \xrightarrow[BAX]{} (remove\ m\ (insert\ k\ (insert\ n\ s))).$$

Together with (A3') we obtain the critical pair

$$cp5 = \langle (remove\ m\ (insert\ k\ s)) \Leftarrow \{m \equiv n\}, (remove\ m\ (insert\ k\ (insert\ n\ s)))\rangle.$$

The conditions $m \equiv k$ and $m \not\equiv k$ lead to common reducts of the terms of cp5:

(1) $(remove\ m\ (insert\ k\ s)) \xrightarrow[NAX]{} (remove\ m\ s) \Leftarrow \{m \equiv k\}$
  $(remove\ m\ (insert\ k\ (insert\ n\ s))) \xrightarrow[NAX]{} (remove\ m\ (insert\ n\ s)) \Leftarrow \{m \equiv k\}$
  $\xrightarrow[NAX]{} (remove\ m\ s) \Leftarrow \{m \equiv n\}$.

(2) $(remove\ m\ (insert\ k\ s)) \xrightarrow[NAX]{} (insert\ k\ (remove\ m\ s)) \Leftarrow \{m \not\equiv k\}$
  $(remove\ m\ (insert\ k\ (insert\ n\ s)))$
    $\xrightarrow[NAX]{} (insert\ k\ (remove\ m\ (insert\ n\ s))) \Leftarrow \{m \not\equiv k\}$
    $\xrightarrow[NAX]{} (insert\ k\ (remove\ m\ s)) \Leftarrow \{m \equiv n\}$.

Let f be a ground substitution such that fm≡fn is NAX-reduced and thus a base theorem. Meta-knowledge about the base specification FINSET implies that fm≡fk or fm≠fk is a base theorem as well. Therefore fm≡fk or fm≠fk is NAX-reduced, and we conclude from (1) and (2) that cp5 is ground NAX-convergent modulo BAX.

Together with (A4) we obtain the critical pair

$$cp6 = \langle t'[(insert\ k\ s)/s'] \Leftarrow \{m \not\equiv n\}, (remove\ m\ (insert\ k\ (insert\ n\ s)))\rangle.$$

The conditions $m \equiv k$ and $m \not\equiv k$ lead to common reducts of the terms of cp6:

(1) $t'[(insert\ k\ s)/s'] \xrightarrow[NAX]{} (insert\ n\ (remove\ m\ s)) \Leftarrow \{m \equiv k\}$
  $(remove\ m\ (insert\ k\ (insert\ n\ s))) \xrightarrow[NAX]{} (remove\ m\ (insert\ n\ s)) \Leftarrow \{m \equiv k\}$
    $\xrightarrow[NAX]{} (insert\ n\ (remove\ m\ s)) \Leftarrow \{m \not\equiv n\}$.

(2) $t'[(insert\ k\ s)/s'] \xrightarrow[NAX]{} (insert\ n\ (insert\ k\ (remove\ m\ s))) \Leftarrow \{m \not\equiv k\}$
  $(remove\ m\ (insert\ k\ (insert\ n\ s)))$
    $\xrightarrow[NAX]{} (insert\ k\ (remove\ m\ (insert\ n\ s))) \Leftarrow \{m \not\equiv k\}$
    $\xrightarrow[NAX]{} (insert\ n\ (insert\ k\ (remove\ m\ s))) \Leftarrow \{m \not\equiv n\}$.

Let f be a ground substitution such that fm≠fn is NAX-reduced and thus a base theorem. Again, meta-knowledge about FINSET implies that fm≡fk or fm≠fk is a base theorem as well. Therefore fm≡fk or fm≠fk is NAX-reduced, and we conclude from (1) and (2) that cp6 is ground NAX-convergent modulo BAX.

Thus all most general critical pairs of $\xrightarrow[BAX]{}$ into NAX are ground NAX-convergent modulo BAX. ∎

9.5 Confluence of NAX

The following criterion for this property requires the convergence of critical pairs. Its proof refers to Lemmata 9.3.2 (1), 9.4.4 and 9.4.5.

Theorem 9.5.1 *Criterion for confluence of NAX*

Suppose that
- the NAX-reduction relation is Noetherian (on ground terms),
- all feasible most general critical pairs of $\xrightarrow[NAX]{}$ into NAX are (ground) NAX-convergent.

Then NAX is (ground) confluent.

Proof. Let u,t,t' be (ground) terms such that

$$u \underset{NAX}{\overset{NAX}{\swarrow \searrow}} \begin{matrix} t \\ t'. \end{matrix}$$

We establish v with

(1)
$$\begin{matrix} t \\ t' \end{matrix} \underset{NAX}{\overset{NAX}{\searrow \nearrow}} v$$

by Noetherian induction on u w.r.t. $\supset\!\!\mid\!^{RD}_{NAX}$ (cf. Lemma 9.4.5).

Case 1. u = t or u = t'. Choose v = t' or v = t, respectively.

Case 2. There are terms u_o, v_o and NAX-reducible goals γ, γ' such that

$$|u \underset{NAX}{\Rightarrow} u_o \Leftarrow \gamma| = 1, \quad u_o \underset{NAX}{\Rightarrow} t$$

and

$$|u \underset{NAX}{\Rightarrow} v_o \Leftarrow \gamma'| = 1, \quad v_o \underset{NAX}{\Rightarrow} t'.$$

Suppose that $\langle u_o, v_o \rangle$ is NAX-convergent, say $u_o \underset{NAX}{\Rightarrow} u'$ and $v_o \underset{NAX}{\Rightarrow} u'$. Since u_o and v_o are smaller than u w.r.t. $\supset\!\!\mid\!^{RD}_{NAX}$, the induction hypothesis supplies us with v',v" such that

(2)
$$t \xrightarrow{\text{NAX}} v'$$
$$u' \xrightarrow{\text{NAX}} v'$$

and

$$u' \xrightarrow{\text{NAX}} v''$$
$$t' \xrightarrow{\text{NAX}} v''.$$

Since $u \sqsupset\!\!\!\mid_{\overline{NAX}}^{RD} u'$, the induction hypothesis establishes v with

(3)
$$v' \xrightarrow{\text{NAX}} v$$
$$v'' \xrightarrow{\text{NAX}} v$$

(1) results from (2) and (3). It remains for us to show that $\langle u_o, v_o \rangle$ is NAX-convergent.

Case 1. There are $t_o \equiv t_1 \Leftarrow \delta \in \text{NAX}$ and a (ground) substitution f such that $t_o[f] = u$, $t_1[f] = u_o$ and $\delta[f] = \gamma$. We have two subcases:

Case 1.1. $u \overrightarrow{\text{NAX}} v_o \Leftarrow \gamma'$ affects t_o (cf. Section 9.2). Since $u \overrightarrow{\text{NAX}} v_o \Leftarrow \gamma'$ is obtained by one application of the Single Reduction Rule, $u \overrightarrow{\text{NAX}} v_o \Leftarrow \gamma'$ is t_o-overlapping. Thus $\langle u_o \Leftarrow \gamma, v_o \Leftarrow \gamma' \rangle$ is a critical pair of $\overrightarrow{\text{NAX}}$ into NAX. Since $\mid_{\overline{NAX}}^{RD}$ is Noetherian, NAX is normalizing. Moreover, $u \overrightarrow{\text{NAX}} u_o \Leftarrow \gamma$ and $u \overrightarrow{\text{NAX}} v_o \Leftarrow \gamma'$ imply that all subterms v of $\gamma u \gamma'$ are smaller than u w.r.t. $\sqsupset\!\!\!\mid_{\overline{NAX}}^{RD}$. Hence by the induction hypothesis, if $v \overrightarrow{\text{NAX}} v'$ and $v \overrightarrow{\text{NAX}} v''$, then $\langle v', v'' \rangle$ is NAX-convergent. Since $\gamma u \gamma'$ is NAX-reducible, Lemma 9.4.4 implies that $\langle u_o, v_o \rangle$ is NAX-convergent.

Case 1.2. $u \overrightarrow{\text{NAX}} v_o \Leftarrow \gamma'$ does not affect t_o. Since $u \overrightarrow{\text{NAX}} u_o \Leftarrow \gamma$, all subterms v of $\gamma = \delta[f]$ are smaller than u w.r.t. $\sqsupset\!\!\!\mid_{\overline{NAX}}^{RD}$. Hence by the induction hypothesis, if $v \overrightarrow{\text{NAX}} v'$ and $v \overrightarrow{\text{NAX}} v''$, then $\langle v', v'' \rangle$ is NAX-convergent. Thus by Lemma 9.3.2 (1), $\langle u_o, v_o \rangle = \langle t_1[f], v_o \rangle$ is NAX-convergent.

Case 2. There are $t_o \equiv t_1 \Leftarrow \delta \in \text{NAX}$ and a (ground) substitution f such that $t_o[f] = u$, $t_1[f] = v_o$ and $\delta[f] = \gamma'$. By interchanging u_o and v_o as well as γ and γ', case 1 implies that $\langle v_o, u_o \rangle$ and thus $\langle u_o, v_o \rangle$ are NAX-convergent.

Case 3. $u = \sigma \langle t_1, ..., t_n \rangle$, $u_o = \sigma \langle u_1, ..., u_n \rangle$, $v_o = \sigma \langle v_1, ..., v_n \rangle$ and for all $1 \leq i \leq n$

$$t_i \xrightarrow{\text{NAX}} u_i$$
$$t_i \xrightarrow{\text{NAX}} v_i.$$

Since t_i is a proper subterm of u and thus $u \sqsupset\!\!\!\mid_{\overline{NAX}}^{RD} t_i$, the induction hypothesis implies

$$u_i \xrightarrow{NAX} t_i'$$
$$v_i \xrightarrow{NAX}$$

for some t_i'. Hence $u \circ \xrightarrow{NAX} \sigma \langle t_1',...,t_n' \rangle$ and $v \circ \xrightarrow{NAX} \sigma \langle t_1',...,t_n' \rangle$. ∎

From Theorems 9.5.1 and 7.8.2 we obtain the first "tractable" Church-Rosser criterion:

(∗) If BAX is empty, $\vdash^{RD}_{NAX}$ is Noetherian (on ground terms), all feasible most general critical pairs of $\xrightarrow{NAX}$ into NAX are (ground) NAX-convergent and AX preserves (ground) NAX-normalizability, then ⟨SIG,AX⟩ is (ground) NAX-Church-Rosser.

Using Lemma 7.7.8 (2), one infers a corresponding inductive theory criterion:

(∗∗) Let CAX be a set of conditional equations and AX' = NAX∪CAX. If $\vdash^{RD}_{AX'}$ is Noetherian on ground terms, all feasible most general critical pairs of $\xrightarrow{AX'}$ into AX' are ground AX'-convergent, for all $u \equiv u' \Leftarrow \vartheta \in AX'$, u is not a base term, and AX∪CAX preserves ground AX'-normalizability, then CAX is a partial inductive ⟨SIG,AX⟩-theorem.

This criterion reduces inductive proofs to proofs of critical pair convergence.

Example 9.5.2 Let ⟨BSIG,BAX⟩ = NAT (cf. Section 3.2),

⟨SIG,AX⟩
   base :   NAT
   opns :   _+_ : nat,nat→nat
   vars :   m,n : nat
   axms :   m+0 ≡ m
            m+n| ≡ (m+n)|

and CAX = {(x+y)+z ≡ x+(y+z)}. On one hand, CAX may be proved directly by induction on the ground instances of z. Then the proof steps are as follows.

(1)   (x+y)+0 ≡ x+y ≡ x+(y+0)
(2)   (x+y)+n| ≡ ((x+y)+n)|
          ≡ (x+(y+n))| ≡ x+(y+n)| ≡ x+(y+n|)   (by the induction hypothesis)

On the other hand, we recognize term overlapping reductions such as

$(x+y)+0 \xrightarrow{(x+y)+z}_{NAX} x+y$ and $(x+y)+n| \xrightarrow{(x+y)+z}_{NAX} ((x+y)+n)|$, which induce two critical pairs of $\xrightarrow[NAX]{}$ into CAX:

$$\langle x+(y+0), x+y\rangle \text{ and } \langle x+(y+n|), ((x+y)+n)|\rangle.$$

Both critical pairs are (NAX∪CAX)-convergent:

$$x+(y+0) \xrightarrow[NAX]{} x+y$$

$$x+(y+n|) \xrightarrow[NAX]{} x+(y+n)|$$
$$\downarrow NAX$$
$$((x+y)+n)| \xrightarrow[CAX]{} (x+(y+n))|$$

There is a strong correspondence between this convergence proof and the inductive proof given by (1) and (2). However, (**) compels us to show the convergence of further critical pairs of $\xrightarrow[NAX]{}$ into CAX, which have no counterpart in the inductive proof. For instance, there are term overlapping reductions

$$(x+0)+z \xleftarrow[NAX]{(x+y)+z} x+z \text{ and } (x+n|)+z \xleftarrow[NAX]{(x+y)+z} (x+n)|+z,$$

which generate the critical pairs

$$\langle x+(0+z), x+z\rangle \text{ and } \langle x+(n|+z), (x+n)|+z\rangle. \blacksquare$$

It would relieve us of a lot of work if convergence proofs could be restricted to those critical pairs of $\xrightarrow[NAX]{}$ into CAX which correspond to inductive proof steps. Indeed, these critical pairs may be fixed by a function that assigns to each ground left-hand side instance of a CAX-equation a particular NAX-redex.

Definition Let CAX be a set of conditional equations. A partial function

$$SEL : T(SIG) \times GT(SIG)^X \longrightarrow Pos(SIG)$$

is called a *critical pair selector for CAX* if for all $u \equiv u' \Leftarrow \delta \in$ CAX and ground reductions $u[f]^u \xrightarrow[NAX]{} t' \Leftarrow \delta$ with NAX-reducible goal δ,

$$SEL(u,f) = t \bullet v' \quad \text{iff} \quad \exists v \neq v' : t \bullet v \text{ is a position of } u[f] \text{ and } v \xrightarrow[NAX]{} v'$$

(cf. Section 7.9). $\blacksquare$

In Example 9.5.2, a critical pair selector for CAX is given by

$$SEL((x+y)+z,f) = \begin{cases} x_o \bullet (fx+fy) & \text{if } fz \xrightarrow{NAX} 0 \\ x_o \bullet ((fx+fy)+t)| & \text{if } fz \xrightarrow{NAX} t| \text{ for some } t. \end{cases}$$

The following lemma is needed for an inductive argument in the proof of Theorem 9.5.4, which weakens Theorem 9.5.1 by taking into account only selected critical pairs. The lemma verifies the crucial conjecture that ground confluence of NAX and ground convergence of selected critical pairs are sufficient for the ground convergence of *all* critical pairs of $\xrightarrow{NAX}$ into CAX.

Lemma 9.5.3 Let CAX be a set of conditional equations, AX' = NAX∪CAX and SEL be a critical pair selector for CAX. Suppose that NAX is ground confluent. Let $u \equiv u' \Leftarrow \delta \in$ CAX, $u[f]^u \xrightarrow{NAX} t' \Leftarrow \delta$ be a ground reduction with NAX-reducible δ and SEL(u,f) = t•v'.

If $\langle u'[f], t[v'/x_o] \rangle$ is AX'-convergent and for all terms t" with $u[f] \xmapsto{RD}_{NAX} t"$, $t" \xrightarrow{AX} v$ and $t" \xrightarrow{AX} v'$ imply that $\langle v, v' \rangle$ is AX'-convergent, then $\langle u'[f], t' \rangle$ is AX'-convergent as well.

Proof. Since $u[f] \xrightarrow{NAX} t'$ and

$$u[f] = t[v/x_o] \xrightarrow{NAX} t[v'/x_o] \text{ for some } v,$$

confluence of NAX implies

(1) $\qquad t' \xrightarrow{NAX} u_o \text{ and } t[v'/x_o] \xrightarrow{NAX} u_o$

for some u_o. Let $\langle u'[f], t[v'/x_o] \rangle$ be AX'-convergent. Then

(2) $\qquad u'[f] \xrightarrow{AX} u_1 \text{ and } t[v'/x_o] \xrightarrow{AX} u_1$

for some u_1. By assumption, (1), (2) and $u[f] \xmapsto{RD}_{NAX} t[v'/x_o]$ imply

(3) $\qquad u_o \xrightarrow{AX} v_o \text{ and } u_1 \xrightarrow{AX} v_o$

for some v_o. Finally, (1), (2) and (3) yield

$$u'[f] \xrightarrow{AX} u_1 \xrightarrow{AX} v_o \text{ and } t' \xrightarrow{NAX} u_o \xrightarrow{AX} v_o. \blacksquare$$

Theorem 9.5.4 *Criterion for confluence of NAX∪CAX*

Let CAX be a set of conditional equations, AX' = NAX∪CAX and SEL be a critical pair selector for CAX. Suppose that

(1) the AX'-reduction relation is Noetherian on ground terms,
(2) NAX is ground confluent,
(3) for all u≡u'⇐ϑ ∈ CAX and ground substitutions f, SEL(u,f) = t•v' implies that ⟨u'[f],t[v'/x$_o$]⟩ is AX'-convergent,
(4) for all v≡v'⇐ϑ ∈ NAX and u≡u'⇐ϑ' ∈ CAX, if root(u) occurs in v, then root(u) = root(v),
(5) all feasible most general critical pairs of $\overrightarrow{CAX}$ into CAX are ground AX'-convergent.

Then AX' is ground confluent.

Proof is nearly the same as the proof of Theorem 9.5.1 (with AX' instead of NAX). Only case 1.1, u$\overrightarrow{AX}$v$_o$⇐γ' affects t$_o$, is now split into four subcases.

Case 1.1.1. t$_o$≡t$_1$⇐ϑ ∈ NAX and u$\overrightarrow{NAX}$v$_o$⇐γ'. Then by (2), ⟨u$_o$,v$_o$⟩ = ⟨t$_1$[f],v$_o$⟩ is NAX- and thus AX'-convergent.

Case 1.1.2. t$_o$≡t$_1$⇐ϑ ∈ CAX and u$\overrightarrow{NAX}$v$_o$⇐γ'. Let t$_o$[f] $\overset{RD}{\underset{NAX}{\longmapsto}}$ t'. Then u = t$_o$[f] ⊃$\overset{RD}{\underset{AX'}{\longmapsto}}$ t'. Hence by the induction hypothesis, if t'$\overrightarrow{NAX}$v and t'$\overrightarrow{NAX}$v', then ⟨v,v'⟩ is NAX-convergent. Since u$\overrightarrow{NAX}$v$_o$⇐γ' is t$_o$-overlapping, (3) and Lemma 9.5.3 imply that ⟨u$_o$,v$_o$⟩ = ⟨t$_1$[f],v$_o$⟩ is AX'-convergent.

Case 1.1.3. t$_o$≡t$_1$⇐ϑ ∈ NAX and u$\overrightarrow{CAX}$v$_o$⇐γ'. Since u$\overrightarrow{CAX}$v$_o$⇐γ' is t$_o$-overlapping, we conclude by (4) that there are u$_1$≡v$_1$⇐ϑ' ∈ CAX and a substitution h with u = u$_1$[h] and v$_o$ = v$_1$[h]. Let t$_o$[f] $\overset{RD}{\underset{NAX}{\longmapsto}}$ t'. Then t$_o$[f] ⊃$\overset{RD}{\underset{AX'}{\longmapsto}}$ t'. By the induction hypothesis, if t'$\overrightarrow{NAX}$v and t'$\overrightarrow{NAX}$v', then ⟨v,v'⟩ is NAX-convergent. Since u$_1$[h] = u = t$_o$[f], t$_o$[f]$\overrightarrow{NAX}$t$_1$[f]⇐ϑ[f] is u$_1$-overlapping. Hence by (3) and Lemma 9.5.3, ⟨v$_o$,u$_o$⟩ = ⟨v$_1$[h],t$_1$[f]⟩ and thus ⟨u$_o$,v$_o$⟩ are AX'-convergent.

Case 1.1.4. t$_o$≡t$_1$⇐ϑ ∈ CAX and u$\overrightarrow{CAX}$v$_o$⇐γ'. Then ⟨u$_o$⇐γ, v$_o$⇐γ'⟩ is a critical pair of $\overrightarrow{CAX}$ into CAX. By (1), AX' is normalizing on ground terms. Moreover, u$\overrightarrow{AX}$u$_o$⇐γ and u$\overrightarrow{AX}$v$_o$⇐γ' imply that all subterms v of γuγ' are smaller than u w.r.t. ⊃$\overset{RD}{\underset{AX'}{\longmapsto}}$. Hence by the induction hypothesis, if v$\overrightarrow{AX}$v' and v$\overrightarrow{AX}$v", then ⟨v',v"⟩ is AX'-convergent. By (5) and Case 1.1.2, all feasible most general critical pairs of $\overrightarrow{AX}$ into CAX are ground AX'-convergent. Since γuγ' is AX'-reducible, we conclude from Lemma 9.4.4 (with CAX instead of NAX) that ⟨u$_o$,v$_o$⟩ is AX'-convergent. ∎

Example 9.5.2 (continued) There is a term overlapping reduction

$$((x'+y')+y)+z \overset{(x+y)+z}{\underset{CAX}{\longrightarrow}} (x'+(y'+y))+z$$

that generates a critical pair of $\overrightarrow{CAX}$ into CAX:

$$cp = \langle (x'+y')+(y+z), (x'+(y'+y))+z \rangle.$$

Both terms of cp have a common "reduct":

$$(x'+y')+(y+z) \xrightarrow{CAX} x'+(y'+(y+z))$$
$$\uparrow CAX$$
$$(x'+(y'+y))+z \xrightarrow{CAX} x'+((y'+y)+z).$$

Hence cp is CAX-convergent.
We conclude from Theorem 9.5.4 that NAX∪CAX is ground confluent. ∎

Lemma 7.7.8 (2) and Theorems 7.8.2, 9.5.1 and 9.5.4 yield a stronger version of the inductive theory criterion (**) given above.

Corollary 9.5.5 *Inductive theory criterion based on a critical pair selector*

Let BAX be empty, CAX be a set of conditional equations, AX' = NAX∪CAX and SEL be a critical pair selector for CAX. Suppose that
- the AX'-reduction relation is Noetherian on ground terms,
- all feasible most general critical pairs of $\xrightarrow{NAX}$ into NAX are ground NAX-convergent,
- for all u≡u'⇐𝔰 ∈ CAX and ground substitutions f, SEL(u,f) = t•v' implies that <u'[f],t[v'/x_o]> is AX'-convergent,
- for all v≡v'⇐𝔰 ∈ NAX and u≡u'⇐𝔰' ∈ CAX, if root(u) occurs in v, then root(u) = root(v),
- all feasible most general critical pairs of $\xrightarrow{CAX}$ into CAX are ground AX'-convergent,
- for all u≡u'⇐𝔰 ∈ AX', u is not a base term,
- AX∪CAX preserves ground AX'-normalizability.

Then CAX is a partial inductive <SIG,AX>-theorem. ∎

By Example 9.5.2 and Corollary 9.5.5, the associativity of + is an inductive theorem.

Generalizations of Corollary 9.5.5 are presented at the end of Section 9.9.

9.6 Strong Confluence of NAX

If the NAX-reduction relation is not Noetherian, strong confluence provides an alternative to Theorem 9.5.1:

Definition NAX is *strongly confluent* if for all terms u,t,t'

$$\begin{array}{c} \text{NAX} \nearrow t \\ u \\ \text{NAX} \searrow t' \end{array} \quad \text{implies} \quad \begin{array}{c} t \searrow \text{NAX} \\ \searrow v \\ t' \nearrow \text{NAX} \end{array}$$

for some v such that  ∎

Strong confluence not only requires that $\langle t,t'\rangle$ be convergent. In addition, the parallel lengths of the two converging reductions $t\overline{\scriptscriptstyle NAX}\!\!\!\rightarrow v$ and $t'\overline{\scriptscriptstyle NAX}\!\!\!\rightarrow v$ must not be greater than the parallel lengths of their "opposites" $u\overline{\scriptscriptstyle NAX}\!\!\!\rightarrow t'$ and $u\overline{\scriptscriptstyle NAX}\!\!\!\rightarrow t$, respectively.

Why should this be the parallel rather than the simple length? To see this, let $u \equiv u' \in NAX$ and x be a variable occurring once in u and twice in u'. Together with a reduction $t\overline{\scriptscriptstyle NAX}\!\!\!\rightarrow t'$ with simple length 1, we obtain the branching

$$u[t/x] \begin{array}{c} \xrightarrow{NAX} u'[t/x] \\ \xrightarrow[NAX]{} u[t'/x]. \end{array}$$

The two terms resulting have the common reduct $u'[t'/x]$, but the simple length of $u[t'/x]\overline{\scriptscriptstyle NAX}\!\!\!\rightarrow u'[t'/x]$ is 1, while that of $u'[t/x]\overline{\scriptscriptstyle NAX}\!\!\!\rightarrow u'[t'/x]$ is 2. We conclude that even a one-step branching that comes from two *independent* reductions cannot always be made convergent by two individual applications of the Single Reduction Rule. But on the other hand, each of the two converging reductions $u[t'/x]\overline{\scriptscriptstyle NAX}\!\!\!\rightarrow u'[t'/x]$ and $u'[t/x]\overline{\scriptscriptstyle NAX}\!\!\!\rightarrow u'[t'/x]$ have parallel length 1.

In general, a set of equations where the right-hand side of one of its elements is not linear would not be strongly confluent if we had defined strong confluence with the simple length instead of the parallel length.

The definition of NAX-convergent critical pairs is strengthened accordingly.

Definition A critical pair $\langle t \Leftarrow \gamma, t' \Leftarrow \gamma' \rangle$ is *strongly NAX-convergent* if for all substitutions f, $(\gamma \cup \gamma')[f] \vdash^{RD}_{NAX} \emptyset$ implies

$$\|t'\overline{\scriptscriptstyle NAX}\!\!\!\rightarrow t\| \leq 1 + \|\gamma[f] \vdash^{RD}_{NAX} \emptyset\|. \blacksquare$$

Given a critical pair $\langle t,t' \rangle$ of NAX into $\overline{\scriptscriptstyle NAX}\!\!\!\rightarrow$ that comes from the branching

$$u \begin{array}{c} \xrightarrow{NAX} t \\ \xrightarrow[NAX]{} t', \end{array}$$

strong convergence of $\langle t,t' \rangle$ implies that t is reachable from t' by applying the Parallel Reduction Rule at most once. (For simplicity we omit axiom premises for the moment.) Do we really need such a strong critical pair condition to ensure that NAX is strongly confluent?

The reductions $u \twoheadrightarrow_{NAX} t$ and $u \twoheadrightarrow_{NAX} t'$ have simple length 1. If there is a variable x in u, which does not belong to the reduction redex that generates $u \twoheadrightarrow_{NAX} t'$, we may compose $u \twoheadrightarrow_{NAX} t'$ with a reduction $v \twoheadrightarrow_{NAX} v'$ such that $u[v/x] \twoheadrightarrow_{NAX} t'[v'/x]$ has parallel length 1. Hence one obtains the diagram

$$u[v/x] \begin{array}{c} \overset{NAX}{\nearrow} t[v/x] \\ \underset{NAX}{\searrow} t'[v'/x] \end{array}$$

where both reductions have parallel length 1. Thus strong confluence of NAX requires a term u' with $\|t[v/x] \twoheadrightarrow_{NAX} u'\| \leq 1$ and $\|t'[v'/x] \twoheadrightarrow_{NAX} u'\| \leq 1$. Indeed, strong convergence of the critical pair $\langle t, t' \rangle$ implies $t' \twoheadrightarrow_{NAX} t$, and thus u' can be defined as $t[v'/x]$:

(∗)
$$\begin{array}{c} t[v/x] \searrow_{NAX} \\   \searrow t[v'/x]. \\ t'[v'/x] \nearrow^{NAX} \end{array}$$

On the other hand, if strong convergence of $\langle t, t' \rangle$ only meant that t and t' have a common reduct, say u", we would get

$$\begin{array}{ccc} t[v/x] & \twoheadrightarrow_{NAX} & t[v'/x] \\ & & \downarrow NAX \\ t'[v'/x] & \twoheadrightarrow_{NAX} & u"[v'/x] \end{array}$$

instead of (∗), but there would be no guarantee that the parallel length of $t[v/x] \twoheadrightarrow_{NAX} u"[v'/x]$ is at most 1. The direction of $t' \twoheadrightarrow_{NAX} t$ matters as well: if we had $t' \twoheadrightarrow_{NAX} t$ instead of $t \twoheadrightarrow_{NAX} t'$, then

$$\begin{array}{c} t[v/x] \searrow^{NAX} \\   \nearrow t[v'/x] \\ t'[v'/x] \nearrow^{NAX} \end{array}$$

instead of (∗). Again, we cannot conclude that $\|t[v/x] \twoheadrightarrow_{NAX} u"[v'/x]\|$ is at most 1.

Therefore, the definition of strong critical pair convergence is just as strong as complying with strong confluence. Strong confluence, on the other hand, supplies us with a substitute for the Noetherian property of $\vdash^{RD}_{NAX}$: induction on the parallel length of NAX-reductions takes the place of Noetherian induction on terms.

Theorem 9.6.1 *Criterion for strong confluence of NAX*
Suppose that
- NAX is left-linear,
- all feasible critical pairs of $\overrightarrow{NAX}$ into NAX are strongly NAX-convergent.

Then NAX is strongly confluent.

Proof. Let

$$u \;\begin{array}{c} \xrightarrow{NAX} t \\ \xrightarrow{NAX} t' \end{array}$$

We establish v with

(1) $\quad \|t\overrightarrow{_{NAX}}v\| \leq \|u\overrightarrow{_{NAX}}t'\|$ and $\|t'\overrightarrow{_{NAX}}v\| \leq \|u\overrightarrow{_{NAX}}t\|$

by induction on the pair $\langle\|u\overrightarrow{_{NAX}}t\| + \|u\overrightarrow{_{NAX}}t'\|, \text{size}(u)\rangle$ w.r.t. the lexicographic extension of $>$ on $\mathbb{N}$ to an ordering on $\mathbb{N}\times\mathbb{N}$.

Case 1. $u = t$ or $u = t'$. Choose $v = t'$ or $v = t$, respectively.

Case 2. There are terms u_o, v_o and goals γ, γ' such that

(2) $\quad \|u\overrightarrow{_{NAX}}t\| = \|u\overrightarrow{_{NAX}}u_o\| + \|u_o\overrightarrow{_{NAX}}t\|$,
$\|u\overrightarrow{_{NAX}}u_o\Leftarrow\gamma\| = 1$, $\|u\overrightarrow{_{NAX}}u_o\| = 1 + \|\gamma \vdash\!\!\!\xrightarrow{RD}_{NAX} \varnothing\|$,

(3) $\quad \|u\overrightarrow{_{NAX}}t'\| = \|u\overrightarrow{_{NAX}}v_o\| + \|v_o\overrightarrow{_{NAX}}t'\|$,
$\|u\overrightarrow{_{NAX}}v_o\Leftarrow\gamma'\| = 1$, $\|u\overrightarrow{_{NAX}}v_o\| = 1 + \|\gamma' \vdash\!\!\!\xrightarrow{RD}_{NAX} \varnothing\|$.

Suppose that there is u' such that

(*) $\quad \|u_o\overrightarrow{_{NAX}}u'\| \leq \|u\overrightarrow{_{NAX}}v_o\|$ and $\|v_o\overrightarrow{_{NAX}}u'\| \leq \|u\overrightarrow{_{NAX}}u_o\|$.

Since $\|u_o\overrightarrow{_{NAX}}t\| < \|u\overrightarrow{_{NAX}}t\|$, (*) and the induction hypothesis yield v' with

(4) $\quad \|u'\overrightarrow{_{NAX}}v'\| \leq \|u_o\overrightarrow{_{NAX}}t\|$,

(5) $\quad \|t\overrightarrow{_{NAX}}v'\| \leq \|u_o\overrightarrow{_{NAX}}u'\|$.

Since $\|v_o\overrightarrow{_{NAX}}t'\| < \|u\overrightarrow{_{NAX}}t'\|$, (*) and the induction hypothesis provide v" with

(6) $\quad \|u'\overrightarrow{_{NAX}}v''\| \leq \|v_o\overrightarrow{_{NAX}}t'\|$,

(7) $\quad \|t'\overrightarrow{_{NAX}}v''\| \leq \|v_o\overrightarrow{_{NAX}}u'\|$.

By (2), (3), (4) and (6), $\|u'\overrightarrow{NAX}v'\|+\|u'\overrightarrow{NAX}v''\| < \|u\overrightarrow{NAX}t\|+\|u\overrightarrow{NAX}t'\|$. Hence the induction hypothesis establishes v with

(8) $\qquad\qquad\qquad \|v'\overrightarrow{NAX}v\| \le \|u'\overrightarrow{NAX}v''\|,$

(9) $\qquad\qquad\qquad \|v''\overrightarrow{NAX}v\| \le \|u'\overrightarrow{NAX}v'\|.$

By (3), (∗), (5), (6) and (8),

$$\|t\overrightarrow{NAX}v\| \le \|t\overrightarrow{NAX}v'\| + \|v'\overrightarrow{NAX}v\| \le \|u_o\overrightarrow{NAX}u'\| + \|u'\overrightarrow{NAX}v''\|$$
$$\le \|u\overrightarrow{NAX}v_o\| + \|v_o\overrightarrow{NAX}t'\| = \|u\overrightarrow{NAX}t'\|.$$

By (2), (∗), (4), (7) and (9),

$$\|t'\overrightarrow{NAX}v\| \le \|t'\overrightarrow{NAX}v''\| + \|v''\overrightarrow{NAX}v\| \le \|v_o\overrightarrow{NAX}u'\| + \|u'\overrightarrow{NAX}v'\|$$
$$\le \|u\overrightarrow{NAX}u_o\| + \|u_o\overrightarrow{NAX}t\| = \|u\overrightarrow{NAX}t\|.$$

Hence (1) holds true, and it remains for us to show (∗).

Case 1. There are $t_o \equiv t_1 \Leftarrow \vartheta \in NAX$ and a substitution f such that $t_o[f] = u$, $t_1[f] = u_o$ and $\vartheta[f] = \gamma$. We have two subcases:

Case 1.1. $u\overrightarrow{NAX}v_o \Leftarrow \gamma'$ affects t_o (cf. Section 9.2), i.e. there are a t_o-overlapping reduction $t_o[f']\overrightarrow{NAX}v_1 \Leftarrow \delta$ and a conditional reduction $f''\overrightarrow{NAX}g \Leftarrow \varphi$ such that $f'+f'' = f$,

(10) $\qquad\qquad\qquad \|f''\overrightarrow{NAX}g \Leftarrow \varphi\| \le \|u\overrightarrow{NAX}v_o \Leftarrow \gamma'\|$

$v_1[g] = v_o$ and $\delta[f'']\cup\varphi = \gamma'$. By (2) and (10), the parallel length of $f''\overrightarrow{NAX}g \Leftarrow \varphi$ is at most 1. Since $\vartheta[f'+f'']$ and $\delta[f'']$ are NAX-reducible,

$$cp = \langle t_1[f'] \Leftarrow \vartheta[f'], v_1 \Leftarrow \delta\rangle$$

is a feasible critical pair of $\overrightarrow{NAX}$ into NAX. By assumption, cp is strongly NAX-convergent. Since $v_o = v_1[g]$,

$$\|v_o\overrightarrow{NAX}t_1[f'+g]\| \le \|v_1\overrightarrow{NAX}t_1[f']\| \le 1 + \|\vartheta[f'+f'']\overset{RD}{\overrightarrow{NAX}}\varnothing\|$$
$$= 1 + \|\gamma\overset{RD}{\overrightarrow{NAX}}\varnothing\| = \|u\overrightarrow{NAX}u_o\|.$$

Furthermore, $u_o = t_1[f] = t_1[f'+f'']$, $f''\overrightarrow{NAX}g$ and $\varphi \subseteq \gamma'$ lead to

$$\|u_o\overrightarrow{NAX}t_1[f'+g]\| \le \|f''\restriction var(t_1)\overrightarrow{NAX}g\restriction var(t_1)\|$$
$$\le \|f''\overrightarrow{NAX}g \Leftarrow \varphi\| + \|\varphi\overset{RD}{\overrightarrow{NAX}}\varnothing\|$$

$$\leq 1 + \|\gamma' \xrightarrow[NAX]{RD} \emptyset\| = \|u \xrightarrow[NAX]{} v_0\|.$$

Hence we conclude (*) for $u' = t_1[f'+g]$.

Case 1.2. $u \xrightarrow[NAX]{} v_0 \Leftarrow \gamma'$ does not affect t_0. Let us verify the assumptions of Lemma 9.3.1. Except for the last, all of them are consequences of (2) and (3). For the last assumption, let v be a subterm of $\vartheta[f]$ and let v', v'' be terms such that

(11) $\qquad \|v \xrightarrow[NAX]{} v'\| + \|v \xrightarrow[NAX]{} v''\| < \|t_0[f] \xrightarrow[NAX]{} v_0\| + \|t_0[f] \xrightarrow[NAX]{} t_1[f]\|.$

We have to establish t'' with

(12) $\qquad \|v' \xrightarrow[NAX]{} t''\| \leq \|v \xrightarrow[NAX]{} v''\| \text{ and } \|v'' \xrightarrow[NAX]{} t''\| \leq \|v \xrightarrow[NAX]{} v'\|.$

Since $t_0[f] = u$ and $t_1[f] = u_0$, (2), (3) and (11) imply

$$\|v \xrightarrow[NAX]{} v'\| + \|v \xrightarrow[NAX]{} v''\| < \|u \xrightarrow[NAX]{} t'\| + \|u \xrightarrow[NAX]{} t\|.$$

Thus (12) follows by the induction hypothesis. Hence Lemma 9.3.1 implies

(13) $\quad \|t_1[f] \xrightarrow[NAX]{} u'\| \leq \|t_0[f] \xrightarrow[NAX]{} v_0\| \text{ and } \|v_0 \xrightarrow[NAX]{} u'\| \leq \|t_0[f] \xrightarrow[NAX]{} t_1[f]\|$

for some u'. Since $t_0[f] = u$ and $t_1[f] = u_0$, (13) coincides with (*).

Case 2. There are $t_0 \equiv t_1 \Leftarrow \vartheta \in NAX$ and a substitution f such that $t_0[f] = u$, $t_1[f] = v_0$ and $\vartheta[f] = \gamma'$. By interchanging u_0 and v_0 as well as γ and γ', case 1 implies (*).

Case 3. $u = \sigma\langle t_1,\ldots,t_n\rangle$, $u_0 = \sigma\langle u_1,\ldots,u_n\rangle$, $v_0 = \sigma\langle v_1,\ldots,v_n\rangle$ and for all $1 \leq i \leq n$

$$\|t_i \xrightarrow[NAX]{} u_i\| \leq \|u \xrightarrow[NAX]{} u_0\| \text{ and } \|t_i \xrightarrow[NAX]{} v_i\| \leq \|u \xrightarrow[NAX]{} v_0\|.$$

Since $size(t_i) < size(u)$, the induction hypothesis implies

$$\|u_i \xrightarrow[NAX]{} t_i'\| \leq \|t_i \xrightarrow[NAX]{} v_i\| \text{ and } \|v_i \xrightarrow[NAX]{} t_i'\| \leq \|t_i \xrightarrow[NAX]{} u_i\|$$

for some t_i'. Let $u' = \sigma\langle t_1',\ldots,t_n'\rangle$ and $1 \leq j,k \leq n$ such that

$$\|u_j \xrightarrow[NAX]{} t_j'\| = \max\{\|u_i \xrightarrow[NAX]{} t_i'\| \mid 1 \leq i \leq n\}$$

and

$$\|v_k \xrightarrow[NAX]{} t_k'\| = \max\{\|v_i \xrightarrow[NAX]{} t_i'\| \mid 1 \leq i \leq n\}.$$

Hence

and
$$\|u \circ \overrightarrow{_{NAX}} u'\| \leq \|u_j \overrightarrow{_{NAX}} t_j'\| \leq \|t_j \overrightarrow{_{NAX}} v_j\| \leq \|u \overrightarrow{_{NAX}} v_0\|$$

$$\|v \circ \overrightarrow{_{NAX}} u'\| \leq \|v_k \overrightarrow{_{NAX}} t_k'\| \leq \|t_k \overrightarrow{_{NAX}} u_k\| \leq \|u \overrightarrow{_{NAX}} u_0\|.$$

Thus (∗) holds true. ∎

9.7 Confluence of ~NAX

The confluence criterion Theorem 9.5.1 presumes both the convergence of critical pairs and the Noetherian property of $\vdash^{RD}_{\sim NAX}$. Theorem 9.6.1, on the other hand, requires that NAX be left-linear and that critical pairs be strongly convergent. Both criteria aim at the NAX-Church-Rosser property. In this section, we develop a confluence criterion based on the Congruence Class Approach (cf. Section 7.3), which will be used to derive sufficient conditions for the ~NAX-Church-Rosser property. These are mainly the Noetherian property of $\vdash^{RD}_{\sim NAX}$ and the linearity of conditional base equations. The first condition is needed because $\supset(\overrightarrow{_{\sim BAX}} \cdot \vdash^{RD}_{\sim NAX})$ will replace the induction ordering $\supset \vdash^{RD}_{\sim NAX}$ used in the proof of Theorem 9.5.1. The second condition implies – together with the Definition Principle of NAX (cf. Section 7.8) – that $\vdash^{RD}_{\sim NAX}$ commutes with ~BAX.

Definition A binary term relation R *commutes with ~BAX* if for all terms u,t,t' there is a term v such that

$$\langle u,t \rangle \in R \text{ and } u \overrightarrow{_{\sim BAX}} t' \text{ implies } t \overrightarrow{_{\sim BAX}} v \text{ and } \langle t',v \rangle \in R^=$$

where $R^=$ denotes the reflexive closure of R. ∎

Lemma 9.7.1 Suppose that
- CE(BAX) is linear and has no isolated variables (cf. Section 7.8),
- CE(BAX) is variable-preserving (cf. Section 7.7) or NAX consists of unconditional equations.
- CE(BAX) is empty or NAX satisfies the Definition Principle.

Then $\vdash^{RD}_{\sim NAX}$ and $\overrightarrow{_{\sim NAX}}$ commute with ~BAX.

Proof. We first show that $\vdash^{RD}_{\sim NAX}$ commutes with ~BAX. Let $u \vdash^{RD}_{\sim NAX} t$ and $u \overrightarrow{_{\sim BAX}} t'$. A term v with

(1) $|t \overrightarrow{_{\sim BAX}} v| \leq |u \overrightarrow{_{\sim BAX}} t'|$ and $|t' \vdash^{RD}_{\sim NAX} v| \leq |u \vdash^{RD}_{\sim NAX} t|$

is found by induction on the pair $\langle |u \vdash^{RD}_{\sim NAX} t| + |u \overrightarrow{_{\sim BAX}} t'|, \text{size}(u) \rangle$ w.r.t. the lexicographic extension of > on $\mathbb{N}$ to an ordering on $\mathbb{N} \times \mathbb{N}$.

Case 1. $u = t'$. Choose $v = t$.

Case 2. There are terms u_0, u', v_0, a ~NAX-reducible goal γ and a ~NAX-reduced goal γ' such that $u' \in \{u_0\} \cup \{u_i \mid \in P\langle u_1,\ldots,u_n\rangle \in \gamma, 1 \le i \le n\}$,

(2) $\qquad |u \vdash^{RD}_{\sim NAX} t| = |u \vdash^{RD}_{\sim NAX} u'| + |u' \vdash^{RD}_{\sim NAX} t|,$
$\qquad |u \vdash^{RD}_{\sim NAX} u'| = |u \vdash^{RD}_{\sim NAX} u_0 \Leftarrow \gamma| = 1.$

(3) $\qquad |u \Rrightarrow_{\sim BAX} t'| = |u \Rrightarrow_{\sim BAX} v_0| + |v_0 \Rrightarrow_{\sim BAX} t'|,$
$\qquad |u \Rrightarrow_{\sim BAX} v_0| = 1.$

Suppose that there is a term v_1 such that

(*) $\qquad |u' \Rrightarrow_{\sim BAX} v_1| \le |u \Rrightarrow_{\sim BAX} v_0|$ and $|v_0 \vdash^{RD}_{\sim NAX} v_1| \le |u \vdash^{RD}_{\sim NAX} u'|.$

Since $|u' \vdash^{RD}_{\sim NAX} t| < |u \vdash^{RD}_{\sim NAX} t|$, (*) and the induction hypothesis provide v' with

(4) $\qquad |t \Rrightarrow_{\sim BAX} v'| \le |u' \Rrightarrow_{\sim BAX} v_1|,$

(5) $\qquad |v_1 \vdash^{RD}_{\sim NAX} v'| \le |u' \vdash^{RD}_{\sim NAX} t|.$

Since $|v_0 \Rrightarrow_{\sim BAX} t'| < |u \Rrightarrow_{\sim BAX} t'|$, (*) and the induction hypothesis supply v'' with

(6) $\qquad |v_1 \Rrightarrow_{\sim BAX} v''| \le |v_0 \Rrightarrow_{\sim BAX} t'|,$

(7) $\qquad |t' \vdash^{RD}_{\sim NAX} v''| \le |v_0 \vdash^{RD}_{\sim NAX} v_1|.$

By (2), (3), (5) and (6), $|v_1 \vdash^{RD}_{\sim NAX} v'| + |v_1 \Rrightarrow_{\sim BAX} v''| < |u \vdash^{RD}_{\sim NAX} t| + |u \Rrightarrow_{\sim BAX} t'|$. Hence the induction hypothesis establishes v with

(8) $\qquad |v' \Rrightarrow_{\sim BAX} v| \le |v_1 \Rrightarrow_{\sim BAX} v''|,$

(9) $\qquad |v'' \vdash^{RD}_{\sim NAX} v| \le |v_1 \vdash^{RD}_{\sim NAX} v'|.$

By (3), (*), (4), (6) and (8),

$|t \Rrightarrow_{\sim BAX} v| \le |t \Rrightarrow_{\sim BAX} v'| + |v' \Rrightarrow_{\sim BAX} v| \le |u' \Rrightarrow_{\sim BAX} v_1| + |v_1 \Rrightarrow_{\sim BAX} v''|$
$\qquad \le |u \Rrightarrow_{\sim BAX} v_0| + |v_0 \Rrightarrow_{\sim BAX} t'| = |u \Rrightarrow_{\sim BAX} t'|.$

By (2), (*), (5), (7) and (9),

$|t' \vdash^{RD}_{\sim NAX} v| \le |t \vdash^{RD}_{\sim NAX} v''| + |v'' \vdash^{RD}_{\sim NAX} v| \le |v_0 \vdash^{RD}_{\sim NAX} v_1| + |v_1 \vdash^{RD}_{\sim NAX} v'|$

$$\leq |u \vdash^{RD}_{\sim NAX} u'| + |u' \vdash^{RD}_{\sim NAX} t| = |u \vdash^{RD}_{\sim NAX} t|.$$

This implies (1), and it remains for us to show (*).

Case 1. There are $t_0 \equiv t_1 \Leftarrow \delta \in$ NAX and a substitution f such that $u \Rightarrow_{BAX} t_0[f]$, $t_1[f] = u_0$ and $\delta[f] = \gamma$. Since $u \Rightarrow_{BAX} v_0$ and BAX is symmetric, we obtain $v_0 \Rightarrow_{BAX} t_0[f]$ and thus $|v_0 \Rightarrow_{NAX} u_0 \Leftarrow \gamma| = 1$. Hence $|v_0 \vdash^{RD}_{\sim NAX} u'| = 1 = |u \vdash^{RD}_{\sim NAX} u'|$ and thus (*) holds true for $v_1 = u'$.

Case 2. There are $t_0 \equiv t_1 \Leftarrow \delta \in$ BAX and a substitution f such that $u = t_0[f]$, $t_1[f] = v_0$ and $\delta[f] = \gamma'$.

Assume that $u \Rightarrow_{NAX} u_0 \Leftarrow \gamma$ affects t_0. Then $t_0[f_1] \stackrel{t_0}{\Rightarrow}_{NAX} t_1 \Leftarrow \gamma_1$ for some f_1, t_1, γ_1. Hence there are a proper subterm t_0' of t_0 and $v \equiv v' \Leftarrow \delta \in$ NAX such that $t_0'[f_1] \Rightarrow_{BAX} v[g]$ for some g. Since CE(BAX) has no isolated variables and NAX satisfies the Definition Principle or $t_0'[f_1] = v[g]$, neither t_0' nor v is a variable. Since root(v) $\in$ NOP, we conclude that root(v) coincides with root(t_0'). Thus root(v) occurs in t_0. But this contradicts the fact that t_0 is a base term.

Therefore $u \Rightarrow_{NAX} u_0 \Leftarrow \gamma$ does not affect t_0. Since $u = t_0[f]$ and t_0 is linear, Lemma 9.2.2 (1) yields $f \Rightarrow_{NAX} g \Leftarrow \gamma$ and $u_0 = t_0[g]$ for some g. From $\sim$NAX-reducedness of $\delta[f] = \gamma'$ we conclude $\delta[f] = \delta[g]$. Hence $\delta[g]$ is $\sim$NAX-reduced. Let $g' = g \restriction var(t_0) + f \restriction (X - var(t_0))$. Then

$$|u_0 \Rightarrow_{BAX} t_1[g']| = |t_0[g] \Rightarrow_{BAX} t_1[g']| \leq 1 = |u \Rightarrow_{BAX} v_0|$$

and

$$|v_0 \vdash^{RD}_{\sim NAX} t_1[g']| = |t_1[f] \vdash^{RD}_{\sim NAX} t_1[g']| \leq |t_0[f] \vdash^{RD}_{\sim NAX} t_0[g]| = |u \vdash^{RD}_{\sim NAX} u_0|.$$

Case 2.1. $u' = u_0$. By the previous equations, (*) holds true for $v_1 = t_1[g']$.

Case 2.2. There are $P\langle u_1,...,u_n\rangle \in \gamma$ and $1 \leq i \leq n$ such that $u' = u_i$. Then γ is not empty and thus by assumption, var(t_0) = var(t_1). Hence $t_0[f] \vdash^{RD}_{\sim NAX} u'$ and $f \Rightarrow_{NAX} g \Leftarrow \gamma$ imply

$$|v_0 \vdash^{RD}_{\sim NAX} u'| = |t_1[f] \vdash^{RD}_{\sim NAX} u'| = |t_0[f] \vdash^{RD}_{\sim NAX} u'| = |u \vdash^{RD}_{\sim NAX} u'|.$$

Therefore (*) is valid for $v_1 = u'$.

Case 3. $u = \sigma\langle u_1,...,u_n\rangle$, $v_0 = \sigma\langle t_1,...,t_n\rangle$ and for all $1 \leq i \leq n$

$$|u_i \Rightarrow_{BAX} t_i| \leq |u \Rightarrow_{BAX} v_0|.$$

Case 3.1. $u' = u_0 = \sigma\langle u_1',...,u_n'\rangle$ and for all $1 \leq i \leq n$, $|u_i \vdash^{RD}_{\sim NAX} u_i'| \leq |u \vdash^{RD}_{\sim NAX} u'|$. Since size($u_i$) < size($u$), the induction hypothesis implies

$$|t_i \overset{RD}{\vdash_{\sim NAX}} t_i'| \le |u_i \overset{RD}{\vdash_{\sim NAX}} u_i'| \text{ and } |u_i' \overset{}{=_{\sim BAX}\Rightarrow} t_i'| \le |u_i =_{\sim BAX}\Rightarrow t_i|$$

for some t_i'. Let $v_1 = \sigma\langle t_1',\ldots,t_n'\rangle$ and $1 \le j,k \le n$ such that

$$|t_j \overset{RD}{\vdash_{\sim NAX}} t_j'| = \max\{|t_i \overset{RD}{\vdash_{\sim NAX}} t_i'| \mid 1 \le i \le n\}$$

and

$$|u_k' =_{\sim BAX}\Rightarrow t_k'| = \max\{|u_i' =_{\sim BAX}\Rightarrow t_i'| \mid 1 \le i \le n\}.$$

Then

$$|u' =_{\sim BAX}\Rightarrow v_1| \le |u_k' =_{\sim BAX}\Rightarrow t_k'| \le |u_k =_{\sim BAX}\Rightarrow t_k| \le |u =_{\sim BAX}\Rightarrow v_0|$$

and

$$|v_0 \overset{RD}{\vdash_{\sim NAX}} v_1| \le |t_j \overset{RD}{\vdash_{\sim NAX}} t_j'| \le |u_j \overset{RD}{\vdash_{\sim NAX}} u_j'| \le |u \overset{RD}{\vdash_{\sim NAX}} u'|.$$

Hence (*) holds true.

Case 3.2. $u' = u_i'$ for some $P\langle u_1',\ldots,u_m'\rangle \in \gamma$ and $1 \le i \le m$, and for all $1 \le i \le n$,

$$|u_i \overset{RD}{\vdash_{\sim NAX}} u'| \le |u \overset{RD}{\vdash_{\sim NAX}} u'|.$$

Since $size(u_i) < size(u)$, the induction hypothesis implies

$$|t_i \overset{RD}{\vdash_{\sim NAX}} t_i'| \le |u_i \overset{RD}{\vdash_{\sim NAX}} u'| \text{ and } |u' =_{\sim BAX}\Rightarrow t_i'| \le |u_i =_{\sim BAX}\Rightarrow t_i|$$

for some t_i'. Let $v_1 = u'$ and $1 \le j \le n$ such that

$$|t_j \overset{RD}{\vdash_{\sim NAX}} t_j'| = \max\{|t_i \overset{RD}{\vdash_{\sim NAX}} t_i'| \mid 1 \le i \le n\}.$$

Then

$$|v_0 \overset{RD}{\vdash_{\sim NAX}} v_1| \le |t_j \overset{RD}{\vdash_{\sim NAX}} t_j'| \le |u_j \overset{RD}{\vdash_{\sim NAX}} u'| \le |u \overset{RD}{\vdash_{\sim NAX}} u'|,$$

and (*) holds true.

Therefore $\overset{RD}{\vdash_{\sim NAX}}$ commutes with ~BAX. The commutativity of $=_{\sim NAX}\Rightarrow$ with ~BAX can be established by the same proof steps. Here only those subcases, which presume that u' is equal to u_0, must be considered. ∎

Let us now generalize Proposition 7.3.2 to conditional equations. Therefore we denote the composition of $=_{\sim BAX}\Rightarrow$ with $\overset{RD}{\vdash_{NAX}}$ by $\sim\overset{RD}{\vdash_{NAX}}$, i.e.

$$\sim\overset{RD}{\vdash_{NAX}} = =_{\sim BAX}\Rightarrow \circ \overset{RD}{\vdash_{NAX}}.$$

Lemma 9.7.2 If $\overset{RD}{\vdash_{NAX}}$ is Noetherian (on ground terms) and $\overset{RD}{\vdash_{\sim NAX}}$ commutes with ~BAX, then $\sim\overset{RD}{\vdash_{NAX}}$ is Noetherian (on ground terms) as well.

Proof is the same as the proof of Proposition 7.3.2, provided that $\xrightarrow[\sim NAX]{}$, $\sim\xrightarrow[NAX]{}$ and BAX are replaced by $\vdash\xrightarrow[\sim NAX]{RD}$, $\sim\vdash\xrightarrow[NAX]{RD}$ and ~BAX, respectively. ∎

Together with the following lemma, Lemma 9.7.1 will result in a criterion for the confluence of ~NAX.

Lemma 9.7.3 Suppose that
- $\vdash\xrightarrow[\sim NAX]{RD}$ is Noetherian (on ground terms),
- $\vdash\xrightarrow[\sim NAX]{RD}$ and $\xrightarrow[\sim NAX]{}$ commute with ~BAX,
- CE(BAX) is empty or NAX satisfies the Definition Principle,
- all feasible most general critical pairs of $\xrightarrow[\sim NAX]{}$ into NAX are (ground) ~NAX-convergent modulo ~BAX.

Then ~NAX is (ground) confluent modulo ~BAX and ~BAX respects (ground) ~NAX-normal forms (cf. Section 7.8).

Proof. That ~BAX respects ~NAX-normal forms is a simple consequence of the first two assumptions.

Let t be a ~NAX-normal form and $t\xrightarrow[\sim BAX]{}t'$. From the Noetherian property of $\vdash\xrightarrow[\sim NAX]{RD}$ we obtain a ~NAX-normal form u with $t'\xrightarrow[\sim NAX]{}u$. By the symmetry of BAX, $t'\xrightarrow[\sim BAX]{}t$. Hence $u\xrightarrow[\sim BAX]{}t$ because $\xrightarrow[\sim NAX]{}$ commutes with ~BAX and t is ~NAX-irreducible. Again by the symmetry of BAX, $t\xrightarrow[\sim BAX]{}u$.

Secondly, we show that ~NAX is (ground) confluent modulo ~BAX. Let

$$u \begin{matrix} \sim NAX \rightarrow t \\ \sim NAX \rightarrow t'. \end{matrix}$$

Two terms v,v' with

(1)
$$\begin{matrix} t \xrightarrow[\sim NAX]{} v \\ \downarrow \sim BAX \\ t' \xrightarrow[\sim NAX]{} v' \end{matrix}$$

are established by Noetherian induction on u w.r.t. $\supset\sim\vdash\xrightarrow[NAX]{RD}$. (By assumption, Lemma 9.7.2 and Lemma 9.4.5, $\supset\sim\vdash\xrightarrow[NAX]{RD}$ is Noetherian.)

Case 1. u = t or u = t'. Choose v = v' = t' or v = v' = t, respectively.

Case 2. There are terms u',u_o and a ~NAX-reducible goal γ such that

(2) $\quad u_o\xrightarrow[\sim NAX]{}t$, $u\xrightarrow[\sim BAX]{}u'$, $|u'\xrightarrow[NAX]{}u_o\Leftarrow\gamma| = 1$ and thus $u\xrightarrow[\sim NAX]{}u_o$.

Since $\underset{\sim NAX}{\Rightarrow}$ commutes with $\sim BAX$, we obtain v_1 with

$$\begin{array}{c} u' \overset{\sim NAX}{\searrow} \\   v_1. \\ t' \underset{\sim BAX}{\nearrow} \end{array}$$

Hence there are a term v_0 and a $\sim NAX$-reducible goal γ' such that

(3) $\qquad |u' \underset{\sim NAX}{\Rightarrow} v_0 \Leftarrow \gamma'| = 1 \;$ and $\; v_0 \underset{\sim NAX}{\Rightarrow} t'$.

Suppose that $\langle u_0, v_0 \rangle$ is $\sim NAX$-convergent modulo $\sim BAX$, say

(*) $\qquad \begin{array}{c} u_0 \underset{\sim NAX}{\Rightarrow} u_0' \\ \downarrow \sim BAX \\ v_0 \underset{\sim NAX}{\Rightarrow} u_1'. \end{array}$

By (2), $u \underset{\sim NAX}{\Rightarrow} u_0$. By (2) and (3), $u \underset{\sim BAX}{\Rightarrow} u' \underset{\sim NAX}{\Rightarrow} v_0$. Hence both u_0 and v_0 are smaller than u w.r.t. $\supset \sim \overset{RD}{NAX}$. Thus by the induction hypothesis, $u_0 \underset{\sim NAX}{\Rightarrow} t$, $v_0 \underset{\sim NAX}{\Rightarrow} v_1$ and (*) imply

(4) $\qquad \begin{array}{c} t \underset{\sim NAX}{\Rightarrow} v_0' \\ \downarrow \sim BAX \\ u_0' \underset{\sim NAX}{\Rightarrow} v_0" \end{array}$ and $\begin{array}{c} v_1 \underset{\sim NAX}{\Rightarrow} v_1' \\ \downarrow \sim BAX \\ u_1' \underset{\sim NAX}{\Rightarrow} v_1" \end{array}$

for some $v_0', v_0", v_1', v_1"$. Since $\underset{\sim NAX}{\Rightarrow}$ commutes with $\sim BAX$, $u_0' \underset{\sim BAX}{\Rightarrow} u_1'$, $v_1 \underset{\sim BAX}{\Rightarrow} t'$ and (4) imply

(5) $\qquad \begin{array}{c} v_0" \overset{\sim BAX}{\searrow} \\   t_0 \\ u_1' \underset{\sim NAX}{\nearrow} \end{array}$ and $\begin{array}{c} v_1' \overset{\sim BAX}{\searrow} \\   t_1 \\ t' \underset{\sim NAX}{\nearrow} \end{array}$

for some t_0, t_1. By (2), (3) and (*), $u \underset{\sim BAX}{\Rightarrow} u' \underset{\sim NAX}{\Rightarrow} v_0 \underset{\sim NAX}{\Rightarrow} u_1'$. Hence u_1' is smaller than u w.r.t. $\supset \sim \overset{RD}{NAX}$. By (4), (5) and the induction hypothesis,

(6) $\qquad \begin{array}{c} t_0 \underset{\sim NAX}{\Rightarrow} t_0' \\ \downarrow \sim BAX \\ v_1" \underset{\sim NAX}{\Rightarrow} t_1' \end{array}$

for some t_0', t_1'. Moreover, (4) and (5) imply $t_0 \underset{\sim BAX}{\Rightarrow} v_0" \underset{\sim BAX}{\Rightarrow} v_0'$ and $v_1" \underset{\sim BAX}{\Rightarrow} v_1' \underset{\sim BAX}{\Rightarrow} t_1$. Hence by (6),

(7) $\qquad \begin{array}{c} t_0' \overset{\sim BAX}{\searrow} \\   v \\ v_0' \underset{\sim NAX}{\nearrow} \end{array}$ and $\begin{array}{c} t_1' \overset{\sim BAX}{\searrow} \\   v' \\ t_1 \underset{\sim NAX}{\nearrow} \end{array}$

for some v,v' because $\xrightarrow{\sim NAX}$ commutes with ~BAX. (4)-(7) imply (1):

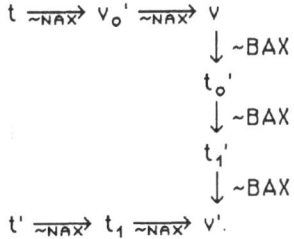

$$t \xrightarrow{\sim NAX} v_0' \xrightarrow{\sim NAX} v$$
$$\downarrow \sim BAX$$
$$t_0'$$
$$\downarrow \sim BAX$$
$$t_1'$$
$$\downarrow \sim BAX$$
$$t' \xrightarrow{\sim NAX} t_1 \xrightarrow{\sim NAX} v'.$$

It remains for us to show that (∗) holds true, i.e., that $\langle u_0, v_0 \rangle$ is ~NAX-convergent modulo ~BAX.

Case 1. There are $t_0 \equiv t_1 \Leftarrow \vartheta \in$ NAX and a (ground) substitution f such that $t_0[f] = u'$, $t_1[f] = u_0$ and $\vartheta[f] = \gamma$. We have two subcases:

Case 1.1. $u' \xrightarrow{\sim NAX} v_0 \Leftarrow \gamma'$ affects t_0. Since $u' \xrightarrow{\sim NAX} v_0 \Leftarrow \gamma'$ is obtained by one application of the Single Reduction Rule, $u' \xrightarrow{\sim NAX} v_0 \Leftarrow \gamma'$ is t_0-overlapping. Thus $\langle u_0 \Leftarrow \gamma, v_0 \Leftarrow \gamma' \rangle$ is a critical pair of $\xrightarrow{\sim NAX}$ into NAX. Since $\vdash^{RD}_{\sim NAX}$ is Noetherian, ~NAX is normalizing. Moreover, $u \xrightarrow{\sim BAX} u'$, $u' \xrightarrow{\sim NAX} u_0 \Leftarrow \gamma$ and $u' \xrightarrow{\sim NAX} v_0 \Leftarrow \gamma'$ imply that all subterms v of $\gamma \cup \gamma'$ are smaller than u' w.r.t. $\supset \sim \vdash^{RD}_{\sim NAX}$. Hence by the induction hypothesis, if $v \xrightarrow{\sim NAX} v'$ and $v \xrightarrow{\sim NAX} v''$, then $\langle v', v'' \rangle$ is ~NAX-convergent modulo ~BAX. Since $\gamma \cup \gamma'$ is ~NAX-reducible, Lemma 9.4.4 implies that $\langle u_0, v_0 \rangle$ is ~NAX-convergent modulo ~BAX.

Case 1.2. $u' \xrightarrow{\sim NAX} v_0 \Leftarrow \gamma'$ does not affect t_0. Since $u \xrightarrow{\sim BAX} u'$ and $u' \xrightarrow{\sim NAX} u_0 \Leftarrow \gamma$, all subterms v of $\gamma = \vartheta[f]$ are smaller than u' w.r.t. $\supset \sim \vdash^{RD}_{\sim NAX}$. Hence by the induction hypothesis, if $v \xrightarrow{\sim NAX} v'$ and $v \xrightarrow{\sim NAX} v''$, then $\langle v', v'' \rangle$ is ~NAX-convergent modulo ~BAX. Thus by Lemma 9.3.2 (2), $\langle u_0, v_0 \rangle = \langle t_1[f], v_0 \rangle$ is ~NAX-convergent modulo ~BAX.

Case 2. There are $t_0 \equiv t_1 \Leftarrow \vartheta \in$ NAX and a (ground) substitution f such that $u' \xrightarrow{\sim BAX} t_0[f]$, $t_1[f] = v_0$ and $\vartheta[f] = \gamma'$. By symmetry of BAX, $t_0[f] \xrightarrow{\sim BAX} u'$. Since $u' \xrightarrow{\sim NAX} u_0 \Leftarrow \gamma$, we have two subcases:

Case 2.1. $t_0[f] \xrightarrow{\sim NAX} u_0 \Leftarrow \gamma$. Either this reduction affects t_0 or it does not affect t_0. Proceeding as in Case 1 one infers that $\langle t_1[f], u_0 \rangle$ and thus $\langle u_0, v_0 \rangle = \langle u_0, t_1[f] \rangle$ are ~NAX-convergent modulo ~BAX.

Case 2.2. $t_0[f] \xrightarrow{\sim NAX} u_0 \Leftarrow \gamma$ does not hold. Since $|u' \xrightarrow{\sim NAX} u_0 \Leftarrow \gamma| = 1$, there are a term u", $x \in$ var(u") and an instance $v \equiv v' \Leftarrow \gamma$ of a conditional NAX-equation such that $u"[v/x] = u'$ and $u"[v'/x] = u_0$. By the Definition Principle of NAX, root(v) is neither a base operation nor a variable. Hence $u' \xrightarrow{\sim BAX} t_0[f]$ can be lifted to a conditional reduction $u'' \xrightarrow{\sim BAX} t'' \Leftarrow \lambda$ such that $t''[v/x] = t_o[f]$ and $\lambda[v/x]$ is ~NAX-reduced. Thus $t_o[f] \xrightarrow{\sim NAX} t''[v'/x] \Leftarrow \gamma$. Again proceeding as in Case 1 one concludes that $\langle t_1[f], t''[v'/x] \rangle$ and thus $\langle t''[v'/x], v_o \rangle = \langle t''[v'/x], t_1[f] \rangle$ are ~NAX-convergent modulo ~BAX, i.e.

(8)
$$\begin{array}{c} v_o \xrightarrow{\sim NAX} v_o' \\ \downarrow \sim BAX \\ t''[v'/x] \xrightarrow{\sim NAX} t_o'' \end{array}$$

for some v_o', t_o''. Since $\lambda[v/x]$ is ~NAX-irreducible, but $v \xrightarrow{\sim NAX} v' \Leftarrow \gamma$ is a conditional reduction, x cannot occur in λ. Hence $\lambda[v'/x] = \lambda[v/x]$ is ~NAX-reduced and thus $t''[v'/x] \xrightarrow{\sim BAX} u''[v'/x]$. Since $\xrightarrow{\sim NAX}$ commutes with ~BAX, (8) implies

(9)
$$\begin{array}{c} t_o'' \searrow \sim BAX \\ v_o'' \\ u''[v'/x] \nearrow \sim NAX \end{array}$$

for some v_o''. By (8) and (9),

$$\begin{array}{c} v_o \xrightarrow{\sim NAX} v_o' \\ \downarrow \sim BAX \\ u_o = u''[v'/x] \xrightarrow{\sim NAX} v_o''. \end{array}$$

Hence $\langle u_o, v_o \rangle$ is ~NAX-convergent modulo ~BAX.

Case 3. $u' = \sigma\langle t_1,...,t_n \rangle$, $u_o = \sigma\langle u_1,...,u_n \rangle$, $v_o = \sigma\langle v_1,...,v_n \rangle$ and for all $1 \leq i \leq n$

$$\begin{array}{c} \sim NAX \nearrow u_i \\ t_i \\ \sim NAX \searrow v_i. \end{array}$$

Since t_i is a proper subterm of u' and $u \xrightarrow{\sim BAX} u'$, t_i is smaller than u w.r.t. $\supset \sim \xrightarrow{RD}_{NAX}$. The induction hypothesis implies

$$\begin{array}{c} u_i \xrightarrow{\sim NAX} \\ \searrow t_i' \\ v_i \xrightarrow{\sim NAX} \end{array}$$

for some t_i'. Hence $u_o \xrightarrow{\sim NAX} \sigma\langle t_1',...,t_n' \rangle$ and $v_o \xrightarrow{\sim NAX} \sigma\langle t_1',...,t_n' \rangle$. ∎

Lemmata 9.7.1 and 9.7.3 amount to

Theorem 9.7.4 *Criterion for confluence of ~NAX*
Suppose that
- CE(BAX) is linear and has no isolated variables,
- CE(BAX) is variable-preserving if for some $u \equiv u' \Leftarrow \vartheta \in$ NAX, ϑ is nonempty,
- CE(BAX) is empty or NAX satisfies the Definition Principle,
- the ~NAX-reduction relation is Noetherian (on ground terms),
- all feasible most general critical pairs of $\overrightarrow{\sim NAX}$ into NAX are (ground) ~NAX-convergent modulo ~BAX.

Then ~NAX is (ground) confluent modulo ~BAX and ~BAX respects (ground) ~NAX-normal forms. ∎

9.8 BAX-compatibility of NAX

The previous three sections dealt with criteria for the confluence of NAX (Theorem 9.5.1), the strong confluence of NAX (Theorem 9.6.1) and the confluence of ~NAX (Theorem 9.7.4). Moreover, the assumptions of the latter criterion also imply that $\overrightarrow{\sim NAX}$ commutes with ~BAX (Lemma 9.7.1) and that ~BAX respects ~NAX-normal forms (cf. Lemma 9.7.3). Since commutativity of $\overrightarrow{\sim NAX}$ with ~BAX is a special case of ~BAX-compatibility of ~NAX (cf. Section 7.8), Theorems 7.8.2 and 9.7.4 supply a ~NAX-Church-Rosser criterion (Theorem 9.9.1). However, in order to obtain a NAX-Church-Rosser criterion by combining Theorem 9.5.1 or 9.6.1 with Theorem 7.8.2 we still need "effective" criteria for BAX-compatibility. Let us recall the definition of BAX-compatibility as given in Section 7.8.

Definition NAX is (ground) *BAX-compatible* if for all (ground) terms t,u,u' and NAX-reduced goals γ such that $t \overrightarrow{NAX} u$ and $|t \overrightarrow{BAX} u' \Leftarrow \gamma| = 1$, ⟨u,u'⟩ is NAX-convergent modulo BAX, i.e.

$$u \overrightarrow{NAX} v$$
$$\downarrow BAX \qquad\qquad (1)$$
$$u' \overrightarrow{NAX} v'$$

for some v,v'. ∎

In Section 9.2 we mentioned that the reduction of BAX-compatibility to a convergence condition for critical pairs calls for a stronger induction hypothesis than (1). We have called it *strong* BAX-compatibility: (1) was strengthened to

$$u \overrightarrow{NAX} v$$
$$\Downarrow BAX \qquad\qquad (2)$$
$$u' \overrightarrow{NAX} v',$$

while the premise of BAX-compatibility, i.e. $|t \overrightarrow{BAX} u' \Leftarrow \gamma| = 1$, is weakened to

the assumption that u' is obtained from t by a fully parallel reduction, i.e. $t \overline{\overline{BAX}} u'$. Since $t \overline{\overline{BAX}} u'$ and $v \overline{\overline{BAX}} v'$ are in the same "class of NAX-reductions", strong BAX-compatibility can be shown by (Noetherian) induction on t if
- strong BAX-compatibility holds for *one-step* reductions $t \overline{NAX} u$ and
- NAX is (strongly) confluent.

Split $t \overline{NAX} u$ into a *one-step* reduction $t \overline{NAX} u_0$ and the remaining reduction $u_0 \overline{NAX} u$. Then by assumption,

$$u_0 \overline{NAX} v_0$$
$$\Downarrow BAX$$
$$u' \overline{NAX} v_0'$$

for some v_0, v_0'. Since NAX is (strongly) confluent, there is v_1 such that $u \overline{NAX} v_1$ and $v_0 \overline{NAX} v_1$ ($\|v_0 \overline{NAX} v_1\| \leq \|u_0 \overline{NAX} u\|$, respectively). Thus

$$\begin{array}{c} NAX \rightarrow v_1 \\ v_0 \\ BAX \searrow v_0', \end{array}$$

v_0 is smaller than t w.r.t. $\overset{RD}{\overline{NAX}}$ and, if NAX is strongly confluent, $\|v_0 \overline{NAX} v_1\| < \|t \overline{NAX} u\|$. Hence, if $\overset{RD}{\overline{NAX}}$ is Noetherian or NAX is strongly confluent, we can apply the induction hypothesis and obtain

$$v_1 \overline{NAX} v$$
$$\Downarrow BAX$$
$$v_0' \overline{NAX} v'.$$

for some v,v'. Therefore $u \overline{NAX} v_1 \overline{NAX} v$ and $u' \overline{NAX} v_0' \overline{NAX} v'$ imply (2).

The question remains whether we need a *fully parallel* BAX-step. The argument for a *parallel* step is the same as in the case of strong confluence (cf. Section 9.6).

Let $u \equiv u' \in$ NAX and x be a variable occurring once in u and twice in u'. Together with a reduction $t \overline{\overline{BAX}} t'$ with simple length 1, there is the branching

$$\begin{array}{c} NAX \rightarrow u'[t/x] \\ u[t/x] \\ BAX \searrow u[t'/x]. \end{array}$$

The two resulting terms have the common reduct u'[t'/x], but the simple length of $u[t'/x] \overline{NAX} u'[t'/x]$ is 1, while that of $u'[t/x] \overline{\overline{BAX}} u'[t'/x]$ is 2. Thus we must start out at least from *parallel* BAX-steps.

However, the *horizontal* parallelism of the Parallel Reduction Rule (cf.

Section 7.7) does not suffice. Imagine a critical pair $\langle u,u'\rangle$ of $\overrightarrow{BAX}$ into NAX that comes from the branching

$$t \begin{array}{c} \overrightarrow{NAX} \ u \\ \\ \overrightarrow{BAX} \ u' \end{array}$$

and can be made convergent by NAX-reductions and one application of the Parallel Reduction Rule for BAX, i.e.

$$\begin{array}{c} u \overrightarrow{NAX} v \\ \downarrow BAX \\ u' \overrightarrow{NAX} v' \end{array} \qquad (3)$$

for some v,v' with $\|v \overrightarrow{BAX} v'\| = 1$. If there is a variable x in t, which does not belong to the reduction redex that generates $t \overrightarrow{BAX} u'$, we may compose $t \overrightarrow{BAX} u'$ with a reduction $v_0 \overrightarrow{BAX} v_1$ such that $t[v_0/x] \overrightarrow{BAX} u'[v_1/x]$ has parallel length 1. This leads to the branching

$$t[v_0/x] \begin{array}{c} \overrightarrow{NAX} \ u[v_0/x] \\ \\ \overrightarrow{BAX} \ u'[v_1/x]. \end{array} \qquad (4)$$

Together with (3), one obtains the converging diagram

$$\begin{array}{c} u[v_0/x] \overrightarrow{NAX} v[v_0/x] \\ \downarrow BAX \\ u'[v_1/x] \overrightarrow{NAX} v'[v_1/x]. \end{array} \qquad (5)$$

$v[v_0/x] \overrightarrow{BAX} v'[v_1/x]$ consists of two BAX-reductions, $v \overrightarrow{BAX} v'$ and $v_0 \overrightarrow{BAX} v_1$, which are supposed to have parallel length 1, but which are composed *vertically*. Thus, although the BAX-reduction in (4) has parallel length 1, the corresponding BAX-reduction in (5) need not have parallel length 1. However, it is a *fully* parallel reduction (cf. Section 9.2).

This prompts us to use $\overrightarrow{BAX}$ in the definition of strong BAX-compatibility.

We present two criteria for this property. The *weak* compatibility criterion rests on the assumption that all feasible most general critical pairs of $\overrightarrow{BAX}$ into NAX are weakly NAX-convergent modulo BAX (cf. Section 9.4). On the other hand, the *strong* compatibility criterion presumes strong instead of weak convergence. The weak compatibility criterion will be combined with Theorem 9.5.1 yielding the *weak NAX-Church-Rosser criterion* (Theorem 9.9.2). This criterion might be applicable to specifications with a

Noetherian NAX-reduction relation. The strong compatibility criterion and the strong confluence criterion (Theorem 9.6.1) result in the *strong NAX-Church-Rosser criterion* (Theorem 9.9.3), which does not require the Noetherian property of $\vdash^{RD}_{NAX}$.

Theorem 9.8.1 *Weak compatibility criterion*
Suppose that
- the NAX-reduction relation is Noetherian (on ground terms),
- NAX is (ground) confluent and left-linear,
- CE(BAX) is empty or NAX satisfies the Definition Principle,
- all feasible most general critical pairs of $\overrightarrow{BAX}$ into NAX are weakly (ground) NAX-convergent modulo BAX (cf. Section 9.4),
- BAX weakly respects (ground) NAX-normal forms (cf. Section 9.2).

Then NAX is strongly (ground) BAX-compatible.

Proof. Let u,t,t' be (ground) terms such that $u \overrightarrow{NAX} t$ and $u \overrightarrow{BAX} t'$. We establish v,v' with

$$t \overrightarrow{NAX} v$$
$$\Downarrow BAX$$
$$t' \overrightarrow{NAX} v'$$

by induction on the pair $\langle u, \|u \overrightarrow{BAX} t'\|\rangle$ w.r.t. the lexicographic extension of $\sqsupset\vdash^{RD}_{NAX}$ on T(SIG) and $>$ on $\mathbb{N}$ to an ordering on T(SIG)×$\mathbb{N}$.

Case 1. u = t. Choose v = t and v' = t'.

Case 2. There are a term u_0, a NAX-reducible goal γ and a NAX-reduced goal γ' such that $u \overrightarrow{BAX} t' \Leftarrow \gamma'$,

(1) $\qquad |u \overrightarrow{NAX} u_0 \Leftarrow \gamma| = 1$ and $u_0 \overrightarrow{NAX} t$.

Suppose that $\langle u_0, t'\rangle$ is strongly NAX-convergent modulo BAX, i.e. there are terms v_0, v_1 with

$$u_0 \overrightarrow{NAX} v_0$$
(*) $$\Downarrow BAX$$
$$t' \overrightarrow{NAX} v_1.$$

Then by (1), (*) and confluence of NAX,

(2)
$$\begin{array}{c} t \searrow^{NAX} \\ \searrow v \\ v_0 \nearrow_{NAX} \end{array}$$

for some v. Since $u \xrightarrow{NAX} u_o \xrightarrow{NAX} v_o$, u_o and v_o are smaller than u w.r.t. $\sqsupset^{RD}_{NAX}$. Hence by (*), (2) and the induction hypothesis, $\langle v, v_1 \rangle$ and thus $\langle t, t' \rangle$ are strongly NAX-convergent modulo BAX. It remains for us to show (*).

Case 1. There are $t_o \equiv t_1 \Leftarrow \delta \in $ NAX and a (ground) substitution f such that $t_o[f] = u$, $t_1[f] = u_o$ and $\delta[f] = \gamma$. We have two subcases:

Case 1.1. $u \xrightarrow{BAX} t' \Leftarrow \gamma'$ affects t_o (cf. Section 9.2). Since $u \xrightarrow{BAX} t' \Leftarrow \gamma'$ is obtained by at least one application of the Fully Parallel Reduction Rule (cf. Section 9.2), $u \xrightarrow{BAX} t' \Leftarrow \gamma'$ is t_o-overlapping. Thus $\langle u_o \Leftarrow \gamma, t' \Leftarrow \gamma' \rangle$ is a critical pair of $\xrightarrow{BAX}$ into NAX. Since $\vdash^{RD}_{NAX}$ is Noetherian, NAX is normalizing. Moreover, $u \xrightarrow{NAX} u_o \Leftarrow \gamma$ implies that all subterms v of γ and all terms v with $u_o \sqsupset^{RD}_{NAX} v$ are smaller than u w.r.t. $\sqsupset^{RD}_{NAX}$. Hence by the induction hypothesis, if $v \xrightarrow{NAX} v'$ and $v \xrightarrow{BAX} v''$, then $\langle v', v'' \rangle$ is strongly NAX-convergent modulo BAX. Since γ is NAX-reducible and γ' is NAX-reduced, Lemma 9.4.6 (1) implies (*).

Case 1.2. $u \xrightarrow{BAX} t' \Leftarrow \gamma'$ does not affect t_o. Since $u \xrightarrow{NAX} u_o \Leftarrow \gamma$, all subterms v of γ are smaller than u w.r.t. $\sqsupset^{RD}_{NAX}$. Hence by the induction hypothesis, if $v \xrightarrow{NAX} v'$ and $v \xrightarrow{BAX} v''$ for some v', v'', then $\langle v', v'' \rangle$ is strongly NAX-convergent modulo BAX. Since $u = t_o[f]$, t_o is linear, $u_o = t_1[f]$, $\gamma = \delta[f]$ is NAX-reducible and γ' is NAX-reduced, (*) follows from Lemma 9.3.2 (3).

Case 2. There are $t_o \equiv t_1 \Leftarrow \delta \in $ BAX, (ground) substitutions f,g and a goal δ such that $f \xrightarrow{BAX} g \Leftarrow \delta$, $t_o[f] = u$, $t_1[g] = t'$ and $\delta[f] \cup \delta = \gamma'$. Since $t_o[f] \xrightarrow{NAX} u_o$, Lemma 9.3.3 implies $f \xrightarrow{NAX} h$ and $u_o \xrightarrow{NAX} t_o[h]$ for some h.

For all $x \in var(t_o)$, fx is a subterm of $u = t_o[f]$ and thus fx = u or $u \sqsupset^{RD}_{NAX} fx$. Moreover, $\|fx \xrightarrow{BAX} gx \Leftarrow \delta\| < \|u \xrightarrow{BAX} t' \Leftarrow \gamma'\|$. Hence fx is smaller than u w.r.t. the induction ordering of this proof (see above). Thus by the induction hypothesis, $\langle hx, gx \rangle$ is strongly NAX-convergent modulo BAX, and (*) follows from (the last statement of) Lemma 9.3.3.

Case 3. $u = \sigma \langle t_1, \ldots, t_n \rangle$, $u_o = \sigma \langle u_1, \ldots, u_n \rangle$, $t' = \sigma \langle v_1, \ldots, v_n \rangle$ and for all $1 \leq i \leq n$ $t_i \xrightarrow{NAX} u_i$ and $t_i \xrightarrow{BAX} v_i$. Since t_i is a proper subterm of u and thus $u \sqsupset^{RD}_{NAX} t_i$, the induction hypothesis implies

$$u_i \xrightarrow{NAX} t_i'$$
$$\Downarrow BAX$$
$$v_i \xrightarrow{NAX} t_i''$$

for some t_i' and t_i''. Hence

$$u_o \xrightarrow{NAX} \sigma \langle t_1', \ldots, t_n' \rangle$$
$$\Downarrow BAX$$
$$t' \xrightarrow{NAX} \sigma \langle t_1'', \ldots, t_n'' \rangle. \blacksquare$$

The strong compatibility criterion assumes strong confluence of NAX (cf. Section 9.6) and linearity of CE(BAX) (cf. Section 7.8) instead of the Noetherian property of $\xrightarrow[NAX]{RD}$:

Theorem 9.8.2 *Strong criterion for strong BAX-compatibility of NAX*
Suppose that
- CE(BAX) is linear,
- NAX is strongly confluent and left-linear,
- CE(BAX) is empty or NAX satisfies the Definition Principle,
- all feasible most general critical pairs of $\xrightarrow[BAX]{}$ into NAX are strongly (ground) NAX-convergent modulo BAX (cf. Section 9.4),
- BAX weakly respects (ground) NAX-normal forms (cf. Section 9.2).

Then NAX is strongly (ground) BAX-compatible.

Proof. Let u,t,t' be (ground) terms such that $u \xrightarrow[NAX]{} t$ and $u \xrightarrow[BAX]{} t'$. We establish v,v' with

$$t \xrightarrow[NAX]{} v$$
$$\Downarrow BAX$$
$$t' \xrightarrow[NAX]{} v'$$

by induction on the triple $\langle \|u \xrightarrow[NAX]{} t\|, size(u), \|u \xrightarrow[BAX]{} t'\| \rangle$ w.r.t. the lexicographic extension of > on $\mathbb{N}$ to and ordering on $\mathbb{N} \times \mathbb{N} \times \mathbb{N}$.

Case 1. u = t. Choose v = t and v' = t'.

Case 2. There are a term u_o, a NAX-reducible goal γ and a NAX-reduced goal γ' such that $u \xrightarrow[BAX]{} t' \Leftarrow \gamma'$,

(1) $\|u \xrightarrow[NAX]{} t\| = \|u \xrightarrow[NAX]{} u_o\| + \|u_o \xrightarrow[NAX]{} t\|$,
$\|u \xrightarrow[NAX]{} u_o \Leftarrow \gamma\| = 1$, $\|u \xrightarrow[NAX]{} u_o\| = 1 + \|\gamma \xrightarrow[NAX]{RD} \emptyset\|$.

Suppose that $\langle u_o, t' \rangle$ is strongly NAX-convergent modulo BAX, i.e. there are terms v_o, v_1 with

$$u_o \xrightarrow[NAX]{} v_o$$
(*) $$\Downarrow BAX$$
$$t' \xrightarrow[NAX]{} v_1.$$

By (1), (*) and strong confluence of NAX, we obtain $t \xrightarrow[NAX]{} v$ and

(2) $$\|v_o \xrightarrow[NAX]{} v\| \leq \|u_o \xrightarrow[NAX]{} t\|$$

for some v. By (1) and (3), $\|v_o \xrightarrow[NAX]{} v\| < \|u \xrightarrow[NAX]{} t\|$. Hence by (*) and induction hypothesis, $\langle v, v_1 \rangle$ and thus $\langle t, t' \rangle$ are strongly NAX-convergent modulo BAX. It remains for us to show (*).

Case 1. There are $t_0 \equiv t_1 \Leftarrow \vartheta \in$ NAX and a (ground) substitution f such that $t_0[f] = u$, $t_1[f] = u_0$ and $\vartheta[f] = \gamma$. Given two terms v,v' with

$$\|v \xrightarrow[NAX]{} v'\| \leq \|\gamma \vdash\xrightarrow[NAX]{RD} \vartheta\|,$$

(1) implies

(3) $\qquad \|v \xrightarrow[NAX]{} v'\| < 1 + \|\gamma \vdash\xrightarrow[NAX]{RD} \vartheta\| = \|u \xrightarrow[NAX]{} u_0\| \leq \|u \xrightarrow[NAX]{} t\|.$

We have two subcases:

Case 1.1. $u \xrightarrow[BAX]{} t' \Leftarrow \gamma'$ affects t_0. Since $u \xrightarrow[BAX]{} t' \Leftarrow \gamma'$ is obtained by at least one application of the Fully Parallel Reduction Rule (cf. Section 9.2), $u \xrightarrow[BAX]{} t' \Leftarrow \gamma'$ is t_0-overlapping. Thus $\langle u_0 \Leftarrow \gamma, t' \Leftarrow \gamma' \rangle$ is a critical pair of $\xrightarrow[BAX]{}$ into NAX. By (3) and the induction hypothesis, if $\|v \xrightarrow[NAX]{} v'\| \leq \|\gamma \vdash\xrightarrow[NAX]{RD} \vartheta\|$ and $v \xrightarrow[BAX]{} v''$, then $\langle v', v'' \rangle$ is strongly NAX-convergent modulo BAX. Since γ is NAX-reducible and γ' is NAX-reduced, Lemma 9.4.6 (2) implies (*).

Case 1.2. $u \xrightarrow[BAX]{} t' \Leftarrow \gamma'$ does not affect t_0. By (3) and the induction hypothesis, if $\|v \xrightarrow[NAX]{} v'\| \leq \|\gamma \vdash\xrightarrow[NAX]{RD} \vartheta\|$ and $v \xrightarrow[BAX]{} v''$, then $\langle v', v'' \rangle$ is strongly NAX-convergent modulo BAX. Since $u = t_0[f]$, t_0 is linear, $u_0 = t_1[f]$, $\gamma = \vartheta[f]$ is NAX-reducible and γ' is NAX-reduced, (*) follows from Lemma 9.3.2 (3).

Case 2. There are $t_0 \equiv t_1 \Leftarrow \vartheta \in$ BAX, (ground) substitutions f,g and a goal δ such that $f \xrightarrow[BAX]{} g \Leftarrow \delta$, $t_0[f] = u$, $t_1[g] = t'$ and $\vartheta[f] \cup \delta = \gamma'$. Since $t_0[f] \xrightarrow[NAX]{} u_0$ and t_0 is linear, Lemma 9.3.3 implies $\|f \xrightarrow[NAX]{} h\| = \|t_0[f] \xrightarrow[NAX]{} t_0[h]\|$ and $t_0[h] = u_0$ for some h. Hence by (1),

$$\|f \xrightarrow[NAX]{} h\| = \|u \xrightarrow[NAX]{} u_0\| \leq \|u \xrightarrow[NAX]{} t\|.$$

For all $x \in var(t_0)$, fx is a subterm of $u = t_0[f]$ and thus size(fx) $\leq$ size(u). Moreover, $\|f \xrightarrow[BAX]{} g \Leftarrow \delta\| < \|u \xrightarrow[BAX]{} t' \Leftarrow \gamma'\|$. Hence fx is smaller than u w.r.t. the induction ordering of this proof (see above). Thus by the induction hypothesis, $\langle hx, gx \rangle$ is strongly NAX-convergent modulo BAX, and (*) follows from (the last statement of) Lemma 9.3.3.

Case 3. $u = \sigma \langle t_1,...,t_n \rangle$, $u_0 = \sigma \langle u_1,...,u_n \rangle$, $t' = \sigma \langle v_1,...,v_n \rangle$ and for all $1 \leq i \leq n$

$$\|t_i \xrightarrow[NAX]{} u_i\| \leq \|u \xrightarrow[NAX]{} u_0\| \quad \text{and} \quad t_i \xrightarrow[BAX]{} v_i.$$

Since size(t_i) < size(u), the induction hypothesis implies

$$u_i \xrightarrow{\mathit{NAX}} t_i'$$
$$\Downarrow \mathit{BAX}$$
$$v_i \xrightarrow{\mathit{NAX}} t_i''$$

for some t_i' and t_i''. Hence

$$u_0 \xrightarrow{\mathit{NAX}} \sigma\langle t_1',\ldots,t_n'\rangle$$
$$\Downarrow \mathit{BAX}$$
$$t' \xrightarrow{\mathit{NAX}} \sigma\langle t_1'',\ldots,t_n''\rangle. \blacksquare$$

9.9 An Algorithm for Church-Rosser Proofs

In summary, we have established three Church-Rosser criteria.

Theorem 9.9.1 *~NAX-Church-Rosser criterion*
Suppose that
- CE(BAX) is linear and has no isolated variables,
- CE(BAX) is variable-preserving or NAX consists of unconditional equations,
- BAX is empty or NAX satisfies the Definition Principle,
- AX preserves (ground) ~NAX-normalizability,
- the ~NAX-reduction relation is Noetherian (on ground terms),
- all feasible most general critical pairs of $\xrightarrow{\mathit{\sim NAX}}$ into NAX are (ground) ~NAX-convergent modulo ~BAX.

Then <SIG,AX> is (ground) ~NAX-Church-Rosser, i.e. all (ground) ~NAX-normalizable <SIG,AX>-theorems are ~NAX-reducible.

Proof. Theorems 7.8.2 and 9.7.4. $\blacksquare$

Theorem 9.9.2 *Weak NAX-Church-Rosser criterion*
Suppose that
- NAX is left-linear,
- BAX is empty or NAX satisfies the Definition Principle,
- AX preserves (ground) NAX-normalizability,
- BAX weakly respects (ground) NAX-normal forms,
- the NAX-reduction relation is Noetherian (on ground terms),
- all feasible most general critical pairs of $\xrightarrow{\mathit{NAX}}$ into NAX are (ground) NAX-convergent,
- all feasible most general critical pairs of $\xrightarrow{\mathit{BAX}}$ into NAX are weakly (ground) NAX-convergent modulo BAX.

Then <SIG,AX> is (ground) NAX-Church-Rosser, i.e. all (ground) NAX-normalizeable <SIG,AX>-theorems are NAX-reducible.

Proof. Theorems 7.8.2, 9.5.1, 9.8.1 and Lemma 9.2.1. $\blacksquare$

Theorem 9.9.3 *Strong NAX-Church-Rosser criterion*
Suppose that
- CE(BAX) is linear,
- NAX is left-linear,
- BAX is empty or NAX satisfies the Definition Principle,
- AX preserves (ground) NAX-normalizability,
- BAX weakly respects (ground) NAX-normal forms,
- all feasible critical pairs of $\xrightarrow[NAX]{}$ into NAX are strongly NAX-convergent,
- all feasible most general critical pairs of $\xrightarrow[BAX]{}$ into NAX are strongly (ground) NAX-convergent modulo BAX.

Then <SIG,AX> is (ground) NAX-Church-Rosser, i.e. all (ground) NAX-normalizeable <SIG,AX>-theorems are NAX-reducible.

Proof. Theorems 7.8.2, 9.6.1, 9.8.2 and Lemma 9.2.1. ■

Provided that one of the above criteria is applicable to <SIG,AX>, the following algorithm orders the assumptions of Theorems 9.9.1-9.9.3 in a way that avoids backtracking as far as possible. It changes between *states* such that the particular actual state represents the set of those criteria which might still be applicable. For instance, the state 23 indicates a point during the check of assumptions where Theorems 9.9.2 and 9.9.3 might still be applicable, while some condition of Theorem 9.9.1 has already been disproved. The following states suffice:

123	:	Theorems 9.9.1, 9.9.2 or 9.9.3 might be applicable.
23	:	Only Theorems 9.9.2 or 9.9.3 might be applicable.
2	:	Only Theorem 9.9.2 might be applicable.
3	:	Only Theorem 9.9.3 might be applicable.
∅	:	No criterion is applicable.
CR	:	<SIG,AX> is NAX-Church-Rosser.
~CR	:	<SIG,AX> is ~NAX-Church-Rosser.

CR-ALG: an algorithm for Church-Rosser proofs

```
begin  state ← 123;
       if CE(BAX) has isolated variables then state ← 23 fi;
       if state = 123
          then if CE(BAX) is not variable-preserving
                  and for some u≡u'⇐𝛿 ∈ NAX, 𝛿 is non-empty
                  then state ← 23 fi fi;
```

```
          if state = 123
            then if CE(BAX) is not linear then state ← 2 fi fi;
          if state = 23 or state = 2
            then if NAX is not left-linear then state ← ∅ fi fi;
          if BAX is non-empty and NAX does not satisfy the Definition
            Principle
            then state ← ∅ fi;
          if state = 123
            then if AX does not preserve (ground) ~NAX-normalizability
                    and NAX is not left-linear
                 then state ← ∅ fi fi;
RETURN:   if state = 23 or state = 2
            then if AX does not preserve (ground) NAX-normalizability
                 then state ← ∅ fi fi;
          if state = 23 or state = 2
            then if BAX does not weakly respect (ground) NAX-normal forms
                 then state ← ∅ fi fi;
          if state = 123
            then if the ~NAX-reduction relation is not Noetherian (on ground
                    terms)
                 then if NAX is not left-linear
                         then state ← ∅
                         else goto RETURN fi fi fi;
          if state = 23 or state = 2
            then if the NAX-reduction relation is not Noetherian (on ground
                    terms)
                 then if state = 23
                         then state ← 3
                         else state ← ∅ fi fi fi;
          if state = 123
            then if all feasible most general critical pairs of $\xrightarrow[\sim NAX]{}$ into
                    NAX are (ground) ~NAX-convergent
                 then state ← ~CR
                 else goto RETURN fi fi;
          if state = 23 or state = 3
            then if CE(BAX) is linear, all feasible critical pairs of $\xrightarrow[NAX]{}$ into
                    NAX are strongly NAX-convergent and all feasible most
                    general critical pairs of $\xrightarrow[BAX]{}$ into NAX are strongly
                    (ground) NAX-convergent modulo BAX
                 then state ← CR
                 else if state = 3 then state ← ∅ fi fi;
```

```
              if state = 2
                then if all feasible most general critical pairs of ⟶_{NAX} into NAX
                           are (ground) NAX-convergent and all feasible most
                           general critical pairs of ⟷_{BAX} into NAX are weakly
                           (ground) NAX-convergent modulo BAX
                      then state ← CR
                      else state ← ∅ fi fi
    end
```

Theorems 9.9.1-9.9.3 immediately yield

Theorem 9.9.4 *Correctness of CR-ALG*
Given a specification <SIG,AX> with base specification <BSIG,BAX>, CR-ALG terminates and,
- if the final state is CR, then <SIG,AX> is (ground) NAX-Church-Rosser,
- if the final state is ~CR, then <SIG,AX> is (ground) ~NAX-Church-Rosser,
- if the final state is ∅, then none of Theorems 9.9.1-9.9.3 is applicable to <SIG,AX> and <BSIG,BAX>. ∎

CR-ALG leads us to a synopsis of all Church-Rosser conditions presented in Chapters 7 and 9:

(1) Base equations do not have isolated variables (cf. Section 7.8).
(2) Base equations are variable-preserving (cf. Section 7.7).
(3) Base equations are linear (cf. Section 7.8).
(4) Non-base equations are left-linear (cf. Section 7.8).
(5) Non-base equations satisfy the Definition Principle (cf. Section 7.8).
(6) All axioms preserve normalizability (cf. Section 7.8).
(7) Base equations weakly respect normal forms (cf. Section 9.2).
(8) Reduction relations are Noetherian (cf. Section 9.4).
(9) Critical pairs are convergent (cf. Section 9.4).

Some remarks on these conditions are still necessary.

(1) Base equations do not have isolated variables.

Lemma 7.8.1 demands (1). For the Congruence Class Approach, this lemma states that each ~NAX-reducible instance $\gamma[f]$ of a base goal γ admits a reduction $f \xrightarrow{=}_{NAX} g$ such that $\gamma[g]$ is ~NAX-reduced. The proof rests on the assumption that ~NAX-redices of $\gamma[f]$ do not overlap γ. Of course, the left-hand side of a *base* equation u≡u' might overlap γ in $\gamma[f]$, i.e. u = t[f] for some proper subterm t of γ. If u' were a variable, say x, then there is the reduction

$t[f] \xRightarrow{\sim BAX} fx$. If, moreover, $fx \xRightarrow{\sim NAX} v$ for some v, then $t[f] \xRightarrow{\sim NAX} v$, i.e. $t[f]$ would be a ~NAX-redex that overlaps γ, and it cannot be ensured that all ~NAX-reducts of $\gamma[f]$ are still instances of γ.

For instance, the Boolean law $x \wedge true \equiv x$ violates (1). Hence we must not attach this axiom to the *base* specification.

(2) Base equations are variable-preserving.

This condition is required in Case 2.2 of the proof that $\vdash^{RD}_{\sim NAX}$ commutes with ~BAX (cf. Lemma 9.7.1). Given a base reduction $t_o[f] \xRightarrow{\sim BAX} t_1[f]$, $x \in var(t_o)$, a conditional reduction $fx \xRightarrow{\sim NAX} u' \Leftarrow \gamma$ and $P\langle u_1,...,u_n\rangle \in \gamma$, we have $t_o[f] \vdash^{RD}_{\sim NAX} u_i$ for all $1 \le i \le n$. It must be guaranteed that $t_1[f] \vdash^{RD}_{\sim NAX} u_i$ holds true as well. Therefore x must occur in t_1 as well. Note that this case can happen only if γ is non-empty. Hence (2) needs to hold only if there are NAX-axioms with a non-empty premise.

For example, axiom (A1) of STORE (cf. Section 3.4) violates (2):

$$s[x \leftarrow m][x \leftarrow n] \equiv s[x \leftarrow n].$$

(3) Base equations are linear.

(3) can be traced back to Lemmata 9.2.2 (1) and 9.3.3. In both statements, one considers (among other things) a base axiom $u \equiv u' \Leftarrow \delta$ and a reduction of the form $u[f] \rightarrow t$ the redex of which does not overlap u. Linearity of u is crucial for obtaining t as an instance of u by, say, g such that $f \rightarrow g$. If u contained two occurrences of the same variable, say x, then the two occurrences of fx in $u[f]$ might have different reducts in t and t would not be an instance of u.

Axiom (A1) of STORE (see above) also violates (3). However, the axiom can be changed into a linear one:

$$s[x \leftarrow m][y \leftarrow n] \equiv s[x \leftarrow n] \Leftarrow x \equiv y.$$

(4) Non-base equations are left-linear.

This assumption is needed in Lemmata 9.3.1 and 9.3.2 (3), which, in turn, refer to Lemma 9.2.2 (1). Thus (4) is justified in the same way as (3).

In Examples 9.4.7 and 9.4.8, we have turned the non-left-linear equations (A3) of ACCESS-FUN (cf. Section 3.4) and (A3) of FINSET-REMOVE (cf. Section 3.10) into left-linear ones:

$$s[x \leftarrow n][y] \equiv n \quad \Leftarrow \quad x \equiv y$$
$$\text{remove } m \text{ (insert } n \text{ s)} \equiv \text{remove } m \text{ s} \quad \Leftarrow \quad m \equiv n.$$

In both examples, NAX is normalizing. But in general, the introduction of new premises might conflict with the requirement that all axioms preserve normalizability (cf. (6)).

(5) Non-base equations satisfy the Definition Principle.

This property is referred to in Lemmata 7.8.1, 9.3.3, 9.7.1 and 9.7.3. The reason for this is always to prevent base terms from being overlapped by the left-hand side of a NAX-axiom. The Definition Principle forbids NAX-equations that consist of base functions (which should be base axioms) as well as axioms of the form $t[\sigma u/x] \equiv t'$ where σ is a non-base operation, while t is a base term that contains (but is not equal to) the variable x. If such an equation contributes to the definition of σ, it expresses the fact that the *value of σ at u* depends on the context of σu, which is here the term t. Without going into a formal elaboration, we claim that this meaning can also be accomplished by keeping to the Definition Principle and using appropriate auxiliary functions. The specification of 2-3 trees (cf. Section 3.13) justifies this conjecture.

Moreover, the Definition Principle makes it easier to implement the Reduction Rule because only non-base operations must be taken into account as possible NAX-reduction redices. This applies to ~NAX-reduction as well, provided that base equations do not have isolated variables (cf. (1)).

(6) All axioms preserve normalizability.

The general Church-Rosser criterion Theorem 7.8.2 demands this condition. Given a derivable as well as normalizable goal γ, the proof of this theorem proceeds by induction on a shortest paramodulating expansion of $\langle \gamma, id \rangle$ to $\langle \emptyset, id \rangle$. The first step of this expansion from $\langle \gamma, id \rangle$ to, say, $\langle \delta, id \rangle$, creates an instance of an axiom premise, say ϑ, as part of δ. To apply the induction hypothesis we must ensure that ϑ is normalizable.

If NAX (or ~NAX) is normalizing, then, of course, AX preserves normalizeability. Otherwise, the axioms must be checked individually. For instance, the stream language interpreter (cf. Section 3.15) confronts us with the axiom

(∗) $\qquad\qquad\qquad t \equiv t' \quad \Leftarrow \quad n \not\equiv 0$

where

and
$$t = (\text{evalAgent s (if (val n) is zero then a else a'))}$$
$$t' = (\text{evalAgent s a'})$$

Given a substitution f such that AXuEAX ⊢ fn≠0, we have to show that fn≠0 is normalizable if t[f] or t'[f] is normalizable.

A close look at the axioms of EVAL-AGENT (cf. Section 3.15) reveals that each reduction $t[f]\xrightarrow{NAX} u$ into a normal form u can be split into reductions $t[f]\xrightarrow{NAX} t[g]$, $t[g]\xrightarrow{NAX} t'[g]$ and $t'[g]\xrightarrow{NAX} u$, where the first does not affect t, i.e. we actually have $f\xrightarrow{NAX} g$, and the second is an application of (∗), i.e. the corresponding premise instance gn≠0 is NAX-reducible. Hence fn≠0 is normalizable.

If, on the other hand, only t'[f] is normalizable, we cannot infer that fn≠0 is normalizable, too, because n does not occur in t'. For instance, let fn be the term

$$(\text{head (evalAgent s (let x be call x)))}|.$$

fn is not normalizable, although fn≠0 is derivable via the axioms

$$0 < n|$$
$$m \neq n \Leftarrow n < m$$

of NAT. A solution to this problem might be drawn from the trick employed in Section 6.3 to make clauses base-representable. We introduce a *definedness predicate* **Def** for *nat*-terms, provide for *partial completeness* (with respect to normalizability: whenever AXuEAX ⊢ (**Def** v), then v must have a normal form) and replace (∗) by

(∗∗) $\quad\quad\quad t \equiv t' \Leftarrow n \neq 0, \text{Def } n.$

Partial completeness would guarantee that each derivable instance of the premise of (∗∗) is normalizable.

(7) **Base equations weakly respect normal forms.**

Lemmata 9.2.1, 9.3.2 (3) and 9.4.6 assume this property. It can often be verified using the following condition which handles each base equation separately.

Definition A set CE of conditional equations *locally respects (ground) NAX-normal forms* if for all u≡u'⇐ϑ ∈ CE the following conditions hold true:

(7.1) For all terms t, x ∈ single(t) and (ground) substitutions f, if t[u/x][f] is NAX-irreducible and ϑ[f] is NAX-reduced, then for all w < occ(x,t), label(w,t) ∈ BOP (cf. Section 8.4).

(7.2) For all z ∈ var(u')-var(u) and (ground) substitutions f, fz is NAX-normalizable. ∎

Proposition 9.9.5 BAX weakly respects (ground) NAX-normal forms if
- CE(BAX) locally respects (ground) NAX-normal forms,
- NAX satisfies the Definition Principle.

Proof. Let t be a (ground) NAX-normal form and $t \Rrightarrow_{BAX} t'$. By induction on $\|t \Rrightarrow_{BAX} t'\|$, we establish a normal form t" with $t' \Rrightarrow_{NAX} t"$ and $t \Rrightarrow_{BAX} t"$.

If $t \Rrightarrow_{BAX} t'$ is generated by a single equation, say u≡u', and var(u')-var(u) consists of a single variable z, then the relationship between t, t' and t" can be sketched as follows.

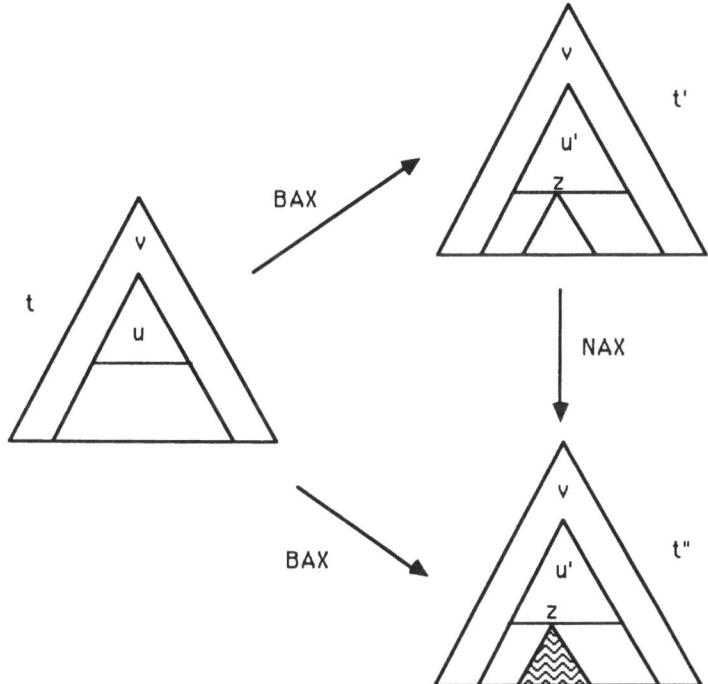

If t = t', the proof is complete with t" = t. Otherwise there are a term v, x ∈ single(v)*, (ground) substitutions f,g, a goal γ, u = ⟨u_1,...,u_n⟩, u' = ⟨u_1',...,u_n'⟩ and $\vartheta = \vartheta_1 \cup ... \cup \vartheta_n$ such that $u_1 \equiv u_1' \Leftarrow \vartheta_1, ..., u_n \equiv u_n' \Leftarrow \vartheta_n$ ∈ BAX,

$$\|f \Rrightarrow_{BAX} g \Leftarrow \gamma\| < \|t \Rrightarrow_{BAX} t' \Leftarrow \vartheta[f]u\gamma\|,$$

t = v[u[f]/x] and t' = v[u'[g]/x] and ϑ[f]uγ is NAX-reduced. Hence for all x ∈

var(u), fx is irreducible. By the induction hypothesis, $gz \xRightarrow{NAX} hz$ and $fz \xRightarrow{BAX} hz$ for some irreducible h and all $z \in var(u)$. By (7.2), $gz \xRightarrow{NAX} h'z$ for some irreducible h' and all $z \in var(u')-var(u)$.

Let $h'' = h\restriction var(u) + h'\restriction(var(u')-var(u))$ and $t'' = v[u'[h'']/x]$. Hence $t' \xRightarrow{NAX} t''$ and $t \xRightarrow{BAX} t''$. Since h" is irreducible and NAX satisfies the Definition Principle, u'[h"] is a normal form.

Let $x = \langle x_1,...,x_n \rangle$. By (7.1), for all $1 \le i \le n$ and $w < occ(x_i,v)$, $label(w,v)$ is a base function. Since u'[h"] is irreducible and NAX satisfies the Definition Principle, we conclude that $t'' = v[u'[h'']/x]$ is a normal form. ∎

As an example, consider the base equations of FINSET (cf. Section 3.10):

(BAX1)   insert m (insert m s) ≡ insert m s
(BAX2)   insert m (insert n s) ≡ insert n (insert m s)

They locally respect ground NAX-normal forms where NAX consists of

(NAX1)   remove m ∅ ≡ ∅
(NAX2)   remove m (insert m s) ≡ remove m s
(NAX3)   remove m (insert n s) ≡ insert n (remove m s)   ⇐ m ≠ n.

Since NAX is ground term reducing (cf. Section 8.4), all ground NAX-normal forms are base terms and thus satisfy (7.1). (7.2) holds true trivially because CE(BAX) is variable-preserving. Since NAX satisfies the Definition Principle, Proposition 9.9.5 implies that BAX weakly respects ground NAX-normal forms.

ACCESS-FUN with STORE as base specification (cf. Section 3.4) is neither ground term reducing nor variable-preserving. Nevertheless the base axioms

(BAX3)   s[x←m][x←n] ≡ s[x←n]
(BAX4)   s[x←m][y←n] ≡ s[y←n][x←m]   ⇐ x ≠ y

locally respect ground NAX-normal forms where NAX consists of

(NAX4)   s[x←n][x] ≡ n
(NAX5)   s[x←n][y] ≡ s[y]   ⇐ x ≠ y.

It is easy to see that each ground NAX-normal form can be written as t[f] such that t is a base term and for all $x \in var(t)$, $fx = \omega[v]$ for some term v over $\{x0,\_|\}$. Since the left- and right-hand sides of BAX3 and BAX4 are instances of the term s[z←k], they cannot be subterms of fx. Hence (7.1) holds true, while (7.2) follows from the fact that NAX is normalizing.

(8) **Reduction relations are Noetherian.**

The Noetherian property of a reduction relation ensures the validity of induction arguments in the proofs of Theorems 9.5.1, 9.8.1 and Lemma 9.7.3. If $\vdash_{NAX}^{RD}$ is Noetherian and CE(BAX) consists of *permutative* equations such as (BAX2) and (BAX4), $\vdash_{NAX}^{RD}$ is Noetherian as well. If CE(BAX) is not variable-preserving, then $\vdash_{NAX}^{RD}$ is not Noetherian: reduction redices may be created just by instantiating those variables which occur only on one side of a base equation (like the variable m in (BAX3)).

A base equation that duplicates a variable may violate the Noetherian property of $\vdash_{NAX}^{RD}$ as well. For instance, (BAX1) generates the reduction

$$\text{remove m (insert m s)} \xrightarrow[BAX]{} \text{remove m (insert m (insert m s))}$$

and thus (NAX2) leads to the *reflexive* reduction

$$\text{remove m (insert m s)} \xrightarrow[NAX]{} \text{remove m (insert m s)}.$$

On the other hand, both FINSET-REMOVE and ACCESS-FUN have a Noetherian *NAX*-reduction relation: the generating set of $\vdash_{NAX}^{RD}$ can be embedded into the recursive path ordering that is induced by the function ordering ≥ given by

$$\text{remove} \geq \emptyset, \quad \text{remove} \geq \text{remove}, \quad \text{remove} \geq \text{insert}$$

and

$$\_[\_] \geq \_[\_],$$

respectively (cf. Section 9.4).

(9) **Critical pairs are convergent.**

With the help of Lemmata 9.4.4, 9.4.6 and Theorem 9.6.1 the confluence and compatibility assumptions of our general Church-Rosser criterion (Theorem 7.8.2) can be reduced to convergence properties of feasible critical pairs.

Example 9.9.6 Let <SIG,AX> be the left-linear version of ACCESS-FUN (cf. Example 9.4.7) or FINSET-REMOVE (cf. Example 9.4.8).

In both cases, NAX is normalizing and satisfies the Definition Principle. Hence AX preserves NAX-normalizability. Above we have shown that BAX weakly respects ground NAX-normal forms (cf. (7)). Furthermore, the NAX-reduction relation is Noetherian (cf. (8)).

All feasible most general critical pairs $\langle t \Leftarrow \gamma, t' \Leftarrow \gamma' \rangle$ of $\xrightarrow[NAX]{}$ into NAX are NAX-convergent because they are reflexive, i.e. $t \Leftarrow \gamma$ and $t' \Leftarrow \gamma'$ are identical (up to a renaming of variables). By Examples 9.4.7 and 9.4.8, all most general critical pairs of $\xrightarrow{BAX}$ into NAX are ground NAX-convergent modulo BAX. We thus conclude from Theorem 9.9.3 that <SIG,AX> is NAX-Church-Rosser. ∎

If no Church-Rosser criterion is applicable because some critical pair <t⇐γ,t'⇐γ'> is not convergent, one may try to *complete* NAX by reducing t and t' to NAX-normal forms u and u', adding either u≡u'⇐γuγ' or u'≡u⇐γuγ' to NAX and restarting CR-ALG. Existing completion procedures refine this process by a number of subtle improvements, which, however, are tailored to a single critical pair notion and a single convergence property. CR-ALG takes into account a variety of such notions and properties in order to meet different requirements. Hence it should be embedded into a *generic* completion procedure, which can be actualized by different Church-Rosser criteria. Describing completion by inference rules seems to be a promising step towards a generic completion procedure (see Bachmair et al.).

In the remarks following Theorem 9.5.1, we have turned this confluence criterion into a set of sufficent conditions for the inductive validity of conditional equations. In the same way, Theorems 9.9.1, 9.9.2 and 9.9.3 give rise to corresponding inductive theory criteria.

Corollary 9.9.7 *Inductive theory criterion based on the ~NAX-Church-Rosser criterion*

Let CAX be a set of conditional equations and AX' = NAX∪CAX. Suppose that
- CE(BAX) is linear, variable-preserving and has no isolated variables,
- AX' satisfies the Definition Principle or
  BAX is empty and for all u≡u'⇐δ ∈ AX', u is not a base term,
- AX∪CAX preserves ground ~AX'-normalizability,
- the ~AX'-reduction relation is Noetherian on ground terms,
- all feasible most general critical pairs of $\xrightarrow{AX'}$ into AX' are ground ~AX'-convergent modulo ~BAX.

Then CAX is a partial inductive <SIG,AX>-theorem.

Proof. Lemma 7.7.8 (2) and Theorem 9.9.1. ∎

Corollary 9.9.8 *Inductive theory criterion based on the Weak NAX-Church-Rosser criterion*

Let CAX be a set of conditional equations and AX' = NAX∪CAX. Suppose that
- AX' is left-linear,
- AX' satisfies the Definition Principle or
  BAX is empty and for all u≡u'⇐δ ∈ AX', u is not a base term,
- AX∪CAX preserves ground AX'-normalizability,
- BAX weakly respects ground AX'-normal forms,

- the AX'-reduction relation is Noetherian on ground terms,
- all feasible most general critical pairs of $\xrightarrow[AX']{}$ into AX' are ground AX'-convergent,
- all feasible most general critical pairs of $\xrightarrow[BAX]{}$ into AX' are weakly ground AX'-convergent modulo BAX.

Then CAX is a partial inductive <SIG,AX>-theorem.

Proof. Lemma 7.7.8 (2) and Theorem 9.9.2. ∎

Corollary 9.9.9 *Inductive theory criterion based on the Strong NAX-Church-Rosser criterion*

Let CAX be a set of conditional equations and AX' = NAX∪CAX. Suppose that
- CE(BAX) is linear,
- AX' is left-linear,
- AX' satisfies the Definition Principle or
  BAX is empty and for all u≡u'⇐δ ∈ AX', u is not a base term,
- AX∪CAX preserves ground AX'-normalizability,
- BAX weakly respects ground AX'-normal forms,
- all feasible critical pairs of $\xrightarrow[AX']{}$ into AX' are strongly AX'-convergent,
- all feasible most general critical pairs of $\xrightarrow[BAX]{}$ into AX' are strongly ground AX'-convergent modulo BAX.

Then CAX is a partial inductive <SIG,AX>-theorem.

Proof. Lemma 7.7.8 (2) and Theorem 9.9.3. ∎

A fourth criterion generalizes Corollary 9.5.5, which uses a *critical pair selector* for reducing the set of critical pairs to be checked for convergence. The generalization admits base axioms.

Corollary 9.9.10 *Inductive theory criterion based on a critical pair selector*

Let CAX be a set of conditional equations, AX' = NAX∪CAX and SEL be a critical pair selector for CAX. Suppose that
- AX' is left-linear,
- AX' satisfies the Definition Principle or
  BAX is empty and for all u≡u'⇐δ ∈ AX', u is not a base term,
- AX∪CAX preserves ground AX'-normalizability,
- BAX weakly respects ground AX'-normal forms,
- the AX'-reduction relation is Noetherian on ground terms,
- all feasible most general critical pairs of $\xrightarrow[NAX]{}$ into NAX are ground NAX-convergent,
- for all u≡u'⇐δ ∈ CAX and ground substitutions f, SEL(u,f) = t•v' implies that <u'[f],t[v'/x_o]> is AX'-convergent,

- for all $v \equiv v' \Leftarrow \delta \in NAX$ and $u \equiv u' \Leftarrow \delta' \in CAX$, if root(u) occurs in v, then root(u) = root(v),
- all feasible most general critical pairs of $\xrightarrow[CAX]{}$ into CAX are ground AX'-convergent,
- all feasible most general critical pairs of $\xrightarrow[BAX]{}$ into AX' are weakly ground AX'-convergent modulo BAX.

Then CAX is a partial inductive <SIG,AX>-theorem.

Proof. Lemmata 7.7.8 (2), 9.2.1 and Theorems 7.8.2, 9.5.1, 9.5.4, 9.8.1. ∎

Corollaries 9.9.7-9.9.10 provide the verification conditions for an *inductive-theorem prover*. If one follows the steps of CR-ALG, the construction is straightforward and thus left to the reader.

9.10 Bibliographic Notes

The notion of a critical pair is due to Buchberger and to Knuth and Bendix and goes along with *completion procedures* to transform equational specifications into Church-Rosser ones (cf. Section 9.9 (9)). Guided by a Noetherian term relation, equations are *oriented*, resulting critical pairs are turned into further axioms, and these steps are repeated until either a confluent set of axioms has been obtained or some equation cannot be oriented because neither orientation would respect the given term relation. The correctness of this procedure was shown by Huet [2], who also uses completion to prove an equation, say $t \equiv t'$, by alternating reduction steps starting out from t and t' with completion steps to enhance the chance that these reductions eventually converge. Completion as a proof method has also been studied by Paul, Dietrich and Bachmair et al. *Inductive completion procedures* extend this idea to the proof of inductive theorems (see Huet and Hullot; Kirchner; Jouannaud and Kounalis; Fribourg [3]). In the latter paper, Fribourg related *induction terms* to complete *NAX-superposition occurrences* and thus invented the concept of critical pair selectors (cf. Section 9.5).

Jouannaud and Kirchner adapted completion to the Congruence Class Approach. A completion procedure for sets of *conditional* equations was outlined by Kaplan [2], who pointed out that only *feasible* critical pairs must be taken into account (cf. Section 9.4). Jouannaud and Waldmann employ narrowing for feasibility proofs and refine Kaplan's procedure by alternating between completion and narrowing steps. Ganzinger equips specifications with *negative assertions* to support the proof that certain critical pairs are not feasible and thus can be removed from convergence checks. Moreover, he introduces *covering assertions,* which are used to derive covering formulas to conclude the convergence of a critical pair from a number of *conditional* reduction diagrams (cf. Section 9.4).

The Church-Rosser criteria developed in this chapter have emerged from confluence criteria for unconditional equations. Jouannaud's Theorem 4 was fundamental to our ~NAX-Church-Rosser criterion (Theorem 9.9.1). The weak NAX-Church-Rosser criterion (Theorem 9.9.2) can be traced back to Huet [1], Theorem 3.2, and Padawitz [2], Theorem 5.14. Fully parallel reductions and strong BAX-compatibility (cf. Section 9.2) are the essential notions for an alternative to the Congruence Class Approach. They were introduced in Padawitz [1,2] and are employed by both NAX-Church-Rosser criteria. Furthermore, the few results on non-terminating rewrite rule systems such as Rosen, Theorem 5.6, and Huet [1], Lemma 3.3, influenced the strong NAX-Church-Rosser criterion (Theorem 9.9.3). In Huet's lemma, NAX is supposed to be *parallel closed,* which just means that all critical pairs of $\overrightarrow{NAX}$ into NAX are strongly convergent (cf. Section 9.6).

References

We use the following abbreviations for proceedings and journals:

CAAP	Colloquium on Trees in Algebra and Programming
CADE	Conference on Automated Deduction
ESOP	European Symposium on Programming
EUROCAL	European Conference on Computer Algebra
ICALP	International Colloquium on Automata, Languages, and Programming
LNCS	Lecture Notes in Computer Science
RTA	Rewriting Techniques and Applications
TAPSOFT	Theory and Practice of Software Development
TOPLAS	Transactions on Programming Languages and Systems

K.R. Apt, M.H. van Emden, Contributions to the Logic of Programming, Journal ACM 29 (1982) 841-862

L. Bachmair, N. Dershowitz, J. Hsiang, Orderings for Equational Proofs, Proc. IEEE Symp. Logic in Computer Science (1986) 346-357

D.W. Barnes, J.M. Mack, An Algebraic Introduction to Mathematical Logic, Springer (1975)

G. Bateson, Mind and Nature: A Necessary Unity, Dutton (1979)

C. Beierle, A. Voß, Theory and Practice of Canonical Term Functors in Abstract Data Type Specifications, Proc. TAPSOFT '87, Springer LNCS 250 (1987) 320-334

J.L. Bell, A.B. Slomson, Models and Ultraproducts: An Introduction, North-Holland (1971)

J.A. Bergstra, J.W. Klop, Conditional Rewrite Rules: Confluence and Termination, Journal of Computer and System Sciences 32 (1986) 323-362

J.A. Bergstra, J.V. Tucker, A Characterization of Computable Data Types by Means of a Finite Equational Specification Method, Proc. 7th ICALP, Springer LNCS 85 (1980) 76-90

R.S. Bird, Using Circular Programs to Eliminate Multiple Traversals of Data, Acta Informatica 21 (1984) 239-250

G. Birkhoff, On the Structure of Abstract Algebras, Proc. Cambridge Philosophical Society 31 (1935) 433-454

D. Bohm, Wholeness and the Implicate Order, Routledge & Kegan Paul plc (1980)

R.S. Boyer, J.S. Moore, A Computational Logic, Academic Press (1979)

M. Broy, On Modularity in Programming, in: H. Zemanek, ed., A Quarter Century of IFIP, North-Holland (1986) 347-362

M. Broy, F.L. Bauer, A Systematic Approach to Language Constructs for Concurrent Programs, Science of Computer Programming 4 (1984) 103-139

M. Broy, C. Pair, M. Wirsing, A Systematic Study of Models of Abstract Data Types, Theoretical Computer Science 33 (1984) 139-174

M. Broy, M. Wirsing, Partial Abstract Types, Acta Informatica 18 (1982) 47-64

B. Buchberger, Basic Features and Development of the Critical-Pair/ Completion Procedure, Proc. RTA '85, Springer LNCS 202 (1985) 1-45

A. Bundy, The Computer Modelling of Mathematical Reasoning, Academic Press (1983)

H.-J. Bürckert, A. Herold, M. Schmidt-Schauß, On Equational Theories, Unification and Decidability, Proc. RTA '87, Springer LNCS 256 (1987) 204-215

R.M. Burstall, Inductively Defined Functions, Proc. TAPSOFT '85, Springer LNCS 185 (1985) 92-96

R.M. Burstall, J. Darlington, A Transformation System for Developing Recursive Programs, Journal ACM 24 (1977) 44-67

R.M. Burstall, J.A. Goguen, Putting Theories Together to Make Specifications, Proc. 5th IJCAI (1977) 1045-1058

C.-L. Chang, R.C.-T. Lee, Symbolic Logic and Mechanical Theorem Proving, Academic Press (1973)

K.L. Clark, Negation as Failure, in: H. Gallaire, J. Minker, eds., Logic and Data Bases, Plenum Press (1978) 293-322

W.F. Clocksin, C.S. Mellish, Programming in Prolog, 3rd edn., Springer (1987)

P.M. Cohn, Universal Algebra, D. Reidel Publishing Company (1981)

A. Colmerauer, Theoretical Model of Prolog II, in: M. v.Caneghem, D.H.D. Warren, eds., Logic Programming and its Applications, Ablex Publishing Corporation (1986) 3-31

N. Dershowitz [1], A Note on Simplification Orderings, Information Processing Letters 9 (1979) 212-215

N. Dershowitz [2], Orderings for Term-Rewriting Systems, Theoretical Computer Science 17 (1982) 279-301

N. Dershowitz [3], Termination of Rewriting, Journal of Symbolic Computation 3 (1987) 69-116

R. Dietrich, Relating Resolution and Algebraic Completion for Horn Logic, Proc. 8th CADE, Springer LNCS 230 (1986) 62-78

E.W. Dijkstra, Notes on Structured Programming, in: O.-J. Dahl, E. W. Dijkstra, C. A. R. Hoare, Structured Programming, Academic Press (1972) 1-82

H.C. Dreyfus, S.E. Dreyfus, Mind over Machine, The Free Press (1986)

R. Echahed, On Completeness of Narrowing Strategies, Proc. CAAP '88, Springer LNCS 299 (1988) 89-101

H.-D. Ehrich, On the Theory of Specification, Implementation and Parametrization of Abstract Data Types, Journal ACM 29 (1982) 206-227

H. Ehrig, B. Mahr, Foundations of Algebraic Specification 1: Equations and Initial Semantics, Springer (1985)

M. Fay, First Order Unification in an Equational Theory, Proc. 4th Workshop on Automated Deduction, Academic Press (1979) 161-167

S. Feferman, Theories of Finite Type Related to Mathematical Practice, in: J. Barwise, ed., Handbook of Mathematical Logic, North-Holland (1977) 913-972

C. Floyd, A Systematic Look at Prototyping, in: R. Budde et al., eds., Approaches to Prototyping, Springer (1984)

R.W. Floyd, Assigning Meanings to Programs, in: J. T. Schwartz, ed., Mathematical Aspects of Computer Science, American Mathematical Society (1967) 19-32

L. Fribourg [1], Handling Function Definitions through Innermost Superposition and Rewriting, Proc. RTA '85, Springer LNCS 202 (1985) 325-344

L. Fribourg [2], Prolog with Simplification, ESPRIT Report METEOR/t11/CGE/PWS, L.I.T.P. Paris (1986)

L. Fribourg [3], A Strong Restriction of the Inductive Completion Procedure, Proc. ICALP '86, Springer LNCS 226 (1986) 105-115

U. Furbach, S. Hölldobler, Modelling the Combination of Functional and Logic Programming Languages, Journal of Symbolic Computation 2 (1986) 123-138

U. Furbach, S. Hölldobler, J. Schreiber, Horn Equality Theories and Paramodulation, Report No. 8801, Fakultät Informatik, UniBw München (1988)

J.H. Gallier, W. Snyder, A General Complete E-unification Procedure, Proc. RTA '87, Springer LNCS 256 (1987) 216-227

H. Ganzinger, Ground Term Confluence in Parametric Conditional Equational Specifications, Proc. STACS '87, Springer LNCS 247 (1987) 286-298

G. Gentzen, Untersuchungen über das logische Schließen, Math. Zeitschr. 39 (1934) 176-210, 405-431

A. Geser, H. Hußmann, Experiences with the RAP System - A Specification Interpreter Combining Term Rewriting and Resolution, Proc. ESOP '86, Springer LNCS 213 (1986) 339-350

V. Giarratana, F. Gimona, U. Montanari, Observability Concepts in Abstract Data Type Specifications, Proc. MFCS '76, Springer LNCS 45 (1976) 576-587

R. Göbel, Ground Confluence, Proc. RTA '87, Springer LNCS 256 (1987) 156-167

J.A. Goguen [1], How to Prove Inductive Hypotheses Without Induction, Proc. 5th CADE, Springer LNCS 87 (1980) 356-373

J.A. Goguen [2], One, None, A Hundred Thousand Specification Languages, Proc. Information Processing '86, North-Holland (1986) 995-1003

J.A. Goguen, J. Meseguer [1], Completeness of Many-sorted Equational Logic, Houston Journal of Mathematics 11 (1985) 307-334

J.A. Goguen, J. Meseguer [2], Remarks on Remarks on Many-Sorted Equational Logic, EATCS Bulletin 30 (1986) 66-73

J.A. Goguen, J. Meseguer [3], Eqlog: Equality, Types, and Generic Modules for Logic Programming, in: D. DeGroot, G. Lindstrom, Logic Programming: Functions, Relations, and Equations, Prentice-Hall (1986) 295-363

J.A. Goguen, J. Meseguer [4], Order-Sorted Algebra I: Partial and Overloaded Operations, Errors and Inheritance, Report, SRI International (1987)

J.A. Goguen, J. Meseguer [5], An Initiality Primer, Report, SRI International (1983)

J.A. Goguen, J.W. Thatcher, E.G. Wagner, An Initial Algebra Approach to the Specification, Correctness and Implementation of Abstract Data Types, in: R. Yeh, ed., Current Trends in Programming Methodology, Vol. 4, Prentice-Hall (1978) 80-149

J.V. Guttag, The Specification and Application to Programming of Abstract Data Types, Ph.D. Thesis, University of Toronto (1975)

J.V. Guttag, J.J. Horning, The Algebraic Specification of Abstract Data Types, Acta Informatica 10 (1978) 27-52

R. Hill, LUSH-Resolution and Its Completeness, DCL Memo 78, Dept. of Artificial Intelligence, University of Edinburgh (1974)

C.A.R. Hoare [1], An Axiomatic Basis for Computer Programming, Communications ACM 12 (1969) 576-580

C.A.R. Hoare [2], Proof of Correctness of Data Representations, Acta Informatica 1 (1972) 271-281

C.M. Hoffmann, M.J. O'Donnell, Programming with Equations, ACM TOPLAS 4 (1982) 83-112

S. Hölldobler, A Unification Algorithm for Confluent Theories, Proc. ICALP '87, Springer LNCS 267 (1987) 31-41

G. Huet [1], Confluent Reductions: Abstract Properties and Applications to Term Rewriting Systems, Journal ACM 27 (1980) 797-821

G. Huet [2], A Complete Proof of Correctness of the Knuth-Bendix Completion Algorithm, Journal of Computer and System Sciences 23 (1981) 11-21

G. Huet, J.M. Hullot, Proofs by Induction in Equational Theories with Constructors, Journal of Computer and System Sciences 25 (1982) 239-266

G. Huet, D.C. Oppen, Equations and Rewrite Rules: A Survey, in R. V. Book, ed., Formal Language Theory: Perspectives and Open Problems, Academic Press (1980)

J.M. Hullot, Canonical Forms and Unification, Proc. 5th CADE, Springer LNCS 87 (1980) 318-334

H. Hußmann, Unification in Conditional-Equational Theories, 2nd edn., Report MIP-8504, Universität Passau (1986); previous version in: Proc. EUROCAL '85, Springer LNCS 204 (1985) 543-553

J. Jaffar, J.-L. Lassez, M.J. Maher, A Theory of Complete Logic Programs with Equality, Journal of Logic Programming 3 (1984) 211-223

A. Josephson, N. Dershowitz, An Implementation of Narrowing: The RITE Way, Report, University of Illinois at Urbana (1986)

J.-P. Jouannaud, Confluent and Coherent Equational Term Rewriting Systems and Application to Proofs in Abstract Data Types, Proc. CAAP '83, Springer LNCS 159 (1983) 269-283

J.-P. Jouannaud, E. Kounalis, Automatic Proofs by Induction in Equational Theories without Constructors, IEEE Symp. on Logic in Computer Science (1986) 358-366

J.-P. Jouannaud, C. Kirchner, H. Kirchner, Incremental Construction of Unification Algorithms in Equational Theories, Proc. ICALP '83, Springer LNCS 154 (1983) 361-373

J.-P. Jouannaud, H. Kirchner, Completion of a Set of Rules Modulo a Set of Equations, SIAM Journal Computing 15 (1986) 1155-1194

J-P. Jouannaud, M. Muñoz, Termination of a Set of Rules Modulo a Set of Equations, Proc. 7th CADE, Springer LNCS 170 (1984) 175-193

J-P. Jouannaud, B. Waldmann, Reductive Conditional Term Rewriting Systems, Proc. Conf. Formal Description of Programming Concepts III, North-Holland (1986) 223-244

S. Kamin, Final Data Type Specifications: A New Data Type Specification Method, ACM TOPLAS 5 (1983) 97-123

S. Kaplan [1], Conditional Rewrite Rules, Theoretical Computer Science 33 (1984) 175-194

S. Kaplan [2], Fair Conditional Term Rewriting Systems: Unification, Termination and Confluence, in: H.J. Kreowski, ed., Recent Trends in Data Type Specification, Springer Informatik-Fachberichte 116 (1985) 136-155

H. Kirchner, A General Inductive Completion Algorithm and Application to Abstract Data Types, Proc. 7th CADE, Springer LNCS 170 (1984) 282-302

H.A. Klaeren, A Constructive Method for Abstract Algebraic Software Specification, Theoretical Computer Science 30 (1984) 139-204

F. Kluzniak, S. Szpakowicz, Prolog for Programmers, Academic Press (1985)

D.E. Knuth, Semantics of Context-Free Languages, Mathematical Systems Theory 2 (1968) 127-145

D.E. Knuth, P.B. Bendix, Simple Word Problems in Universal Algebras, in: J. Leech, ed., Computational Problems in Abstract Algebra, Pergamon Press (1970) 263-297

W.A. Kornfeld, Equality for Prolog, in: D. DeGroot, G. Lindstrom, Logic Programming: Functions, Relations, and Equations, Prentice-Hall (1986) 279-293

R.A. Kowalski, Logic for Problem-Solving, North-Holland (1979)

R.A. Kowalski, D. Kuehner, Linear Resolution with Selection Function, Artificial Intelligence 2 (1971) 227-260

H.-J. Kreowski, Partial Algebras flow from Algebraic Specifications, Proc. ICALP '87, Springer LNCS 267 (1987) 521-530

J.B. Kruskal, Well-quasi-ordering, the Tree Theorem and Vaszonyi's Conjecture, Transactions AMS 95 (1960) 210-225

W. Küchlin, A Confluence Criterion Based on the Generalized Newman Lemma, Proc. EUROCAL '85, Springer LNCS 204 (1985) 390-399

D.S. Lankford, Canonical Inference, Report ATP-32, University of Texas at Austin (1975)

D.S. Lankford, A.M. Ballantyne, Decision Procedures for Simple Equational Theories with Permutative Axioms: Complete Sets of Permutative Reductions, Report ATP-37, University of Texas at Austin (1977)

J.-L. Lassez, V.L. Nguyen, E.A. Sonenberg, Fixed Point Theorems and Semantics: A Folk Tale, Information Processing Letters 14 (1982) 112-116

G. Levi, Logic Programming: The Foundations, the Approach and the Role of Concurrency, in: J. W. de Bakker, W.-P. de Roever, G. Rozenberg, eds., Current Trends in Concurrency, Springer LNCS 224 (1986) 396-441

B. Liskov, S. Zilles, Programming with Abstract Data Types, SIGPLAN Notices 9 (1974) 55-59

J. W. Lloyd, Foundations of Logic Programming, Springer (1985)

B. Mahr, J.A. Makowsky, Characterizing Specification Languages Which Admit Initial Semantics, Theoretical Computer Science 31 (1984) 49-59

Y. Malachi, Z. Manna, R. Waldinger, Tablog: A New Approach to Logic Programming, in: D. DeGroot, G. Lindstrom, Logic Programming: Functions, Relations, and Equations, Prentice-Hall (1986) 365-394

Z. Manna, Mathematical Theory of Computation, McGraw-Hill (1974)

Z. Manna, J. Vuillemin, Fixpoint Approach to the Theory of Computation, Communications ACM 15 (1972) 528-536

A. Martelli, C. Moiso, G.F. Rossi, An Algorithm for Unification in Equational Theories, Proc. IEEE Symp. on Logic Programming (1986) 180-186

A. Martelli, U. Montanari, An Efficient Unification Algorithm, ACM TOPLAS 4 (1982) 258-282

J. Meseguer, J.A. Goguen, Initiality, Induction and Computability, in: M. Nivat, J. Reynolds, eds., Algebraic Methods in Semantics, Cambridge University Press (1985) 459-541

D.L. Musser, On Proving Inductive Properties of Abstract Data Types, Proc. ACM Principles of Programming Languages (1980) 154-162

P. Naur [1], Formalization in Program Development, BIT 22 (1982) 437-453

P. Naur [2], Programming as Theory Building, Microprocessing 15 (1985) 253-261

M. Navarro, F. Orejas, Parameterized Horn Clause Specifications: Proof Theory and Correctness, Proc. TAPSOFT '87, Springer LNCS 249 (1987) 202-216

N.J. Nilsson, Principles of Artificial Intelligence, Tioga Pub. Co. (1980) and Springer (1982)

T. Nipkow, G. Weikum, A Decidability Result About Sufficient Completeness of Axiomatically Specified Abstract Data Types, Proc. 6th GI-Conf. on Theoretical Computer Science, Springer LNCS 145 (1983) 257-268

M. Nivat, On the Interpretation of Recursive Polyadic Program Schemes, Symposia Mathematica 15, Academic Press (1975) 255-281

F. Nourani, On Induction for Programming Logic: Syntax, Semantics and Inductive Closure, EATCS Bulletin 13 (1981) 51-64

M.J. O'Donnell [1], Computing in Systems Described by Equations, Springer LNCS 58 (1977)

M.J. O'Donnell [2], Equational Logic as a Programming Language, The MIT Press (1985)

P. Padawitz [1], Correctness, Completeness and Consistency of Equational Data Type Specifications, Dissertation, Report No. 83-15, FB 20, TU Berlin (1983)

P. Padawitz [2], Parameter Preserving Data Type Specifications, Journal of Computer and System Sciences 34 (1987) 179-209

P. Padawitz [3], The Equational Theory of Parameterized Specifications, Information and Computation 76 (1988) 121-137

P. Padawitz [4], Strategy-Controlled Reduction and Narrowing, Proc. RTA '87, Springer LNCS 256 (1987) 242-255

P. Padawitz [5], ECDS - A Rewrite Rule Based Interpreter for a Programming Language with Abstraction and Communication, Report MIP-8703, Universität Passau (1987)

D.L. Parnas, A Technique for Software Module Specification with Examples, Communications ACM 15 (1972) 330-336

E. Paul, On Solving the Equality Problem in Theories Defined by Horn Clauses, Proc. EUROCAL '85, Springer LNCS 204 (1985) 363-377

G.E. Peterson, M.E. Stickel, Complete Sets of Reductions for Some Equational Theories, Journal ACM 28 (1981) 233-264

U. Pletat, G. Engels, H.-D. Ehrich, Operational Semantics of Algebraic Specifications with Conditional Equations, Report No. 118/81, Abteilung Informatik, Universität Dortmund (1981)

A. Poigné, On Specifications, Theories and Models with Higher Types, Information and Control 68 (1986) 1-46

M. Polanyi, Personal Knowledge, Chicago University Press (1958)

G. Plotkin, Building-in Equational Theories, Machine Intelligence 7 (1972) 73-90

J.-C. Raoult, J. Vuillemin, Operational and Semantic Equivalence Between Recursive Programs, Journal ACM 27 (1980) 772-796

H. Rasiowa, R. Sikorski, The Mathematics of Metamathematics, Polish Scientific Publishers (1968)

U. **Reddy**, Narrowing as the Operational Semantics of Functional Languages, Proc. IEEE Symp. on Logic Programming (1985) 138-151

H. **Reichel**, Structural Induction on Partial Algebras, Akademie-Verlag (1984)

F.-M. **Reisin**, Softwaretechnik oder Die Geschichte einer unbewältigten Krise, in: J. Bickenbach et al., eds., Militarisierte Informatik, FIFF Berlin (1985) 37-50

P. **Réty**, Improving Basic Narrowing Techniques, Proc. RTA '87, Springer LNCS 256 (1987) 228-241

P. **Réty, C. Kirchner, H. Kirchner, P. Lescanne**, NARROWER: A New Algorithm for Unification and its Application to Logic Programming, Proc. RTA '85, Springer LNCS 202 (1985) 141-157

M.M. **Richter**, Logikkalküle, Teubner (1978)

G. **Robinson, L. Wos**, Paramodulation and Theorem-Proving in First-Order Theories with Equality, in: Machine Intelligence 4, Edinburgh University Press (1969) 135-150

J.A. **Robinson** [1], A Machine-Oriented Logic Based on the Resolution Principle, Journal ACM 12 (1965) 23-41

J.A. **Robinson** [2], Notes on Logic Programming, in: M. Broy, ed., Logic of Programming and Calculi of Discrete Design, Springer (1987) 109-144

B.K. **Rosen**, Tree-Manipulating Systems and Church-Rosser Theorems, Journal ACM 20 (1973) 160-187

D. **Sannella, A. Tarlecki**, On Observational Equivalence and Algebraic Specification, Journal of Computer and System Sciences 34 (1987) 150-178

J.R. **Searle**, Minds, Brains and Science. The Reith 1984 Lectures, BBC (1984)

A. **Selman**, Completeness of Calculi for Axiomatically Defined Classes of Algebras, Algebra Universalis 2 (1972) 20-32

J.R. **Slagle**, Automated Theorem-Proving for Theories with Simplifiers, Commutativity and Associativity, Journal ACM 21 (1974) 622-642

L. **Sterling, E. Shapiro**, The Art of Prolog, The MIT Press (1986)

J.W. **Thatcher, E.G. Wagner, J.B. Wright**, Data Type Specification: Parameterization and the Power of Specification Techniques, ACM TOPLAS 4 (1982) 711-732

M. **Wand** [1], Final Algebra Semantics and Data Type Extensions, Journal of Computer and System Sciences 19 (1979) 27-44

M. **Wand** [2], Specifications, Models and Implementations of Data Abstractions, Theoretical Computer Science 20 (1982) 3-32

B.L. Whorf, Language, Thought, and Reality, selected writings, ed. by J.B. Carroll, MIT Press (1956)

F. Winkler, B. Buchberger, A Criterion for Eliminating Unnecessary Reductions in the Knuth-Bendix Algorithm, Proc. Coll. on Algebra, Combinatorics and Logic in Computer Science, Coll. Math. Soc. J. Bolyai 42 (1983) 849-869

P.H. Winston, B.K.P. Horn, Lisp, Addison-Wesley (1984)

M. Wirsing, Structured Algebraic Specifications: A Kernel Language, Theoretical Computer Science 42 (1986) 123-249

M. Wirsing, P. Pepper, H. Partsch, W. Dosch, M. Broy, On Hierarchies of Abstract Data Types, Acta Informatica 20 (1983) 1-33

N. Wirth, The Development of Programs by Stepwise Refinement, Communications ACM 14 (1971) 221-227

L. Wos, G.A. Robinson, D.F. Carson, L. Shalla, The Concept of Demodulation in Theorem Proving, Journal ACM 14 (1967) 698-709

J.-H. You, Outer Narrowing for Equational Theories based on Constructors, Proc. ICALP '88, Springer LNCS 317 (1988) 727-741

J.-H. You, P.A. Subrahmanyam, A Class of Confluent Term Rewriting Systems and Unification, Journal of Automated Reasoning 2 (1986) 391-418

H. Zhang, J.-L. Remy, Contextual Rewriting, Proc. RTA '85, Springer LNCS 202 (1985) 46-62

Notation Index

A, 142
A/~, 8
abs, 84
A^n, A^+, A^*, 7
A_s, 7
At(SIG), 10
AX, 11, 55
A^X, 9
AX', 188
$\overline{AX}^{\rightarrow}$, 164, 167

B, 142
b^*, 12
BAX, 139
$\overline{BAX}^{\rightarrow}$, 164, 167
$\overline{BAX}^{\rightarrow}$, 242
$\overline{\overline{BAX}}^{\rightarrow}$, 167
becomes, 15
$B\vdash_{AX}^{N}$, 210
BOP, 139
$B\vdash_{AX}^{RD}$, 181
BSIG, 139

CE(AX), 121
CE(BAX), 139
CGen, 91
CH, 79
CMod, 91
CR-ALG, 293
C_s, 78
CTh, 78
$\vdash_{cut}$, 106, 114

$\delta \Leftarrow \gamma$, 105
$\delta \bullet t$, 179
DH, 57
DH(c), 108
DTh, 56, 107

EAX, 56
Eq(SIG), 10
eval, 13

f[g], 9
fin, 85
F(SIG,AX), 57
f⌈V, 9

GAt(SIG), 10
GCTh, 79
GDTh, 62
Gen, 61
$|\langle\gamma,f,g\rangle B\vdash_{AX}^{N}\langle\gamma',f',g'\rangle|$, 210
$|\langle\gamma,f,g\rangle R B\vdash_{AX}^{N}\langle\gamma',f',g'\rangle|$, 217
$|\langle\gamma,f\rangle L\vdash_{AX}^{N}\langle\gamma',f'\rangle|$, 232
$|\langle\gamma,f\rangle\vdash_{AX}^{N}\langle\gamma',f'\rangle|$, 189
$|\langle\gamma,f\rangle R\vdash_{AX}^{N}\langle\gamma',f'\rangle|$, 215
$|\langle\gamma,f\rangle S\vdash_{AX}^{N}\langle\gamma',f'\rangle|$, 195
$\vdash_{AX}^{GP}$, 129
$\vdash_{AX}^{GN}$, 192
GNF, 204
Goal(SIG), 10
GoalSub, 220
$\vdash_{AX}^{GR}$, 129
$|\gamma\vdash_{AX}^{RD}\gamma'|, \|\gamma\vdash_{AX}^{RD}\gamma'\|$, 168
GT(SIG), 9

HS, 12

ICTh, 79
id, 10
id^A, 8
IH, 62
INF, 200
ini, 69
I(SIG,AX), 62
ITh, 61

$L\vdash_{AX}^{GR}$, 132
$LM\vdash_{AX}^{GR}$, 134
$L\vdash_{AX}^{N}$, 232

Mod, 13, 55, 105

nat, 8
NAX, 140
$\overline{NAX}$, 164, 167
$\overline{\sim NAX}$, 166
$\vdash_{AX}^{N}$, 189
NBR, 142
NF, 195
NOP, 140

OP, 8
Op, 220
$Op\vdash_{AX}^{N}$, 220
OpT, 220

¬p, 105
$\vdash_{AX}^{P}$, 122
$p \Leftarrow \gamma$, 11
PR, 8
Pre(AX), 121

⊃R, 256
$\vdash_{AX}^{R}$, 115
$RB\vdash_{AX}^{N}$, 217
$\vdash_{AX}^{RD}, \vdash_{NAX}^{RD}, \vdash_{\sim NAX}^{RD}$, 167

rep, 70, 86
$R\vdash_{AX}^{N}$, 215

S, 7
$S\vdash_{AX}^{GN}$, 195
SIG, 8, 55
$S\vdash_{AX}^{N}$, 195
SNF, 235
$S\vdash_{AX}^{RD}$, 180

$|t\overrightarrow{_{AX}}t'|, \|t\overrightarrow{_{AX}}t'\|$, 168
$|t\overrightarrow{_{AX}}t' \Leftarrow \gamma|, \|t\overrightarrow{_{AX}}t' \Leftarrow \gamma\|$, 165
$\|t\overrightarrow{_{BAX}}t'\|, \|t\overrightarrow{_{BAX}}t' \Leftarrow \gamma\|$, 243
$t[f]$, 9
$T(SIG)$, 8
$t \equiv t'$, 10
t/x, 9

VS, 78

X, 8
XG, 114

Z(SIG,AX), 79

∼, 8, 57, 62, 99, 108
≈, 79
<, ≤, 221
⊃, 255
⊥, 204
⊨, 13
⊢, 56, 106

Definition Index

absorbs equations, 226
Absorption Rule, 134
abstraction homomorphism, 84
Abstraction Rule, 242
affects a term, 245
arity, 8
atom, 10

Base Assumption, 139
base representation, 141
base specification, 139
basically reducible, 182
Basic Narrowing Rule, 210
basic reduction, 181
Basic Reduction Rule, 181
Basic Success Rule, 181, 210
BAX-compatible, 173, 285
~BAX-compatible, 173
behavioural equivalence, 79
BOOL-complete, 91

canonical term structure, 72
characteristic function, 93
Church-Rosser, 172
clause, 11
closed world assumption, 119
coarity, 8
commutes with ~BAX
compatible with substitution
  prefixes, 220
complete, 55
Composition Rule, 164
conclusion, 11
conditional equation, 11
conditional function, 95
conditional reduction, 164
conditional reduction calculus, 164,
  166

confluent, 173
conservative extension, 140
consistent set of sequents, 106
consistent structure, 91
constant, 8
Construction Rule, 232
constructs substitutions, 225
contextual theory, 78
convergent critical pair, 251
convergent critical pair modulo
  BAX, 252
convergent term pair, 173
conversion axiom, 93
conversion-complete, 93
coretraction, 70
critical pair, 250
critical pair selector, 268
cut-consistent, 106
Cut Rule, 56, 105

deductive solution, 58
deductive theory, 56, 107
Definition Principle, 174
derivation, 55
detects clashes, 226
domain, 9

empty sequent, 105
equality axiom, 56
equality predicate, 8
equation, 10
equational counterpart, 95
equationally complete, 95
expands variables, 225
Expansion Rule, 134

feasible critical pair, 250
feasible reduction redex, 180

finally correct, 85
final representation function, 86
final structure, 79
follows contextually, 88
free structure, 57
fully parallel reduction, 243
fully parallel reduction calculus, 242
Fully Parallel Reduction Rule, 242
functionally reflexive axiom, 137
functional reflexivity axiom, 93

General Assumption, 8, 55
GN-solution, 192, 195, 213
goal, 10
goal reduction, 167
goal reduction calculus, 167
goal variable, 114
GP-solution, 129
ground, 9, 10
grounding equation, 204
ground term generating, 207
ground term reducing, 201
GR-solution, 129

Herbrand structure, 12
homomorphism, 69
Horn clause calculus, 56

identity, 8, 10
inductionless induction, 150
inductive contextual theory, 79
inductive theory, 61
inference relation, 56
inhabited, 55
initially correct, 69
initial representation function, 70
initial SIG-extension, 142
initial structure, 62
innermost, 201
instance, 9, 10
irreducible, 166
isolated variable, 174

isomorphism, 69

label, 199
lazy narrowing calculus, 231
Lazy Narrowing Rule, 231
lazy resolution calculus, 131
Lazy Resolution Rule, 131
left-linear, 174
length of a parallel reduction, 243
LGR-solution, 132
linear, 9
literal, 105
LMGR-solution, 134
LN-solution, 232
locally correct, 221
locally redex stable, 201
locally respects normal forms, 298
location, 199

Martelli-Montanari rule, 134
most general critical pair, 250
most general expansion, 129, 192, 212
most general reduction, 245
most general unifier, 10

narrowing calculus, 188
narrowing expansion, 189, 195, 210, 214, 217, 232
narrowing redex, 194
narrowing strategy, 195
Narrowing Rule, 188
Negation as Failure, 119
Noetherian, 7
non-sub-unifiable, 202
normal form, 166
normalizable, 171
normalizing, 171
N-solution, 189, 195, 210
N-solution ordering, 220

occurrence, 199

OP-compatible, 13
optimized narrowing tree, 220
optimizing function, 220
overlapping reduction, 244, 245
overlaps, 9

parallel length, 165, 168
Parallel Reduction Rule, 164, 166, 167
paramodulant, 121
paramodulating expansion, 121
paramodulation calculus, 121
Paramodulation Rule, 121
partial inductive theory, 148
partially complete, 149
position, 179
PR-compatible, 13
prefix, 9,10
prefixed axiom, 121
premise of a clause, 11
premise of a critical pair, 250
premise of a reduction, 164
preserves base-representability, 149
preserves normalizability, 176
prime ideal, 99
proper-subterm relation, 255
P-solution, 122

recursive path ordering, 255
redex stable, 200
reduced, 166
Reduced Basic Narrowing Rule, 216
Reduced Narrowing Rule, 214
reducible, 167
reducible by S, 180
reduction mapping, 214
reduction redex, 180
reduction relation, 167
reduction strategy, 180
Reflexivity Rule, 242
refutation, 106
rejects non-narrowable goals, 226

representation condition, 70
resolution calculus, 114
Resolution Rule, 115
resolvent, 115
resolving expansion, 115, 132
respects logical syntax, 96
respects normal forms, 173
Restricted Resolution Rule, 121
root, 9
R-solution, 115

satisfies, 13, 105
s-context, 78
S-controlled Narrowing Rule, 194
S-controlled reduction, 180
S-controlled Reduction Rule, 180
sequent, 105
sequent calculus, 105
<SIG,AX>-theorem, 56, 107
SIG-congruence relation, 13
SIG-model, 13, 55, 105
signature, 8
SIG-structure, 11
simple length, 165, 168
single, 9
Single Reduction Rule, 164, 166, 167
size, 9
SNF-based, 235
solution in a structure, 13
specification, 11
splits equations, 225
Splitting Rule, 134, 232
S-sorted function, 8
S-sorted relation, 8
S-sorted set, 7
strongly BAX-compatible, 243
strongly confluent, 271
strongly convergent critical pair, 272
strongly convergent critical pair modulo BAX, 252

strongly convergent term pair
  modulo BAX, 243
strongly irreducible, 235
subspecification, 11
substitution, 9
Substitution Rule, 56, 105
subsumes, 9
subsumes goals, 225
subsumes solutions, 225
Success Rule, 167, 188
sufficiently complete, 141
Superposition Rule, 245

term, 8
term-generated, 13
term reduction, 167

Unification Rule, 121
unifier, 9
uniform strategy, 200

valid, 13, 105
var, 9
variable, 8
Variable Assumption, 114
variable-preserving, 172
visible atom, 78
visibly initial, 83

weakly convergent critical pair, 252
weakly OP-compatible, 255
weakly respects normal forms, 243